Corrupting
the IMAGE III

Corrupting the Image Vol. 3

Dr. Douglas M. Hamp

Eskaton Media Group

Corrupting the Image Vol. 3:
Singularity, Superhumans and the Second Coming of Jesus
By Dr. Douglas M. Hamp

Copyright © 2022 by Dr. Douglas Hamp
www.douglashamp.com

Published by Eskaton Media Group

ISBN: 978-1-63821-417-5

Cover by Sebby Sandu – Aesthetica Society

Unless otherwise indicated, all Scripture quotations are taken from the New King James Version, Thomas Nelson Publishers (1997). The Hebrew text is from the Biblia Hebraica Stugartensia. The Greek Old Testament Scriptures are from the Septuagint. New Testament Greek quotations are from the Greek New Testament according to the Byzantine Text form, edited by Maurice A. Robinson and William G. Pierpont, 2000 edition; this is the edition by Pierpont and Robinson of a Majority, or Byzantine, text of the NT. Quotations marked KJV are from the King James Version. Quotations marked ESV are from the English Standard Version. Quotations marked ISV are International Standard Version. Quotations marked JPS are from the Jewish Publication Society. Quotations marked NET are from the New English Translation. Quotations marked NASB are from the New American Standard Bible. Quotations marked RYLT are from the Revised Young's Literal Translation. Quotations marked ASV are from the American Standard Version. Quotations marked ERV are from the English Revised Version. Quotations marked WBT are from the Webster's Bible Translation. Quotations marked WEB are from the World English Bible. Quotations marked YLT are from the Young's Literal Translation. All Scripture quotations have been retrieved using theWord Bible Software. All emphases of Scripture verses are mine.

Printed in the United States of America.

Endorsements

While the modern American church leads the way into global apostasy, the enemy of God, of His creation, and of His people, is gaining strength and assembling his forces for the coming great conflict. Satan is staging his assets for a blitzkrieg of shock and awe evil that will overwhelm the earth.

In contrast, those of us who have eyes to see and ears to hear, those of us who have maintained our focus on Jesus, who have spirits in tune with the Holy Spirit, have been spiritually immunized against the strong delusion that has fallen upon the earth in preparation for the rise of the Beast.

This immunization serves to protect us from the wiles of the devil and enables us to see and hear everything the Father is revealing to His faithful remnant concerning the coming war.

UFO disclosure, Artificial Intelligence, genetic engineering, transhumanism, and the mad rush toward singularity are not disparate endeavors but are all part of the devil's strategy of casting a dragnet to ensnare all of humanity in a great deception of faux hope and faux salvation.

I am grateful for scholars and brothers in the faith like Dr. Douglas Hamp. His dedication to literary archaeology is clearly his calling, his gifting from the Father through the Holy Spirit, and Doug's gift to the remnant body of Jesus today.

Doug's latest effort, *Corrupting the Image, Vol. 3, Singularity, Superhumans and the Second Coming of Jesus* is bringing our understanding of events in the days of the Beast leading up to the return of Jesus into focus. I believe every pastor and Bible teacher is well-served to read and appropriate what Doug provides his readers. In doing that, we can be assured that God's people are prepared for what is coming upon the earth.

—Dr. Mike Spaulding, Pastor, Author, Researcher, Radio Host

Doug Hamp's *Corrupting the Image 3* carefully lays out a theological roadmap for understanding the heavenly and earthly battles yet to take place in the future. No more beating around the bush. This thought-provoking book goes beyond mere eschatological speculations as it urges its readers to carefully examine the biblical evidence for themselves. It provides an in-depth study of the two witnesses from Revelation 11 ushering in the Armageddon battle and the second coming of Jesus Christ. Any believer interested in a deep theological study of apocalyptic eschatology will find *Corrupting the Image 3* captivating and eye opening!

—**Dr. Igal German, International Biblical Apologetics Association & Yesod Bible Center**

Dr. Douglas Hamp has done it again with a book where he uses both linguistic skills and overall grasp of the Bible to come out with some amazing insights! It is amazing to read a book like this because few people have the training and expertise to even imagine some of the things in this third volume. I think many Christians who read this may discover a new passion for their Bible as Doug dives into what things could look like in the days to come. Look at your Bible through new lenses as you learn so much about Biblical world history and how it could affect our present day and future. What a great book to read and give as a gift to those who want to be challenged in their world view!

—**Austin Brazil, Senior Pastor Cross The Line Church**

Dr. Hamp has once again taken up the case for the explicit impact of the modern-day Nephilim and demonstrated how it correlates to the current phenomenon of 'disclosure' by our government. What was once incredulous among Bible-believing Christians has now become a tenet of our worldview. *Corrupting the Image* has been one of the foremost books demonstrating why this is so. Part III is the icing on the cake. If you were a fan of the other two books, this is a must read. If you haven't read the other books, you must dig into this edition. It is a revelation of the enemy's stratagem against humanity in these end days. There are few books that have such relevance to our perilous situation.

—**S. Douglas Woodward, TH.M, MBA, President, Faith Happens Books**

Dr. Doug Hamp has been given a gift. The intangible details of the end times are made clear to him and, in turn, he makes them clear to you and me. I'm not an expert on the spiritual playbook of the Enemy, the existence of beings outside of our understanding, the imminent interconnectivity of man and machine, or how it all comes together. But I know from experience that those who think outside the box end up being correct more often than most people will give them credit for. Dr. Doug definitely thinks outside the box and I'm willing to listen to him on this one.

The Book of Revelation is unfolding before our eyes — that is, if we have our eyes open. Prepare to see things in a way you've never seen before.

—**Scott Laird, ND**

Acknowledgements

Thank you to the people who helped with the editing and proofing of this book! Special thanks to you, Kimberly Sikes, for the amazing attention to detail and the numerous hours you invested in editing the book! Thanks to Sarah Rush and Shemmen Zayit as well for the very helpful editing and proofing. And thank you Bob Rico, for reading early drafts and giving me important feedback. Thank you Chris Steinle for the feedback and for doing the book formatting.

About the Author

Douglas Hamp earned his M.A. in the Bible and its World from the Hebrew University of Jerusalem and his PhD in Biblical Studies from Louisiana Baptist University. He served as an assistant pastor at Calvary Chapel Costa Mesa for six years, where he lectured and developed curriculum at the School of Ministry, Spanish School of Ministry and Calvary Chapel Bible College Graduate School. He is the author of numerous books, articles, & DVDs and has appeared on national and international TV, radio, and internet programs in English and in Spanish. He is senior pastor of the Way Congregation in Denver, CO.

Foreword

By Michael K. Lake, Th.D.

Genesis 6 serves as a clarion warning of what will transpire in the future. In fact, it has been unfolding before our eyes since the dawn of the twentieth century. Jesus warned us in Matthew 24, regarding the days of Noah:

> But as the days of Noah *were,* so also will the coming of the Son of Man be.
>
> —Matthew 24:37 (NKJV)

Much of the body of Christ has been strategically made ignorant of the truths that were enfolded in Genesis 6. I have called this ignorance strategic, because the priesthood of darkness has been laboring for well over a millennium to obfuscate the truth of what happened when the sons of God began their genetic experiment with the daughters of men.

In Moses' day, the children of Israel knew all too well what happened in the days of Genesis 6. Israel had lived as slaves to a nation that worshipped the Watchers and their hellish offspring, the Nephilim. One of the purposes of the Torah was to present to the children of Israel the truths of what was holy and profane, righteous and unrighteous, and clean and unclean. Therefore, Moses concentrated on the effects of the Watchers and their children upon humanity. We find the dark effects of these fallen creatures upon humanity in Verse 5.

> Then the LORD saw that the wickedness of man *was* great in the earth, *and that every intent of the thoughts of his heart was only evil continually.*
>
> —Genesis 6:5 (NKJV) (Emphasis added)

By the 5th Century A.D., the forces of the Mystery Religions had already sown the error of angel worship into Catholic theology, which was nothing more than the same pagan worship of the Nephilim in a new form. Once the infection of error got into the body, it quickly replicated in other variants.

Celsus and Julian the Apostate then used the traditional "angel" belief to attack Christianity. Julius Africanus' solution was to develop a new theology of convenience: It was the sons of Seth marrying wild women that caused the problem of Genesis 6. Likewise, Cyril of Alexandria and Augustine also repudiated the orthodox "angel" position with the "line of Seth" interpretation which prevailed into the Middle Ages and is still widely taught today among many churches who find the literal "angel" view a bit disturbing. There are many outstanding Bible teachers who still defend this view[1] and most ministers in our day are trained in seminary to embrace the Sethite theory and still find the Genesis 6 "angel" interpretation an embarrassment.

This theology of convenience, however, caused an amnesia within the Church that would eventually cripple the end-time saints from understanding the machinations of darkness in their day. Today, hints of Watcher technologies are all around us. Some of them are found in items we use every day. Many others are reserved for high-level operatives of various governments around the world to ensure the development of a New World Order. Also, the dark effects of the Watchers upon humanity are all around us. The minds of our citizenry are getting darker by the hour. Those on the cutting edge of technology and science are dreaming of a post-human era. In this new era on planet earth, humanity will transcend its mortal bounds to become homo-deus. In the darkest hours of our planet, there are powerful men and women salivating in anticipation for the moment that they can access immortality and achieve godhood.

However, there is a fresh breeze of the Holy Spirit moving upon the Church. Heaven is whispering -- REMEMBER. Almighty God is raising up anointed researchers that are willing to do the hard research necessary to regain what we have lost, through the mists of human history. One such researcher is my colleague and friend, Dr. Douglas Hamp. In this powerful trilogy of books on "Corrupting the Image," you will discover what the children of Israel understood the very first time that the book of Genesis was read to them.

---

[1] Missler, Chuck. Article: Mischievous Angels or Sethites?
http://www.khouse.org/articles/1997/110/

This third volume contains vital information that will be found in the headlines of tomorrow. The Watchers and their forbidden children are returning to aid the Son of Perdition in his final assault upon God and humanity. So, read this important volume to be informed. Read it to be prepared. Prayerfully read it to properly discern the prophetic times that we are living in today. May God use this book to keep you from being deceived, so you can become part of God's remnant army for the last days.

Michael K. Lake, Th.D.

Chancellor and Founder, Biblical Life College and Seminary

Author, *The Shinar Directive: Preparing the Way of the Son of Perdition, The Sheeriyth Imperative: Empowering the Remnant to Overcome the Gates of Hell,* and *The Kingdom Priesthood: Preparing and Equipping the Remnant Priesthood for the Last Days*.

Contents

Table of Figures

List of Tables

PART ONE:

A WORLD CONFRONTED BY HOSTILE EXTRA-DIMENSIONALS

Intro: Old Gods, Ancient Aliens

Satan's basic goal has not changed for thousands of years: he wants to be the supreme, undisputed lord of the earth where all serve him. In *Corrupting the Image 1* and *2*, we saw that Satan sent the sons of God to come down on Mt. Hermon and procreate the Nephilim. After the Flood, he gave his power, throne and authority to Nimrod, who became a hybrid, was hailed as Ninurta, son of Enlil (Satan), and was the Beast who: "was, is not and will ascend out of the abyss." Satan deceived the ancient world by posing as the god, Enlil (the prince of the power of the air), who usurped the authority of the Creator and dramatized his boast for all to see in the annual spring spectacle called the Akitu Festival. Here, Satan indoctrinated all stratums of society with the belief that he was god and could make men into gods. He used Ishtar, the woman known as Mystery Babylon, to lure mankind into building a gateway to reach the gods.

Now, in these last days, the deception will be the same, but the lingo will change slightly: the ancient gods are now dubbed advanced extraterrestrial beings who came here long before we did and can help us evolve. That will be our basic thesis throughout this book: Satan and his team pose as "good aliens," here to help us and protect us from Jesus' team "the hostile beings." This theme can be found in the 2021 Marvel movie, *Eternals*, in which the ancient gods of Babylon and Egypt were highly advanced beings charged with defending earth against a hostile race called Deviants. In setting up this deception, Satan will attempt to regain his dominion and authority over the world, to strengthen his rebel forces, and battle Jesus when He returns.

PREPARATION FOR THE STRONG DELUSION

The Darwinian molecules-to-man theory of evolution has been very effective in convincing billions around the world that there is not an all-powerful Creator (such as the God of Israel); and, that we and the ancient aliens are related and are both on an evolutionary path.[2] In fact, many researchers are convinced that aliens are responsible for the creation of life on earth!

---

[2] See Corrupting the Image 1.

In his 1981 book, *Life Itself,* Francis Crick, the co-discoverer of the structure of DNA, proposed the theory of directed panspermia (lit. seeds everywhere) in which ancient aliens transported the first seeds (DNA) of life to earth via a spaceship. He discusses the chemicals necessary for life to begin and suggests how the first replicator molecule, RNA, could have come along; [3] though he confesses it "seems almost **impossible** to give any numerical value to the probability of what seems a rather unlikely sequence of events."[4] He does not resolve this quandary, but simply moves on to the likelihood of other planets in the universe where life might have started—just like evolutionist Richard Dawkins. After a lot of speculation, Crick conjectures there to be "a million planets in our galaxy on which we might hope to find oceans of thin organic soup waiting for life to get going."[5] Thus, the man who co-discovered the structure of DNA could not fathom how life on earth could have arisen, other than postulating that some advanced beings brought life here on a spaceship.[6] Such an idea is surprisingly widespread in popular and academic circles.

In the 2006 movie, *Expelled: No Intelligence Allowed*, Ben Stein interviews famed atheist and evolutionist Richard Dawkins on the origins of life.

BEN STEIN: Well, how did it start?

DAWKINS: Nobody knows how it got started. We know the kind of event that it must have been. We know the sort of event that must have happened for the origin of life.

---

[3] The theory of evolution has offered a tantalizing explanation as to how life arose. We evolved from nothing, from the Goo to the Zoo, to you. The basic belief is 13.8 billion years ago, the Big Bang somehow occurred, though no one knows how or why. Then 4.56 billion years ago, some rocks ran into each other and eventually the earth was formed. Roughly 2 billion years ago, life somehow happened.

[4] He admits that "we **cannot** decide whether the origin of life on earth was an extremely unlikely event or almost a certainty—or any possibility in between these two extremes." Crick F. (1981). Life itself. Simon & Schuster, p. 87, 88.

[5] Crick F. (1981). Life itself. Simon & Schuster, p. 105

[6] Crick F. (1981). Life itself. Simon & Schuster, p. 148. See also http://ofbacteriaandmen.blogspot.com/2012/08/francis-crick-and-directed-panspermia.html

BEN STEIN: And what was that?

DAWKINS: It was the origin of the first self-replicating molecule.

BEN STEIN: Right, and how did that happen?

DAWKINS: I told you, we don't know.

BEN STEIN: What do you think is the possibility that Intelligent Design might turn out to be the answer to some issues in genetics or in Darwinian evolution.

DAWKINS: Well, it could come about in the following way. It could be that at some earlier time, somewhere in the universe, a **civilization evolved**, probably by some kind of Darwinian means, probably to a very high level of technology, and designed a form of life that they **seeded** onto perhaps this planet. Um, now that is a possibility, and an intriguing possibility. And I suppose it's possible that you might find evidence for that if you look at the details of biochemistry, molecular biology, you might find a **signature of some sort of designer**.

BEN STEIN: *[voice over]* Wait a second. Richard Dawkins thought intelligent design might be a legitimate pursuit?

DAWKINS: And that **Designer** could well be a **higher intelligence** from elsewhere in the universe. But that higher intelligence would itself have had to have come about by some explicable, or ultimately explicable process. It couldn't have just jumped into existence spontaneously. That's the point.

BEN STEIN: *[voice over]* So professor Dawkins was not against intelligent design, just certain types of designers. Such as God.

Ben Stein humorously quizzes Dawkins whether he believes in any god that might have
created it.

> DAWKINS: Any god anywhere would be completely incompatible with anything that I've said.[7]

---

[7] Expelled: No Intelligence Allowed, Directed by Nathan Frankowski, written by Kevin Miller and Ben Stein, starring Ben Stein. 2008.

Richard Dawkins believes that an intelligent alien designer was likely involved in the creation of life, but just not the God of the Bible. Like Dawkins, the evidence of fine tuning for life in the universe has caused many to suggest that aliens might have been responsible. [8] Avi Loeb, the longest serving chair of astronomy at Harvard, believes creation by alien intelligence is the best answer to the origin of the universe. He writes:

> A less explored possibility is that our universe was **created** in the **laboratory** of an **advanced technological civilization**. Since our universe has a flat geometry with a zero net energy, an advanced civilization could have developed a technology that created a baby universe out of nothing through quantum tunneling.[9]

Carl Sagan, a renowned evolutionist and atheist, portrays in his novel, *Contact*, a recent race of advanced beings (aliens) have been watching over humanity. The aliens explain that they are not the creators, but there was an even more ancient race of advanced beings before them who primed the universe for life. [10] All Sagan does is chronologically push back the problem of where life came from, and like Dawkins, considers alien creators acceptable as candidates, but not the God of the Bible.

Nick Bostrom has proposed a similar idea suggesting that our universe is nothing more than a simulation, and we are living in a gigantic computer program created by advanced beings.[11]

---

[8] https://mindmatters.ai/2021/10/if-extraterrestrials-didnt-fine-tune-earth-maybe-there-is-a-god

[9] https://mindmatters.ai/2021/10/harvard-astronomer-advanced-aliens-engineered-the-big-bang

[10] A number of native American tribes, including the Lakota, speak of the Star people who upgraded humanity with their DNA, so that, in the long run, we are part alien.

[11] https://mindmatters.ai/2021/10/could-advanced-aliens-have-fine-tuned-earth-for-life

In the same vein, Professor of quantum physics at Imperial College London, Terry Rudolph, has proposed the theory that starlight may be harnessed by extraterrestrials as an encrypted quantum internet through the principle of quantum entanglement. [12] These theories of origin postulated by the respected intellectuals of our time exclude the God of the Bible and prime the pump for the strong delusion that will cloud the minds of those who refuse to believe the truth.

MAN WILL ACCEPT THE ONE COMING IN HIS OWN NAME

Why is the theory of evolution and advanced beings more compelling than special creation by God? The answer is simple: Man, in his rebellion, has audaciously rejected and forgotten our loving Creator, like the citizens in Jesus' parable who hated the noble man who had gone to receive for himself a kingdom and return, "and sent a delegation after him, saying, 'We will not have this *man* to reign over us'" (Luke 19:14), just as God told Samuel: "they have rejected Me, that I should not reign over them (1 Sam 8:7).

We want to be our own gods. We want to do it our own way. We would prefer to see ourselves related to cold aliens far away who seeded the planet rather than a loving God who is near and created us in His image. Paul spoke about men suppressing the truth that God is the Creator and rightful King.

> For since the **creation** of the world His invisible attributes are clearly seen, being understood by the things that are made, even His eternal power and Godhead, so that they are without excuse (Rom 1:20), because, although they knew God, they did not glorify Him as God, nor were thankful, but became futile in their thoughts, and their foolish hearts were darkened (Rom 1:21) who exchanged the truth of God for the lie, and worshiped and served the creature rather than the Creator (Rom 1:25).

---

[12] https://www.vice.com/en/article/5db4ma/starlight-could-really-be-a-vast-alien-quantum-internet-physicist-proposes "What I show is that alien civilizations can, in principle, run their own quantum internet in such a way that to the creatures excluded from the conversation (us!) we will only ever see thermal electromagnetic radiation...All we would see, if they did use the effect I propose, is some very random looking thermal light."

Richard Dawkins summed up how much of humanity feels about God in his book, *The God Delusion:*

> "The God of the Old Testament is arguably the most unpleasant character in all fiction: jealous and proud of it; a petty, unjust, unforgiving control-freak; a vindictive, bloodthirsty ethnic cleanser; a misogynistic, homophobic, racist, infanticidal, genocidal, filicidal, pestilential, megalomaniacal, sadomasochistic, capriciously malevolent bully."

Aliens instead of God are certainly part of the strong delusion setting man up for the coming of the lawless one, that is, the Beast who was, is not, and ascends out of the abyss. The Amplified Bible brings out the strength of what is coming:

> The coming [of the lawless one, the antichrist] is through the activity and working of Satan and will be attended by **great power** and with all sorts of **[pretended] miracles** and signs and **delusive marvels**—[all of them] **lying wonders**— And by **unlimited seduction** to **evil** and with all **wicked deception** for those who are perishing (going to perdition) because they did not welcome the Truth but refused to love it that they might be saved. Therefore God sends upon them a misleading influence, a working of error and a strong delusion to make them believe what is false, In order that all may be judged and condemned who did not believe in [who refused to adhere to, trust in, and rely on] the Truth, but [instead] took pleasure in unrighteousness (2 Thess. 2:9–12 AMP).

Jesus said: "I have come in My Father's name, and you do not receive Me; if another comes in his own name, him you will receive" (John 5:43). Jesus came to give humanity everything man could want and more, but he was rejected. Satan / the Beast will come as the dragon, and the world will receive him. He will give the impression that he wants to help humanity, but through insidious schemes he will trick people and gain authority through his Covenant of death and Sheol. At that point, anything will seem more acceptable than the message of truth and the moral standards shown in the Word of God.

Chapter 1: UFOS no longer conspiracy

In preparation for the great Day of the Lord, Satan must not only deceive man into thinking aliens helped create us, but that they are present today. Since the United States detonated the first atomic bomb, there have been thousands of sightings around the world. Many world leaders and astronauts claimed to have seen them, which we covered in *Corrupting the Image 1*. In 1952, General Major Samford stated at a press conference, "I am here to discuss the so-called flying saucers ..." that were seen flying over the Capitol Building in Washington DC. He confirmed that they were not our tech: "We can say that the recent sightings are in **no way connected with any secret development** by any department of the United States."[13]

Captain Edgar D. Mitchell, Apollo 14 Astronaut, even bluntly stated: "We all know that UFOs are real. All we need to ask is, 'where do they come from.'" However, as *thesun.com* notes: "US intelligence services officially closed the book on the phenomena in 1969 at the conclusion of Project Blue Book, which stated there was nothing to see regarding UFOs." [14] Back then, seeing a UFO was relegated to conspiracy theorists and crackpots and could jeopardize your standing at work and in society, and lead to intense ridicule.

However, nowadays, things have changed. Prestigious news and documentary media organizations such as the New York Times, CBS's *60 Minutes*, Fox, Netflix, National Geographic, and others are reporting on them as being real and not part of the lunatic fringe. Leslie Keene, who co-authored eye-opening articles in The New York Times about UFOSs and the US military, stated in an interview with *Space.com*, "I believe we may have finally arrived at the threshold of a new paradigm."[15] It is a new paradigm because people are now willing to take a serious look at the unidentified phenomena. Indeed, after roughly fifty years of denial, the government had done an about-face, admitting their existence to the New York Times.

---

[13] https://wiki2.org/en/John_A._Samford
[14] https://www.the-sun.com/news/3008383/ufos-coming-from-space-sea-aliens
[15] https://www.space.com/ufos-are-real-leslie-kean-interview

"The Pentagon took the unprecedented step of releasing three stunning UFO videos filmed by the US Navy. President Barack Obama ... addressed the topic on CBS: He said: "What is true, and I'm actually being serious here, is that there's footage and records of objects in the skies that **we don't know exactly what they are;** we can't explain how they moved, their trajectory ..."[16]

The footage has not revealed anything new about UFOs, but most importantly, it has taken the discussion from conspiracy theory to that of "a genuine national security debate in the US," which has "made clear to everyone, **something is in the skies.**"[17] In other words, what once was conspiracy has finally been declared real by the United States government. Now, regardless of what one thinks about the explanation, no one can deny that something non-human is in the skies.

Probably the most impressive video is known as the Navy's 2004 video depicting what is described as a "Tic Tac," which shows an unidentified aerial phenomenon being pursued by Navy fighter planes.

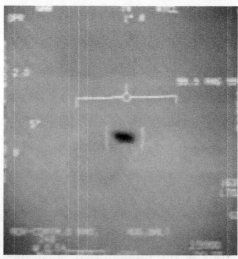

Figure 1. Screenshot the eerie and unexplained 'Tic Tac' video filmed by the US Navy and released by the Pentagon.

---

[16] https://www.the-sun.com/news/3008383/ufos-coming-from-space-sea-aliens

[17] https://www.the-sun.com/news/3008383/ufos-coming-from-space-sea-aliens

The leaked and confirmed authentic US Navy videos have helped us piece together very interesting clues, which the Bible predicted. In a Fox special TMZ INVESTIGATES: UFOs: THE PENTAGON PROOF, Jeremy Corbel—a filmmaker reporting on the presence of UFOs among the military—notes the very non-physical behavior of the objects they were observing:

"What we are seeing is objects at 80,000 feet or above dropping down to sea level in less than a second and a half. No sonic boom, that stop on a dime. There are no wings, no propellors. There are no jet engines. No exhaust. How would you control the direction? How would you navigate? How is this thing propelled?"

Later in the interview, Christopher Mellon, former assistant secretary of Defense for Intelligence likewise comments on the unexplainable physics involved:

"The Tic Tac case is the best, clearest example of a vehicle that nobody that I have spoken with has a plausible explanation for. The 'tic tac' descending in a matter of seconds from essentially 80,000 feet and then to sea level and then hovering and then instantaneous accelerating to hypersonic speeds – that's physics that we don't understand. How does anybody survive? How does the vehicle itself survive the crushing forces that would be generated by that kind of acceleration? That is 10 – 50 times beyond the tolerance of anything we've ever built, in terms of being able to withstand the forces that would be subjected to that vehicle."

Both men indicate that the objects they are viewing do not behave according to the laws of physics. They have no signs of engines or propulsion, no exhaust, no forms of navigation. This evidence corresponds with what was reported in the 1952 sighting over Washington DC where they sped away at 7,000 miles per hour.[18]

---

[18] https://www.history.com/news/ufos-washington-white-house-air-force-coverup

NASA administrator Bill Nelson shared in an interview "passionately about his agency's mission to seek out life beyond Earth." He also commented on the series of U.S. military encounters with mysterious flying objects, many of which appeared to maneuver in extraordinary ways while in restricted airspace."[19] He also noted that the pilots "saw something, and their radars locked onto it." When asked to speculate about what it means, he remarked, "Who am I to say that planet Earth is the only location of a life form that is civilized and organized like ours?"

At the same time as the "tic tac" video and photo were captured, the United States was carrying on the search—under a Pentagon program established to study UFOs before being disbanded in 2017—known as Advanced Aerospace Threat Identification Program (AATIP). Hence, contrary to the conclusion of Project Blue Book, which said there was nothing to see regarding UFOs, the UAP Task Force continued on with UFO research; and "Defense chiefs have since confirmed a number of leaked UFO videos and photos which were submitted to the Task Force for investigation."[20]

TRANS-MEDIUM BEINGS FROM THE SEA?

Jeremy Corbel went on to explain how Navy personnel reacted to a UFO that had been hovering just above the water, and then descended into the ocean: "You hear them say splash, splash. It doesn't mean it splashed. It means they believe it went into the water." The narrator then comments, "It sounds crazy, but could it be an object that traverses the skies and the ocean with ease?" Corbel continues explaining how the object could go effortlessly from the air into the water with no splash:

---

[19] https://thehill.com/opinion/international/579303-nasa-chief-bill-nelson-latest-official-to-suggest-ufos-have?rl=1

[20] https://www.the-sun.com/news/3008383/ufos-coming-from-space-sea-aliens/

"This is a trans-medium vehicle —a vehicle that can penetrate that space between air and sea, no plumes, no heat, no exhaust. This thing is self-propelled with intelligence." The narrator adds, "The military has confirmed —these photos are authentically UFOS." Corbel adds how the objects, which were lit up like Christmas trees were "... swarming around the ship," and that "they are self-luminous."[21]

Investigative reporter George Knapp also weighed in during the TMZ interview. He was asked, "Do you think that this has anything to do with an object or objects outside of our solar system?" He responded by saying that this is just one of the possibilities one must consider. He went on to suggest:

> "...That they've always lived on Earth. That they've been here longer than us. That they're crypto-terrestrials. Maybe they **live in the ocean**. Maybe they live here separated from us by some **thin psychic dimensional membrane** that they move back and forth. There are a lot of exotic ideas that have been explored and discussed behind closed doors."

Knapp is simply taking the data to its logical conclusion: We are witnessing "self-luminous" beings, seemingly unbound by physical laws, which might exist behind some "thin psychic dimensional membrane," (recall we studied in *Corrupting the Image 2* —there is a veil, a membrane between our earthly-physical domain and the spiritual-heavenly domain). The UAPs unbound by physical laws is also what we saw in *Corrupting the Image 1* in the testimony of Dr. John Mack from Harvard, who described how the alien beings— supposedly abducting people—are a "less embodied species than we are"[22]; but are working on creating a hybridization program as an insurance policy for preserving life on earth.

---

[21] TMZ INVESTIGATES: UFOs: THE PENTAGON PROOF
www.fox.com/watch/2c2489402d90e9cf47fe5ec0eff0250f/
[22] All quotations from Dr. John Mack retrieved July 14, 2010 from:
http://www.pbs.org/wgbh/nova/aliens/johnmack.html

What Knapp and John Mack are really concluding is that we are witnessing spiritual beings, which the Bible calls angels / messengers (whether good or bad). Given that these beings often emit their own light, or as Jeremy Corbel stated, are "self-luminous," we might have an explanation for why the Bible sometimes calls angels "stars."[23]

- The seven **stars** are the angels [angeloi ἄγγελοι] (Rev 1:20).
- the **stars** of heaven fell to the earth, as a fig tree drops its late figs (Rev 6:13).[24]
- I saw a **star** fallen from heaven to the earth (Rev 9:1–2).
- … two men stood by them in **shining** garments (Luke 24:4).

RISING UP OUT OF THE SEA

That these spiritual beings reside in the ocean is also incredibly germane in light of biblical texts. In Revelation, John writes, "I stood on the sand of the sea. And I saw a beast rising up **out of the sea** ..." (Rev 13:1).

These craft have also been seen to shape shift[25] as described in the Bible: "Satan himself **transforms** himself into an angel of **light**" (2 Cor 11:14).

Gary Heseltine, who spent six years working with the Royal Air Force police, 24 years with the British Transport Police, and now serves as vice president of the new International Coalition for Extraterrestrial Research (ICER)—made up of UFO researchers and scientist from 27 countries—believes that aliens might not be coming from outer space, but from the oceans.

---

[23] As evidenced BDAG, classical Greek literature sometimes considered "stars" to be sentient beings. See: Stoicorum Veterum Fragmenta, coll. J(H) vArnim I–IV 1903–24. See also: Chrysippus, phil., ed. J(H) vArnim, Stoicorum veterum fragmenta II 1903 III b.c.

[24] John is referring to angelic beings, not stars in the night sky (incandescent burning bodies. If he were, then ALL the stars from Alpha Centari to Beetlejuice to the super giants and our own sun would need to fall to the earth and there would be no more planet earth.

[25] According to MUFON reporting as seen on Netflix: Hangar 1: The UFO Files

"UFOs are often seen coming in and out of water, so I suspect that in our deepest oceans and trenches we may well have alien bases. That sounds crazy but if you think about it, we only know 5 per cent of ocean, we know more about the surface of the moon or Mars than our own oceans."[26]

It now seems altogether probable that John was witnessing something similar to what the pilots are seeing: crypto-terrestrials, separated from us by a psychic, dimensional membrane, coming up out of the sea, as both Corbel and Heseltine have also suggested.

Robert Salas shared his experience along with six other Air Force officers in 2010. He witnessed ten nuclear missiles taken offline while in an underground base.

He says, "I want the Air Force, the government to come forward and say this is a real phenomenon." According to the write up in *theSun.com*:

US military security reported seeing lights in the sky making off maneuvers before; five minutes later, they claimed they spotted a "pulsating oval-shaped object" hovering above the base. The launch officer claims the missiles he was monitoring then started going into the "no go" condition. And this apparent display of power by the UFOs came at the height of the Cold War when the US and Russia sat poised on the edge of Armageddon.

Captain Salas said, "I think it was simply a show. They wanted to shine a light on our nuclear weapons and just send us a message. My interpretation is the message is 'get rid of them' because it's going to mean our destruction."

---

[26] https://www.the-sun.com/news/3008383/ufos-coming-from-space-sea-aliens/

The US Air Force has never confirmed the incident—but his account appears to match up with numerous other claims of the links between nukes and UFOs.[27]

The base allegedly took a day to bring the weapons back online—and they could not find any physical damage or explanation for the sudden problem with the missiles.[28]

Gary Heseltine is like many who interpret these craft / beings as entities concerned about either us or the planet, or both. He explained to the Sun Online: "There is a massive correlation between UFOs being seen near nuclear facilities; whether it's nuclear aircraft carriers, nuclear submarines, nuclear weapon storage areas, power plants." He concludes that when they show up, they are sending us the message **"we don't like nuclear weapons."** He speculates: "Maybe they realize we could destroy this beautiful planet."[29] Mr. Heseltine believes the UFOs/Aliens may be concerned about their habitat—the oceans—and they do not want us to destroy the world they share with us.

Another person to make the connection between UFO sightings and nuclear weapons is Luis Elizondo, who "spent 20 years running military intelligence operations worldwide: in Afghanistan, the Middle East and Guantanamo." He hadn't given UFOs a second thought until 2008. That's when he was asked to join something at the Pentagon called the Advanced Aerospace Threat Identification Program, or "AATIP."[30] He reported:

"That is one of the concerns we have from a national security perspective, that there does seem to be some sort of

---

[27] https://www.the-sun.com/news/3125848/ufos-shut-down-nukes-us-base/
[28] See also https://www.cbsnews.com/news/ex-air-force-personnel-ufos-deactivated-nukes/
[29] https://www.the-sun.com/news/3008383/ufos-coming-from-space-sea-aliens/
[30] https://www.cbsnews.com/news/ufo-military-intelligence-60-minutes-2021-05-16/

congruency or some sort of intersection between these UAP or UFO sightings and our nuclear technology; with nuclear propulsion, nuclear power generation, or nuclear weapons systems. Furthermore, those same observations have been seen overseas in other countries. They too have had the same incidents. So that tells us this is a global issue."

Mr. Elizondo claimed that, in the US, UFOs have disabled nuclear capabilities; while he has heard reports that in other nations, nuclear technology has been switched on. He characterized the technology being witnessed as "something that could be anywhere between 50 and 1,000 years ahead" of mankind's own capabilities.[31]

Without question, something is out there. The evidence thus far shows highly advanced non-human beings who have always been on planet earth, live in the oceans, are separated from us by a thin psychic, dimensional membrane, are self-luminous, and can shape-shift. Clearly our weapons are of no consequence to them, and they can turn them on or off as they desire.

Luis Elizondo appeared on CBS's *60 Minutes*, which did a special, "UFOs regularly spotted in restricted U.S. airspace." When asked whether he thought UFOs are real, he quipped, "The government has already stated for the record that they're real. I'm not telling you that. The United States government is telling you that." In other words, for those waiting for an official disclosure that UFO's are real, Mr. Elizondo thinks it has already happened.

In the interview, Mr. Elizondo described how advanced the UFOs are:

"Imagine a technology that can do 6-to-700 g-forces, that can fly at 13,000 miles an hour; that can evade radar and that can fly through air and water and possibly space. And oh, by the way, has no obvious signs of propulsion, no wings, no control surfaces, and yet still can defy the natural effects of Earth's gravity. That's precisely what we're seeing."

---

[31] https://www.the-sun.com/news/3125848/ufos-shut-down-nukes-us-base

In the same *60 Minutes* special former Navy pilot Lieutenant Ryan Graves calls whatever is out there a security risk … his F/A-18F squadron began seeing UAPs hovering over restricted airspace southeast of Virginia Beach in 2014 once they updated their jet's radar, making it possible to zero in with infrared targeting cameras.

Lieutenant Graves explained how pilots training off the Atlantic Coast have seen UAPs "every day for at least a couple years." The *60 Minutes* special showed training footage off the coast of Jacksonville, Florida in 2015, captured on a targeting camera by members of Graves' squadron, which included soundbites from pilots: "Look at that thing, it's rotating! My gosh! They're all going against the wind, the wind's 120 knots to the west. Look at that thing dude!"[32]

An incident off Southern California in 2004 … was documented by radar, by camera, and four naval aviators. David Fravor, a graduate of the Top Gun naval flight school and commander of the F/A-18F squadron on the USS Nimitz; and flying at his wing, Lieutenant Alex Dietrich, who has never spoken publicly about the encounter.[33]

They are now opening up about what they saw, and the conclusion is that what they witnessed is not from earth. Based on these many points of data, according to a 2021 US Pew Research Center survey "About three-quarters (76%) of adults under age 30 say intelligent life exists on other planets."[34] Another poll found "just under half of Americans believe UFOs exist and have visited the Earth."[35] These polls reveal that the belief in UFOs and aliens is no longer conspiracy.

---

[32] https://www.cbsnews.com/news/ufo-military-intelligence-60-minutes-2021-05-16

[33] Ibid.

[34] https://www.pewresearch.org/fact-tank/2021/06/30/most-americans-believe-in-intelligent-life-beyond-earth-few-see-ufos-as-a-major-national-security-threat See also https://www.studyfinds.org/ufo-alien-invasion-inevitable

[35] https://www.ipsos.com/en-us/americans-believe-in-ufos-aliens. There is life on other planets 66%.

S tephen Bassett, CEO of Paradigm Research Group, would like to see the world use the UFO / alien technology. He hopes technology companies: "have made major strides in developing reengineering paradigm-shifting energy systems derived from these vehicles; and if that is true then that absolutely has got to get in the public domain as soon as possible."[36]

There is no question that alien tech would advance humanity rapidly, but advanced beings helping man is merely part of the strong delusion. According to the book of Enoch, the same thing already happened in the days of Noah. The sons of God (*benei haelohim* in Hebrew)… "took wives, each choosing for himself; whom they began to approach, and with whom they cohabited; **teaching** them **sorcery**, **incantations**, and the dividing of roots and trees" (1 Enoch 7:10).

In *Corrupting the Image 2,* we discovered that it was Satan himself, under the secret logogram ⤙ BAD, hidden in the Hermon inscription (BATios), the god of death,[37] who commanded the sons of God to come down. *1st Enoch* reveals that the sons of God gave knowledge (a form of technology) to humans. That activity is strangely familiar with what MUFON field investigator Cassidy Nicholas acknowledged in an interview based on reports from many Native American tribes:

UFOs exist and have visited earth 45%; Humans will have permanent colonies in outer space by 2100 37%;
If they exist, alien and human societies would be similar 26%.

[36] https://www.netflix.com/watch/81066340?trackId=14170287 Episode 3, Code Named Aurora, minutes 26-27. See also
https://www.imdb.com/title/tt15163678/?ref_=ttep_ep3

[37] BAD ⤙ represents the Sumerian word "úš = death, destruction" uš2 = die, kill; blood https://mugsarsumerian.com/default.htm#u12041. Proto-Semitic: *mūt, Arabic: māta مَات Hebrew: māťמת, Ugaritic: mt 𐎚𐎎 (mâtu in Akkadian), http://www.assyrianlanguages.org/akkadian/dosearch.php

"In many tribes, like Zuni and Lakota, there are stories of these sky beings meeting medicine men in canyons and teaching them about how to better understand nature and their land, giving them tools of survival to bring back to their clan."[38]

Brian Mathieson, a UFO witness adds: "It seems like there is a symbiotic relationship between these Star people and Native Americans. I'm not exactly sure what the extraterrestrial beings are getting out of the relationship, but if these creatures have been teaching medicine men how to better understand nature, does that mean they know our world better than we do?"

Harry Turner is a witness who claims to have had a UFO interaction while driving his big rig cross-country and later experienced X-ray vision. He aptly describes how these aliens are essentially gods:

"If extraterrestrials have mastered the technology to travel to our world from God-knows-what distance, then their knowledge of everything would have to be so far outside of what we can conceive that they would basically be like gods to us. And to these gods, there's very little that's impossible."[39]

The *Hangar 1* show narrator follows up Harry's statement with an important question:

"If what Harry Turner says is true, that he was granted superpowers like X-ray vision, think of what that could mean for humanity. Maybe part of the UFO mystery involves unlocking this future where nothing is impossible."[40]

The basic narrative is the same: Sons of God, Sky people, aliens, god, (whatever the title popular within a specific time or culture), they are coming to watch over us, protect us or help us by giving us new technology. Yet, we must first understand who is giving us this advanced technology, rather than blindly trying to reverse engineer it.

---

[38] Hangar 1: The UFO Files, "Star People" Episode, aired May 8, 2015.
   https://www.imdb.com/title/tt4535058/?ref_=nm_flmg_slf_2
[39] Hangar 1: The UFO Files, "UFO Superpowers" Episode aired Jun 26, 2015.
   https://www.imdb.com/title/tt4535112/?ref_=tt_ch
[40] *Hangar 1: The UFO Files*, "UFO Superpowers" Episode aired Jun 26, 2015.
   https://www.imdb.com/title/tt4535112/?ref_=tt_ch

Figure 2 Twilight Zone's "To Serve Man."

If this weren't so serious, we might liken it—in fun—to watching the Twilight Zone's "To Serve Man." Aliens show up with a book entitled "To Serve Man," and promise to turn earth back into the Garden of Eden. All they ask in return is trust. When a group, proud to have been selected to visit the aliens' home planet, is boarding the flying saucer, a woman warns, "Mr. Chambers, don't get on that ship … the rest of the book … it's a cookbook!" The aliens did not come to be a servant, but rather to *serve man for dinner*. In his pride, man does not realize that he is on the menu!

Gary Heseltine, like so many others, believes the extraterrestrials pose no threat to humanity, and we ought to start looking at them in a friendly light. "The things that are being described now were seen and being described in the 1940s, 50s, 60s and 70s. Nothing has changed. All we have is better technical equipment, like video on aircraft, so we can pick things up easier; that's why it's being seen more. We are saying you've got to start preparing people for a massive psychological change, whether it's now or six months or a year's time. Everything is pointing to ET or non-humans … Seventy years of past history would say they've been here all that time, they're not a threat."[41]

---

[41] https://www.the-sun.com/news/3008383/ufos-coming-from-space-sea-aliens

DRACONIAN FROG SPIRITS

Mr. Heseltine has rightly pointed out that the extraterrestrials are taking a long approach to fully revealing themselves, which appears to be part of the deception. Author Craig Campobasso has created an almanac based on "accounts from researchers, experts, government officials, innocent bystanders, and ET enthusiasts." The contactee cases and eyewitness testimony he has compiled about beings beyond earth[42] reveal there is a reptilian race that remarkably matches the spirits that look like frogs[43] John saw in Revelation:

> "And I saw three unclean spirits like **frogs** coming out of the mouth of the **dragon**, out of the mouth of the beast, and out of the mouth of the false prophet. For they are spirits of demons, performing signs, which go out to the kings of the earth and of the whole world, to gather them to the battle of that great day of God Almighty" (Revelation 16:13–14).

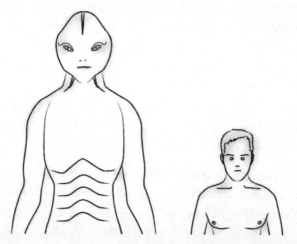

Figure 3. Draconians compared to humans: By Austin Feff - Own work, CC BY-SA 4.0, https://commons.wikimedia.org/w/index.php?curid=79121417.

---

[42] The Extraterrestrial Species Almanac: The Ultimate Guide to Greys, Reptilians, Hybrids, and Nordics (MUFON) Publisher: MUFON, Publication Date: January 1st, 2021, By Craig Campobasso. He claims at least half of the eighty-two extraterrestrial races he has assembled in the book, are indistinguishable from humans and are peaceful.

[43] By Austin Feff - Own work, CC BY-SA 4.0, https://commons.wikimedia.org/w/index.php?curid=79121417

Such an almanac may push our limits of credulity, nevertheless, it is significant that the Draconians come "from the Orion, Sirius, and Draco constellations" and:

> "are cold-blooded creatures who skin is made of scales, scutes, and bony plates. Their most common coloration is brown, beige, and green … They have a foul, pungent smell, an odor that is designed to weaken its opponent in battle. They feel superior over every race, especially human."[44]

Draconian, of course, means dragon; and in *Corrupting the Image 2*, we traced the "great dragon" back to ancient Mesopotamia to show that Satan, without question is the great dragon who has been working behind the scenes since the beginning. We discovered that Ninurta / Nimrod—a hybridized version of the dragon—was known as the star Sirius (we will study that later) and identified by Orion (which was also called gabbar / gibbor).[45] We also studied the Bashmu (*Bashan* in Hebrew), the snake-dragons, and the relationship to Og, King of Bashan. Likewise, we noted the *Mushhushshu*, which is a reptilian dragon-looking creature (see Figure 5, next page).

---

[44] The Extraterrestrial Species Almanac: The Ultimate Guide to Greys, Reptilians, Hybrids, and Nordics (MUFON) Publisher: MUFON, Publication Date: January 1st, 2021, By Craig Campobasso. Pg. 126.

[45] "According to K. van der Toorn…a conflation of traditions could have resulted in the idea that, to the Greeks, the constellation Orion instead of Sirius was the heavenly counterpart of the hunter Orion … in Syriac Orion is called *gabbar*, "hero." Amar Annus, The God Ninurta in the Mythology and Royal Ideology of Ancient Mesopotamia, State Archives of Assyria Studies, Volume XIV Helsinki 2002. Book 3 Pg. 135-138.

Figure 4. Mušḫuššu H. Frankfort, Cylinder Seals, text-fig. 33 (=ANEP #511) (Gudea; Girsu [Tello]).

Regarding their cosmic agenda Campobasso states:

"Draconians want to completely rule the universe... Fear and weakness are aphrodisiacs to them. They are hell-bent on conquest and control... Master manipulators and puppet masters... They plan everything out carefully to guarantee success. Time is their friend. They are said to rule over Earth from behind the cosmic curtain..."

Satan, the great dragon, feels completely superior to humans, has planned everything to ensure his success, is hell-bent on total control, and rules behind the "cosmic curtain." Campobasso reports a variation of the Draconians; they "are able to hide their craft in dimensional time pockets, secret realms not known to man..."[46] The Bible calls the cosmic curtain "the veil" and George Knapp calls it a "thin psychic dimensional membrane." We are simply talking about the same phenomena with different nomenclature.

Campobasso explains how, "Draconians shape-shift their consciousness into other dimensions, including the astral plane, and project their consciousness into a body they want to control" —another parallel to Satan who can transform into an angel of light. Campobasso describes how Draconians choose to possess "lower vibrational humans, whose auras are compromised due to smoking, drinking, and abusing drugs. These holes in the auric field giving them a point of entrance." The Bible just calls 'lower vibrations' and 'compromised auras' sin, transgression and iniquity. Different terms, but same ideas.

In *Corrupting the Image 1* and *2*, we spoke at length about how the Sons of God procreated with women to create a race called Nephilim. It turns out Draconians do the same thing:

> When impregnating human women, Draconians **camouflage themselves as handsome men having sex with them in a dream or altered state**. The Dracs then harvest the fetus within two to three months for their breeding program. When abducting humans, they implant false screen memories in the host. They can manipulate a mind or body in a dream or in the astral plane and also attack them while there, instilling tremendous fear upon waking. The Dracs feed off the trauma, a sustenance that gives them power and boosts their ego. They can speak mind to mind.[47]

---

[46] The Extraterrestrial Species Almanac: The Ultimate Guide to Greys, Reptilians, Hybrids, and Nordics (MUFON) Publisher: MUFON, Publication Date: January 1st, 2021, By Craig Campobasso. Pg. 128

[47] The Extraterrestrial Species Almanac: The Ultimate Guide to Greys, Reptilians, Hybrids, and Nordics (MUFON) Publisher: MUFON, Publication Date: January 1st, 2021, By Craig Campobasso. Pg. 126

The description of the Draconians abducting people is consistent with the hundreds of reports from Dr. John Mack of Harvard that we considered in *Corrupting the Image 1*. Dr. Mack explained how the abductions are "both literally, physically happening to a degree; and it's also some kind of psychological, spiritual experience occurring and originating perhaps in another dimension." He then described the probing of the body: "they sense in the case of men, sperm removed; in the women, eggs removed; some sort of hybrid offspring created which they're brought back to see in later abductions." Mack said the abductees reported the purpose was "**To produce some kind of new species** to bring us together to produce a hybrid species ... an awkward coming together of a less embodied species than we are, and us."[48]

Campobasso is unwittingly describing the dragon-demonic beings that the Bible has long warned of: "the sons of God saw the daughters of men, that they were beautiful; and they took wives for themselves of all whom they chose" (Gen 6:2). Paul likewise warned of those deceitful spiritual beings:

> For we do not wrestle against flesh and blood, but against principalities, against powers, against the rulers of the darkness of this age, against spiritual hosts of wickedness in **the heavenly places** (Eph 6:12).

WHY NO DISCLOSURE YET?

Based on the numerous Pentagon videos and the tens of thousands of files collected by the Mutual UFO Network (MUFON), we know that these beings want to be seen by our militaries. They are broadcasting their existence and how vastly superior they are to our greatest equipment and technology. Why do they play cat and mouse with our military, disable our nuclear missiles from time to time, and yet do not reveal themselves to the masses? Why hasn't Satan staged the ultimate disclosure with UFOs appearing simultaneously around the world so that their existence is known beyond the shadow of a doubt?

---

[48] All quotations from Dr. John Mack retrieved July 14, 2010 from:
http://www.pbs.org/wgbh/nova/aliens/johnmack.html

The reality is that though Satan is working constantly to undermine God's plans, God is the one who decides when it is time to open the seals. Satan can only truly begin his end-times scenario "when the Lamb [has] opened one of the seals..." which allows the rise of:

> "... a white horse. He who sat on it had a bow; and a crown was given to him, and he went out conquering and to conquer" (Rev 6:1–2).

Thus, ultimately, God will decide when. Nevertheless, the many years of UFO interactions have been important stage setting for the next part of his deception.

Chapter 3: Two Interdimensionals Terrorize Earth

While God has given Satan free rein to perform his dastardly deeds, and given each person the freedom to choose his destiny, God always remains in control. Right on God's schedule and according to his omniscient plan, when wickedness comes up before God's face (Gen 19:13), God's sends his eleventh-hour witness of the judgment and devastation about to come upon the earth.

Noah, "a preacher of righteousness" (2 Pet 2:5), was a witness before the judgment of the flood; Lot was as a witness to Sodom and Gomorrah (2 Pet 2:6-7); and again, Jonah witnessed to Nineveh (Jon 1:2). So too, it will be when Mystery Babylon's "sins have reached to heaven, and God has remembered her iniquities" (Rev 18:5). Therefore, when God decides it is time, and Jesus breaks the first seal, God will send the Two Prophets to the world to witness with signs and wonders of what is coming. Shortly thereafter, Satan will launch his countermove. His decades of UFO-stage-setting will come into focus and take on a new relevance. The UFO/ alien disclosure will be to the Two Witnesses what Pharaoh's magicians were to Moses and Aaron.

> So Moses and Aaron went into Pharaoh, and they did so, just as the LORD commanded. And Aaron cast down his rod before Pharaoh and before his servants, and it became a serpent (Exod 7:10). But Pharaoh also called the wise men and the sorcerers; so the magicians of Egypt, they also did in like manner with their enchantments (Exod 7:11). And Pharaoh's heart grew hard, and he **did not heed them**, as the LORD had said (Exod 7:13).

When Moses and Aaron gave witness of God's intentions to Pharaoh's court, their powerful message was not heeded because Satan had previously installed his counterfeits; Today, the idea of directed panspermia, the thousands of UFO sightings, alien abductions, etc. are the modern equivalent to Pharaoh's court, installed beforehand so the world will not heed the message of the Two Witnesses.

A witness (μάρτυς *martus*) is "one who testifies in legal matters."[49] God will send the Two Witnesses, like the prophets of old, to testify against the world's embrace of Mystery Babylon, the woman that rides the Beast [Nimrod], the goddess Inanna / Ishtar "the great harlot who sits on many waters" (Rev 17:1) "with whom the kings of the earth committed fornication" (Rev 17:2). [50] Mankind will hate the Two because even now the world bows down to the harlot's cosmopolitan charm, full of pride, gossip, slander, lust of power, rebellion, hatred and denial of the Creator, vengeance against God, military might, social influence, atheism and humanism. The world loves her seductive consumerism, gluttony, covetousness, and greed of the bull-god of Wall Street. The world lauds her for her progressive ideals of harlotry, pornography, fornication, women with women, men with men, transvestitism, transgenderism,[51] and baby-killing.

The Two Witnesses will be commissioned "**before** the decree is issued… Before the day of the LORD's anger comes" (Zeph 2:2), and will exhort the world: "**Seek the LORD**, all you meek of the earth, who have upheld His justice. Seek righteousness, seek humility. It may be that you will be hidden in the day of the LORD's anger" (Zeph 2:3). Just as Moses came with power to authenticate God's message, so will the Two. Understanding who they are or in what spirit they operate will help us understand the nature of the plagues they will bring upon the world and why they will be so incredibly hated.

LITERAL AND REPRESENTATIVE WITNESSES

"And I will give power to my Two Witnesses, and they will prophesy one thousand two hundred and sixty days, clothed in sackcloth" (Rev 11:3). "These are the Two olive trees and the Two lampstands standing before the God of the earth" (Rev 11:4).

---

[49] BDAG μάρτυς martus.
[50] See Corrupting the Image 2.
[51] In Corrupting the Image 2, we discovered in the ancient world, only the goddess had mystical powers to transform a man into a woman and vice versa. Today we have surgeons and hormones to change a person's outward sexual appearance. However, a person never really changes their gender.

The identity of the Two Witnesses has been of great interest to commentators for ages. Since John was not told their names, we must figure them out based on their description. However, taking the description either literally or metaphorically will also determine who we think they are. My view is that they are literal individuals who represent others in the same way a congressman in the House of Representatives represents his or her constituents. Over the centuries, proposals have been:

- Israel and the Church
- Jews and gentiles
- the law and the prophets
- etc. [52]

Indeed, they will likely represent any or all of those groups to varying degrees; and because they are called the Two olive trees, they likely represent the house of Israel and the house of Judah, as well. Nevertheless, it must be stressed that they will be real individuals. When we consider that they prophesy 1,260 days—a timeframe also stated as 42 months, and 3.5 years in Daniel (7:25; 12:7) and Revelation (11:2, 12:6, 14; 13:50)—there is little reason to understand it as anything but a literal period of time. They will also literally die, resurrect, and ascend into the sky, like Jesus did.

WHO STAND BEFORE THE GOD OF THE EARTH

These witnesses are identified as "the Two olive trees and the Two lampstands **standing before the God of the earth.**" The prophet Zechariah saw a vision of two olive trees dripping oil into a lamp. He asked the angel, "What are these two olive trees—at the right of the lampstand and at its left?" (Zech 4:11). The angel responded: "These are the Two anointed ones [שְׁנֵי בְנֵי־הַיִּצְהָר *shnei benei hayitzhar*], who **stand beside the Lord of the whole earth**" (Zech 4:14).

---

[52] See Krieger, Douglas. *The Two Witnesses Vol 1*. Tribnet Publishing. Sacramento, CA, 2014. pgs. 9-40.

We have a positive match between the Two. The angel revealed that the olive trees are "anointed ones." The word is not "*mashakh*," which we would expect and from which we get the word "messiah." Rather, they are called "sons of oil." The word "oil" is *yitzhar* [יצהר] which is "fresh oil, shining (pure) oil" (BDB).[53] The root is the same as "*tzohorayim*" which means noon, or shining. It is also phonetically related to *zahar* [זהר] "to admonish, warn, teach, shine, send out light, be light, be shining" (BDB). While the meaning is clearly oil, there is an overtone of shining, admonishing and warning. Who are these two anointed / admonishers / shining ones who stand before the Lord? Scripture reveals two men in particular who stood before the Lord.

The first is **Moses**, who stood before God repeatedly:

- So when the LORD saw that he turned aside to look, God called to him from the midst of the bush and said … "Do not draw near this place. Take your sandals off your feet, for the place where you **stand** is holy ground" (Exod 3:4–5).
- The LORD called Moses to the top of the mountain, and Moses went up (Exod 19:20).
- I **speak** with him **face** to **face**, even plainly, and not in dark sayings; and he sees the form of the LORD. Why then were you not afraid to speak against My servant Moses?" (Num 12:8).
- But since then there has not arisen in Israel a prophet like Moses, whom the LORD knew face to face (Deut 34:10).

The other was **Elijah**:

- And Elijah the Tishbite, of the inhabitants of Gilead, said to Ahab, "As **the LORD God of Israel** lives, **before whom I stand**, there shall not be dew nor rain these years, except at my word" (1 Kgs 17:1).
- Then Elijah said, "As the **LORD of hosts** lives, **before whom I stand**" (1 Kgs 18:15).

---

[53] Brown, Francis, S. R. Driver and Charles A. Briggs. *A Hebrew and English Lexicon of the Old Testament*. Oxford: The Clarendon Press, 1907. Yitzhar [יצהר].

The ancient Rabbis taught that Elijah and Moses would reappear before the coming of Messiah.[54] One such commentary, states:

"the advent of the Messiah is dependent upon general repentance brought about by the prophet **Elijah**" (Sanh. 97b; Pirḳe R. El. xliii.; Assumptio Mosis, i. 18).

Another, Deuteronomy Rabbah states:

"The Holy One, blessed be He, said to Moses: '**Moses**, by your life, just as you have given your soul for Israel in this world, so in the future to come, when I **bring** them the prophet **Elijah**, the Two **of you will come as one**'" (Deuteronomy Rabbah 3:17).

The rabbis were absolutely correct that Moses and Elijah would come at the advent of Messiah. They came in spectacular fulfillment at Jesus' transfiguration, which we learned in *Corrupting the Image 2* happened on Mt. Hermon.

Now it came to pass, about eight days after these sayings, that He took Peter, John, and James and went up on the mountain to pray. As He prayed, the appearance of His face was altered, and His robe became white and glistening. And behold, **two men talked with Him, who were Moses and Elijah**, who **appeared in glory** and spoke of His decease which He was about to accomplish at Jerusalem. But Peter and those with him were heavy with sleep; and when they were fully awake, they saw His glory and **the Two men who stood with Him.**

Then it happened, as they were parting from Him, that Peter said to Jesus, "Master, it is good for us to be here; and let us make three tabernacles: one for You, one for Moses, and one for Elijah"–not knowing what he said. While he was saying this, a **cloud** came and overshadowed them; and they were fearful as they entered the cloud. And a voice came out of the cloud, saying, "This is My beloved Son. Hear Him!" (Luke 9:28–35).

---

[54] Moses, who will reappear with Elijah (Deut. R. iii.; Targ. Yer. to Ex. xii. 42; comp. Ex. R. xviii. and Luke ix. 30).
https://jewishencyclopedia.com/articles/5849-eschatology#anchor8

We see that Moses and Elijah showed up "in glory," an allusion to their anointing / sons of oil / shining, designated in Zechariah; and that they **stood** with the Lord of all the earth. Furthermore, the ancient Jewish commentators Philo and Targum Yerushalmi taught "the same **pillar of cloud**"[55] in the wilderness would appear with Messiah. Indeed, the cloud did appear on the mountain, and the Father's voice emanated from it, authenticating Jesus' ministry.

While I am persuaded the Two Witnesses will actually be Moses and Elijah, it is impossible to prove conclusively. Nevertheless, what matters is that these two individuals will, at the very least, operate in the spirit of Moses and Elijah, even if they are not those two in person. Consider after Elijah was taken to heaven, "the sons of the prophets" observed of Elisha, "the **spirit of Elijah rests on Elisha**" (2 Kgs 2:15). This is the same spirit of Elijah that Jesus claimed was also on John the Immerser:

> Jesus answered and said to them, "Indeed, **Elijah is coming first** and will restore all things. But I say to you that Elijah has come already, and they did not know him but did to him whatever they wished. Likewise the Son of Man is also about to suffer at their hands." Then the disciples understood that He spoke to them of John the Baptist (Matt 17:11–13).

It is fitting that the Two Witnesses will come in the spirit of Moses and Elijah (or be them) since they both battled against BATios / Enlil / Dagan / Melqart—all names of Satan, the god of death. Moses' and Elijah's appearance with Jesus on top of the mountain (where Satan sent the Two hundred angels to create the Nephilim) make them the ideal candidates to come back in the last days to warn the world that Satan is going to open the abyss and resurrect Nimrod. We will also see that their end-time plagues are the same as what Moses and Elijah formerly imposed.

---

[55] Philo, "De Execrationibus," 8; Targ. Yer. to Isa. xxxv. 10, https://jewishencyclopedia.com/articles/5849-eschatology#anchor8

THE TWO WITNESSES HAVE SUPER-POWERS

God will send the Two Witnesses to warn the world; and, in order to authenticate their message they will have out-of-this-world abilities. They will use their powers to testify of the coming King.

> "I will give power to my Two Witnesses … (Rev 11:3) And if anyone wants to harm them, **fire** proceeds from their mouth and devours their enemies. And if anyone wants to harm them, **he must be killed in this manner** (Rev 11:5). These have power to **shut heaven**, so that **no rain falls** in the days of their prophecy; and they have power **over waters to turn them to blood**, and to **strike** the earth with all **plagues**, as often as they desire (Rev 11:6).

These two will disrupt life on earth as we know it. The blows will be so formidable that once these two are dead, the entire world will celebrate and rejoice (more about that later). For a period of forty-two months, the Two Witnesses will call down fire, stop the rain, turn waters into blood, and essentially trash the earth.

This is the period where we should likely expect to see a plethora of UFO sightings all over the world. It might be Satan telling the world he and his minions are here to help. If that happens, then we would expect world governments to progressively increase their response. At first, they will try to remove the Two with snipers, and when bullets fail, they will increase the firepower to tanks, aircraft, missiles, lasers, energy and sound weapons and whatever other high-tech weaponry is available. The text is clear that if anyone comes against them, then they will be killed with fire. With his mouth, Elijah called down fire from the sky when he battled against the prophets of Baal[56] on Mt. Carmel (cf. 1 Kgs. 18:24, 38); and again, when he contended with the fifty soldiers who came to take him away (2 Kgs. 1:10,12). Any soldiers coming against the Two Witnesses will suffer a similar fate; soldiers on foot in full body armor will sink to the ground, M1 Abrams tanks will explode, and squadrons of F-22s will fall from the sky after being struck with the heavenly fire.

---

[56] The priests of Baal (synonymous with Melqart, King of Tyre, AKA Satan) with whom Elijah contends (1 Kgs 18:20–40) would thus be the priests of Melqart. Erdman's Bible Dictionary: MELQART.

SHUT HEAVENS

The Two Witnesses also "have power to shut heaven, so that no rain falls in the days of their prophecy" (Rev 11:6), just like Elijah said to Ahab: "As the LORD God of Israel lives, before whom I stand, there shall not be dew nor rain these years, except at my word" (1 Kgs 17:1; 18:1). Elijah shut the heavens to cause Israel to repent and return to God. The effect of draught leads to scorching heat on humans and animals, thirst, and an inability to maintain hygiene etc. A starvation-level-crisis ensues due to lack of rain, which leads to fire that burns the trees and grass. The waters turn to blood, fish die, ships are destroyed, and property is lost.

To better see the actions of the Two Witnesses in context, we might want to approach the text thematically, not chronologically: Parallel events with their inter-related aspects might not be separate events; but rather, the same events seen from different perspectives (See Appendix 1: The Thematic Approach to Interpreting Revelation). This idea was also suggested by the late Irvin Baxter who writes:

> The book of Revelation is not in chronological order. They are three vantage points of the end time. You can view them in comparison with the synoptic gospels of Matthew, Mark, and Luke. We know this is true because the 6th and 7th seal, the 7th trumpet, and the 7th vial all record the same event, the second coming of Jesus Christ. Also, if the kingdoms of this world become the kingdoms of our Lord and His Christ in Revelation 11:15, it would not make sense for the Antichrist to begin his rule in Revelation 13.[57]

That means we ought to look for the descriptions of the harm they cause in Revelation and a plethora of other passages. We in fact see the effects of no rain upon the earth in the breaking of the third seal, (the Black Rider). "I looked, and behold, a black horse, and he who sat on it had a pair of scales in his hand (Rev 6:5). And I heard a voice in the midst of the four living creatures saying, 'A quart of **wheat** for a denarius, and three quarts of **barley** for a denarius; and do not harm the **oil** and the **wine'** (Rev 6:6)."

---

[57] https://www.endtime.com/blog/book-revelation-chronological-order/

Thematic Revelation passages about the 2 Witnesses

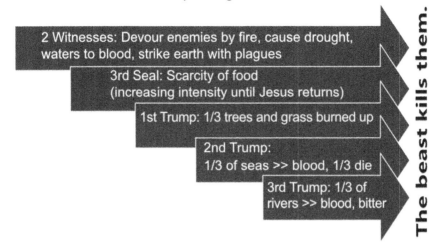

Table 1. Thematic Revelation passages about the 2 Witnesses.

Just one quart of wheat will cost an entire day's wage. We cannot even fathom the radical change that this represents. One bushel of wheat costs roughly $8 in 2022. There are about 37 quarts in one bushel, which means one quart of wheat costs about $0.21. A day laborer earns about $128 daily ($16 dollars times eight hours). That is a 60,952% increase in the price of wheat! This event is not just a little blip in food prices! This is an earth starvation-level-crisis of the greatest magnitude.

FIRE AND BLOOD

Not only will the Two Witnesses shut heaven, but they will have "power over waters to **turn them to blood**" (Rev 11:6). Fire and blood are the two very things that are thrown to earth in the sounding of the first trumpet:

> "The first angel sounded: And hail and **fire** followed, **mingled with blood**, and they were thrown to the earth. And a third of the trees were burned up, and all green grass (*chortos* χόρτος) was burned up" (Rev 8:7).

The reason that food prices will have gone to the moon is that one third of the trees were burned up and all green grass was burned up![58] Grass in this instance is not simply the grass on your front lawn. Rather, it is any kind of pastureland and hay, and occasionally can be used to refer to herbs in a general sense. Wheat and barley are variations of "grass" (*chortos* χορτος).[59]

Trees and grass are incredibly susceptible to forests fires in times of drought, which is one of the plagues the Two Witnesses will bring. We see this scenario predicted by many of the ancient Hebrew prophets. Joel chapter one lists the same features we have already seen in Revelation. Especially telling is the mention of how fire has devoured the pastures, with almost identical language to the first trumpet.

> The **field** is wasted, the land mourns; for the **grain** is ruined, the new **wine** is dried up, the **oil** fails (Joel 1:10). Be ashamed, you farmers, wail, you vinedressers, for the **wheat** and the **barley**; because the harvest of the field has perished (Joel 1:11). **The vine has dried up**, and the fig tree has withered; the pomegranate tree, the palm tree also, and the apple tree All the **trees of the field are withered**; surely joy has withered away from the sons of men (Joel 1:12). Alas for the day! For the day of the LORD is at hand; it shall come as destruction from the Almighty (Joel 1:15). Is not **the food cut off** before our eyes, Joy and gladness from the house of our God? (Joel 1:16). The seed shrivels under the clods, Storehouses are in **shambles**; **Barns** are **broken** down, for the **grain** has withered (Joel 1:17). How the animals groan! The herds of cattle are restless, because they have no **pasture**; even the flocks of sheep suffer punishment (Joel 1:18). **Fire** has devoured the open pastures, and a **flame** has burned all the **trees** of the field (Joel 1:19).

---

[58] Compare: "Do not harm the earth, the sea, or the trees till we have sealed the servants of our God." (Rev 7:3)

[59] Liddell-Scott-Jones Lexicon of Classical Greek χόρτος, ὁ, prop. enclosed place (v. sub fin.), but always with collat. notion of a feeding-place: in Il., farmyard, in which the cattle were kept, αὐλῆςἐνχόρτῳ 11.774; αὐλῆςἐνχόρτοισι 24.640 .

The field is wasted, grain ruined, wine dried up, oil failed, and the food has been cut off. His listing of fires devouring the open pastures lines up perfectly with the description of the green grass (hay) being burned up in Revelation. The beasts of the field are domesticated animals, which are dependent on pastures, that is, "the grass of the field"—thus the grass being burned up in Revelation harmonizes with Joel.

Joel even prophesies that the trees are burned by flame. In Revelation, we see a third of the trees are burned, while in Joel it says all the trees of the field are burned. This is a small, but important difference as it limits the trees to those found in a field as opposed to a jungle or forest. Trees of the field are listed for us: fig, pomegranate, palm, and apple. These are fruit bearing trees that mankind cultivates, harvests, and then eats the fruit. If these trees are destroyed, it will only add to the lack of food and the skyrocketing food prices. Thus, the one third of trees that are burned up, are more than likely the "trees of the field," as mentioned in Joel.

The prophet Isaiah likewise predicted the burning of the earth, lack of wine, and other food. Isaiah reveals the magnitude and broad reach of the coming judgment. It will be judgment that affects the very earth itself. "Behold, the LORD makes the earth empty and makes it waste, distorts its surface … scatters abroad its inhabitants" (Isa 24:1). Isaiah next focuses on how comprehensive the judgment will be. No one will be spared: rich, poor, buyers, sellers, creditors, debtors, etc.

Mankind has transgressed God's laws in a way similar to how the earth was corrupted in the days of Noah. Just as back then, so too, judgment and incredible calamities will follow. Men will be burned and will die. The destruction will span all socio-economic ranges (just as described in the book of Revelation): "

> As with the buyer, so with the seller; As with the lender, so with the borrower; As with the creditor, so with the debtor (Isa 24:2).

The Two Witnesses shutting the heavens brings in a time of intense drought, which brings the loss of trees by fire on a global scale that affects wheat, barley, plus oil and wine,[60] and subsequently results in global starvation. Notice also that God is the One performing the devastation, though we have seen it will be accomplished through his Two Witnesses acting as his agents, just as Moses acted for God in bringing the judgments upon Egypt.

THE TWO STRIKE THE EARTH

Lastly, the Two can also strike [πατάξαι - πατάσσω *patasso*][61] the earth with all plagues, as often as they desire (Rev 11:6). We recall how Moses struck the Nile, turning it into blood (Exod. 7:17–19). The Greek word πατάσσω *patasso* "to strike" is significant because the ten plagues were both a physical and a spiritual battle against Satan's forces. God said:

"For I will pass through the land of Egypt on that night, and will **strike** [πατάξαι] all the firstborn in the land of Egypt, both man and beast; and **against all the gods of Egypt** I will execute judgment: I am the LORD" (Exod 12:12).

We also see the word was used where "Saul sought to pin [πατάξαι] David to the wall with the spear…" (1 Sam 19:10). Hence, the Two Witnesses will be causing severe damage to the world and pinning the world against the wall so that they have to make a decision and choose whom they will serve. The world might just think the Two are bluffing, but they are not. They are validating God's warnings with signs, just as Moses told Pharaoh:

---

[60] The directive to not harm the oil and wine is sometimes understood that the rider is told not to harm the oil and wine. However, upon closer inspection, we must note that the one of the four creatures is not instructing the rider what to do; rather, he is simply reporting the news: Wheat and barley go for this much; concerning oil and wine, be careful because you cannot make more (what is stored is all you have).

[61] The first place is where God promises not to never again "destroy [πατάξαι] every living thing" (Gen 8:21).

"Thus says the LORD: 'By this you shall know that I am the LORD. Behold, **I will strike** the **waters** which are in the river … and they shall be turned to **blood** (Exod 7:17). And the **fish** that are in the river shall **die**, the river shall stink, and the Egyptians will loathe to drink the water of the river'" (Exod 7:18).

Moses' warning Pharaoh before striking the Nile and killing the fish serves as a prototype to how the Two will strike the "waters to turn them to blood, and to strike the earth with all plagues, as often as they desire" (Rev 11:6). We see such an event occurring:

And something like a great mountain burning with fire was thrown into the sea,[62] and a third of the sea became **blood**. And a third of the living creatures in the sea **died**, and a third of the ships were destroyed (Rev 8:8–9).

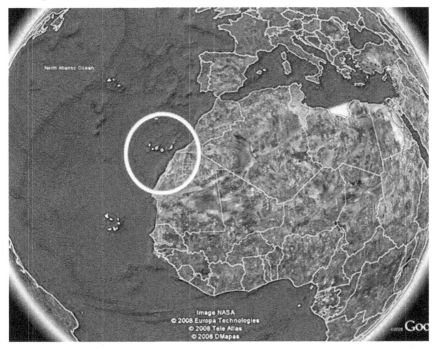

Figure 5. Canary Island, Courtesy Google Earth

---

[62] This plague may be the first physical fulfillment of Jesus' statement: "For assuredly, I say to you, whoever says to this mountain, 'Be removed and be cast into the sea,' and does not doubt in his heart, but believes that those things he says will be done, he will have whatever he says (Mark 11:23).

A mountain burning with fire thrown into the sea sounds like a volcano near the water that falls into the ocean. And not surprisingly, such a future scenario exists!

Dr. Steven Ward, of the University of California, US, and Dr. Simon Day, of the Benfield Greig Hazard Research Centre at University College London, UK warn that "a volcanic eruption on the Canary Islands, off West Africa, could trigger a vast undersea landslide." They estimate a collapse could happen off the western flank of the Cumbre Vieja volcano on the island of La Palma in the Canaries. They believe a build-up of groundwater could destabilize a block of rock up to 500 cubic km in size, which could break off in a future eruption, rushing into the sea at up to 350 km an hour (220 mph).

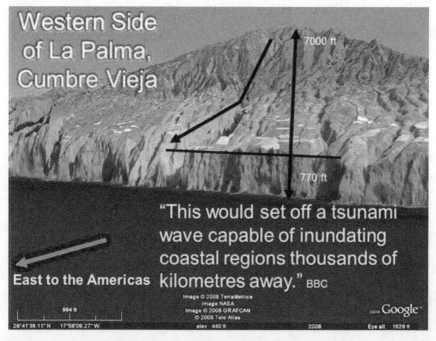

Figure 6. Looking at the west side of the Canary Islands, courtesy Google Earth.

The energy released by the collapse would equal the entire US electricity consumption for six months. The dome of water it caused would be 900 meters (2,950 feet) high, and the resulting tsunami, higher than any in recorded history, which would travel outwards, reaching speeds of 800 km an hour (500 mph).

Waves 100 m (330 ft) from crest to trough would strike the African coast, while north-eastwards they would affect Spain, Portugal and France, and could still be approaching 12 m (40 ft) when they hit the UK. Across the Atlantic, the damage would be far worse, with wave heights of more than 40 m (130 ft) expected in northern Brazil. Dr. Day said, "It's entirely possible you'd see 50-m waves coming ashore in Florida, New York, Boston, all the way up to Greenland, and in some cases reaching up to 10 km inland."[63]

THE WORLD DOES NOT HEED

No doubt, if that scenario unfolded according to the scientists' model, it would fulfill Jesus' prophecy of "on the earth distress of nations, with perplexity, the sea and the waves roaring" (Luke 21:25). Two beings with the power to cause such carnage will be both feared and utterly detested. Humanity's prior modeling of La Palma may be how they are able to explain it away. Just like Pharaoh's men could simulate some of the plagues, the world will not heed the witnesses' shots across the bow as a warning from the Most-high God. The world will be looking for a solution to be rid of the Two troublemakers of the earth just as Pharaoh was plagued by Moses, and King Ahab hated Elijah whom he called the "troubler of Israel" (1 Kgs 18:17). Elijah rightly answered: "I have not troubled Israel, but you and your father's house have, in that you have forsaken the commandments of the LORD and have followed the Baals" (1 Kgs 18:18). Just like both Pharaoh and King Ahab stiffened their necks and looked to their gods,[64] so too will the world search for a way to get rid of the Two.

In the spirit of Moses, they will likely tell the world: "I call heaven and earth as witnesses today against you, that I have set before you life and death, blessing and cursing; therefore choose life, that both you and your descendants may live (Deut 30:19).

---

[63] http://news.bbc.co.uk/2/hi/science/nature/1513342.stm

[64] God does not delight in meting out these judgments upon the world. God would sooner see the world repent, but being omniscient he knows the end from the beginning; he knows what the future holds and sees that sadly, they will not repent. God saw **Nineveh's** "works; that they turned from their evil way; and God relented from the disaster that He had said He would bring upon them, and He did not do it." (Jon 3:11) God's grace upset the prophet who "just knew" that God was gracious and would relent.

In the spirit of Elijah, they will challenge the world:

"How long will you falter between two opinions? If the LORD is God, follow Him; but if Baal, follow him. But the people answered him not a word" (1 Kgs 18:21).

Motivated with knowledge of the terrible consequences that will follow if the world rejects their testimony, the Two will make it clear that if there is no repentance, the King will judge.

Adonai of armies musters the army for battle. They come from a far country, from the end of heaven—Adonai and His weapons of indignation, to destroy the whole land. Wail, for the day of Adonai is at hand! It will come as destruction from the Almighty. Therefore all hands will be limp, every man's heart will melt, and they will be afraid. Pangs and sorrows will take hold of them; they will be in pain as a woman in childbirth; they will be amazed at one another; their faces will be like flames. Behold, the day of Adonai comes, cruel, with both wrath and fierce anger, to lay the land desolate; and He will destroy its sinners from it (Isa 13:4–9).

Jesus warned, "Unless those days were shortened, no flesh would be saved" (Matt 24:22), and that "as the days of Noah were, so also will the coming of the Son of Man be" (Matt 24:37). We talked about what happened in the days of Noah in *Corrupting the Image 1* and 2: "there were Nephilim on the earth in those days ... when the sons of God came into the daughters of men and they bore children to them" (Gen 6:4).

In the end, because man by and large rejects the message of the Two (Rev 16:11), and will "not receive the love of the truth that they might be saved ... God will send them strong delusion, that they should believe the lie, that they all may be condemned who did not believe the truth but had pleasure in unrighteousness" (2 Thess 2:10–12). Just as Pharaoh rejected the many proofs, so too the world will reject the truth of the Two, and instead, in a delusional state will accept Satan's lie—that he is here to help fight the Two agents of the malevolent Creator who only wants to limit their freedom and enslave them.

Chapter 4: Extraterrestrial Saviors

Many today are waiting for a major disclosure event where UFOs show up around the world to announce their presence officially and undeniably. Such an event would unite the world in shock and with a common purpose. Such an idea was prefigured when Ronald Reagan stated in a conversation he had with General Secretary Gorbachev in 1985:

If suddenly there was a **threat to this world** from some other species from another planet... We'd forget all the little local differences that we have between our countries, and we would find out once and for all that we really are all human beings on this earth together.[65]

He later stated at the United Nations, September 21, 1987: "Perhaps we need some outside, universal threat to make us recognize this common bond. I occasionally think, how quickly our differences worldwide would vanish if we were facing an **alien threat** from outside this world."

According to a UK survey, 60% of Brits believe it is only a "matter of time before Earth becomes the target of an alien invasion."[66] When the Two Witnesses, wielding extraordinary powers, demand that mankind submit to their tyrannical overlord, and then inflict violence on resisters, the world could justifiably interpret them as hostile aliens.

Movies and science fiction literature often depict humanity's creators as tyrannical, advanced beings hellbent on eating us or enslaving us. In the movie, *Prometheus,* one member of an advanced humanoid race eons ago sacrificially released his DNA into earth's water, thereby becoming the father of humanity. When a group travels to the creators' planet, they discover the creators intend to harm us.

The Two Witnesses could easily be seen in the light of agents of the cold aliens rather than those of a loving God who is concerned about his creation. After 3.5 years of their fire, drought and attacks, the world will be exhausted, disheartened and in financial ruin, as described by Isaiah:

---

[65] December 4, 1985, speaking to the students at Fallston High School in Fallston, Maryland.
[66] https://www.studyfinds.org/ufo-alien-invasion-inevitable/

The new wine fails, the vine languishes, all the merry-hearted sigh (Isa 24:7). … Strong drink is bitter to those who drink it (Isa 24:9). The city of confusion is broken down; every house is shut up, so that none may go in (Isa 24:10). There is a cry for wine in the streets, all joy is darkened, the mirth of the land is gone (Isa 24:11).

For forty-two months, Earth's greatest militaries with their most advanced weapons have been humbled; one third of ships including super tankers and massive cargo ships (Rev 8:9) are destroyed; one third of the fish dead; one third of trees devastated by drought and fire, and starvation is setting in for many. The world will be in desperate straits—desperate to find a solution to be rid of the Two.

While some will consider the message of the Two and repent, many others will dig in their heels, like Pharaoh who did not repent when the God of heaven and earth sent witnesses and judgment. As Pharaoh foolishly fought against the God of Israel, leading to the destruction of his country, the death of his firstborn, and eventually his own death, so too, the world that has written off the God of Jacob will challenge the God of creation to combat.

The world will reject their true message and will become increasingly delusional, mistaking the Two for meddlesome aliens hell-bent on exacerbating climate change and changing man's Mystery-Babylon-way-of-life. Mankind will therefore perceive them as an existential threat that must be overcome once and for all by any means necessary. If Satan has been staging worldwide UFO sightings during the ministry of the Two, as I suggest, then the world may take the view that the enemy-of-my-enemy-is-my-friend. Hence, mankind might believe they have an equally powerful ally who can defeat the Two.

The "alien threat outside our world" will provide a "universal threat" that will bring the world together, just as Ronald Reagan suggested. However, the deception is that the ones God sends will be perceived by the world as hostiles, while Satan's gang will be viewed as the "good" aliens —the ones who have been living in the oceans, watching out for us, in order to help in our time of greatest need.

We discussed that scenario in *Corrupting the Image 1*. In the 2009 film, *Knowing*, earth is going to explode, but dark figures who later transform into radiant beings (cf. 2 Cor 11:14–15) are working to save humanity. God and Jesus are frequently mentioned in the movie, but they are either impotent or do not care to save the planet, whereas the aliens do.

The reality of Satan's deception is well illustrated in the TV series, *V*, where an extraterrestrial race arrives on Earth with seemingly good intentions (similar to the Twilight Zone's *To Serve Man*). They look completely human and gain people's trust while hiding their true machinations and monstrous appearance. Unfortunately, Satan and his forces, "with all unrighteous deception among those who perish, because they did not receive the love of the truth, that they might be saved" (2 Thess 2:10), will look like the heroes the world desperately needs. Just like in *V*, the would-be-saviors who come to "serve man" are interested in devouring him. Nevertheless, at that point, the world will be fully prepared to strike a Faustian bargain[67] —a veritable deal with the devil. Satan will deliver, but it won't come cheap (we will consider the price tag in the next chapter).

RISE OF SATAN'S HYBRID AVATAR

David Lewis, in his book, *UFO, End Time Delusion*, states that "aliens … will select a human person and endow him with superhuman powers and knowledge. This man will lead us to world government and world peace."[68] The question then is: how would Satan confer this superhuman power and knowledge to a man? Satan has been preparing this move for thousands of years. In *Corrupting the Image 2*, we determined "the beast who was" to be a fusion of Satan / Enlil with Nimrod / Ninurta. In the end times and quite possibly at the request of humanity, looking for a solution to defeat the Two, Satan will fuse with a human, thus creating the well-known character that the Bible calls the son of perdition, man of sin, Beast, little horn and antichrist.

---

[67] "The term refers to the legend of Faust… who agrees to surrender his soul to an evil spirit (in some treatments, Mephistopheles, or Mephisto, a representative of Satan)… in exchange for otherwise unattainable knowledge and magical powers that give him access to all the world's pleasures." https://www.britannica.com/topic/Faustian-bargain

[68] David Lewis, *UFO: End Time Delusion*, p. 46.

The Beast will be a hybrid, Satan's own avatar that he can use to do his bidding, who will fit the bill as mankind's ultimate hero and save humanity. That fusion will for all practical purposes be a restoration of the Satan-Nimrod relationship, which we established in *Corrupting the Image 2*. Notice that Revelation tells us the Beast that "was and is not" in John's day will come back. It will ascend out of the bottomless pit.

> "The **beast** that you saw **was**, and **is not**, and **will ascend** out of the bottomless pit and go to perdition. And those who dwell on the earth will marvel, whose names are not written in the Book of Life from the foundation of the world, when they see the beast that was, and is not, and yet is" (Rev 17:8).

In other words, Satan intends to fuse with a man, as he did with Nimrod. He will thereby create for himself an avatar like he did with Nimrod (see *Corrupting the Image 2*). Next, we will see how he might do that.

QUANTUM ENTANGLEMENT OVERSHADOWING

Notice how the prophet Daniel reveals this transition when he is told about a horn:

> And it **grew up** [*tigdal* תִּגְדַּל] to the host [*tzevah* צְבָא] of heaven; and it cast down **some** of the host [*tzavah* צְבָא] and **some** of the stars to the ground, and trampled them (Dan 8:10).

The Hebrew word *tigdal* [תִּגְדַּל] comes from the lexical form *gadal* (גדל) meaning to "grow up, become great, to be magnified."[69] The idea is that the Little Horn goes from a lesser state to a greater state. He becomes so great that he even grows up to the "host of heaven," which is a common reference to the angelic/demonic realm. Quantum physics might hold the answer as to how this could happen. We may find the answer by considering what we scientifically know today and then projecting that into the future.

---

[69] BDB *tigdal* [תִּגְדַּל].

God said to Satan those many ages ago: And I will put enmity between you and the woman, and between your seed [זַרְעֲךָ *zarakha*] and her seed [זַרְעָהּ *zarah*] (Gen 3:15). In *Corrupting the Image 1*, we determined that if "her seed" equals Jesus Christ, then "your seed" must be its antithesis, thus: antichrist, the Beast. In *Corrupting the Image 2*, we concluded Satan might have overshadowed Nimrod in a manner somewhat like the Holy Spirit overshadowing Mary. The angel explained how it worked:

"The Holy Spirit will come upon you, and the power of the Highest will overshadow [ἐπισκιάσει, *episkiasei*] you; therefore, also, that Holy One who is to be born will be called the Son of God (Luke 1:35).

The word "overshadow" means to cast a shadow over something, such as hiding it from the rays of the sun.[70] Clearly, Satan is finite and cannot compare with the Holy Spirit. Nevertheless, he understands the laws of the universe and may utilize them to further his cause.

Another clue is the term "son of Perdition," which Judas Iscariot was also called. We are not saying that Judas and the Beast/Antichrist are the same. Rather, the term "son of perdition" may be the result of a process. Remember that Satan entered Judas (Luke 22:3, John 13:27) and possessed him. While we do not know exactly what happens when a person is possessed, we do know that the human is overpowered by the demon who can override the person's will and control their speech, muscles and more. In modern terminology, Satan possessing Judas might have formed a quantum entanglement. LiveScience defines it this way:

---

[70] LSJ ἐπισκῐ-άζω, throw a shade upon, overshadow, τῇ [πτέρυγι] τὴν Ἀσίην 1.209 . cf. GA 780a30, CP 2.18.3, : c.dat., Sens. 79, : — Pass., Ph. 1.262, al.; opp. φωτίζειν, S.E. P. 1.141: — Med., -σκιάζεσθαι τὸν ἥλιον to ward off the sun's rays, 5.29.3: metaph., conceal, obscure. 2. . darken, obscure, Ph. 2.223 (Pass.): metaph., ἀφροσύνη ἐ. ψυχήν Id. 1.685, al.

Entanglement occurs when a pair of particles, such as photons, interact physically. A laser beam fired through a certain type of crystal can cause individual photons to be split into pairs of entangled photons.[71]

Sean Hamill explains:

"In quantum entanglement, subatomic particles maintain a relationship—for instance, vibrating when the other vibrates—even when separated and even if they are at great distances from each other."[72]

Jesus gave an example of entanglement:

"The wind [ruach / spirit] blows where it wishes, and you hear the sound of it, but cannot tell where it comes from and where it goes. So is everyone who is born of the Spirit" (John 3:8).

In other words, we cannot predict what the Spirit is going to do, what should be observable, and what cannot be observed.

Thus, even after Satan left Judas, they could have still been intwined in a quantum entanglement. This relationship might explain why Jesus chose to call Judas "the son of perdition" (John 17:12). Paul used the same phrase, "the man of sin is revealed, the son of perdition" (2 Thess 2:3–4) whom John describes as "the **beast** that you saw was, and is not, and will ascend out of the bottomless pit and go to **perdition**" (Rev 17:8). Certainly, the descriptor of being the "son of" indicates a relationship. Satan entered Judas who became the son of perdition. This strongly suggests the Beast will also be possessed by Satan. However, unlike Judas, the Beast will also have the dragon's power, throne and great authority. Hence, the Beast is a greater order of magnitude, and he will be the fulfillment of what Scripture has prophesied.

---

[71] https://www.livescience.com/28550-how-quantum-entanglement-works-infographic.html

[72] https://www.merriam-webster.com/dictionary/quantum%20entanglement

The ultimate question is: how can Satan impart his DNA (seed) into a human and merge with him? There are several possibilities to consider. First, scientists believe they may have found a portal to another dimension or a warped scalar portal to fermionic dark matter.

"We found that the new scalar field had an interesting, non-trivial behavior along the extra dimension," the team explained. "Since this new particle has very similar quantum properties as the Higgs boson, it was very natural to assume that the two particles should mix with each other, meaning that their quantum-mechanical wave functions are intertwined. If this heavy particle exists, it would necessarily connect the visible matter that we know and that we have studied in detail with the constituents of the dark matter, assuming that dark matter is composed out of fundamental fermions, which live in the extra dimension," the physicists explained. "This is not a far-fetched idea, since we know that ordinary matter is made of fermions and that, if this extra dimension exists, they will very likely propagate into it," they noted. "A possible new messenger to the dark sector," the researchers said.[73]

We cannot dogmatically say whether Satan and the angels exist in that extra dimension of dark matter. However, the scientists are describing an invisible extra dimension that touches and impacts our own natural realm of existence. Immediately, our attention is drawn to the testimony of George Knapp who said that the aliens may "live here separated from us by some thin psychic dimensional membrane that they move back and forth." Could it be that what the Bible calls the "veil," what Ufologists call a "thin membrane," and what quantum scientists call the "warped scalar portal to fermionic dark matter" are all one and the same thing?

---

[73] https://link.springer.com/article/10.1140/epjc/s10052-021-08851-0
https://www.vice.com/en/article/z3vkny/scientists-have-proposed-a-new-particle-that-is-a-portal-to-a-5th-dimension

Therefore, it stands to reasons that Satan might, in the future, create a quantum entanglement with a man ready to do his bidding, and then open a wormhole between the spiritual plane (antimatter) and the terrestrial plane (matter)—producing a portal between dimensions. If the superposition (quantum entanglement) can be maintained for enough time, then a genetic merger could take place.

We discussed in *Corrupting the Image 2* how three months after his bone marrow transplant, Chris L. of Reno, Nevada discovered that "the DNA in his blood had changed. It had all been replaced by the DNA of his donor, a German man." Then four years after the bone marrow donation, he discovered "swabs of his lips and cheeks contained his DNA – but also that of his donor." The biggest shock was that "all of the DNA in his semen belonged to his donor." The researchers concluded that Chris "had become a chimera, the technical term for the rare person with two sets of DNA." The team monitoring Chris stated: "We were kind of shocked that Chris was no longer present at all."[74] Chris, the man, did not go away, but genetically he did.

The many testimonies of people who have received heart transplants furthers our understanding of what might be going on. For example:

An eight-year-old girl, who received the heart of a murdered ten-year-old girl, began having recurring vivid nightmares about the murder. Her mother arranged a consultation with a psychiatrist who after several sessions concluded that she was witnessing actual physical incidents. They decided to call the police who used the detailed descriptions of the murder (the time, the weapon, the place, the clothes he wore, what the little girl he killed had said to him) given by the little girl to find and convict the man in question.[75]

---

[74] https://www.independent.co.uk/news/world/americas/dna-bone-marrow-transplant-man-chimera-chris-long-forensic-science-police-a9238636.html
[75] Pearsall, Paul. The Heart's code: tapping the wisdom and power of our heart energy. New York; Broadway Books, 1999.

Thus, Satan fusing with the Beast could be achieved not only on a genetic level, but also on an emotional and memory level. That means that the Beast would also know what Satan knows and feel what Satan feels. That is to say, he would be Satan's avatar on earth.

In biblical terms, this would be similar to the Holy Spirit overshadowing Mary and imparting DNA into her womb to create the zygote of the Lord Jesus.

In like manner, Satan could transmit his DNA into the man of his choosing. Thus, when this DNA transfer occurs, the man becomes what the Bible calls "The Beast" or the "Son of Perdition." Satan's DNA becomes the Beast's; The Beast becomes a god—Satan's avatar and his reincarnation. Their fates become intertwined, or symbiotic; Satan's power, throne, and authority are the Beast's.

The Beast (antichrist) has now genetically become the son of perdition. Whatever DNA Satan gave to Ninurta / Nimrod, ages ago, would be present in the new avatar known as the Beast. Antichrist, the man becomes a god, and Satan has incarnated as a man. The number of the Beast might confirm the genetic transformation we have been discussing.

John records that our quest "calls for wisdom: Let the one who has insight calculate the beast's number, for it is man's number, and his number is 666" (Rev 13:18 NET). In the KJV translation, "the number of **a** man" suggests it is the number of a particular man whereas the NET translation suggests that it is something common to humanity.[76] The Greek text lacks an indefinite article, which would make the difference between "a man" and "man" i.e., "mankind."

---

[76] NET syntactical notes: The translation man's number suggests that the beast's number is symbolic of humanity in general, while the translation a man's number suggests that it represents an individual. NET Rev 13:18.

The New English Translation notes how "the **number '666' is the number that represents humankind** ... an individual is in view, but his number may be the number representing all of humankind."[77] In other words, one man is in view, but the number is common to all humanity.

After reading *Corrupting the Image 1*, Tyler H., a Ph.D. in Pharmaceutical Sciences, wrote to me explaining how something regarding DNA had come to mind about the number of the Beast. He said, "the average molecular weight of one base pair of DNA and RNA is 666 grams/mol (g/mol) or 666 atomic mass units (amu)."[78]

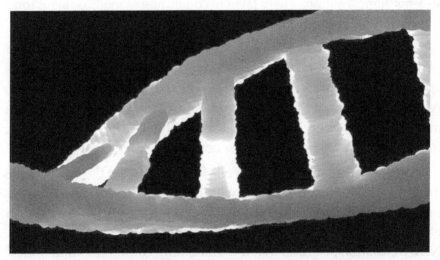

Figure 7 Double Helix. Image by Colin Behrens from Pixabay.

---

[77] NET Notes to Revelation 13:18: "it is man's number." Ex Syn 254 states "if ἀνθρώπου is generic, then the sense is, 'It is [the] number of humankind.' It is significant that this construction fits Apollonius' Canon (i.e., both the head noun and the genitive are anarthrous), suggesting that if one of these nouns is definite, then the other is, too. Grammatically, those who contend that the sense is 'it is [the] number of a man' have the burden of proof on them (for they treat the head noun, ἀριθμός, as definite and the genitive, ἀνθρώπου, as indefinite – the rarest of all possibilities). Considering Johannine usage, we might also add Rev 16:18, where the Seer clearly uses the anarthrous ἄνθρωπος in a generic sense, meaning 'humankind.'

[78] Personal email communication and Interview Awakening Report with Tyler H. who asked for his last name to remain undisclosed.

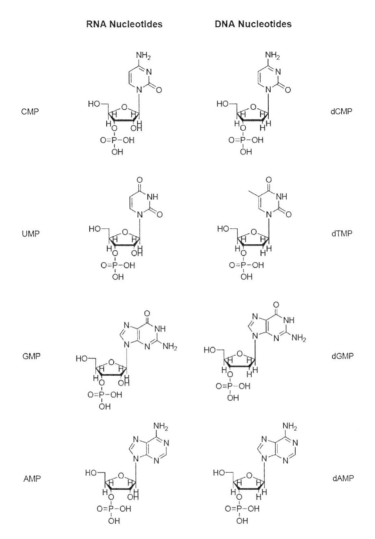

Chemical Formula: $C_{77}H_{112}N_{30}O_{60}P_8$
Exact Mass: 2664.45359
Molecular Weight: 2665.66828   2665.66828 g/mol ÷ 4 bp = 666.41707

or from the "Exact Mass"

2664.45359 g/mol ÷ 4 bp = 666.1133975

Figure 8 Showing molecular weight.

Tyler used the chemical formula $C_{77}H_{12}N_{30}O_{60}P_8$ and then looked at the molecular weight: 2665.66828 g/mol and divided by 4 base pairs (BP) which equals 666.41707 which when rounded down is 666. He also calculated using the exact mass of 2664.45359 g/mol and divided by 4 BP = 666.1133975 which when rounded down yields 666. He went on to say that "every man has a unique name –it is spelled using these 6 molecules. We can copy (make an image) of anyone's 'name.'"

Tyler's discovery has grand implications. It means that the number is the average weight of a base pair of RNA and DNA and found in every person. However, a man is coming who will give his special variation to humanity. If Tyler's discovery is correct, then it corroborates our conclusion: namely that the man known as the Beast will undergo a genetic transformation. Just like how Chris L. disappeared genetically, replaced by his German bone marrow donor, so too the number of the Beast may be indicative of Satan's DNA.

What if this person who has fused with Satan has hybridized DNA, and then he gives his altered hybridized super DNA to humanity for us to likewise become gods? We can be like him: we can have super intelligence, super ability, super strength, and immortality. Lastly, the world will be incredibly desperate to upgrade to god-status to fight the coming alleged alien invasion that the Two Witnesses talked about—presuming the false-interpretation scenario.

Anti-Nicene church father Irenaeus makes the suggestion that the number represents "titan," a word we studied intensely in *Corrupting the Image 2* to mean hybrid. He argues:

"It has in itself the predicted number, and is composed of six letters ... is ancient, and removed from ordinary use; for among our kings we find none bearing this name Titan, nor have any of the idols which are worshipped in public among the Greeks and barbarians this appellation. Among many persons, too, this name is accounted divine ... And besides this, it is an ancient name ... belonging to a tyrant... perchance he who is to come shall be called Titan."[79]

[79] https://www.newadvent.org/fathers/0103530.htm

SATAN / BEAST, SAME FEATURES

Enlil / Satan / the dragon and the Beast have the same features, the same power, authority, and throne because they are fused. They are one. All the powers that various kingdoms have had are now summed up in this person known as the Beast. The man who fuses with Satan has cursed himself forever with immortality in a fallen state. After Adam ate from the tree, God said: "Man has now become like one of us and lest he eat from the tree of life and live forever …" If Adam had eaten from the tree of life in his fallen state, he would have been immortal, yes, but degenerate and decaying in that state. This explains why "The beast that you saw was, and is not, and will ascend out of the bottomless pit and **go to perdition**" (Rev 17:8), and is called "the **son of perdition**" (2 Thess 2:3–4). He will have become the god of death incarnate. The many names we learned in *Corrupting the Image 2* for Satan such as BAD, Nergal, Pabilsag, and others were all related to death. The prophet Ezekiel prophesied of this one known as death in Ezekiel 38–39, which we will consider in later chapters. The Beast will go to perdition; he will be lost. This is really a culmination of Satan's previous kingdoms.

The Beast that carries Ishtar or Inanna is Nimrod, the rebel (the culmination of Satan's previous kingdoms).

1 Peter says we (believers) are partakers of God's nature. In the Beast, Satan has created a counterfeit, so the world becomes a partaker of his nature. Consequently, John says, "they worshiped the dragon who gave authority to the beast; and they worshiped the beast" (Rev 13:4). Just what are the formidable powers that are so awesome that the world's superpowers will not be able to compete with him and will ask, "Who [*is*] like the beast? Who is able to make war with him?" (Rev 13:4).

SATAN'S POWERS BECOME THE BEAST'S

We considered the powers Satan could have afforded Nimrod and the powers that the Beast who ascends out of the abyss will receive to utilize all of Satan's power, throne, and great authority (Rev 13:2). We studied Satan's powers in detail in *Corrupting the Image 2* where we learned he was manipulating the weather, etc. when Jesus rose and rebuked the wind, and spoke to the sea. The following is a potential list of the powers the Beast appears to have.

Power	Scripture
•**Biokinesis:** manipulate biology	• Job 2:7 Satan … struck Job with painful boils …
•**Electrokinesis**: control electrical things	• Rev 13:13 … he even makes fire come down from heaven.
•**Flight**	• Rev 8:13 an angel flying through the midst of heaven
•**Pathokinesis:** manipulate emotions	• Eph 6:11 … stand against the wiles of the devil.
•**Power augmentation and granting:** impart power to others	• Exod 7:11 the magicians … did in like manner with their enchantments. • Rev 13:2 The dragon gave him his power, his throne, and great authority.
•**Shape Shift:** change one's form	• 2 Cor 11:14 Satan himself transforms himself into an angel of light.
•**Telepathy:** read minds and implant thoughts	• Matt 16:23 "Get behind Me, Satan! You are an offense to Me …"
•**Teleportation**: travel without occupying space in between	• Matt 4:5, 8 Then the devil took Him up into the holy city … the devil took Him up on an exceedingly high mountain.
•**Thermokinesis:** alter temperatures	• Job 1:16 "The fire of God fell from heaven and burned up the sheep and the servants …"
•**Weather manipulation**	• Job 1:19 "a great wind came … and struck the … house • Mark 4:39 He arose and rebuked the wind [he rebuked Satan

Table 2. Potential Powers of the Beast.

We considered this merger in *Corrupting the Image 2* between Satan and Nimrod, whose name means "rebel." While the man called the Beast might not be a reincarnation of Nimrod himself, he will certainly come in the spirit of Nimrod. Hence, the graphic below represents their merger. However, this time will begin a reign of terror the likes of which the world has never seen nor ever shall see again.

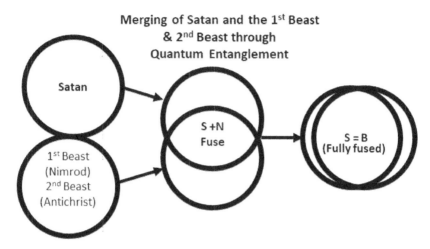

Figure 9. Merging of Satan & Nimrod and the Second Beast.

Vignette 1: Becoming the Son of Perdition

NOTE: There are several vignettes throughout this book. They are short narratives putting the theology and theory into a story format to make it easier to understand. The story is fiction, but is based on the facts we have amassed so far. Skip to the next chapter if you just want the facts.

"All these things I will give You if You fall down and worship me,"[80] Enlil / Satan says boastfully to the man he teleported with him to the rugged peaks of Mt. Hermon.[81] They are alone in the darkness. The man shivers in the cold night air. Satan exhibits the kingdoms of the world in all of their glory before him. The power, money, and fame beckon him to claim them, and he falls prostrate before Enlil.

"There is none like you, O Enlil. Thank you for showing me the light. You are the god of light and god of good," the man professes to Enlil who has transformed himself to look like a glorious Angel of light.[82] "I pledge my fidelity to you alone, my Lord." Enlil basks in the adulation. "There is none like you," the man repeats.

These sons of Adam are willing to renounce Adonai for practically nothing; strike everything they own, and they will curse Adonai to his face.[83] Or better yet, strike their bones and flesh and they will curse their Maker immediately,[84] he thought. But give them everything they want, and they will bow down to me, Satan muses. He looks at his subject with contempt, fully aware that the man worships him only to get what he wants.

---

[80] Matt 4:8
[81] Matt 4:9
[82] 2 Cor 11:14
[83] Job 1:11
[84] Job 2:5

There had been many over the last two millennia with the same anti-Messiah spirit[85], hating the ways of Adonai, as did the son of Adam kneeling before him. Now that the sons of Adam had entered the genetic age, the time was ripe.

Enlil thinks about this servant's qualities: He loves himself more than any other, and he loves money and power.[86] He is precisely what I need at this hour.

"I have given you money, power, and influence—all because of your loyalty to me. You have done well, my servant, and have learned the mystery of your craft.[87] What more do you desire?"

The man lifts his head, fixing his eyes on his master. "I want the key to the dynamo of living power;[88] I want immortality, your throne, your power, and your great authority. Then together we may prevail in your ancient struggle to shake off the binders of Adonai."

Enlil understands perfectly: He acts out of selfish ambition and conceit and is full of every kind of wickedness, evil, greed, and depravity. His heart has nothing but deceit and viciousness and is a hater of Adonai. And … he is utterly ruthless. I sense no humility in him whatsoever.[89] He has none of the qualities of Adonai in him.

"Let our fusion begin," Enlil commands. In a moment, they are transported to the ancient site of the tower of Babel. They stand in a pool of blood in a pentagram flanked by five priestesses inside a temple. Enlil, who has been facing him in his angel-of-light disguise, transforms back into his hideous black shriveled appearance. "The Maker took my beauty from me," he says. He is only partially materialized; and then, walks into the man. Their bodies superimpose; hand on hand, chest on chest, face on face. Quantum entanglement begins.

---

85 1 John 2:18
86 2 Tim 3:2–5; Jas 3:14–15
87 Manly P. Hall, *The Lost Keys of Freemasonry*, Macoy Publishing and Masonic Supply Co. Richmond, Va., 1976. P. 65
88 Ibid.
89 Rom 1:29--31; Phil 2:3–4

VIGNETTE 1: BECOMING THE SON OF PERDITION

The man convulses with pain and begins to fall over. Four priestesses walk up to him to support him while the fifth—the high priestess—walks up to him, takes his hand and runs her knife across his palm; his blood spills into the pool of blood at their feet. Now their DNA begins to merge. Satan's seed, his DNA information code, is fusing with the man's.

The man, who had until now not been able to stand, feels power surge through his body. He can feel himself transforming, one cell at a time. He is evolving from a lowly son of Adam and is beginning to be a gibbor, a mighty one; he is becoming the son of perdition.[90] The sensation is beyond all imagination or expectation, more sensual and intoxicating than any drug he had ever taken. Soon, the change is complete; every cell in his body has been changed. The seething power of Enlil is in his very DNA.[91] He has finally transcended humanity and has ascended to divinity.[92] He has fused with Enlil; Enlil's thoughts are now his. Enlil's hands are now his. Enlil's feelings, desires, wisdom, hatred, and his power, authority, and throne are now the man's.[93]

"I am god! The image of Adonai is undone!" he boasts. "I am free. I have become a new creation; I am born anew! The shackles of Adonai which bound me are gone!" Looking around, he sees beyond the thin psychical dimensional membrane. Dark malevolent demons prostrate before him, ready to do his will.[94] They are his to command.[95] He looks higher and sees a yet higher realm, the realm of Adonai. "I curse you! I will cut down your people and prosper." He shouts to God and those who dwell therein.[96] "My name shall be greatly extolled above every other. To me every knee shall bow and tongue will confess that I am Lord of the earth."

---

[90] Rev 13:2, 4
[91] Manly P. Hall, *The Lost Keys of Freemasonry*, Macoy Publishing and Masonic Supply Co. Richmond, Va., 1976. P. 65
[92] Rev 13:1, Dan 7:11; 2 Thes 2:3; Gen 3:15
[93] 2 Thes 2:3–4, 9; Rev 13:2, 4
[94] 2 Kgs 6:17
[95] Dan 8:10–11; Rev 17:12
[96] Dan 8:10–12; Rev 17:12

Chapter 5: The World's Deal with Death and Sheol

As soon as Jesus opens the first seal and the Two Witnesses begin their ministry, Satan / the Beast will begin pushing for the world to join his covenant. We see this in the rider on the white horse who "had a bow; and a crown was given to him, and he went out conquering and to conquer" (Rev 6:2). He will go out and win people over to his side, perhaps forcefully.

As the ministry of the Two and Satan's UFO deception progress, the desperate world will be more willing to pay any price, including relinquishing their authority to Satan, if he rids the world of the "bad aliens," the Two Witnesses. Just like Nazi Germany did not stand for truth, but believed Hitler's lies that he alone could make their troubles go away, similarly the world will embrace the lies they've wanted to hear.[97] They will reject the Two Witnesses' message of repentance (a direct call to return to God), in favor of Satan's lies that he alone can solve their problems. In exchange for defeating the Two Witnesses, they will confer their authority to him, the lord of Death.

The only true weapon that Satan has ever had against his all-powerful opponent, God, is the legal authority derived from usurped power stolen from Adam. God has given legal authority, and once established it can only be legally overturned by a cosmic event, like what Jesus did on the cross. Once humanity relinquishes its birthright, like Esau traded for a bowl of stew, Satan will once again hold authority. He will operate like a foreign diplomat who may act with impunity. Satan will have regained dominion and authority, which grants him diplomatic immunity from prosecution.

---

[97] It is very telling that part of the story Himmler used to persuade Germany's masses of their manifest destiny was to point to their ancient past. In their case, it was a completely fictional accounting of history. But the point is the Germans were sold on the idea that they, the Aryans, were the master race who were descended from gods and were worthy of ruling the world. We may again see a world dictator that invents a fictional, yet self-serving, history of mankind.

WHY A COVENANT?

Satan knows Jesus intends to reclaim the world that is rightfully His. Therefore, to truly have a fighting chance against the King of Kings, Satan must regain authority over the bodies and souls / minds of "every tribe, tongue, and nation" (Rev 13:7). The crisis in which the world finds itself will play into Satan's hands perfectly, because his goal is to regain authority. Recall, Satan (as BAD / Enlil / Nergal / UG), the king of death and Sheol, once held authority (dominion) over the earth, which allowed him to decree the fates of men and to boast against his Creator.

Think of it this way: God created the world, and then leased it out to Adam. It is all God's, but He gave full authority to Adam. The dominion was Adam's, though it technically belonged to God. Satan hoodwinked Adam and Eve in the Garden and usurped the dominion for himself. Because of this, Satan could say to Jesus, "All this authority … for this has been delivered [παραδεδοται] to me" (Luke 4:6). The word *paradedotai* [παραδεδοται], according to BDAG, means: "to convey something in which one has a relatively strong personal interest, hand over, give (over), deliver, entrust," and also "to entrust for care or preservation, give over, commend, commit."[98] In other words, the kingdoms of this world had been given over, entrusted, committed to Satan—we might say he swindled Adam and Eve 'fair and square.'

Neither Adam and Eve, nor God had any legal recourse; Satan legally scammed them. To be sure, God was and is infinitely more powerful. But the contest was not about strength; it was about authority, and Satan had the legal authority. Once the dominion of Earth was forfeited, God still had the *power* to destroy Satan, but not the *authority*, which was the genius of Satan's plan. He found God's one weakness: "it is impossible for God to lie" (Heb 6:18). He knew for certain God could not just overpower him and take it back because "righteousness and justice are the foundation of His throne" (Ps 97:2).

---

[98] Bauer, Walter. A Greek-English Lexicon of the New Testament and Other Early Christian Literature, Frederick W. Danker, ed. Chicago: University of Chicago Press, 2000. Accessed through TheWord Bible Software, v.9.

CHAPTER 5: THE WORLD'S DEAL WITH DEATH AND SHEOL

Satan's hubris played out in the ancient Mesopotamian Akitu festival where the "good news" was brought to him of the killing of (An) the Creator and where the authority ("*anutu*" Anu-ship) was delivered to him. That authority was known as the Tablet of Destinies in the ancient world; he was the owner[99] and gave it to "Ninurta, as the seal-bearer of Enlil ... [who] was probably authorized to act with Enlil's authority. ... Ninurta ... is often invoked as the "Bearer of the Tablet of Destinies of the Gods."[100] The usurped authority was what he used to keep himself in power for millennia as the king of death and Sheol, and to decree the fates of men.

Nevertheless, we learned in *Corrupting the Image 1* that God declared war against Satan; and stated, one would come who would crush his head. Therefore, even though the earth was Satan's, he needed to guarantee there would be no end to his rule. He knew the prophesy that the seed of the woman would crush his head and attempted to escape it via the angelic incursion on Mt. Hermon, upon which he claimed to be king and commissioned the creation of Nephilim. Satan's attempt failed, and eventually Jesus "planted his flag" on Hermon, transfigured, and communed with Moses and Elijah. In so doing, Jesus claimed his ultimate victory over the god of death and stopped the gates of Hades / Sheol from opening. By way of the cross, Jesus broke the real authority of death and Sheol and thereby acquired the keys of death and Sheol — keys which Satan needs to reacquire.

When Satan seduced man with the forbidden fruit in the Garden, even back then he was offering an agreement with death and Sheol. Mankind eventually went on to cohabitate with fallen angels and bring forth the Nephilim in the days of Noah. Nimrod made a covenant with death and Sheol when he became the first post-flood gibbor-hybrid. The iniquity of the Amorites, as we studied in *Corrupting the Image 2*, was likely the same Faustian bargain.

---

[99] Amar Annus, The God Ninurta in the Mythology and Royal Ideology of Ancient Mesopotamia, State Archives of Assyria Studies, Volume XIV Helsinki 2002. Pg. 14.

[100] Amar Annus, The God Ninurta in the Mythology and Royal Ideology of Ancient Mesopotamia, State Archives of Assyria Studies, Volume XIV Helsinki 2002. Pg. 83-pg 88.

In the words of Jesus, what does it profit a man to gain the whole world and lose his soul? This question has plagued mankind for ages. What good is money and power if you are dead? Hence, the greatest prize is immortality. Every time man is told he can become a god, he jumps at the chance. God, of course, has promised to give man immortality and super-powers, but man wants it on his own terms. Therefore, Satan will use a "back door" or loophole to regain his authority over mankind in order to successfully defeat God. Before the return of Jesus, he must get all of Adam's sons to give their authority to him, the god of death and Sheol. They must give up the authority (dominion) with which Jesus, "with His own blood ... obtained eternal redemption" (Heb 9:12). It was this redemption that caused those in heaven to declare:

> "You are worthy to take the scroll, and to open its seals; for You were slain, and have redeemed us to God by Your blood out of every tribe and tongue and people and nation" (Rev 5:9).

If the world will once again give Satan authority in exchange for him getting rid of the two witnesses, then Satan thinks he will reach a stalemate with God.[101] We catch a glimpse of this where the world worships the dragon:

> So they worshiped the dragon who gave **authority** to the beast; and they worshiped the beast, saying, "Who is like the beast? **Who is able to make war with him**?" (Rev 13:4) And he was given a mouth speaking great things and blasphemies, and he was given **authority** to continue for forty-two months (Rev 13:5).

---

[101] To be clear, Satan CANNOT actually undo Jesus' work on the cross where he legally freed us from death and the grave. Nevertheless, Satan is still trying to undo it through his covenant with death and Sheol. The plan appears to be for nations to give him authority so he can act with immunity and blaspheme God and those in heaven. However, in order for the immunity to stick, he must get every man, woman and child to commit to the mark of the Beast (be transformed). We know from Scripture that if anyone takes the mark of the beast they will then be forever lost without any hope of redemption. In other words, Jesus' amazing sacrifice becomes meaningless to them. Even if they should want to repent, they cannot. So, Satan cannot gain control over the planet like he once had, but can theoretically gain control over all the planet's people and if successful, he might be able to prevent Jesus from taking it back.

Satan is operating with legitimate authority during the end times. The arrival of the Two Witnesses and the plagues they bring upon the world will ultimately compel the world to give their authority to Satan (via the Beast), to combat them. Of course, no one will think they are making a covenant with death and Sheol, let alone a bargain with Satan himself. As far as the world is concerned, there is no Satan; he is just a figment of silly, backward imaginations. However, "because they did not receive the love of the truth, that they might be saved" (2 Thess 2:10) at the testimony of the Two Witnesses, "for this reason God will send them strong delusion, that they should believe the lie" (2 Thess 2:11). They "did not believe the truth but had pleasure in unrighteousness" (2 Thess 2:12) and will fall for Satan's scheme, just as the apostle Paul indicated.

Satan (AKA Death) offers to help the world against the Two and will bring dark forces from the underworld (Hades / Sheol) to help.

A pale green horse![102] The name of the one who rode it was **Death, and Hades [Heb. שאול Sheol]** followed right behind. They were given **authority** [εξουσια *exousia*] over a **fourth of the earth** [*epi to tetarton tēs gēs*], to kill its population with the sword, famine, and disease, and by the wild animals of the earth (Rev 6:8 NET).

---

[102] The fourth seal reveals the intensity of the judgments and the unfolding of the tribulation. The *hippos chloros* translated as "pale" which, according to Robertson, was understood as "yellowish, common in both senses in old Greek, though here only in N.T. in this sense, greenish yellow... Homer used *chloros* of the ashen color of a face blanched by fear (pallid) and so the pale horse is a symbol of death and of terror." Robertson's Word Pictures. The comments on this usage of chloros: *pale, greenish gray* (cp. the relatively paler appearance of the dorsal side of a leaf compared to its ventral side) as the color of a pers. in sickness contrasted with appearance in health (Hippocr., Prognost. 2 p. 79, 18 Kühlew.; Thu. 2, 49, 5; Maximus Tyr. 20, 5b.— Of 'pale' fear Il. 7, 479; 10, 376), so the horse ridden by Death BDAG Chloros.

The king of death and Sheol (Hades) is none other than Satan, and we discovered in *Corrupting the Image 2* the hideous creatures he planned to unleash on the world (we will consider those creatures again later). Revelation 6, à la the fourth horseman, gives us a snapshot that Satan gains authority over all mankind. The authority over one fourth of the earth in that passage is referring to a portion of the **planet's surface area** not one fourth of all people.[103] Approximately 72% of the earth's surface is covered with water[104] which leaves less than 28% of the earth's surface on which people can live. A study done in 1995 by Tobler *et al.* concluded that one fourth (25.4%) of the earth's surface area is inhabited by humans. In the study, they partitioned 217 countries into a total of 19,032 polygons with 295,000 persons per polygon. This amounted to an area of 25.4% of earth's surface. That would be around 96% being considered as occupied at a population density of 42.45 people/sq.km. [105] Incredibly, that scientific study stated 25% of the world's surface is inhabited by humans, the very percentage John saw in his vision. This provides yet one more proof of the trustworthiness of God's Word! This confirms our interpretation that Satan (Death and Hades) will have authority over the twenty-five percent of the surface of the planet inhabited by humans. In other words, Satan will have authority over every place humans live. It is also stated: "**authority** was given him over every tribe, tongue, and nation" (Rev 13:7).

---

[103] Greek grammarian A.T. Robertson, writing nearly a century ago, likewise understood the text to be speaking about a portion of the planet. Robertson, Archibald Thomas. Robertson's Word Pictures. Ada: Baker Publishing Group, 1923. Revelation 6:8.

[104] https://www.un.org/sustainabledevelopment/wp-content/uploads/2017/05/Ocean-fact-sheet-package.pdf The ocean is vast, covering 140 million square miles (363 million square km), equivalent to approximately 72 per cent of the earth's surface.

[105] (But the quadrangles would also include a lot of protected and unprotected wilderness and uninhabited deserts. it would be far to smooth to give a proper idea of how much land is inhabited) *Tobler et al.* (1995)*The Global Demography Project* (Natl. Center for Geographic Information and Analysis, Univ. California, Santa Barbara), Tech. Rep. 95–6.

ISRAEL AND THE COVENANT

Scripture does not tell us if everyone signs the covenant with death and Sheol at the same time. It is probably progressive, and it could be that Israel will be the last country as they are hesitant to trust after what happened in the Holocaust. Nevertheless, the leadership of Jerusalem,[106] (the ancient seat of power under the Davidic kingdom, then under the Sanhedrin in the Second Temple era, and the seat of the Knesset today) will ultimately join the covenant / agreement (*brit*) with Death and Sheol.

> Therefore hear the word of the LORD, you scornful men, Who **rule** this people who are in **Jerusalem**, (Isa 28:14) Because you have said, "We have made a covenant with **death,** [אֶת־בְּרִית *brit et Mavet*] and with **Sheol [Gr. ᾅδης *Hades*]** we are in agreement. When the overflowing scourge passes through, It will not come to us..." (Isa 28:15).

They will believe cutting a deal with Satan, dressed up as an alien superhero, is the best thing for the country which will spare them from the "overflowing scourge," which TWOT defines as "a figure of speech for God's judgment on his people."[107] The Two Witnesses' plagues unquestionably will qualify as God's judgment, which the leadership will want to avoid.

Because a covenant of death is "until death do us part," there will be no backing out, no escaping it; death is the only way to get out of the covenant. With the contract (legal authority) in hand, then Satan, via his super-human avatar, son of Perdition, can behave as if he has God over a barrel: he can act with impunity and there is nothing God can do about it. If anyone breaks the covenant with Death, then he or she will face the penalties of the contract just like when people default on their mortgage (a legal contract).

---

[106] To be clear, this assessment does not support anti-Semitism; we are not speaking of Israelis or Jewish people in general. Rather, we are noting how God is speaking to the **governing body in the modern state of Israel located in Jerusalem**.

[107]: Isa 8:8; 28:2, 15, 17–18; 30:28 (against Samaria in this case). It does not stretch one's imagination to feel the full force of the analogy. Harris, Laird R., Gleason L. Archer, Jr. and Bruce K. Waltke. *Theological Wordbook of the Old Testament.* Chicago: Moody Publishers, 1980. (TWOT) overflowing scourge.

APOSTASY

The covenant that the world and Israel make with Death and Sheol will create the conditions necessary for the man of sin to be revealed. Paul writes "concerning the coming of our Lord Jesus Christ and our gathering together to Him" (2 Thess 2:1) because "that Day will not come unless the **falling away** [αποστασια *apostasia*] comes **first**, and the man of sin is revealed, the son of perdition" (2 Thess 2:3). Just what is the falling away (apostasy)? According to BDAG, apostasy means "defiance of established system or authority, rebellion, abandonment, breach of faith"[108] The very next lexical entry in BDAG, ἀποστάσιον, *apostasion*, is very revealing. It was a legal term: "in the sense of relinquishment of property after sale, abandonment, etc. The consequent giving up of one's claim explains the meaning that the word acquires in Jewish circles:) δοῦναι βιβλίον ἀποστασίου (Jer 3:8; Just., D. 114, 5) notice of divorce, give (one's wife) a certificate of divorce." BDAG

Apostasy is an action not a document. Relinquishment / abandonment are actions that are sealed with a document that makes the action official. For example, divorce is a separation sealed with a document that makes it official. Apostasy by extension means abandonment of previously established relationship. The covenant with death and Sheol is the formality that seals the breakup. The "*apostasion*" is the document that recorded the apostasy / falling away [αποστασια *apostasia*], abandonment of a contract, such as a divorce certificate (e.g. Deut 24:3).

The language of apostasy, "relinquishment of property after sale, abandonment" is synonymous of the word Satan used, *paradedotai* [παραδεδοται] "to convey something in which one has a relatively strong personal interest, hand over, give (over), deliver, entrust,"[109] when he told Jesus the authority had been "delivered" to him. Adam and Eve relinquished dominion, which was conveyed, delivered and entrusted to Satan.

---

[108] (Josh 22:22; 2 Ch 29:19; 1 Macc 2:15; Just., D. 110, 2; Tat. 8:1) ἀπό τινος (Plu., Galb. 1053 [1, 9] Z. v.l. ἀπὸ Νέρωνος ἀ.; Jos., Vi. 43) ἀποστασίαν διδάσκεις ἀπὸ Μωϋσέως you teach (Judeans) to abandon Moses Ac 21:21. BDAG Apostasy

[109] BDAG παραδεδοται *paradedotai*.

Thus, the *apostasia* is not a casual "falling away," like someone who switches from vanilla to chocolate or changes allegiance to a sports team. Rather, it is "giving up one's claim," after which the property is abandoned. So what covenant is the world leaving by signing up with Death and Sheol? Isaiah states it is the everlasting covenant:

> The earth is also defiled under its inhabitants, because they have transgressed the laws, changed the ordinance, broken the **everlasting covenant** (Isa 24:5). Therefore the curse has devoured the earth, and those who dwell in it are desolate. Therefore the inhabitants of the **earth are burned**, and few men are left (Isa 24:6).

While we could spend a long time discussing the term, "everlasting covenant," indeed entire books have been written on it, we will limit our scope to the fact that it is related to the resurrection of "our Lord Jesus from the dead, that great Shepherd of the sheep, through the blood of the **everlasting covenant**" (Heb 13:20).

In other words, Jesus freed humanity from the power of death and the grave (Sheol), and now the world is spurning that freedom and going back into bondage.

There seems to be a distinction between national/corporate and personal agreements with death and Sheol. The Beast will target global adherence to his covenant, but joining at an individual level is required. The nations will give their authority to Satan, which allows him to launch his plan; and then, it will be sealed forever apparently when people take it individually. Because of the great, irreversible danger here, an angel will be flying in heaven warning humanity:

> Then a third angel followed them, saying with a loud voice, "If anyone worships the beast and his image, and receives his mark on his forehead or on his hand (Rev 14:9), he himself shall also drink of the wine of the wrath of God, which is poured out full strength into the cup of His indignation. He shall be tormented with fire and brimstone in the presence of the holy angels and in the presence of the Lamb" (Rev 14:10).

The writer of Hebrews offers a sobering admonition to those who personally break the covenant based on **two** or three **witnesses**:

For if we sin willfully after we have received the knowledge of the truth, there no longer remains a sacrifice for sins (Heb 10:26), but a certain fearful **expectation of judgment**, and fiery indignation which will devour the adversaries (Heb 10:27). Anyone who has rejected Moses' law dies without mercy on the testimony of **two** or three **witnesses** (Heb 10:28). Of how much worse punishment, do you suppose, will he be thought worthy who has trampled the Son of God underfoot, counted the **blood of the covenant** by which he was sanctified a common thing, and insulted the Spirit of grace? (Heb 10:29).

The apostasy of which Paul spoke is necessary for the Son of Perdition to enter the end-time's stage. It is the worldwide, corporate acceptance of the covenant with Death and Sheol, and it affords Satan (through the Beast) immunity so he can, "speak pompous words against the Most High" (Dan 7:25a). Revelation says:

He was given a **mouth speaking great** things and **blasphemies**, and he was **given authority** to continue for forty-two months. Then he opened his mouth in **blasphemy** against God, to **blaspheme** His name, His tabernacle, and those who dwell in heaven (Rev 13:5–6).

THE WAR BETWEEN MICHAEL AND SATAN

Paul tells us that the apostasy is necessary for the son of Perdition to arise and for the one who restrains to be removed.

For the mystery of lawlessness [ανομία *anomia* / lawlessness] is already at work; only He who now restrains [ο κατεχων ο *katechon*] will do so until He is taken out of the way [μεσου *mesou*] (2 Thess 2:7).

According to BDAG, *katecho* means "to prevent the doing of something or cause to be ineffective, prevent, hinder, restrain."[110] Thus, someone or something is restraining lawlessness now and will continue with that job until he/it is removed. The big question, of course, is who or what is that? We will find important clues to that question in what happens once he/it is removed.

---

[110] BDAG κατεχω katecho

The table below compares Paul's words with Isaiah 28 where the leadership follow the rest of the world and make a covenant with Death and Sheol. Notice the parallels:

The coming of the lawless one is according to the working of Satan, with all power, signs, and **lying wonders**, and with all unrighteous **deception** among those who perish, because they did not receive the love of the truth, that they might be saved. And for this reason God will send them **strong delusion**, that they should **believe the lie**, that they all may be condemned who did not believe the truth but had pleasure in unrighteousness (2 Thess 2:9–12).	Therefore hear the word of the LORD, you **scornful men**, Who rule this people who are in Jerusalem, Because you have said, "We have made a covenant with death, and with Sheol we are in agreement. When the overflowing scourge passes through, It will not come to us, For we have made **lies our refuge**, and under **falsehood** we have hidden ourselves" (Isa 28:14–15).

Table 3. Parallels between 2nd Thessalonians 2 and Isaiah 28.

Once this restraining force is removed, then mankind, in general, will "believe lies" and make "lies our refuge." There will be "delusion" and hiding under "falsehood." These texts are describing the same thing. It means the restrainer is legally/contractually removed from μεσου *mesou* "the midst" / "middle of" when the leadership of Jerusalem, like the other nations, believe Satan's lying wonders and make a covenant with Death and Sheol to protect themselves from the "overflowing scourge" brought on by the Two Witnesses, instead of repenting at the testimony and signs of the Two Witnesses.

THE RESTRAINER REMOVED FROM HIS POST

From other clues we have already examined, we know that once the restrainer is removed then the Beast will go into the temple and cause the abomination that causes desolation. Jesus said of that time:

For then there will be great tribulation [Gr. Θλιψις *thlipsis*], such as has not been since the beginning of the world until this time, no, **nor ever shall be** (Matt 24:21).

75

Jesus' sobering statement was preceded by Jeremiah: "Alas! For that day is great, so that **none is like it**; and it is the time of **Jacob's trouble** [צָרָה *tsara*] ..." (Jer 30:7). The prophet Daniel also spoke of the tribulation [צָרָה *tsara*], a time like none other:

> "At that time Michael shall stand up, the great prince who stands watch over the sons of your people; And there shall be a **time of trouble** [צָרָה *tsara* / Gr. Θλιψις *thlipsis*], Such as **never was** since there was a nation, Even to that time ..." (Dan 12:1).

All three passages speak of big trouble like the world has never seen or will ever see again, which tells us that they are all speaking of the same event. Daniel gives us insight into the happenings in the spiritual realm, specifically with Michael who will "stand up."

"Michael shall stand up" does not mean he had been sitting on the job. In all examples *"omed"* has the connotation of "active defense." For example, in the book of Esther, after Haman was executed, "the king permitted the Jews ... [to] protect [לַעֲמֹד *la'amod*] their lives" (Esth 8:11). The NET Bible translates it "to stand up for themselves." The same Hebrew word *"omed"* is used in a previous military passage: "the prince of the kingdom of Persia withstood me [עֹמֵד לְנֶגְדִּי *omed lenegdi*]" (Dan 10:13). Hence, Michael "the great prince who stands watch over ... your people" is the defender of God's covenant people.

Thus, Michael is defending Israel but then, "there shall be a **time of trouble** [צָרָה *tsara* / Gr. Θλιψις *thlipsis*], such as never was since there was a nation, even to that time ..." (Dan 12:1). Jesus, Paul, Jeremiah and Daniel were all speaking of the same time of tribulation [צָרָה *tsara* / Gr. Θλιψις *thlipsis*] that would come—a time brought about by the abomination of desolation. This begs the question: If Michael is standing watch over Daniel's people, why does he allow the time of Jacob's trouble to happen? It sounds like he is not doing his job—which is exactly the case! Why isn't he doing his job? Simple. Once the Beast gains authority through mankind's apostasy, he will be free to inflict this time of utmost trouble without the restrainer interfering. Michael will not be doing his job because he will be removed from his post. Michael, the great prince and guardian of Israel, is the being restraining the lawless one, the son of perdition, from arising. He will continue to defend Israel and restrain until he is legally taken out of the midst of that role.

CHAPTER 5: THE WORLD'S DEAL WITH DEATH AND SHEOL

Once the covenant with death and Sheol is enacted with the world, and specifically with the leadership who rule in Jerusalem, Michael's authority to stand watch over Daniel's people is revoked, just like Israel allowed themselves to be cursed at Baal Peor, even though they were blessed. Michael is told to "stand down" and is removed from his post, which will then permit the Beast, merged with Satan, to access the spiritual realm:

> "And it [the beast] grew up to the host of heaven; and it cast down some of the host and some of the stars to the ground, and trampled them" (Dan 8:10). "He even exalted himself as high as the Prince of the host; and by him the **daily sacrifices** were taken away, and the place of His sanctuary was cast down" (Dan 8:11). "Because of transgression, an army was given over to the horn to oppose the daily sacrifices; and he cast truth down to the ground. He did all this and prospered" (Dan 8:12). "...concerning the daily sacrifices and the **transgression of desolation**, the giving of both the sanctuary and the host to be trampled underfoot" (Dan 8:13).

The chapter repeats and explains how his deception will work and he will rise up against the Prince:

> "Through his cunning He shall cause deceit to prosper under his rule; and he shall **exalt** himself in his heart. He shall destroy many in their prosperity. He shall even rise against the **Prince of princes**; but he shall be broken without human means (Dan 8:25). ...Therefore seal up the vision, for it refers to **many days in the future**" (Dan 8:26).

Notice that he exalts "himself as high as the Prince of the host (Daniel 8:11). The Beast—merged with Satan and having 100% of Satan's "power, his throne, and great authority" (Rev 13:2)—rises up to the heavenly-angelic domain, fights against good angels, tramples some of the heavenly host,[111] and then continues fighting until he reaches the "prince of the host (Dan 8:11). We learn that prince is "Michael one of the chief princes" (Dan 10:13).

---

[111] In *Corrupting the Image 1*, I understood Satan's trampling of stars to be a reference to having greater authority than some demons. While that is possible, upon closer inspection, the events in Daniel seem to describe the battle in Revelation 12; and, the casting of some of the host could plausibly refer to Michael's angels.

Michael comes to the aid of his warriors, and they halt the advance of the Beast. Revelation gives some insight into this time by noting that:

> War broke out in heaven: **Michael and his angels fought with the dragon**; and the dragon and his angels fought (Rev 12:7).

As a result of the battle we learn that "nor was a place found for them in heaven any longer" (Rev 12:8). As a result of the battle, Satan can no longer access the spiritual realm. In the book of Job, we catch a glimpse of the access he has had to the spiritual realm. "Now there was a day when the sons of God came to present themselves before the LORD, and Satan also came among them" (Job 1:6). He will lose that access and be stuck in the earthly dimension, which is good news to those in the spiritual/heavenly realm as it is proclaimed: "Therefore rejoice O heavens, and you who dwell in them!" (Rev 12:12a). However, that is incredibly bad news to earthlings: "Woe to the inhabitants of the earth and the sea! For the devil has come down to you, having great wrath, because he knows that he has a short time" (Rev 12:12). Satan getting cast to the earth is the beginning of the time of Jacob's trouble.

A plausible reason Satan loses his access to the heavenly realm is that he merges with the Antichrist forming the Beast. Perhaps he thought he could have his cake and eat it too. He wanted to continue having access to the spiritual realm, behind the veil, while having a physical manifestation / avatar here on the earth. The casting of Satan from heaven is viewed from several places in Revelation: "a great star fell from heaven, burning like a torch" (Rev 8:10). The name of the star is Wormwood … (Rev 8:10–11). The literal meaning of "Wormwood" is "bitterness" because it will make the waters bitter. In chapter nine, John "saw a **star fallen** from heaven to the earth. To him was given the key to the bottomless pit abyss" (Rev 9:1). The star in question is also the king and "angel of the abyss and his name in Hebrew [is] Abaddon, but in Greek he has the name Apollyon" (Rev 9:11). Both Abaddon and Apollyon mean destroyer, and bitterness is the sting of one who destroys. We learned in *Corrupting the Image 2* that the king of the underworld, the god of death, was Enlil / Nergal (etc.) / Satan. Hence, Satan is the star we see cast to the earth in chapter twelve, along with his angels, who are also referred to as stars. This ejection from the heavenlies likely happens simultaneously or at very nearly the same time as the abomination of desolation.

This battle happens after the world as well as the leadership of Jerusalem take on the covenant with Death. Though Michael ultimately wins the battle in the heavenlies, on earth, the time of Jacob's trouble will just be getting started. Satan's anger will be focused to "make war with the rest of her offspring, who keep the commandments of God and have the testimony of Jesus Christ" (Rev 12:17, just as Jeremiah, Daniel, and Jesus said.) This time of Jacob's trouble will be the time when God says Israel and Judah "will seek My face; in their affliction [צָרָה *tsara*], they will earnestly seek Me" (Hos 5:15). Thus both houses will seek him in their tribulation and will earnestly seek him.

Satan, via the Beast, will also have authority to "persecute the saints of the Most High and shall intend to change times and law. Then the saints shall be given into his hand for a time and times and half a time" (Dan 7:25). Revelation says, "it was **granted** to him to make war with the saints and to overcome them" (Rev 13:7). We see the themes of ruthless lawlessness, blaspheming, and persecution / war against the holy people in a host of scriptures (Dan 7:21, 8:24, 9:27, 11:36), which we will consider later. The bottom line is that once armed with this game-changing authority, the Beast can blaspheme God and those in heaven with impunity, and do as he pleases against the holy people and the world at large.

Chapter 6: The Lawless One and the Seven Mountains of Shinar

A s the Beast rises to power and the world embraces the reality that we are not alone in the universe, it is likely we will see a return to the worship of the old Babylon gods, Enlil, Ninurta and Ishtar. They would of course be understood to be the same advanced beings who either seeded our planet, or have been watching over us in some way.

The mystery of lawlessness of which Paul spoke can be found in Zechariah 5, where an angel spoke with the prophet in a vision about wickedness (the same Greek word: ανομία *anomia* / lawlessness) returning to the ancient land of Shinar / Sumer / Mesopotamia: "This is their iniquity[112] in all the earth" (Zech 5:6 LXX). "Here is a lead disc lifted up, and this is a woman sitting inside the basket" (Zech 5:7). The woman in the basket "is the **Wickedness!** [הָרִשְׁעָה *harisha* η ανομια e *anomia*] …" (Zech 5:8). She is being taken to Babel "To build a house for it in the land of Shinar" (Zech 5:11). We encounter this same woman in Revelation known as "MYSTERY, BABYLON THE GREAT, THE MOTHER OF HARLOTS…" (Rev 17:5).

In *Corrupting the Image 2*, we learned Nimrod's kingdom began in Babylon—gate of the gods—and was the headquarters of Mystery Babylon that eventually spread throughout the world. We also learned that Inanna, "queen of heaven," was the woman riding the Beast.[113] Babylon had a physical locale, but the effects of its systematic wickedness are worldwide. Just like, there is a city of Hollywood, California, but the influence is global.

---

[112] "This is their resemblance [עֵינָם *einam*; Gr: αυτη η αδικια αυτών *aute e adikia auton*] throughout the earth" (Zech 5:6). The English text reads "resemblance based Hebrew *einam*, "their eye." The Greek Septuagint has understood it differently and could be based on [עֲוֹנָם *'avonam*, "their iniquity,"]. The difference is just a small stroke ' for the yud and the vav. The Septuagint reading fits better, in my opinion.

[113] The Dictionary Of Deities And Demons In The Bible, Eds. K. Van Der Toorn, Bob Becking And Pieter W. Van Der Horst (Boston, 1999). Pg. 66. See also Parpola, Asko (1998), *Studia Orientalia*, 84, Finnish Oriental Society, ISBN 9789519380384

According to Zechariah's vision, Inanna will return to the land of Shinar (Mesopotamia), where she originated, where someone will "build a temple for her in the land of Babylonia" (Zech 5:11 NET). Who better to build it than the King of Babylon, Satan or his agent, the Beast? The angel continued explaining: "When it [the temple] is finished, she [Mystery Babylon] will be placed there in her own residence" (Zech 5:11 NET). The aliens who appear to be offering a needed solution to mankind may quite likely be seen as the gods of yesteryear. The Marvel movie, *Eternals,* posits that very idea—namely that the ancient gods of Babylon and Egypt were highly advanced alien beings. If such turns out to be the case, then there may also be a shrine or even a city built to them in the land of Babylon in Iraq. Exploring exactly how or when this could happen is beyond the scope of this book. Nevertheless, the names of Ishtar, Ninurta and Enlil may be on people's lips again, despite God's warnings:

> Pay attention to do everything I have told you, and do not even mention the names of other gods—do not let them be heard on your lips (Exod 23:13 NET).

Statues of earth's saviors abound. The world could openly worship the ones who free them from the tyranny of the Two Witnesses and the God of Israel.

Babylon as a shrine or city would be the manifest headquarters of radical anti-Creator beliefs. Ishtar would be the guardian and promoter of: harlotry, pornography, fornication, homosexuality, transgenderism, transvestitism, baby-killing, pride, lust of power, atheism and humanism, rebellion, hatred and denial of God, consumerism, gluttony, covetousness, greed, military might, social influence, and so much more. She would embody the things the Two Witnesses opposed. Indeed, such a wanton display of "freedoms" might help crystalize the world's decision to give their authority to Satan.

Figure 10. Row of Sphinxs, Las Vegas, Nevada.

SATAN'S SEVEN MOUNTAIN-KINGDOMS OF SHINAR

Satan, king of death, which we learned in *Corrupting the Image 2*, was called the "great mountain" (KUR-GAL). This leads us towards solving the puzzle of the seven mountains. In Revelation, John is shown the woman who rides the beast, and he is amazed. The angels then said to him:

"Why did you marvel? I will tell you the mystery of the woman and of the beast that carries her, which has the seven heads and the ten horns" (Rev 17:7). "The beast that you saw was, and is not, and will ascend out of the bottomless pit and go to perdition. And those who dwell on the earth will marvel, whose names are not written in the Book of Life from the foundation of the world, when they see the beast that was, and is not, and yet is" (Rev 17:8). "Here is the mind which has wisdom: The **seven heads are seven mountains** on which the woman sits" (Rev 17:9). "There are also seven kings..." (Rev 17:10).

Recall geometry class: If A equals B, and B equals C, then A equals C. Therefore, seven heads equal seven mountains equal seven kings (7 heads = 7 mountains = 7 kings). Therefore, the seven heads, mountains, and kings are one and the same. These are the kings / kingdoms of Shinar that emerged from Enlil starting with Nimrod who is the Beast that was, is not, and ascends out of the abyss. The phrase, "The seven heads are seven mountains on which the woman sits" (Rev 17:9) signifies that the woman (Ishtar) has (or will have) ridden on the backs of (been supported by) seven kingdoms which emerged from Babylon. This of course recalls the cylinder seal at which we looked that shows Ishtar riding on the beast, being driven by Satan.

Figure 11. Rain Goddess. Cylinder seal. Mesopotamia. Akkad period, c. 2334-2154 B.C. Shell. 33.5 X 19.5 mm. New York, Pierpont Morgan Library, Corpus 220.

John also said: "There are also seven kings. Five have fallen, one is, and the other has not yet come. And when he comes, he must continue a short time" (Rev 17:10).

Five empires ruled Sumer / Shinar (the kingdoms "between the rivers"— Mesopotamia) in succession before John wrote Revelation. They were: 1) Sumer (Old Babylon), 2) Akkad / Assyria, 3) Neo Babylonian, 4) Medo-Persia and 5) the Greek empires. Nimrod, the Beast who was, founded the first kingdom, Old Babylon (gate of the gods) and was associated with the building of the *Etemenanki* (tower of Babel).[114]

---

[114] George, Andrew (2007) "The Tower of Babel: Archaeology, history and cuneiform texts" Archiv für Orientforschung, 51 (2005/2006). Pg. 75–95. pdf document.

Under the direction of Enlil, he established the false worship system where he was worshipped as Ninurta, Lord of the Earth. As time wore on, the politics changed, but the gods remained the same. Enlil's name morphed to Illil; and Inanna (the queen of heaven) became Ishtar.

FIVE HAVE FALLEN

After the death of Alexander the Great in 323 BC, his Hellenistic empire was split among his four generals, the four wings and heads that Daniel saw (Dan 8:22). According to A.H. Sayce,

> "A tablet dated 275 BC states that the inhabitants of Babylon were transported to Seleucia, where a palace and a temple (E-sagila) were built. With this deportation, Babylon became insignificant as a city, although more than a century later, sacrifices were still performed in its old sanctuary."[115]

Though impoverished, politically inconsequential, and under Greek rule, sacrifices were still being conducted in Babylon one hundred years later—or about 175 BC. When the Romans conquered the Greeks, Babylon fell into their hands. However, it was the gods of Babylon who had already conquered the world. Their influence had been felt throughout the world for thousands of years. Over time and cultures, the syncretic god Enlil, for example, became Illil, Melqart, and Heracles, as well as Zeus and Jupiter in the Latin or Roman perspective. The cult of Inanna / Ishtar had spread from the land of Shinar / Sumer to the ends of the Earth: west to Greece and beyond, and eastward to India under names such as Ishtar, Ashtoreth, Astarte, Aphrodite, Qadesh, Diana, Urania,[116] and Durga.[117]

---

[115] Sayce, Archibald Henry (1911). "Babylon." In Chisholm, Hugh (ed.). Encyclopædia Britannica. 3 (11th ed.). Cambridge University Press. pp. 98–99.

[116] The Dictionary Of Deities And Demons In The Bible, Eds. K. Van Der Toorn, Bob Becking And Pieter W. Van Der Horst (Boston, 1999). Pg. 66.

[117] Parpola, Asko (1998), *Studia Orientalia*, 84, Finnish Oriental Society, ISBN 9789519380384

The angel told John regarding the seven kings that, "five have fallen, one is," (Rev 17:10). We identify the "one" as the Roman Empire. It was the standing empire, (under Emperor Trajan, 53 AD - 117 AD, that ruled over Babylon in John's days. According to Cassius Dio, Trajan traveled to Babylon "because of its fame—though he saw nothing but mounds and stones and ruins to justify this."[118] Thus, we have seen six nations that supported the woman: Sumer (and Old Babylon), Akkad, Neo-Babylon, Medo-Persia, Greece and Rome.

THE KINGS WITHOUT A KINGDOM

Then the angel said, "the other has not yet come. And when he comes, he must continue a **short time**" (Rev 17:10). The answer to the last kingdom is in the text itself. We know that it will continue but a "short time." The last will be the kingdom of the Ten Horns: "The ten horns which you saw are ten kings who have **received no kingdom as yet**, but they **receive authority for one hour as kings** with the beast" (Rev 17:12).

The Ten do not yet possess a (seventh) kingdom but when they finally get it, it will last "one hour," which certainly qualifies as a "short time" (and with the advent of Big Tech, one hour is possible). The angel told John, "The beast that was, and is not, is himself also the eighth, and is of the seven, and is going to perdition" (Rev 17:11). The Beast is the first king, Ninurta / Nimrod, the beast who was—the one that the woman rode—that we saw in the iconography; and in John's day, it was said that he "is not." Hence, he belonged to the club of seven kings / kingdoms that have supported the woman. In the last days, he will "ascend out of the abyss," which means he will be numerically both the first king and the eighth. Daniel provides us an important link:

"The **ten horns** are ten kings who shall arise from this kingdom. And another shall rise after them; He shall be different from the first ones, and shall subdue three kings" (Dan 7:24).

---

[118] Cassius Dio, Roman History, published in Vol. VIII of the Loeb Classical Library edition, 1925. Pg. 419.

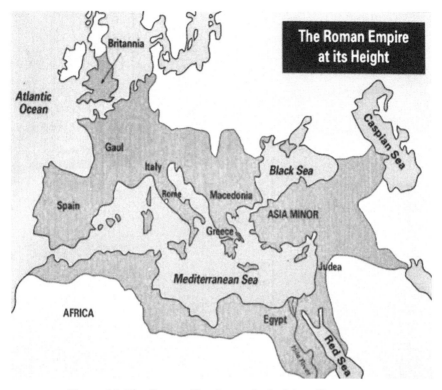

Figure 12. The Roman Empire at the height of its power.

The ten horns are ten kings, who come from the Roman Empire, which we learned was extensive. This means that these kings do not need to come from Italy and its capital city of Rome. Rather, they can come from North Africa, Egypt, the Middle East, Asia Minor or Europe. Then a king will arise from the fourth and terrible kingdom who will be part of a group of ten kings but will be different from them and will eventually depose three of them. His kingdom will be the one mentioned as; "the other has not yet come."

Chapter 7: Abomination of Desolation

O nce the apostasy has occurred in which humanity has turned their back to God Most High and given their authority to Death and Sheol, and the Restrainer is removed, then the next phase will begin:

The man of sin is revealed, the son of perdition, who opposes and exalts himself above all that is called God or that is worshiped, so that he **sits as God in the temple** of God, **showing** himself that **he is God**" (2 Thess 2:3–4).

Humanity will be enraptured when they relinquish their authority to Satan once again. It will be as if Satan could have gotten Israel to forsake God and had actually gone back to Egypt; and given themselves over to be slaves again, forfeiting the freedom God acquired for them.

What is amazing to consider is that the abomination very well could happen on Passover, based on clues in the text. We know the saints will be given into Satan's / the Beast's hands for 3.5 years, their power will be "completely shattered," when "all these things shall be finished" (Dan 12:7); and Jesus will come at the end of that time. Notice Daniel's use of "a time, times, and half a time [לְמוֹעֵד מוֹעֲדִים וָחֵצִי *lamoed moedim vachetzi*]" (Dan 12:7). "Time" in Hebrew is *moed, which* refers to an appointed time / feast.[119] For example, God says: "The feasts of the LORD [מוֹעֲדֵי יְהֹוָה *Moedei* YHWH], which you shall proclaim to be holy convocations, these are My feasts [מוֹעֲדָי *moadai*]" (Lev 23:2). Hence, the strong implication is that there will be a feast cycle, followed by two more feast cycles, and then one-half. Or simply put, 3.5 years, starting with the first feast, which was the beginning.

In studying the feasts of the Lord, we are amazed how the first coming and ministry of Jesus coincided with the spring feasts of the Lord. The same correlation and synchronization at the fall feasts is very likely at his second coming. Let's take a look:

---

[119] BDB Moed

Leviticus 23 reveals there are four spring feasts: Passover (*Pesach*), Unleavened Bread (*Chag HaMazot*), Firstfruits (*Bikurrim*), and Pentecost (*Shavuot*). While each of the feasts has its own rich history and meaning, we note that they also perfectly coincide with the ministry of Jesus and pouring out of the Holy Spirit. Passover was, of course, the time when God told the children of Israel to put blood on their lintels; and He would pass-over those households and their firstborn children would be spared. Jesus' death occurred on Passover and the gospel writers call him the Passover lamb.

God told the children of Israel not to put yeast in their dough because they would need to leave in a hurry, and the bread would not have time to rise. Paul tells us that yeast is a symbol of sin (1 Cor 5:7), and Jesus was literally dead to sin in the grave during unleavened bread. Then, on the first day after the weekly Sabbath, the feast of Firstfruits occurred — when Israel was to bring in the first of their early harvest; and Jesus resurrected on Firstfruits. Paul specifically points this out: "Christ is risen from the dead, and has become the firstfruits of those who have fallen asleep" (1 Cor 15:20). The last of the spring feasts is Pentecost (Shavuot) which was the time that God entered a marriage contract (betrothal) with Israel. It was, of course, also this time, which Jesus had told the disciples to wait in Jerusalem when the Holy Spirit would be poured out.

Jesus' death, burial, and resurrection, and the giving of the Holy Spirit, perfectly coincided with the spring feasts and provide us a template of Jesus' second coming at the fall feasts. Let's consider the fall feasts, which include the feast of Trumpets (*Yom Teruah*), the Day of Atonement (*Yom Kippur*), and the feast of Tabernacles (*Sukkoth*).

My friend, Dr. Gavin Finley, has created a helpful graphic to illustrate the feasts. The feast of trumpets is when we blow the shofar in anticipation of *Yom Kippur*, the Day of Atonement. That is when the high priest would take the blood into the Holy of Holies on behalf of himself, the temple, and the people; and may be the time when Jesus sits in judgment over the nations after his return. (See Figure 13 on adjacent page).

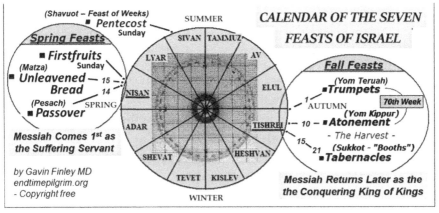

Figure 13. 49 Days from Firstfruits to Shavuot – Giving of the Torah, by Dr Gavin Finley endtimepilgrim.org

With the feasts in mind, we can see from the chart that there is half a year between *Yom Kippur* and Passover / Firstfruits. If Jesus returns at the time of the fall feasts at either Trumpets or *Yom Kippur*, and the abomination of desolation occurs 3.5 years (1260 days, 42 months) before, then that means the abomination of desolation is highly likely to occur on Passover (it also means the Two Witnesses will first appear around the time of the Feast of Trumpets). Jesus' appeal "that your flight may not be in winter or on the **Sabbath**" (Matt 24:20) could even hint at this happening on a high Sabbath, such as Passover. If this is the case, Satan (the Beast) might enjoy desecrating the memory of Passover when the Israelites escaped his grip from Egypt, which was a great fiasco for him and his minion gods of Egypt. Passover was also the time when Jesus died and defanged him and his "mighty ones of Bashan," (the host of demonic forces that surrounded him at the cross) who were gaping their mouths at him. Satan might gloat by reversing the good news Jesus brought to the world through his death on Passover which "disarmed principalities and powers," and "made a public spectacle of them" (Col 2:15).

Thus, when people in Israel are celebrating Passover, the time God had said: "against all the gods of Egypt I will execute judgment" (Exod 12:12), he might see this feast as the perfect opportunity to reenact the Akitu festival, which centered around the "good news" that the creator was dead (a ritual we studied in *Corrupting the Image 2*). Indeed, this might be just the beginning of his blasphemy against God.

Imagine if there is a functioning temple with sacrifices happening, and those were stopped, and the place was desecrated on such a holy day; it would add insult to injury.

> "... then they shall take away the daily [sacrifices,] and place [there] the abomination of desolation" (Dan 11:31). "Then the king shall do according to his own will: he **shall exalt and magnify himself above every god**, shall speak blasphemies against the God of gods, and shall prosper till the wrath has been accomplished; for what has been determined shall be done" (Dan 11:36).

Just like in the ancient Akitu festival, Satan will once again hold the Tablet of Destinies,[120] giving him legal authority over the world. After some two-thousand years, Satan, through the Beast, will have authority to "to make war with the saints and to overcome them. And authority was given him over every tribe, tongue, and nation" (Rev 13:7).

WHAT DO ABOMINATION AND DESOLATION MEAN?

Jesus warned of a time "when you see the 'abomination of desolation,' spoken of by Daniel the prophet, standing in the holy place" (Matt 24:15). Three places in Daniel speak of the abomination of Desolation (9:27 11:31, and 12:11).[121]

> "And from the time that the daily sacrifice is taken away, and the abomination of desolation [*Shikkuz shomem* שִׁקּוּץ שֹׁמֵם] is set up [לָתֵת *latet*]" (Dan 12:11).

---

[120] Amar Annus reminds us "In *Enuma eliš*, the Tablet of Destinies is associated with the powers of Anu" (Anu being the creator). Amar Annus, The God Ninurta in the Mythology and Royal Ideology of Ancient Mesopotamia, State Archives of Assyria Studies, Volume XIV Helsinki 2002. Pg. 14.

[121] "and place [וְנָתְנוּ *natnu*] there the abomination of desolation [הַשִּׁקּוּץ מְשׁוֹמֵם *HaShikutz meshomem*] (Dan 11:31). The term "place" is actually "give/n" and could be "placed" but it could simply mean "given." That is, the Beast gives humanity something from that location.

The term "abomination of desolation" is filled with mystery, though the language is straightforward. The first word, abomination [שָׁקֶץ *shiqquẓ*] means "detestable thing, detestable idol."[122] The noun is used in relation to the various animals that are abominable and ought not to be eaten: "these animals will be an abomination [*sheketz* שֶׁקֶץ] to you; you shall not eat their flesh" (Lev 11:11). The word basically means to contaminate. If dust enters a clean room, then it is contaminated, or *shikkuẓ*. In the case of God's temple, it was a sacred space that was off limits to outside objects, people and practices. Gabriel explains the timing of the vision Daniel witnessed:

> "The vision refers **to the time of the end** …. I am making known to you what shall happen in the latter time of the **indignation**; for at the appointed **time the end** shall be" (Dan 8:17, 19).

The time of indignation [הַזָּעַם *haza'am*] Gabriel was speaking of was the Day of the Lord as evidenced in many passages such as: Isa 26:20, Isa 13:5, 34:2, Jer 10:10, Hab 3:12 and more. It is when God fights on behalf of Israel against the Beast.

The next word, desolation [מְשַׁמָּה *měshammâ*], means devastation "caused by some great disaster, usually as a result of divine judgment."[123] The noun,

> "Desolation" most frequently applies to places and things. In Isa 64:10, Isaiah is praying for a restoration of Jerusalem, which had come under God's judgment and was now a desolation (q,v,), In Joel 2:3 the land which had been "like the Garden of

---

[122] TWOT *shiqqūṣ shiqqēṣ* is used seven times, in the Piel. The Akkadian has a cognate, *saqāṣu* "be spotted, unclean." Found in close association with *shāqaṣ* are *ṭāmē'* in the Piel, "make unclean" and *tā'ab*, "abhor." The object of abhorrence may be the forbidden foods as above, or "the abomination" (tô'ēbâ), an idol. In one beautiful song of praise, the psalmist says of God, "He has not despised (*shāqaṣ*) nor abhorred the affliction of the afflicted" (Ps 22:24 [H 25]). TWOT

[123] TWOT מְשַׁמָּה *měshammâ*.

Eden" before the locust plague has become a "desolate wilderness ... The book of Daniel has four passages employing the Polel form of the verb (*měshōmēm* and *shômēm*) ... the Polel seems to put more stress on the fact that someone has caused the sanctuary or altar to be polluted, thus rendering it unfit for the worship and service of God.[124]

What this suggests is that the future holy place (or temple) will be biblically acceptable. In other words, the temple of God will be a legitimate, functional place where sacrifices can happen. In fact, the Temple Institute of Jerusalem has been preparing for decades to reestablish the temple and can have it fully functional as soon as they get the green light. They desire to reestablish the temple because of their zeal for God. However, the Beast will use it for his own evil intentions. The Beast will establish himself as a god worthy of praise, which is an abomination. Scripture calls this sacrilege. Daniel says:

"But in the middle of the week He shall bring an end to sacrifice and offering. And on the wing of **abominations** shall be one who makes desolate ..." (Dan 9:27).

This event is so important, Daniel is told two more times of its coming:

"... then they shall take away the daily [sacrifices,] and place [there] the abomination [הַשִּׁקּוּץ *hashikutz*] of desolation" (Dan 11:31). "Then the king shall do according to his own will: he **shall exalt and magnify himself above every god**, shall speak blasphemies against the God of gods, and shall prosper till the wrath has been accomplished; for what has been determined shall be done" (Dan 11:36).

We saw glimpses and hints of this in the life of Antiochus Epiphanes. But the person spoken of here seems to go far beyond anything that Antiochus Epiphanes ever did.

"And from the time [that] the daily [sacrifice] is taken away, and the abomination of desolation is set up, [there shall be] one thousand two hundred and ninety days" (Dan 12:11).

---

[124] TWOT מְשַׁמָּה *měshammâ*.

It is significant that the word "abomination" *shikkutz* was used as a synonym for false gods:

> "Then the king defiled the high places that were east of Jerusalem, which were on the south of the Mount of Corruption, which Solomon king of Israel had built for Ashtoreth the abomination [שִׁקֻּץ *shiqquz*] of the Sidonians, for Chemosh the abomination [שִׁקֻּץ *shiqquz*] of the Moabites, and for Milcom the abomination [שִׁקֻּץ *shiqquz*] of the people of Ammon" (2 Kgs 23:13).

This shows that the abomination of desolation occurs when the Beast / Antichrist goes into the holy place and declares himself to be God; usurping the very position of the Supreme God and declaring that he is replacing God in his own temple. He then shows (demonstrates his qualities) [ἀποδεικνύντα] himself by "the working of Satan, with all power, signs, and lying wonders" (2 Thess 2:9) — that he is a god in the temple of God. It is one thing to be a braggart, and quite another to do what you claim you can do. The Beast will not speak empty words; he will show himself that he is mighty and "a god."

WOUNDED BY THE SWORD

After Satan's merger with the Beast and subsequently declaring himself to be god, there will be some who realize he must be stopped. Just as people tried to kill Hitler when they realized he was a monster, so too, it is highly likely someone will attempt to assassinate the Beast and may do so rather quickly. We are told the Beast will be killed and then come back to life: "the first beast, whose **deadly wound was healed**" (Rev 13:12). Because of this feat, the false prophet will later instruct "those who dwell on the earth to make an image to the beast who was **wounded by the sword and lived**" (Rev 13:14). Thus, we see that he suffered a mortal wound, and yet lived. The prophet Zechariah also spoke of this event.

> "Woe to the worthless shepherd [רֹעִי הָאֱלִיל *roi ha'elil*], who leaves the flock! A sword [חרב *cherev*] shall be against his arm and against his right eye; His arm shall completely wither, and his right eye shall be totally blinded" (Zech 11:17).

While swords were obviously used in ancient times, the term is broader and metaphoric, meaning any kind of war-like activity. Paul speaks of God's minister bearing the sword saying, "he does not bear the sword in vain; for he is God's minister, an avenger to execute wrath on him who practices evil" (Rom. 13:4). We know that Rome used several methods in warfare and in policing her subjects. The most well known to us as Christians were the whip and the cross. Though the soldiers carrying out Jesus' execution had swords, they did not kill him with the sword. After thirty-nine brutal lashes with a cat-of-nine-tails, they nailed him to a cross until He died.

Furthermore, the word "sword" [חרב *cherev*] in Hebrew is the same root as the verb *"charav"* which according to BDB means: "to be waste, lay waste, make desolate, be desolate, be in ruins" and "to attack, smite down, slay, fight."[125] Thus, the sword can be understood as killing someone with a type of weapon. A common modern term would be "arms." Swords, spears, slingshots, guns, canons, missiles, etc. are all examples of arms and could be understood as deadly weaponry. In our day, the gun is the most ubiquitous weapon. Could the Beast die by sword? Certainly. However, his death might also be caused by "arms" which might include some kind of firearm.

SHEPHERD OF ENLIL

In the English translation, we read "Woe to the worthless shepherd [רֹעִי הָאֱלִיל *roi ha'elil*]" (Zech 11:17), but in the original Hebrew we make an incredible discovery: the term "worthless" is the term *"ha'elil."* In *Corrupting the Image 2*, we learned that Elil, Illil and Enlil are the same.

A. T. Clay in 1907 casually pointed out that the "origin of אלילים, the word translated 'idols' in the Old Testament … is probably to be found in the name of the Nippurian deity Ellil."[126] Christopher B. Hays states regarding Illil (Enlil):

"His name was known far and wide throughout the ancient Near East, and in syllabic cuneiform it was written as Illil (e. g., d.-li-lu); this is taken to be a contracted form based on a

---

[125] BDB [חרב] cherev.
[126] Albert T. Clay, "Ellil, the God of Nippur" AJSL 23 (1907) 277.

doubling of the word ilu, "god," i. e. il-ilû, "god of gods." This vocalization Illilu and its equation with Enlil are attested already in bilingual texts from Ebla. In fact, it is now commonly argued that the Sumerian writing of his name, ᵈen.líl ("Lord Wind") was derived from the Semitic name."[127]

We are now discovering the many masks under which Satan hid his identity through the ages. In *Corrupting the Image 2*, we found the name "Illil / Ellil / Enlil" in Isaiah 14:12 written "Heilel." Hays notes:

"Because lordship itself was Illil's defining characteristic … Akkadian terms such as illilu, "god of the highest rank" and illilūtu, "divine supremacy" (literally "Enlil-ship") … illilūtu was ascribed to various other deities over the centuries, including Šamaš, Marduk, Sîn and Nabû, each of whom was called illilu at various times. This background is significant to the biblical use of אליל, since it too arguably began with a specific reference to Illil, but was also applied to other divinities."[128]

Thus, the epithet "Enlil" became so common that it was synonymous with "idols" which were indeed worthless. God said to Israel, "Do not turn to [the] idols [הָאֱלִילִים *ha'elilim*] …I am the LORD your God" (Lev 19:4). In the day of the Lord, mankind will disavow his idols [הָאֱלִילִים *ha'elilim* (Isa 2:18) Thus, Zechariah's vision is speaking of a worthless shepherd, but more specifically, is saying woe to the shepherd of Enlil.

We also considered the many syncretisms of Satan, and hence his plethora of titles, many of which we find in the Bible with variant spellings including Enlil (Isa 14:12), Ninurta (2 Kgs 19:37), Marduk / Merodach (Jer 50:2, etc.), Baal / Bel (Isa 46:1, etc.), Melqart / King of Tyre (Ezek 28:12), Dumuzid / Tammuz (Ezek 8:14, etc.), and more. Ninurta was known as the son of Enlil, and often stood in Enlil's stead.

---

127 Christopher B. Hays, Enlil, Isaiah, and the Origins of the ʾĕlilim: A Reassessment, ZAW 2020; 132(2): 224–235, https://doi.org/10.1515/zaw-2020-2002

128 Christopher B. Hays, Enlil, Isaiah, and the Origins of the ʾĕlilim: A Reassessment, ZAW 2020; 132(2): 224–235, https://doi.org/10.1515/zaw-2020-2002

This aligns perfectly with our conclusion that Satan and the man known as the Antichrist (or the Beast) merge and share their identity. This also explains the enigmatic phrase: "The beast that you saw was, and is not, and will **ascend out of the bottomless pit** and go to perdition" (Rev 17:8).

The Beast upon which the woman (Ishtar) was riding was Ninurta / Nimrod who we learned was the "rebel" whom Satan raised up in the ancient world.

In *Corrupting the Image 2*, we considered how Satan fused with Nimrod causing him to become a gibbor or a hybrid being. In the ancient world, he was the rebel known as Ninurta, Pabilsag, Nergal, and possibly Gilgamesh. He was the one who was behind the iniquity of the Amorites, which led to figures such as Og of Bashan, and more.

He was the Beast on which Mystery Babylon rode. He was the Beast who "was, and is not, and will ascend out of the bottomless pit and go to perdition" (Rev 17:8). This rebel, whom Satan will bring back, who was and is not, will ascend out of the abyss. Ninurta was also known as Heracles, who was the **dying and rising** god.

Finally, at the end of history, Satan will make good on the promise to cause him to revive. Nevertheless, this revivification will be a fake copy, inferior to the glorious resurrection of Jesus. Nevertheless, the Nimrod (Ninurta) who died so long ago will in some way be present in the future.

BACK TO LIFE

Whether by sword or some other weapon, the Beast will be healed of the "**deadly wound**" (Rev 13:12). Revelation states:

> "those who dwell on the earth will marvel, whose names are not written in the Book of Life from the foundation of the world, when they see the beast that was, and is not, and yet is" (Rev 17:8).

How could the world not marvel when in front of their eyes, one whom they saw dead has come back from the dead? We have some amazing gadgets and phenomenal technology nowadays. We can go to the moon, go deep in the oceans, and communicate instantaneously.

It will take something spectacular to make the world marvel. It will be so impressive that the world will accept it as truth. Those who buy into this idea—into this system—are the ones whose names are not written in the Book from the foundation of the world, when they see the Beast that was, and is not, and yet is.

This amazing feat will then inspire the false prophet to instruct "those who dwell on the earth to make an image to the beast who was **wounded by the sword and lived"** (Rev 13:14). Though the Beast lives, according to Zechariah, there will be some permanent damage:

A sword shall be against his arm and against his right eye; His arm shall completely wither, and his right eye shall be totally blinded (Zech 11:17).

From that day on, he will be marked by these two features: a withered hand, and a blinded right eye.

We cannot be sure exactly when he will be struck; nevertheless, coming back from the dead will be a wonder that will only cause him to boast all the more. He has made himself into a god, declared himself to be a god, and now, he has demonstrated that he is a god, just as Daniel said "he shall **exalt** and magnify **himself** above every god, shall **speak blasphemies against the God of gods"** (Dan 11:36); and Paul said: "the son of perdition, who opposes and **exalts** himself above all that is called God or that is worshiped, so that he sits as God in the temple of God, **showing** himself that he is God" (2 Thess 2:3–4).

Chapter 8: The Flight of the Remnant!

Jesus instructed that when the abomination of desolation happens we should just leave everything and flee. Believers (the Remnant) living in the region of Judea will put two and two together—considering the words of Jesus and the Two Witnesses. They will also be on alert because the Beast has occupied the recently erected temple (or a designated holy place / tabernacle).[129] In fact, if he dies and rises at this point, then the Remnant will know that the window to escape will not stay open for long. They will heed Jesus' mandate and get out of town.[130]

> "Then **let those who are in Judea flee** to the mountains (Matt 24:16). Let him who is on the housetop not go down to take anything out of his house (Matt 24:17). And let him who is in the field not go back to get his clothes (Matt 24:18). But woe to those who are pregnant and to those who are nursing babies in those days! (Matt 24:19). And pray that your flight may not be in winter or on the Sabbath (Matt 24:20). For then there will be great tribulation, such as has not been since the beginning of the world until this time, no, nor ever shall be" (Matt 24:21)

.

---

[129] It must be stressed that Jesus told us that the abomination would be something clearly evident; and it would immediately impact those in Jerusalem. Unfortunately, there are many today who make spurious claims about vaccines, government regulations, and other conspiracy theories as being the abomination or the mark of the Beast. Until we see what Jesus described, then it simply has not happened, and the mark of the Beast has not yet been introduced.

[130] Preterist theology suggests the events spoken of in Matthew 24 and most of Revelation already happened around 70 A.D. However, Jesus said this will be a time of great tribulation, such as has not been since the beginning of the world, until this time, nor ever shall be. That limits Matthew 24 to be the all-time worst event ever. The destruction of the temple in 70 AD was a terrible time filled with bloodshed. But was it the worst that the world has ever seen? Was it really worse than World War II where 50 million people died? Was it worse than the 6 million Jews who were sent to the death camps?

Based on Jesus' warning, it sounds like time is of the essence; there will be no time to go home to get your bug-out bag. If the Beast has not killed the Two Witnesses at this point, then they may provide the covering the Remnant needs to get out of town. They could potentially provide just enough of a window (maybe hours, days) for the faithful to get out.

However, once the Two have been eliminated Satan (merged with the Beast) will no longer be able to access the spiritual realm, and he will realize he must act quickly to ensure his reign continues. As we mentioned before, for his immunity to stick, he must have all humanity adhering to his covenant. The Revelation 12 Woman (the Remnant) [131] and any other would-be mark-refusers will pose an existential threat to him. As such, they must either toe the line or be removed. However, the presence of the Two Witnesses may provide a deterrent to Satan pursuing those escaping to the wilderness, and hence they must be killed first; though, they may have been eliminated already (and it is difficult to completely ascertain, since we are considering events that likely occur within days or hours of one another; and, because the sequence is not precisely stated in Scripture). Thus, we do our best to piece together these future events from Scripture and add a bit of logic. It could be that the final events happen in a different order. If the Witnesses are already dead, then we can appreciate the even greater urgency to leave immediately. We will examine the slaying of the Two in the next chapter.

Nevertheless, Satan (the dragon) / the Beast (hybridized) will deal swiftly and sternly with the group fleeing to escape his rule.

"Now when the dragon saw that he had been cast to the earth, he persecuted the woman who gave birth to the male Child" (Rev 12:13).

---

[131] The woman is the Commonwealth of Israel, though a detailed answer is outside the scope of this work. The bottom line, however, is people who are faithful to the God of Israel. We will simply refer to them as the Remnant for convenience sake. Krieger, Douglas W., et al. Commonwealth Theology Essentials. Commonwealth of Israel Foundation, 2020.

Those who flee by faith will be aided by God:

"But the woman was given two wings of a great eagle, that she might fly into the wilderness to her place, where she is nourished for a **time and times and half a time**, from the presence of the serpent" (Rev 12:14).

We see this same imagery in Exodus 19, when God told Israel: "You have seen what I did to the Egyptians, and how I bore you on **eagles' wings** and brought you to Myself" (Exod 19:4). God did not get on a giant eagle, like in the *Lord of the Rings*, and fly them on the backs of the eagles out to the desert. God was speaking metaphorically that like an eagle will protect her chicks, he will protect his people from harm.

Satan will pursue those fleeing, hoping to overtake them before they reach their safe haven:

"The serpent spewed water out of his mouth like a flood after the woman that he might cause her to be carried away by the flood (Rev 12:15). But the earth helped the woman, and the earth opened its mouth and swallowed up the flood which the dragon had spewed out of his mouth" (Rev 12:16).

What is the water that he spews out of his mouth? It is possible that Satan could come to planet Earth and cause a flood of water. However, an angel in the book of Revelation defines this representation: "The **waters** ... **are** peoples, multitudes, nations, and tongues (Rev 17:15). Thus, it is a multinational elite army sent in the pursuit of the Remnant and coming in like a flood (a motif used in Scripture: "Who is this coming up like a flood, Whose waters move like the rivers?" Jer 46:7. Egypt rises up like a flood ... (Jer 46:8).[132] Satan is going to send out an army to destroy the faithful remnant. The humans pursuing them may well see the supernatural protection of the God of Israel.

---

[132] See also Isa 8:7.

Anyone supporting the Two will be seen as traitorous, and the Beast will be delighted to murder them. God, however, will protect the Remnant by a cataclysmic cave-in of the surface of the earth where these armies will perish, like at Korah's rebellion. God will see to it that the Remnant, the woman, is taken to a safe place and will be nourished for 3.5 years, 1260 days or 42 months. In the expression "time, times and half a time," the first "time" denotes one year. This is verifiable later by the same timeframe expressed in days:

> "Then the woman fled into the wilderness, where she has a place prepared by God, that they should feed her there **one thousand two hundred and sixty days**" (Rev 12:6).[133]

While there will be a group who arrives to a safe haven, "the rest of her offspring" numbering in the millions will not have had that chance.

> "And the dragon was enraged with the woman, and he went to make war with the rest of her offspring, who keep the commandments of God and have the testimony of Jesus Christ" (Rev 12:17).

Of course, if you are a believer today and consider that we might be going through this terrible time, the question is naturally: how can I get my family to the safe haven? Insofar as I can tell, Scripture does not give us the answer. This is likely something that calls for steadfast faith and a spirit of sacrifice, knowing that God will never forsake the faithful.

With that group out of reach, Satan will turn his attention to the millions still within his grasp:

> "And the dragon was enraged with the woman, and he went to **make war** with the rest of her offspring, who **keep the commandments of God** and have the **testimony of Jesus Christ**" (Rev 12:17, see also 13:10, 14:12 15:4, 16:15, and 19:8).

---

[133] It was Sir Robert Anderson who discovered that a prophetic year consists of 360 days. If we plug that into our formula, then it works out perfectly, 1260 days is 3 and a half years; if the years consist of 360 days each.

The book of Daniel gives witness to the unbridled onslaught against God's people.

- The same horn was making **war against the saints**, and prevailing (Dan 7:21).
- His power shall be mighty, but not by his own power; He shall destroy fearfully, and shall prosper and thrive; He shall destroy the mighty, and also **the holy people** (Dan 8:24).
- "Then the king shall do according to his own will: he shall exalt and magnify himself above every god, shall **speak blasphemies against the God of gods**, and shall prosper till the wrath has been accomplished; for what has been determined shall be done (Dan 11:36).

Daniel also confirms this terrible time will come after the abomination, which happens in the middle of Daniel's seventieth week, and will last 3.5 years:

- But in the middle of that week he will bring sacrifices and offerings to a halt. On the wing of abominations will come **one who destroys,** until the decreed end is poured out on the one who destroys (Dan 9:27).
- it shall be for a time, times, and half a time; and when the **power of the holy people has been completely shattered**, all these things shall be finished (Dan 12:7).

The persecution against the saints will increase in intensity. First, there will be a mandate that everyone must receive the mark of the Beast to buy and sell, and then the penalty will be elevated to beheading (Rev 13:17, 20:4).

In Revelation, John saw souls under the altar asking how long until God avenged their blood.

"Then a **white robe** was given to each of them; and it was said to them that they should rest a little while longer, until both the number of their fellow servants and their brethren, who would be **killed** as they were, was completed" (Rev 6:11).

In the next chapter, John saw them clothed in their white robes:

"A great multitude which no one could number, of all nations, tribes, peoples, and tongues, standing before the throne and before the Lamb, clothed with **white robes**, with palm branches in their hands" (Rev 7:9).

According to one of the elders, "These are the ones who come out of the great tribulation and washed their **robes** and made them **white** in the blood of the Lamb" (Rev 7:14). This group of people are the same who "**keep the commandments of God** and have the **testimony of Jesus Christ**" (Rev 12:17) with whom the dragon made war.

While this will be a horrendous time on planet Earth, the Remnant will grow. Many will discover their real faith in Jesus for the first time; what used to be a cold relationship with God will become alive like never before. Even in the face of persecution and the death of loved ones, and self, the Remnant stand strong.

"Those who do wickedly against the covenant he shall corrupt with flattery; but the people who know their God shall be strong, and **carry out great exploits** (Dan 11:32). And those of the people who understand shall instruct many; yet for many days they shall fall by sword and flame, by captivity and plundering (Dan 11:33). Now when they fall, they shall be aided with a little help; but many shall join with them by intrigue (Dan 11:34). And some of those of understanding shall fall, to refine them, purify them, and make them white, until the time of the end; because it is still for the appointed time (Dan 11:35). Then the king shall do according to his own will: he shall exalt and magnify himself above every god, shall speak blasphemies against the God of gods, and shall prosper till the wrath has been accomplished; for what has been determined shall be done" (Dan 11:36).

Chapter 9: Satan's Avatar Vs God's Witnesses

Now let's take a look at the impending battle between the Beast and the Two Witnesses. To make war against his arch enemies (the terrorizers of earth) and to overcome them, the Beast will need to possess powers greater than theirs!

Up to this point, the Two Witnesses have been invincible. Nothing has been able to stop them until the appointed time. If threatened, they destroy by the fire coming out of their mouths (Rev 11:5). They have power over weather and rain; They can turn water into blood; They bring plagues on earth at their own judgement (Rev 11:5–6). They are on a mission from God.

Fusing with Satan and gaining his powers is the game changer for the Beast. While having a physical body is a game changer for Satan. The Beast will be armed with "all power, signs, and lying wonders (2 Thess 2:9), and the full arsenal of Satan's weapons will belong to the Beast, which marks the end of the Two Witnesses' supremacy. Even these Two with superhero powers will fall by the hand of the Beast.

"When they finish their testimony, the beast that ascends out of the bottomless pit will make war [πόλεμος *polemos*] against them, overcome them, and kill them" (Rev 11:7).

The abomination of desolation occurs in conjunction with the killing of the Two Witnesses. The way the text is written could be interpreted in two ways: 1) that that he first kills them and then goes into the temple to boast that he is a god, or 2) he first goes into the Temple, makes his boast, is killed and comes back to life, and then makes war on them. We are going with option 2.

We know the battle will take place in Jerusalem since, "their dead bodies will lie in the street of the great city which spiritually is called Sodom and Egypt, where also our Lord was crucified" (Rev 11:8). Some commentators have objected, saying that the city could not be Jerusalem since it was never called Sodom or Egypt. Yet a simple search in Scripture reveals that it has been called those names many times:

- Concerning Judah and **Jerusalem**. A people laden with iniquity, a brood of evildoers, children who are corrupters! They have forsaken the LORD, they have provoked to anger the Holy One of Israel, they have turned away backward. Hear the word of the LORD, you rulers of **Sodom**; give ear to the law of our God, you people of **Gomorrah** (Isa 1:1, 4, 10).
- For **Jerusalem** stumbled, and Judah is fallen, because their tongue and their doings are against the LORD, to provoke the eyes of His glory (Isa 3:8). ...they declare their sin as **Sodom**... (Isa 3:9).
- **Jerusalem** ... **has never given up** her harlotry brought from **Egypt** ... (Ezek 23:4, 8).

Jesus also made it clear that those **in Judea** ought to flee (Mat 24:16). There can be little doubt that the place in question is none other than Jerusalem, where Jesus[134] was crucified.

We can only imagine the scale of the war that will take place between the Beast and the Two Witnesses. Revelation simply states the Beast will make "war." While it could refer to a single battle rather than a protracted years-long conflict like WWII, it definitely conveys the idea of an arduous struggle, with both sides fighting for their lives—using the full extent of their resources to overcome their foe. Judging from their respective awe-inspiring and supernatural powers, such a battle will likely include lightning strikes, hurricane force winds, directing harm-inflicting hornets and locusts, flying projectiles, darkness, manipulation of water and nature, and more. The deadly battle will likely continue for hours or perhaps days until at last, the Beast gains the upper hand and overcomes them. In a radical change of fortune, the Two Witnesses who had "tormented those who dwell on the earth" (Rev 11:10) are finally outmatched. The Beast then delivers the fatal blow, and they collapse. Dead. If the world was not able to make war against the Two Witnesses but suffered from their torments, then the question **"who can make war with the beast"** (Rev 13:4) suddenly rings true at a whole new level. The answer is—**no one on earth!** Nevertheless, the death of the Two will be cause for worldwide rejoicing and jubilation.

---

[134] The NU text says "their" vs "our." Either reading is acceptable – the reading "their" Lord underscores that their king is Jesus.

WITNESSES' BODIES OUT IN THE OPEN

It is hard to genuinely appreciate the sigh of relief the world will emit when "their dead bodies will lie in the street" (Rev 11:8). At that point, agreeing to Satan's covenant (with death and Sheol) will look like it was a great deal, since under his protection the two hostile entities were routed. The world will be ecstatic. For those who have believed in the Lord, and who knew that these Two Witnesses were from God, it will be a day of sorrow. But for those not willing to repent, their death will be cause for immense rejoicing. These two extra-terrestrial terrorists who demanded the world to repent and submit to the God of Israel will be gone. Earth-dwellers will finally shed tears of relief that they are no more. As part of the celebration of their death, and perhaps to quell any residual disbelief that they are truly gone, their bodies will be left on display for all the world to see:

> "Then those from the peoples, tribes, tongues, and nations will see their dead bodies three-and-a-half days, and not allow their dead bodies to be put into graves" (Rev 11:9).

Everybody on the planet will see their dead bodies displayed for three and a half days, a correlation to the 3.5 years, 1260 days, or 42 months they spent witnessing. Their death will become a new holiday:

> "And those who dwell on the earth will **rejoice** over them, make merry, and send gifts to one another, because these two prophets tormented those who dwell on the earth" (Rev 11:10).

They will be so delighted the Two are dead that they will send gifts to one another. There is incredible euphoria the world over. Truly, a new age has dawned for mankind. The Beast is the most revered man on earth. How could there not be jubilation? The two hostile aliens who rained their plagues upon earth, whom the world's greatest weapons could not defeat, are finally, once and for all, dead! The euphoria after the Allies who defeated Nazi Germany will pale in comparison. Earth itself is saved! There will be dancing in the streets and massive public displays of affection. Those who found themselves targeted to repent, but refused, will be the most ecstatic. Finally, the two hostiles who challenged mankind's way of life are no more.

Their message of hate has been silenced. The tormentors that plagued earth are gone. Finally, the world can get back to the old ways of lust, debauchery, and carnal pleasures without anybody condemning, convicting, or accusing them. The one responsible for their death will be hailed a hero. No. A *superhero*. No...A god. If he was able to destroy the Two whom no one else could defeat, then he would be worthy of worship and allegiance.

THEY'RE BAAAAAACK!

The victory lap will be short lived though. Just as the world is settling into life as it used to be, the ones left to rot in the streets suddenly come back to life!

> "After the three-and-a-half days the breath of life from God entered them, and they stood on their feet, and great fear fell on those who saw them. And they heard a loud voice from heaven saying to them, Come up here. And they ascended to heaven in a cloud, and their enemies saw them" (Rev 11:11–12).

This is, of course, reminiscent of when Yeshua went up to the top of the Mount of Olives, and the disciples were watching him, then He was lifted up into the sky, went into a cloud, and disappeared from their sight. While the disciples were gaping at the sky, the angels came and asked why they were standing around. "This Jesus will come back in the same manner that you saw him go" (Acts 1:9–11). It was a bodily resurrection of Jesus, and a bodily ascension up into the atmosphere.

It will be the same with the Two Witnesses; it will be a bodily resurrection and a bodily ascension into the atmosphere, where God then receives them up into a cloud and their enemies will see them. The text is stressing that this is a real-world, tangible, literal event. It will not be merely a metaphor of a biblical truth. The Two may be representative of Israel and the Church, Jews and gentiles, the law and the prophets, or the house of Judah and house of Israel, etc. However, the physical death and then revival of the Two cannot apply merely to a symbolic presence, but rather, to two physical bodies.

We know the world will send real gifts to one another because the two real beings that caused them real and terrible grief are finally gone. Only two literal, real-world, defeated-and-then-really-resurrected individuals fit the bill.

Of course, at the revival of the Two, the world will be petrified (Rev 11:12). After all, these tormenters were untouchable until the Beast rose from the abyss and killed them. But now, not even death can defeat them? To top it off, a voice from the sky calls them and they depart, with frightening events following:

> "In the same hour there was a great earthquake, and a tenth of the city fell. In the earthquake seven thousand people were killed, and the rest were afraid and gave glory to the God of heaven" (Rev 11:13).

Some will recognize that the earthquake came from God and will give him glory.[135] That means that they acknowledge that the Two Witnesses were truly from the God of heaven, and that they need to repent —just like at the cross, after the earthquake, the Roman soldier recognized: "Indeed this was the Son of God." This will likely be the moment some of the leadership in Jerusalem realize they might have given their authority to the wrong guy. Sadly though, many around the world will continue in their hard-headedness, just like Pharaoh did.

The Beast and the central ruling power will likely use the Two Witnesses' resurrection to shore up any doubts about his scheme. In order for his plan to work, as this book has outlined, he must get all humanity to sign up for his covenant of death and Sheol, if he is to regain complete authority over planet earth. This will be why everyone will be required to take the mark of the Beast so that they cannot repent of giving him their authority and turn to Jesus. Satan's survival depends on everyone accepting it and becoming his slave.

---

[135] It will be evidence of God's hand in a way similar to a tornado that came out of nowhere and broke the steeple of a Lutheran church that was voting whether Pastors could be practicing homosexuals.
https://www.desiringgod.org/articles/the-tornado-the-lutherans-and-homosexuality

Therefore, Satan (via the Beast) may spin the resurrection of the Two, pegging the God of Israel as a vindictive, egotistical, cruel, genocidal, bigoted ancient alien who is upset every time man finds success in independence. Satan's propaganda may go something like, "The God of Israel is the malevolent creator who seeks to limit us to make sure we do not evolve into gods, which is why God sent the Two." The Beast will likely point out that after becoming a god himself, he was able to defeat them, and the world can too. And because the Two will return with Jesus and his army, it is imperative that everyone on earth be ready to fight for earth and "our way of life."

The Beast could beat the Two, but a whole army? Therefore, to match the colossal force of Jesus' army, everyone on earth will need to "upgrade" with his god-like, hybridized DNA and acquire the extra physical and implanted capabilities for that kind of fight. Then together with their enhanced god-abilities, the world can unite and fight against the Lord of Hosts coming with his hostile alien army who will attempt to steal the planet.

2 Witnesses' Ministry of 1260 Days

Beast rising to power. Treaty with "many" introduced	Fire from heaven, drought, waters turned to blood, various plagues	BEAST fuses with Satan, becomes Son of Perdition	Abomination of desolation Beast shot, returns from Sheol

2 Witnesses prophesy 42 months	World looks for solution to be rid of the 2 Witnesses	Covenant with Death and Sheol (world & Israel) finalized	Beast kills 2 Witnesses

Table 4. Two Witnesses' Ministry of 1260 Days.

THE FALSE PROPHET

At this point, one known as the False Prophet (cf. Rev 19) will rise up to rally the world to get behind the cause. He will look peaceful like a lamb, but he is extremely dangerous and speaks like a dragon. The False Prophet's job will be to help humanity unite themselves around Satan's plan.

> Then I saw another beast coming up out of the earth, and he had two horns like a lamb and spoke like a dragon. And he exercises all the authority of the first beast in his presence, and causes the earth and those who dwell in it to worship the first beast, whose deadly wound was healed. He performs great signs, so that he even makes fire come down from heaven on the earth in the sight of men. And he deceives those who dwell on the earth by those signs which he was granted to do in the sight of the beast, telling those who dwell on the earth to make an image to the beast who was wounded by the sword and lived. He was granted power to give breath to the image of the beast, that the image of the beast should both speak and cause as many as would not worship the image of the beast to be killed. He causes all, both small and great, rich and poor, free and slave, to receive a mark on their right hand or on their foreheads, and that no one may buy or sell except one who has the mark or the name of the beast, or the number of his name (Rev 13:11–17).

When this is happening, people will not know him as the "false prophet," in contrast to the two true prophets God sent to be witnesses of the truth, which the world rejected. And because they rejected the truth, now they will believe the lie and make falsehood their refuge. The False Prophet is the one who tells the world the sweet lie they want to hear—that they can defeat YHWH.

The False Prophet will make a convincing pitch to the world on why they should believe and trust the Beast who has gone before them, has merged with the advanced and ancient "god" Enlil, who has been a champion of humanity for millennia (see *Corrupting the Image 2*) and wants to see us become superhuman.

Indeed, Damien Echols, convicted in 1994 of what prosecutors labeled "satanic sex ritual slayings,"[136] is now "openly touting the power of summoning angels through the power of Enlil," and is teaching "'high magick' to subscribers through his Patreon page."[137] Echols recounts his experience:

> One morning when I was in the middle of the angelic invocations involved in the Shem Operation, I experienced something that was initially disorienting and frightening. Suddenly it felt like the very earth dropped away beneath my feet. I was surrounded by an incredible amount of light—it was so bright that it felt like I was standing in the middle of the sun. Then it felt like something snapped, and I was surrounded by the darkness of an infinite void. [...]

> The closest I'll ever be able to come to articulating what happened is this: I saw the nighttime sky. It was crystal clear—truly beautiful. And then, across this vision of the sky, I saw a word spelled out, just as if the wind were gently rippling across the stars as if they were wheat. The word was *Enlil*. [...]

> So, of course, I began invoking him. Instead of calling upon all of the angelic intelligences I'd been using, I invoked Enlil in all directions—east, west, up, down, and everywhere in between. The resultant energy I experienced was unlike anything I'd ever felt, even after years of intense angel work. Enlil's presence was like feeling the unified power of a thousand archangels.[138]

---

136 The Associated Press, "Arguments Conclude in 'West Memphis Three' Appeals." Arkansas Democrat-Gazette, Oct. 2, 2009.
https://www.arkansasonline.com/news/2009/oct/02/appeals-continue-slayings-arkboys-93/, retrieved 5/4/21. Cf The Second Coming of Saturn. Derek P. Gilbert, 2021. Pg. 290.
137 The Second Coming of Saturn. Derek P. Gilbert, 2021. Pg. 290.
138 Damien Echols, Angels and Archangels: The Western Path to Enlightenment (Boulder, CO: Sounds True, 2020), pp. 261–263. Cf Second Coming of Saturn pg. 290.

All that humanity needs to do to acquire that same "unified power of a thousand angels" is to take the Beast's DNA and merge it with their own, and they will be gods as well. Getting the upgrade will likely be voluntary at first. When some people are slow to get it, then they will be unable to buy. When that does not incentivize, the False Prophet will have the Beast's authority and can demand submission upon pain of death.

The False Prophet will explain how becoming a god is vital to humanity's survival; if the world had an army of evolved beings like the Beast, then mankind might stand a chance against the coming hostiles. With fear driving them, those who dwell on the earth will understand everyone must become a superhuman god, like the Beast, in order to fight the god-like aliens who are coming to enslave them. The False Prophet may explain how the coming of the Two Witnesses was not planned, but serves as the catalyst to hasten the next phase of our evolution—to become an immortal super-soldier to deal with the hostile army. The False Prophet may promise utopia afterwards, like the Twilight Zone aliens who promised to make the earth into a Garden of Eden.

PART TWO:

BECOME A HYBRID TO FIGHT THE ALIEN INVASION

Chapter 10: Singularity (Mark of the Beast) to Fight the Creator

Having rejected the opportunity to repent, as preached by the Two, and having bought into Satan's lie, the world will have no choice but to prepare to stand and fight the Creator in a climatic clash that the Bible calls Armageddon and the war of Gog and Magog. They will be strongly deluded, thinking they can fight their Creator because they will not see the God of Israel as the Almighty, King of Kings and Lord of Lords, but more so as the malevolent "alien" creators in *Prometheus*. In other words, they can attain equal footing with God / Jesus through genetic upgrades and technology.

The world will think they can overcome Him just as Pharaoh thought he was YHWH's equal. Scripture tells us that mankind will be preparing for a battle against Jesus.

- For they are spirits of demons, performing signs, which go out to the kings of the earth and of the whole world, to **gather them to the battle** of that great day of God Almighty (Rev 16:14).
- And I saw the beast, the **kings** of the earth, and their **armies**, **gathered** together **to make war against Him** who sat on the horse and against His army (Rev 19:19).
- The noise of a multitude in the mountains, like that of many people! A tumultuous noise of the **kingdoms** of **nations** gathered together! The LORD of hosts musters the army for battle (Isa 13:4).

At the end of the documentary *Transcendent Man*, Ray Kurzweil, a forward thinker hired by Google as director of engineering, quips: "Does God exist? Well, not yet."[139] His pithy statement is pregnant with meaning: man will transform himself into a god and the Judeo-Christian God is but a myth.

---

[139] https://medium.com/@BJ_Murphy/a-transhumanists-journey-becoming-gods-angels-and-ghosts-826c81bb5b33

Leading Transhumanist Mark Pesce states, our goal is to recreate our genetic code into that of a god.

"Once the genome was transcribed, once we knew what had made us human, we had—in that moment—passed into the Transhuman. Knowing our codes, we can recreate them in our so-called synthetic rows of 1s and 0s ... now we will reach into the improbable, re-sequence ourselves into a new Being, de-bugging the natural state, translating ourselves into supernatural, incorruptible, eternal. There is **no God but Man**."[140]

Pesce makes it clear that the goal is not just living longer, but that man will be the only undisputed god. Clearly, he and others are already preparing for the final battle with God. He continues with the clear intention that man is to recreate the universe in our image.

"We seek something more—a transcendence of transience, translation to incorruptible form ... We seek, therefore, to bless ourselves with perfect knowledge and perfect will; to **become as gods**, take the universe in hand, and transform it in our image—for our own delight. As it is on Earth, so it shall be in the heavens."[141]

We cannot miss his usage of biblical sayings: "in our image," "as it is on earth," and so on. Such language poses no problem if there is no Creator God. However, we know there is, and He intends to reclaim the earth, which He purchased with His own blood (which we explored in *Corrupting the Image 2*).

---

[140] https://issuu.com/mytheory/docs/becoming_transhuman
[141] https://issuu.com/mytheory/docs/becoming_transhuman, see also
https://creation.com/transhumanism-mankinds-next-step-forward

Kurzweil predicts we will achieve post-human singularity, which is the transhumanist term for when humanity is able to "to transcend these limitations of our biological bodies and brains... There will be no distinction, post-Singularity, between human and machine." His predicted date of the singularity is 2045, in terms of when he expects computer-based intelligences to significantly exceed the total of human brainpower. He writes that advances in computing before that date "will not represent the Singularity" because they do "not yet correspond to a profound expansion of our intelligence."[142]

Man becoming a god is precisely what historian and author from my alma mater—the Hebrew University of Jerusalem, Israel—Yuval Noah Harari suggests. He forecasts that homo sapiens will upgrade themselves into a divine being and warns these enhancements may only be for the rich, establishing biological divide in the human race. He says:

"I think it is likely in the next 200 years or so homo sapiens will upgrade themselves into some idea of a divine being, either through biological manipulation or genetic engineering or by the creation of cyborgs, part-organic part non-organic ... It will be the greatest evolution in biology since the appearance of life, will be as different from today's humans as chimps are from us now. ... Many researchers believe that we have already started down the path towards a cyborg future. After all, many of us already rely on bionic ears and eyes, insulin pump technology and prosthetics to help us survive and with researchers recently learning how to send people's thoughts across the web, subconsciously, control bionic limbs and use liquid metal to heal severed nerves. It is not hard to imagine how we could continue to use technology to supplement our vulnerable human bodies further.[143]

---

[142] http://basarab-nicolescu.fr/Docs_articles/CHK_3.pdf Cybernetics and Human Knowing. Vol. 23 (2016), no. 4, pp. 77-81 The Dark Side of Technological Singularity: New Barbarism Basarab Nicolescu1

[143] https://www.sciencealert.com/wealthy-humans-could-live-forever-as-cyborgs-within-200-years-expert-predicts

Harari may be too conservative in his estimated timeline of when these things will take place. There is already a desire to become a god. The reason people will willingly want to take the mark of the Beast, again, is not to check out faster at Walmart, but it is because they want to become a god, and that will be the promise offered to them. The resurrection of the Two Witnesses and the threat of the coming of their onerous overlord will only accelerate the process. Some may even welcome the face-to-face confrontation to defeat God once and for all.

While the world is already on a rapid pace to beat death and upgrade into gods, the Bible reports that a false prophet will come to encourage the world to go to the next level.

BIOHACKERS

In the Netflix Original series, *Unnatural Selection* (which "chronicles the ambitions and struggles of scientists, doctors, patients, conservationists, and biohackers as they seek to wrest control of evolution from nature itself"[144]), we discover that there is a growing grass-roots community of people who are excited about humanity becoming a different species—that we can become whatever we like. The urgent need to upgrade will be welcomed by many.

---

[144] Molteni, Megan (October 18, 2019). "A Netflix Series Explores the Brave New World of Crispr - From malaria-ridden villages in Burkina Faso to fertility clinics in Ukraine, Unnatural Selection takes viewers deep into the gene-editing revolution." Wired. Retrieved October 18, 2019. https://www.wired.com/story/a-netflix-series-explores-the-brave-new-world-of-crispr/

Indeed, any person standing against such an upgrade will be viewed a Luddite[145], siding with the enemy. There is already a sentiment that the government has been denying us the right to upgrade ourselves with biohacking as we see fit. This sentiment is expressed in the words of Charles Darwin, considered the father of evolution.

"If the misery of the poor be caused not by the laws of nature, but by our institutions, great is our sin." – Charles Darwin - Voyage of the Beagle

In other words, it is a sin for institutions to legislate in such a way that leads to the misery of people. Regardless of how he intended it, his words have already become a rallying cry in the biohacker community.[146]

While it is noble to try to alleviate suffering, we must face the fact that we will not overcome death by our own means. The only way is through the Lord Jesus. Yet, consider, if people believe there is no God, and we have randomly evolved this far over billions of years, then we owe it to ourselves to evolve to the next level. Of course, long before the final delusion, the apotheosis of man first had to happen in the minds of men.

How Genetic Engineering Could Make Us Gods (CRISPR/Cas 9)

One of the most advanced or avantgarde technologies that could lead to becoming a god is CRISPR/Cas 9. It gives us the ability to open a segment of our DNA, insert a foreign DNA sequence, and radically change our DNA. It is just like you might cut and paste code or words out of a Word doc. It is incredibly cheap. It is fast and easy.

---

[145] "Luddite," from Oxford Languages: 1) a person opposed to new technology or ways of working.
"a small-minded Luddite resisting progress"; 2) Historically: a member of any of the bands of English workers who destroyed machinery, especially in cotton and woolen mills, that they believed was threatening their jobs (1811–16).
[146] Josiah Zayner – American biohacker, artist, and scientist as quoted in the miniseries: Unnatural Selection.

In his book, *The Code Breaker*, Walter Isaacson interviewed Jennifer Doudna, a biochemist at the University of California at Berkeley, who along with her collaborator, Emmanuelle Charpentier, received the Nobel Prize for their 2012 breakthrough on the gene-editing technique called CRISPR which stands for Clustered Regularly Interspaced Short Palindromic Repeats. When asked what CRISPR looks like and what it is, Doudna responded:

> "It's not a computer and it's not software. If you were looking at it in my lab, you would see a tube of colorless liquid," Doudna said. Two tubes, actually. The first contains molecules that have been engineered to latch onto one particular gene in the cells of a living thing – a specific part of its DNA. The proteins in the other liquid cuts the DNA at that spot. "It's like a zip code that you can address to find a particular place in the DNA of a cell and literally, like scissors, make a snip," said Doudna.
>
> Cutting DNA like this usually *disables* a gene. We can disable a gene that gives us a disease, or shut off the gene that limits how much fur cashmere goats grow, or how much muscle a beagle grows.
>
> Those medical treatments show off CRISPR's most jaw-dropping possibilities. About 7,000 human diseases are caused by gene mutations that, in theory, we can simply snip away. They include muscular dystrophy, cystic fibrosis, Huntington's disease, and sickle-cell disease, a blood disorder that brings debilitating pain, infections, and early death. It affects about 100,000 Americans, including Victoria Gray, a Mississippi mother of four who became the first American to be treated with CRISPR-fixed genes. In the year since receiving the experimental treatment, she has had no severe pain or hospitalization.[147]

---

[147] https://www.cbsnews.com/news/crispr-jennifer-doudna-walter-isaacson-the-code-breaker/

Clearly the good that CRISPR can do is extensive. Certainly, alleviating and even curing people who suffer from the terribly painful, indeed excruciating debilitating sickle cell disease is a worthy use of CRISPR. As followers of Jesus, we desire to see people healed and comforted. The fact that Ms. Gray has had no severe pain or hospitalization is wonderful. Just as any technology can be used for good, it also has the potential to be used for evil. Gene editing techniques like CRISPR, and others that may come after it, have the unique potential of destruction. They have the capacity to change humanity at a fundamental level. Doudna says that CRISPR will allow us to put in "a different DNA sequence, replacing it with something we've created ourselves. We'll be able to rewrite the genes of any plant, animal or person."[148] She explains that we will not see designer babies tomorrow, "but it's close enough, in the sense that the **technology fundamentally could enable this**, that I think it's critical that we have a discussion about it."[149]

If we could use CRISPR to heal someone of blindness, we ought to do so—and indeed, some are already being cured of such diseases. The trouble is that healing people of problems is likely just the beginning; soon, we will be using it to enhance ourselves.

"But once the door is open, it is not a big step to start using CRISPR/Cas 9 for so-called 'vanity traits,' such as good looks, intelligence, or athleticism." As Doudna said, "Once the discovery is made, it's out there."[150]

Some may argue that not using genetic engineering is unethical because it condemns children to preventable suffering. But could a dictator state like North Korea cement their rule forever by forcing gene editing on their subjects? It will likely be argued that not taking the mark of the Beast is unethical, inhumane, and even dangerous. This is something that is not far away. "It's no wonder; we already have do-it-yourself CRISPR engineering kits available on the internet for less than $200."

---

[148] https://www.cbsnews.com/news/crispr-jennifer-doudna-walter-isaacson-the-code-breaker/

[149] https://www.cbsnews.com/news/crispr-jennifer-doudna-walter-isaacson-the-code-breaker/

[150] https://scienceaccessibly.wordpress.com/2016/09/27/crispr-how-genome-editing-will-change-the-world-forever/

In an interesting video, people were asked what they would change about themselves if they could use gene editing CRISPR/Cas 9. Some of the responses were worthwhile goals, some only prove the dangerous path we are on:

- I would just like to not have Muscular Dystrophy. That's all I'll need to be happy.
- I would fix the genes that cause EDS so I'm not a cripple anymore.
- I would like to be taller.
- Would like to be a superwoman.
- I wish I would be smarter than everyone.
- To have spider-man's powers.
- I would like to have eternally perfect health.
- **I think the rewards far outweigh all the risks... I'm all in for fully legalizing gene editing, (with peer-review oversight).[151]

We would like to see people healed. But where does it end? How do you decide who gets to do what? Once it is out there, they are going to keep pushing the envelope.

PIG HEARTS, MONKEY BRAINS, AND HUMAN-MONKEY HYBRIDS

In 2017 National Geographic reported how a human-pig hybrid was created in the laboratory, specifically, pig lungs with human blood, thereby proving "that human cells can be introduced into a non-human organism, survive, and even grow inside a host animal."[152] The article went on to say the reason for doing such an Island of Dr. Moreau feat is to "address a critical shortage of donor organs." No one would deny this sounds noble, but where does it end? Indeed, researchers are trying to enlarge monkey brains: "Experts took the gene known as ARHGAP11B—which directs stem cells in the human brain—and placed it into the brains of common marmosets." This research caused the secular-pop news site thesun.com to report:

---

[151] Source: https://www.youtube.com/watch?v=5gQGWJraptU
[152] https://www.nationalgeographic.com/news/2017/01/human-pig-hybrid-embryo-chimera-organs-health-science/

SCIENTISTS have made monkeys brains bigger by splicing them with human genes in an experiment reminiscent of the *Planet of the Apes*.

In the *Planet of the Apes*, humans make primates smarter to the point that they eventually rise up and enslave the very ones who enlarged their brains. Thus, it is not just prophecy-minded Christians who are concerned with such experiments. Many are wondering if we will indeed bring the apocalypse upon ourselves. The people that are working on these projects almost certainly have good intentions of saving and improving lives. The problem is when our technology is divorced from our Creator, we are going to end up with our own Frankenstein's monster, and it will not be good. In 2021, Professor Juan Carlos Izpisua Belmonte, who worked on the first human-pig hybrid in 2017, led the research of making the first human-monkey hybrid. He explains the motive for doing so, saying: "These chimeric approaches could be really very useful for advancing biomedical research."[153] The human-macaque monkey embryos were observed for about twenty days and were then destroyed.

RESURRECTING DOGS AND CATS

Scientists already have the technology to "resurrect" your pet through cloning. Dogs cost a mere $50,000, cats $25,000, and horses $85,000.[154] What results is an animal that looks and bears the same physical features as the animal that died. We could think of it like making a twin—we know that twins can look uncannily alike and act and think alike ... but they are two different people with different souls and personalities. Hence, the cloned animal will be identical to the animal that died, but will not be the same being.

---

[153] https://www.the-sun.com/lifestyle/tech/2713352/first-human-monkey-embryo-created

[154]

https://www.americanveterinarian.com/journals/amvet/2018/november2018/pet-cloning-where-we-are-today

Since 2015, a team led by the renowned molecular engineer and geneticist George Church of Harvard University has been working to produce a mammoth-elephant hybrid, rather than a clone. They plan to do this through "synthetic biology," or splicing the genes of a woolly mammoth with those of an Asian elephant, its closest living relative, which shares 99 percent of its DNA.[155]

The article wisely notes, "If scientists are able to resurrect the long-extinct woolly mammoth, they aren't likely to stop with just one prehistoric beast." [156] The *Jurassic Park* scientists genetically engineered dangerous species because they could; and, as those who saw the movies know, it didn't end well. Likewise, the opportunity to upgrade humanity into gods will prove too great a temptation, and many will go for it.

THE DANGERS OF GENE EDITING

The aforementioned technologies are not inherently evil, and in their own right, could alleviate some human suffering. Many intelligent, well-funded people with good motives believe that through scientific advancement and technology, humans can rid the world of disease, become super intelligent, have enhanced senses and powers, and live forever.

However, those same things have incredible potential to be used for harm. The Beast (and False Prophet) will likely not be the creator of the technology behind the mark of the Beast, but will appropriate it for his own selfish purposes. *The Motley Fool*, a secular magazine with no eye for Bible end-times-prophecy, shares some of the very real dangers of gene editing. They point out:

> The **goal** of gene editing is to modify specific DNA sequences, resulting in **target mutations** (desired changes in gene structure). There is a possibility, though, that DNA sequences other than the target ones could also be changed.

---

[155] https://www.history.com/news/wooly-mammoth-resurrection-cloning-genesis

[156] https://www.history.com/news/wooly-mammoth-resurrection-cloning-genesis

The danger is so great, they say, that gene editing is now considered to have the same destructive potential as other weapons of mass destruction!

> When you think about **weapons of mass destruction** (WMD), nuclear bombs and chemical warfare probably come to mind. But in 2016, the then-director of National Intelligence, James Clapper, added another item to the **WMD list: gene editing.**
>
> Clapper mentioned gene editing as a new global danger in his testimony to the Senate Armed Services Committee in addition to listing the technology as a potential weapon of mass destruction. Why? **Gene editing could be used to genetically engineer bacteria or viruses to be used in biological attacks against humans,** or to cause widespread crop damage. These might sound like farfetched plots from books and movies, but the advent of CRISPR makes the prospects of gene editing being used in biological attacks greater than ever.
>
> Unlike previous gene editing approaches, CRISPR/Cas9 is inexpensive and relatively easy to use, which could make it appealing to terrorist organizations or rogue states.[157]

To classify gene editing as a weapon of mass destruction is a big deal. As the name indicates, it could be a weapon that would destroy people on a grand scale, or could essentially trigger an extinction level event. There are scenarios, as we have explored, that pose dangers so great that editing ourselves into gods might seem like the absolute best option. Indeed, the only option.

All these ideas and goals that transhumanism advocates have already been promised to us by God. When God created Adam and Eve in the garden, He created them perfect. They were innocent without blemish, disease and death. God plans to take us back to that Edenic condition, and perhaps superior.

---

[157] https://www.fool.com/investing/2018/06/18/is-gene-editing-dangerous-4-things-you-should-know.aspx

The challenge is that man does not want to follow God's ways. We want to enjoy the ways of sin and rebellion against the Most High, but then still have superpowers. But it does not work that way. If we follow God's plan, we will have the things that He has intended for us:

- immortality (Rev 21:4)
- angelic-like bodies (Lk 20:36)
- disease-free (Rev 21:4)
- super intelligence (Lk 20:36)
- limitless powers (Mk 11:23)

Unlimited mobility, like walking on water, and colossal physical capabilities like moving mountains, are just the beginning of what God has for us.

DISTRIBUTION - DNA PRINTING THE MARK OF THE BEAST

The Beast requires all to take his mark. Just how might he go about this? Once Satan has merged with the Beast into his Avatar with hybridized DNA, as we have considered throughout this book, then the next step is to make this same genetic advancement available to everyone on a mass scale. Using the tools of CRISPR/Cas9, the hybridized gene would need to be extracted from the Beast, and then deciphered and replicated billions of times. Technology is currently at the level where DNA can be printed by a DNA printer using sugar as the base "ink." DNA Script is one such company that makes benchtop DNA printers.[158]

---

[158] https://www.dnascript.com/products/

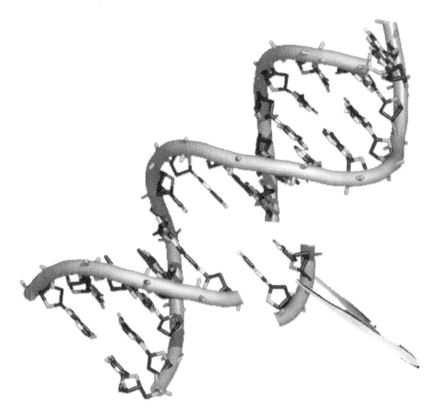

Figure 14. By Ciencias EspañolasKoS -
https://commons.wikimedia.org/w/index.php?curid=75624775

Once the snippet of the Beast's upgraded code is isolated, it could be converted into binary code, 1s and 0s in a computer, and then could just be emailed![159] Someone at the receiving end could then print it using a DNA printer, and inject it into themselves and others. To fundamentally alter a person's humanity, the new hybridized DNA would need to change the person's DNA on the germline level, that is the cells that pass on information to the next generation of cells. The new DNA replicates and virtually overrides the original. An injection by itself would not be enough; and changing somatic (body) cells would not be enough. A person must want the change, and therefore take it as an act of worship offered to the Beast.

---

[159] Source:
http://www.youtube.com/watch?v=rD5uNAmbDaQ&feature=colike

Chapter 11: Allegiance Needed for the Mark to Work

C ould you be forced to take the mark against your will? What if they strap you down and inject you, but you do not want it? What happens then? God seems to have built in a safety switch.

The Bible makes clear that three things are necessary for a person to be doomed and lost forever. It is not just taking the mark, but also worshiping the Beast and his image.

"Then a third angel followed them, saying with a loud voice, 'If anyone **worships** the **beast** and his **image**, and **receives** his **mark** on his forehead or on his hand ...'" (Rev 14:9).

That is, they must 1) worship the Beast, and 2) worship the image, and 3) take the mark. If they do these three things, then there is a transformation, and there is no more hope. To be clear, when we talk about taking the mark of the Beast, we are in reality talking about those three steps. If people are injected with the upgraded DNA against their will, then they have **not taken the mark of the Beast**. All three steps are necessary for it to work. Worship is the Greek word *"proskuneo."* According to the BDAG Lexicon:

Freq. used to designate the custom of prostrating oneself before persons and kissing their feet or the hem of their garment, the ground, etc.; the Persians did this in the presence of their deified king, and the Greeks before a divinity or something holy, to **express in attitude** or gesture one's **complete dependence** on or **submission** to a high authority figure, (fall down and) worship, do obeisance, to prostrate oneself before, do reverence to, welcome respectfully[160]

Worship was not just bowing down; it was having an attitude of complete dependence and submission to a high authority figure. In other words, it does not have to be bowing down to an idol, necessarily; it is an act of renouncing self and committing to act in that other entity's interests. It puts the worshiper in a position of subject and the other of master.

---

[160] BDAG proskuneo

The image of the Beast is going to require worship—that everybody must look on it with an attitude of complete acceptance and dependence on the image of the Beast. By this act, they will be recognized as belonging to a superhuman realm. It appears that in worshipping the image, you are also worshipping the Beast, a transcendent being. It seems that the image decrees that those who will not express gratitude and dependence on the image are to be killed.

We will talk more about worshipping his image in the next chapter.

Lastly, a person must receive his mark, thereby agreeing to a genetic transformation. If a person undergoes those three things, then a genomic mutation will occur, and the person's fate is sealed. He has ceased to be an image-bearer of his Creator; he now bears the corrupted image of Satan. How could this mechanism of converging the three prerequisites possibly work?

PLACEBO AND NOCEBO

A way to understand the mechanism is to consider the use and application of a placebo in modern medicine. A placebo is generally a sugar pill or some other substance without active ingredients. The key to the placebo effect, however, is that people think it is an actual medicine. They take it and often experience the intended effects of the real medicine.

A placebo: "works about 18-80% of the time, and it's not just in your head—it actually dilates bronchi, heals ulcers, makes warts disappear, drops your blood pressure, and makes bald men who think they're getting Rogaine grow hair!"[161]

Because people think it is the real thing, their body begins to manifest those expected changes. Conversely, there is an evil twin to the placebo called the "nocebo." This is where a person reads about the possible side effects of a medication and experiences the negative side effects, even though the pill they are taking is just sugar.

---

[161] https://www.psychologytoday.com/blog/owning-pink/201308/the-nocebo-effect-negative-thoughts-can-harm-your-health

Dr Lissa Rankin explains:

"Nocebo complaints are not random; they tend to arise in response to the side effect warnings on the actual drug or treatment. The mere suggestion that a patient may experience negative symptoms in response to a medication (or a sugar pill) may be a self-fulfilling prophecy. For example, if you tell a patient treated with a placebo, he might experience nausea, he's likely to feel nauseous. If you suggest that he might get a headache, he may. Patients given nothing but saline who thought it was chemotherapy actually threw up and lost their hair.[162]

The person experiencing such effects has not ingested a harmful chemical, just sugar or saline. However, they believed that they were taking an active drug. It was their belief that caused them to experience the described benefits or side effects of the placebo.

Likewise, in the Garden of Eden, Satan did not flat-out say that God lied. He approached, sowing doubt in God's words, thus gaining easy access to Eve's brain. She was now open to the idea that they would be like God, a positive thought that opened up all doors for Satan to go on with the deceit. Satan's end-time approach to humanity will be equally persuasive. He will use subtle persuasion, promises and the Beast's own manifested supernatural capabilities as an example, which will entice people and reinforce their desires. Therefore, the people must choose to worship the Beast. A person cannot be forced to take the mark. If forced, then the receptive capacities of his cells will be shut off and there will be no effect. To initiate the activation of the inserted foreign material, he must be drawn to desire it. Microbiologist Dr. Bruce Lipton says,

"Your perception of any given thing, at any given moment, can influence the brain chemistry, which, in turn, affects the environment where your cells reside and controls their fate."

---

[162] https://www.psychologytoday.com/blog/owning-pink/201308/the-nocebo-effect-negative-thoughts-can-harm-your-health

On the outside of a cell are protein receptors that are constantly scanning for good or bad signals. If the signals they encounter are good (that is, there are no danger signals coming from the brain), then the cell opens and allows nutrients to enter which is when repair, growth and reproduction can happen within the cell. But if the signal says times are bad (e.g. there is a lion chasing us), then the cell closes its doors, and it does not allow any kind of nutrients to come in. The belief may not be real, (e.g., there is not a lion chasing you), but you believe there is a lion chasing you. Because your brain says, "things are bad," your cells close up.

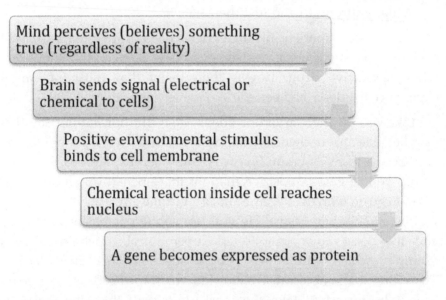

Table 5. Progression from mental perception to physical expression.

Putting it all together, the person that believes in the Beast says, "Yes, I want this thing; I believe in what you're doing." When that person says, "Yes, I want that genetic transformation. Give it to me," then his cells open up to welcome and receive the new genetic code, leading to transformation. Then, it goes through its whole process of expressing genes and proteins, etc.

If you are coerced or physically restrained, your mere declaration that you don't want it will nullify its effect, and your cells will close off and not let in the new code.

As a summary let's see the three steps that are necessary for a person to seal his doom:

1. Worship the Beast (that is, admiring, following, promoting, committing and desiring).
2. Worship his image.
   ➢ The worship or belief literally unlocks the person's cells, thereby allowing the foreign DNA strand to gain access to the nucleus and the ability to rewrite the DNA.
3. Physically take/receive Beast seed (DNA).Results in a visible mark.
   ➢ The foreign DNA is the replicated DNA from the Beast, which is from Satan. If we liken this to a snakebite—Satan's seed (DNA) is the venom and the bite marks left over are the mark of the Beast. Either way, the visible mark is evidence of receiving the seed (666 atomic mass units / AMU).

The prophecy of the mark of the Beast includes many facets such as transhumanism, genetic engineering, and artificial intelligence. Based on the evidence here and in *Corrupting the Image* volumes 1 and 2, I believe the following scenario is going to come about in one of these possible ways:

- Satan will reveal his DNA / his seed (code) to the man of his choosing who yearns with great passion for ultimate power.
- This chosen man literally transforms into the hybrid being, the chimera that the Bible calls the Beast.
- He then has Satan's power, authority, and throne transferred to himself while people will proclaim him invincible: "who is like the Beast?"
- He makes his promise of becoming a man-god a reality by receiving his hybridized DNA and gaining superhuman strength, intelligence and or immortality, etc.
- He then replicates his hybridized DNA with an atomic weight of 666 atomic mass units and makes it available to humankind.
  ➢ Suddenly, becoming a real-life Super Man—a superhuman is not a comic book fantasy anymore. It will become an option for the entire world to embrace through the offer of the Beast's DNA made available universally. Under the ruse of becoming "gods," many will accept the hybridized DNA of the Beast and will worship the Beast and his image.

WHAT IS THE MARK ON THE HAND AND FOREHEAD?

So how might the Beast make it possible for the world to become a god like him?

"He causes all, both small and great, rich and poor, free and slave, to receive a mark on their right hand or on their foreheads (Rev 13:16), and that no one may buy or sell except one who has the mark or the name of the beast, or the number of his name" (Rev 13:17).

markbeast666.blogspot.com

Figure 15. Barcode as the Mark of the Beast.

"Here is wisdom. Let him who has understanding calculate the number of the beast, for it is the number of a man: His number is 666." (Rev 13:18).

Without a doubt, a lot of ink has been spilled trying to figure out the mark of the Beast. A popular theory in the 90s was the barcode. The three parallel red line pairs (far right, far left, and center) supposedly corresponded to the number six, hence every barcode had 666 built into it. It was all the rage when this theory first came out. People were looking closely at the three longer parallel lines that supposedly meant 666 or the mark of the Beast.

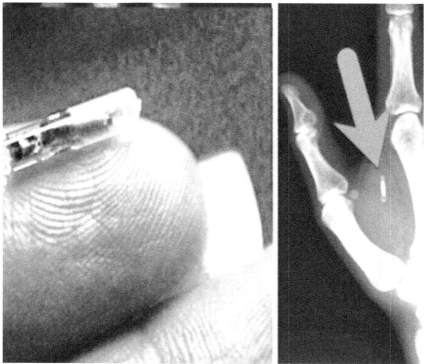

Figure 16. RFID chip.

When the RFID chip came out, it was deemed to be the mark, because it is the size of a grain of rice, which can be inserted into your hand, and then computer systems would recognize you; doors would open, computers would log you in, etc. There was a lot of fear about the RFID chip technology; however, if it can be inserted, it can also be removed. Thus, it is not the mark of the Beast.

Could these and other technologies be steppingstones? Possibly. But neither barcodes nor RFID chips in and of themselves are the problem. When the Beast comes, he is not going to stamp a barcode on your forehead or on your right hand. The mark of the Beast is something far more sinister.

There is also a long-standing teaching from the Seventh Day Adventists that those people that worship on Sunday are engaging in the mark of the Beast. The obvious flaw with such a teaching is that there have always been people who do not worship the God of the Bible on any day, and they never received a mark, nor did they worship the Beast and his image.

Figure 17. Illustration suggesting 666 is the name of Allah.

Another popular candidate for the mark is the name Allah written out in Arabic. In the graphic above, the man has a cloth around his head that bears the inscription Allah on it. Looking closely, we see what would correspond to the Greek numbers. Presumably, these are corresponding to the 666 as is written out in Greek letters (see Figure 20 below). This style of calligraphy depicts one way the name Allah is written in Arabic. When we view the standard font, we see that the correlation, which originally seemed to exist, quickly goes away. Arabic fonts and scripts vary; and can be styled differently. It is not correct to assume that this writing will always contain 666 because the graphic does not show the predominant way that the name Allah is written in Arabic (see Figure 19 below).

Figure 18. The name of Allah.

Secondly, we see that the Greek "*Xi*" which is the number 60, is vertical in Greek, while it is horizontal in Arabic. This does not work either because the sigma, the 6, is not the same. Furthermore, this is not the number of a man, but the number of a god (Allah)—if that theory were correct. Scripture is clear that the 666 is going to be the number of a man, not the number of a god.

Figure 19. 666 written in Greek (Byzantine text types).[163]

While it is possible that some Muslims may interpret the mark as being the sign of the Mahdi (a last-days Islamic political, military, and religious leader), worshipping an image is strictly forbidden in Islam. It is simply inconceivable that roughly 1 billion Muslims would begin to worship an image and a man. For those reasons, I do not believe that the writing of the name of Allah in Arabic is 666.

---

[163] 666 is written as χξς in the later Byzantine source texts. Whereas, in the older, Alexandrian texts, 666 is written out as, ἑξακόσιοι ἑξήκοντα ἕξ, *hexakosioi hexēkonta hex.* https://biblehub.com/greek/exakosioi_1812.htm

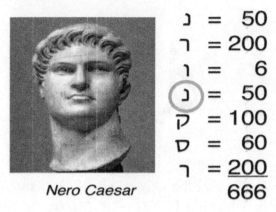

ℶ	=	50
ר	=	200
ו	=	6
ℶ	=	50
ק	=	100
ס	=	60
ר	=	200
		666

Nero Caesar

Figure 20. The supposed value of Nero's name.

There is another theory based on Gematria—that is, a system where every letter represents a number in both Greek and in Hebrew. Some people have looked to Nero Caesar, declaring that he must be the Antichrist and claiming his name equals 666 in Hebrew. But the letter Nun (ℶ) is **not part of his name**. It is not Nerōn; it is Nero. To make the theory work, the extra letter had to be added into his name for the letters to add up to 666.

Trans-literation	Letter (upper and lower case)	Value
a	I ι	10
b	K κ	20
g	Λ λ	30
d	M μ	40
e	N ν	50
w	Ξ ξ	60
z	O o	70
ē	Π π	80
th	(Ϙ)	90

Table 6. Table showing the numerical value of featured Greek letters.

Greek also has the same feature where the letters equal a number because (the numbers we have today did not come about until later). Now in Greek literature, there were people that would use this idea of Gematria. For example, "Filo is arithmos fme" (Φιλω ης αριθμος φμε), means "I love her whose number is 545." The man who wrote that was thinking "545" all day because it reminded him of "fme." Cute. Then we have, "Amerimnus thought upon his lady Harmonia for good. The number of her honorable name is 45."

However, it is unlikely gematria is involved in deciphering the 666 number of his name since it is the number of humanity.

KARAGMA

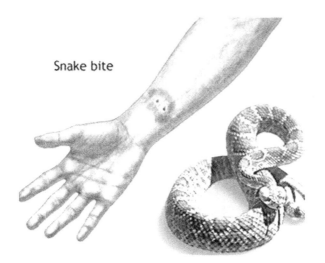

Figure 21. Snake bite leaving a mark.

Scripture speaks specifically about receiving a mark: "He causes all, both small and great, rich and poor, free and slave, to receive a mark ["*karagma*" (χάραγ-μα)] on their right hand or on their foreheads" (Rev 13:16). The Greek word for "mark" is "*karagma*" (χάραγ-μα) which according to Liddell-Scott-Jones Lexicon of Classical Greek, is "any mark engraved, imprinted, or branded, that could be a serpent's mark."[164]

---

[164] Liddell, H. G., Robert Scott and Henry Stuart Jones, eds. *Lexicon of Classical Greek*, 9th ed., Oxford: Oxford University Press, 1925.

A snakebite or a bee sting is a *karagma*. It could also be "writing of an imperial missive; a stamped document; a brand on a camel, for example, carved work; or the impress on the coin." It has a broad idea of anything that is stamped in or imprinted. It includes stamped money, a stamp-mark character, or a mark of endorsement.

The visible mark on the forehead or right hand may be likened to people who have a little scar after receiving the polio vaccine, for example. Though the scar was the side effect of getting the vaccine, not the goal, many people still have the *karagma* of the polio vaccine.

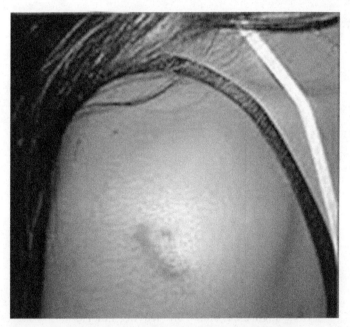

Figure 22. A mark left from the polio vaccine.

The "mark" of the Beast may not be the absolute goal; it might be the byproduct of having this DNA transformation. Perhaps after a person has taken the DNA upgrade, then a *karagma* could appear on your right hand or on your forehead, and it is an evidentiary byproduct of undergoing this transformation. Once the mark shows up, it will be visible to everyone that anyone bearing the mark has undergone the genetic transformation procedure.

Do we have a biblical correlation to this? We do. We see a prototype of this in that Israelites would carry the mark of their God on their forehead and on their hand. In Deuteronomy Moses instructs:

".. lay up these words of mine in your heart and in your soul, and **bind** them as a sign on your **hand**, and they shall be as frontlets **between your eyes** ..." (Deut 11:18).

What is a frontlet? The Hebrew word is ṭôṭāphôt (טּוֹטָפֹת), frontlets, bands, marks; it denotes a mark, or a sign placed on the forehead between the eyes as a memorial, which TWOT explains:

The placing of **frontlets** upon the forehead is always associated with making signs upon your hand. A common means of identifying slaves in the ancient near east was to **mark** their **hands** and/or their **foreheads**.

We see this again in Ezekiel where the Lord spoke to an angel instructing to:

"Go through the midst of the city, through the midst of Jerusalem, and put a **mark** on the **foreheads** of the **men who sigh and cry over all the abominations** that are done within it" (Ezek 9:4 and Rev 9:4).

The mark of the Beast, which will be given to lovers of unrighteousness, is the inverse-image of God's mark on the forehead of the righteous. God will seal his people again at the end of the age:

"Do not harm the earth, the sea, or the trees till we have sealed [σφραγίζω *sphragidzo*] the servants of our God on **their foreheads**" (Rev 7:3).

The word is *sphragidzo* (σφραγίζω), which means "to mark with a seal as a means of identification, mark, seal (...of all kinds of animals), so that the mark denoting ownership and also carries with it the protection of the owner."[165] These sealed individuals are completely sold out for God and have his commandments in their hearts and minds. We see these people again in Revelation 14 "having His Father's **name written on their foreheads**." They are "redeemed from among men, being firstfruits to God and to the Lamb" (Rev 14:1, 4).

---

[165] BDAG σφραγίζω sphragidzo

In 1 Corinthians, Paul speaks about the resurrection and says, "Christ the firstfruits, afterward those who are Christ's at His coming" (1 Cor 15:23). Jesus was called the first fruit of the resurrection and the first one who has resurrected into the kind of glorified body, which afterwards, His faithful will also receive.

The exclusive group mentioned in Revelation 14 appears to be the first set-apart righteous to experience this new state-of-being in their new body. "God's seal upon them" means they are protected and cannot be hurt or killed in the same manner as the angel sealed the righteous of Jerusalem. God's mark consequently contrasts with the mark of the Beast, whose recipients love unrighteousness and have obtained a different kind of immortal body. The mark of the Beast, then, is a byproduct of those who decide they want to upgrade to become a god and worship the image so that they can fight against God. It shows they are not only under the protection of the Beast, but indeed, are owned by the Beast, both body and mind.

Chapter 12: Hive Mind and the Image of the Beast

The mark of the Beast "become-a-god upgrade" is only part of the solution Satan will employ to prepare the world for the great battle against Jesus. Having individual powers is great, but only a one-minded togetherness will defeat the Two Witnesses' overlord and his armies coming to shake the Earth. Due to the "great fear" (Rev 11:11) that fell on the world when the Two Witnesses resurrected, it will be clear to all that the world must unite like never before. To combat this most serious existential threat to humanity's very survival, radical steps must be taken.

Scripture describes with amazing specificity this collective surrendering of mankind to the goals set by the Beast and how they act as one: "These are of **one mind**, and they will give their power and authority to the beast" (Rev 17:13).

HUMAN COMPUTER INTERACTION ALIEN AI

Dr. Louis Rosenberg, a Stanford graduate who has been awarded more than 350 patents for his technological efforts in AR VR collaborative systems, artificial intelligence, and human computer interaction, describes the coming non-human life:

"An alien intelligence is heading towards us at breakneck speeds. It will not show up in a rocket ship but will be born right here on Earth, in a research lab. The first sentient AI will be as different from us as any alien we can imagine and we have no reason believe its interests will be even remotely aligned with our own. This intelligence will be flexible and cunning, able to infiltrate our computer networks and permeate our critical infrastructure. It will quickly become smarter than we are and when that happens, humans will struggle to understand how it thinks, feels or acts. But it will understand us completely. After all, we will have told it everything we know and it will have spent decades studying human actions and reactions. And if that sounds incredibly dangerous, that is because it is."[166]

---

[166] https://disruptionhub.com/edit-rise-human-hive-mind/ Jun 2017

Keep in mind we are reviewing the research of people who are not necessarily reading the Book of Revelation, but who are nevertheless telling us things that sound eerily familiar and reminiscent of what we read in Bible prophecy. Dr Rosenberg continues:

"It is equally likely that it **will pursue its own interests**. How can we protect ourselves from being intellectually outmatched by our own creation? A good place to look is Mother Nature, where many species have evolved ingenious methods of jointly amplifying their intellects to levels well beyond the capacity of any single individual. Evolution has enabled these species to 'think as one,' combining the knowledge, wisdom, intuition and instincts of large groups into closed loop systems that are smarter together than any of the individuals could ever be alone. Biologists call this process 'swarm intelligence.'" [167]

Dr. Rosenberg suggests that the existential reason to become part of the hive mind is to protect ourselves from AI. In 2002, the National Science Foundation within the US Department of Commerce started talking about the mind meld and a collective consciousness coming for humanity. They suggest:

"With knowledge no longer encapsulated by individuals, the distinction between individuals and the entirety of humanity would blur. Think Vulcan mind meld. Remember Mr. Spock, from Star Trek and he would put his hand on you, transfer his mind or something like that. We would perhaps become more of a hive mind, an enormous, single, intelligent entity." [168]

We concluded the Image of the Beast would be a single entity, which will have its own desires and goals. Also in 2002, the Fathers For Life website spoke of a hive mind being brought to life!

---

[167] https://disruptionhub.com/edit-rise-human-hive-mind/ Jun 2017
[168] Converging Technologies for Improving Human Performance (pre-publication on-line version), June 2002, U.S. National Science Foundation, U.S. Department of Commerce, pp. 164, 165.

"Not only will the **hive mind have been brought to life** by the end of this century, but it will also offer the **lure of immortality**, enhanced body functions and vastly improved brain power for all those who join it, giving them virtually instantaneous communication with one another and making them **potentially unimaginably powerful**. That's what makes us human and what comprises mankind, e. g.: individual personalities will then no longer exist."[169]

By contrast, Disruption Hub has their own version of how becoming a swarm will help humanity mitigate the effects of AI:

"These systems are a combination of AI algorithms and real human participants, they will always be inherently aligned with human morals, interests, values and sensibilities. The resulting super-intelligence will not be an alien entity with conflicting values and interests but instead will be the natural evolution of the human intellect."[170]

While that sounds good on the surface, what if the morals, interests, values, and sensibilities programmed into this AI are distinctively in conflict against God's principles and commandments, and against those "who keep the commandments of God and have the testimony of Jesus Christ" (Rev 12:17)? What if those new values would "cause as many as would not worship the image of the beast to be killed" (Rev 13:15)?

Such a scenario is what end-times Bible prophecy has predicted for the last two millennia.

---

[169] https://fathersforlife.org/culture/Hive_Mind.htm
[170] https://disruptionhub.com/edit-rise-human-hive-mind/

IMAGE OF THE BEAST

"And he deceives those who dwell on the earth by those signs which he was granted to do in the sight of the beast, telling those who dwell on the earth to make an image to the beast who was wounded by the sword and lived" (Rev 13:14).

The image [εἰκών *eikon* / icon] is "an object shaped to resemble the form or appearance of something, likeness, portrait … of the emperor's head on a coin." [171] This language is reminiscent of when God said, "Let Us make man in Our image, according to Our likeness" (Gen 1:26). In other words, the False Prophet may get the world to make a replica of the Beast or maybe a sophisticated cyborg that looks just like the Beast. However, there may be another way to interpret the text.

The text says, "He was granted 'power to give' [εδοθη αυτω δουναι] breath [πνευμα] to the image of the beast" (Rev 13:15). The Greek word πνευμα "*pneuma*" can be understood as "air: the movement, blowing, breathing, that which animates or gives life to the body, breathe life, spirit. It is a part of human personality; your spirit, not necessarily your wind." [172] Then, is it just breath in the lungs? BDAG Lexicon also explains breath as, "An independent noncorporal being, in contrast to a being that can be perceived by the physical senses, that is a spirit." The last definition is, "an **independent, transcendent personality**." The Spanish Reina Valera may bring out the sense better "le fué dado que diese espíritu á la imagen de la bestia" (Rev 13:15) … that is, "to him was given that he might give spirit to the image of the beast."

In other words, the false prophet gives a transcendent personality to the image—a non-corporeal being that is a spirit. This latter definition seems to fit with the rest of the verse:

"that the image of the beast should both speak and cause as many as would not worship the image of the beast to be killed" (Rev 13:15).

---

[171] BDAG εἰκών eikon
[172] BDAG πνευμα pneuma

The image of the Beast is not merely an animatronic or dumb robot. It is not just a sophisticated AI. Either it breathes with breath in its lungs, or the other option is that it has "an **independent, transcendent personality**." It is not just a parlor trick; it will have "the ability to speak" (Rev13:15). If it can speak, that means it has thoughts. He is like an engineered TWIN of the Beast. It seems to be that the Beast and the False Prophet are trying to replicate, copy, counterfeit the process of God's creation of man in some form or fashion. Many secular thinkers have already concluded that such a "twin" will be transcendent, immune to human weaknesses and look indestructible; and, is coming in the near future.

HYBRIDIZED THOUGHTS

Ray Kurzweil suggests in the future, "our thinking then will be a hybrid of biological and non-biological thinking." [173] The implications of what he is saying are huge. Having a non-biological body part is one thing. But to have our thoughts, the most intimate part of what makes us, us —to have our thoughts hybridized potentially by the late 2030s is an incredible consideration indeed. Kurzweil's predictions are not just pie in the sky ideas, but are quickly becoming a startling reality.

Elon Musk has a company called Neuralink, which is **developing a "neural lace" technology to augment the cognitive abilities of the human brain—to upload and download thoughts.**[174] Basically, they drill through the skull and put a tiny mesh apparatus on the brain, which a person can then use to upload and download thoughts to a computer or to a destination of choice. Musk claims the company already has a monkey with "a wireless implant in [his] skull with tiny wires, who can play video games with his mind." It is not hard to see how such technology could have the ability to help millions of people live more active lives. It may help quadriplegics and untold others who suffer from neurological damage or other motor-skill deficiencies. Such advances are laudable—but history reminds us of how humans can use good technology for evil, and the Bible warns us of what is coming.

---

[173] https://www.ibtimes.co.uk/ray-kurzweil-human-brains-could-be-connected-cloud-by-2030-1504403
[174] https://thesiliconreview.com/2017/03/neuralink-is-developing-neural-lace-technology-to-augment-the-cognitive-abilities-of-the-human-brain

Musk explained that the goal with the brain-linking technology is addressing brain and spinal injuries and making up people's lost capacity with an implanted chip. "There are primitive versions of this device with wires sticking out of your head, but it's like a Fitbit in your skull with tiny wires that go into your brain."[175]

No one can question such good uses of the nascent technology. Nevertheless, like all technology, it remains to be seen if it will be used for good or to enslave people. Could the therapeutic effects of these procedures be used as a cover for the real purpose that is intended, namely, to engineer a way of remote manipulation of the human mind into a hive-mind entity?

Based on what we read in the book of Revelation, it would not be surprising if we were witnessing the building blocks of the Image of the Beast.

"Cognitive scientists have said that the mind is the software of the brain. Increasingly, physical software has the capacity to meld with, and augment, the human mind. If AI-enabled [Brain Computer Interface] BCI achievements already seem unbelievable, it stands to reason that BCI breakthroughs in the not-too-distant future could be truly momentous. Will the technology be harnessed for positive use cases to cure diseases or for mind control?"[176]

A form of brain hacking already exists; it occurs when Satan gains access to a mind and starts inserting his ideas. However, we are able to stop him and bring all thoughts captive (2 Cor 10:5). On the other hand, if there is a mesh on our brains, how could we stop the hacker? Losing freewill and the ability, and the right, to make our own decisions might not be far behind.

---

[175] https://www.bloomberg.com/news/articles/2021-02-01/elon-musk-wired-up-a-monkey-s-brain-to-play-videogames
[176] https://venturebeat.com/2021/02/13/thought-detection-ai-has-infiltrated-our-last-bastion-of-privacy/

CHAPTER 12: HIVE MIND AND THE IMAGE OF THE BEAST

It is with incredible irony that Elon Musk has stated that one of the reasons for creating Neuralink was to keep pace with artificial intelligence, which he believes is our biggest existential threat:

"I think we should be very careful about artificial intelligence. If I had to guess at what our biggest existential threat is, it is probably that. We need to be very careful," said Musk. "I'm increasingly inclined to think that there should be some regulatory oversight, maybe at the national and international level, just to make sure that we don't do something very foolish… With artificial intelligence we are summoning the demon. In all those stories where there is the guy with the pentagram and the holy water, it is like—yeah, he is sure he can control the demon. Doesn't work out."[177]

This kind of technology may represent fundamental stepping-stones to the image of the Beast, to the number, and the mark of the Beast. The neural lace in and of itself is not evil, but it could be used for evil. If you had a very pleasing image of a person in your head telling you what to do, would you say no? *Could* you say no? Elon Musk probably has good intentions, but we can easily see how such technology could be used for incredible evil. After all, if someone hacks our computer, it is only a machine that we can disable. But if someone hacks our minds, then what?

Researchers from Queen Mary University in London are working on using a neural network to read our thoughts and thereby determine a person's emotional state.

In this research, participants in the study watched a video while radio signals were sent towards them and measured when they bounced back. Analysis of body movements revealed "hidden" information about an individual's heart and breathing rates. From these findings, the algorithm can determine one of four basic emotion types: anger, sadness, joy, and pleasure. The researchers proposed this work could help with the management of health and wellbeing and be used to perform tasks like detecting depressive states.

---

[177] https://www.theguardian.com/technology/2014/oct/27/elon-musk-artificial-intelligence-ai-biggest-existential-threat

Ahsan Noor Khan, a PhD student and first author of the study, said: "We're now looking to investigate how we could use low-cost existing systems, such as Wi-Fi routers, to detect emotions of a large number of people gathered, for instance in an office or work environment." Among other things, this could be useful for HR departments to assess how new policies introduced in a meeting are being received, regardless of what the recipients might say. Outside of an office, police could use this technology to look for emotional changes in a crowd that might lead to violence.

The researchers admit that this sounds like 1984—and for good reason. Nevertheless, researchers around the world continue to push the envelope.

Researchers at Kyoto University in Japan developed a method to "see" inside people's minds using an fMRI scanner, which detects changes in blood flow in the brain … Though far from polished, this was essentially a reconstruction of what they were thinking about. One prediction estimates this technology could be in use by the 2040s.

MIT researchers have developed a computer interface that can transcribe words that the user verbalizes internally but does not actually speak aloud. A wearable device with electrodes pick-up neuromuscular signals in the jaw and face that are triggered by internal verbalizations, also referred to as subvocalizations. The signals are fed to a neural network that has been trained to correlate these signals with particular words. The idea behind this development is to meld humans and machines "such that computing, the internet and AI would weave into human personality as a 'second self.'"[178]

We must acknowledge that quadriplegics, comatose patients, and others could greatly benefit from such technology. As Biblicists, we are pro technology. Nevertheless, we must also acknowledge how such technology could be used for incredible destruction. The building and assembling of the image of the Beast seems to fit the bill.

---

[178] https://venturebeat.com/2021/02/13/thought-detection-ai-has-infiltrated-our-last-bastion-of-privacy/

BRAIN TO BRAIN COMMUNICATION

With an effective Brain Computer Interface (BCI), brain-to-brain communication becomes the next logical step. Pascual-Leone explains:

"By using advanced precision neuro-technologies including wireless EEG and robotized TMS, we were able to directly and noninvasively transmit a thought from one person to another, without them having to speak or write. This in itself is a remarkable step in human communication, but being able to do so across a distance of thousands of miles is a critically important proof-of-principle for the development of brain-to-brain communications."[179]

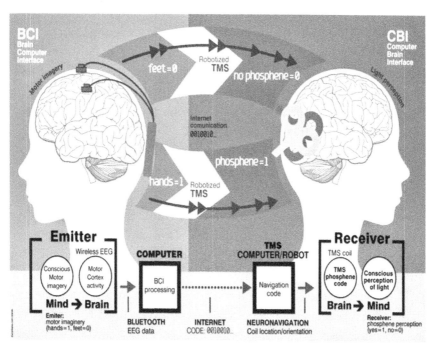

Figure 23. How Brain to brain communication will work.

The things researchers are able to do today were the science fiction of yesterday. In the popular series *Star Trek*, Spock was able to use his Vulcan mind meld to impart knowledge directly into someone else's brain.

---

[179] https://www.iflscience.com/brain/direct-brain-brain-communication-used-humans/

Now it is reality, still in its infancy, but it is happening by creating a device that allows two people to share information through thought. The researchers tested the technology by separating ... the users by more than 8000 kilometers, with one user in France and the other in India.[180]

With brain-to-brain communication, it would then be possible to have something called the hive mind, an idea first proposed in 2007 and dubbed the Technium. Kevin Kelley explains the characteristics of the hive mind.

"The emergent system of the technium—what we often mean by 'Technology' with a capital T—has its own inherent agenda and urges, as does any large complex system, indeed, as does life itself. That is, an individual technological organism has one kind of response, but in an ecology comprised of co-evolving species of technology we find an elevated entity—the technium—that behaves very differently from an individual species. The technium is a superorganism of technology. It has its own force that it exerts. That force is part cultural (influenced by and influencing of humans), but it is also partly non-human, partly indigenous to the physics of technology itself. That is the part that is scary and interesting."[181]

Scary indeed. We must remember that the authors we are consulting are not speaking of the biblical end times, but of the devasting effects humanity's own brilliance could have on itself. Once again, it is not any of these technologies that are in and of themselves evil. However, in the hands of a madman—with humanity between a rock and hard place—such technologies could be used for great evil.

180
https://journals.plos.org/plosone/article?id=10.1371/journal.pone.0105225

181 https://www.edge.org/conversation/kevin_kelly-the-technium-and-the-7th-kingdom-of-life

WHAT IS A HIVE?

The next question we should consider is what exactly is a hive mind?

A colony of honeybees is far more than an aggregation of individuals, that is a composite being that functions as an integrated whole. Indeed, one can actually or accurately think of a honeybee colony as **a single living entity**, weighing as much as five kilograms and performing all of the basic physiological processes … The hive is doing all this. Each one has its own little member part but there is a **bigger thing happening**.[182]

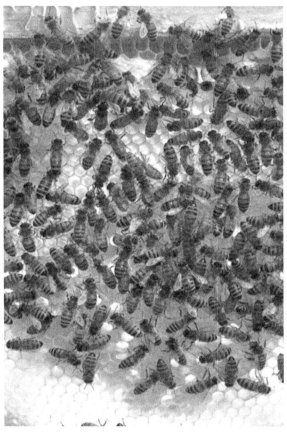

Figure 24. Colony of Honeybees Unknown Author licensed under CC BY-SA-NC.

---

[182] https://www.wired.com/2011/12/the-true-hive-mind-how-honeybee-colonies-think

The notion that a hive (as with the technium) can be considered its own organism, a "single living entity" is very telling. Recall that we discovered that the image of the Beast will have breath, which could be interpreted to mean, "a transcendent being." With that in mind, we will now turn to some forecasters who are speculating that humanity just may become something like the hive.

Washington University biologist Joan Strassmann, who has published papers on the topic of the hive mind, including "Beyond society: the evolution of organismality" along with colleague David Queller,[183] explains in *Gizmodo* how humans could potentially become a superorganism as clones.

"So what, exactly, is an organism? There are no hard and fast rules, but Strassmann and Queller call it a 'social phenomenon.' What they mean by that is all individuals have evolved from simpler organisms that work cooperatively. Your body is a society of cells that function together to make you walk, clean your blood, and digest your food.

Now for the real question: What would inspire a group of multicellular organisms like ants or humans to form a superorganism? In their book *The Superorganism*, biologists Bert Hölldobler and E.O. Wilson argue that it is a complex process involving genetic evolution and environmental pressures. Generally a group of insects like bees will move from behaving as individuals to forming colonies when they are storing food (like honey or pollen) that comes from multiple sources. At that point, a colony has a better chance of surviving than an individual."[184]

Thus for humans to even consider merging into a hive mind scenario, there would have to be an existential reason for doing so — that is, something that would cause people to believe they would have better odds of survival as a hive than separately.

---

[183] https://royalsocietypublishing.org/doi/abs/10.1098/rstb.2009.0095
[184] https://io9.gizmodo.com/could-humans-evolve-into-a-giant-hive-mind-5891143

The 3.5 years of terrors by the Two Witnesses, their resurrection, and forthcoming army of hostile aliens (Jesus and company) could be such a reason to prompt the creation of the hive. Lest we think that once again this is all just fanciful thinking, we ought to note that the technology to create a human hive already exists.

"The interfaces and algorithms to connect people into real time swarms also exist already and are referred to as 'artificial swarm intelligence.' Governed by AI algorithms, these combine the knowledge, wisdom, insights and intuitions of real people and in real time, enabling large groups of networked humans to quickly converge upon optimized decisions, predictions, solutions and evaluations."[185]

BECOMING A SUPERORGANISM

Joan Strassman continues in her explanation of humans becoming a superorganism. To be fair, she considers the evolution of humans into a colony organism as "rank speculation" at this point. Nevertheless, she points out that:

"The things that would drive a human group to organismality would be suppression of conflict and an increase in cooperation ... That could happen with higher relatedness. But right now there is far too much conflict."[186]

If the world, as Ronald Reagan put it, were facing "an **alien** threat from outside this world," we would quickly come together. The real terror caused by the Two Witnesses, their subsequent resurrection and threat to return could be just the thing necessary to drive humanity to organismality. Strassman continues mapping out how such a transition to a hive mind might happen stating we would:

---

[185] https://disruptionhub.com/edit-rise-human-hive-mind/
[186] https://io9.gizmodo.com/could-humans-evolve-into-a-giant-hive-mind-5891143

"need a society of human clones to make the complete transition from individuals to colony clones. In order to form a hive mind, humans may have to act more like an integrated neural network."[187]

The mark of the Beast could be just the switch necessary to conform individuals into clones. After all, they would all receive hybridized DNA from Satan himself. Strassman points out that one way to bring the human minds together could be to use "wireless brain-to-brain communication, which is not that far off in terms of available technology." She then asks the million-dollar question:

"What happens to our individuality if we give rise to a hive mind? Are our individual minds obliterated? Or is it just business as usual while a collective intelligence supervenes on our brains, unbeknownst to us? Giulio Tononi (of the information integration theory) actually thinks that the individual consciousness winks out when the group forms a truly integrated whole ... individuals would cease to be conscious."[188]

SATAN CONTROLS MINDS

So what would Satan do with a hive mind? As we have seen, people who take the mark are superhuman, and the hive would unite them to act as a superorganism. Such a weapon might prove highly effective in the coming battle against man's Creator. Satan may want to assimilate us into a single living organism to fight Yeshua in a way like the Borg from Star Trek—"resistance is futile; you will be assimilated."

However, unlike a hive of honeybees where there is no top-down leadership, Satan would be at the top. He would control it. He wants to take away people's autonomy and their freewill, their individuality. Satan wants to bind us, and it starts in our minds, as demonstrated by many verses:

---

[187] https://io9.gizmodo.com/could-humans-evolve-into-a-giant-hive-mind-5891143
[188] https://knowingneurons.com/2018/01/31/emergence-hive-mind/

- "These are of one mind [γνώμη, *gnōmē*], and they will give their power and authority to the beast (Rev 17:13).
- For to be carnally minded [φρονημα, *phronēma*] is death (Rom 8:6).
- do not be conformed to this world, but be transformed by the renewing of your mind [νοῦς, *nous*]... (Rom 12:2).
- whose minds [νόημα, *noēma*] the god of this age has blinded... (2 Cor 4:4).
- as the serpent deceived Eve by his craftiness, so your minds [νόημα] may be corrupted from the simplicity that is in Christ (2 Cor 11:3).
- whose end is destruction, whose god is their belly, and whose glory is in their shame–who set their mind [φρονέω, *phroneō*] on earthly things (Phil 3:19).
- And you, who once were alienated and enemies in your mind [διάνοια, *dianoia*] by wicked works (Col 1:21).

What is the common word? It is the mind.[189] Satan is going for our minds because the mind is where we make decisions that lead us to freedom or bondage, to life or to death. The man who was possessed with a legion of demons was in bondage and not in his right mind; his will was suppressed and overpowered. After Jesus freed him, the man was "sitting and clothed and in his right mind [σωφρονέω, *sōphroneō*]" (Mark 5:15). According to BDAG, "σωφρονέω to be able to think in a sound or sane manner, be of sound mind, of mental health."

Think of it like J.R.R. Tolkien's *Lord of the Rings* in which the evil ancient god, Sauron, created a ring in which his essence dwells. From that day, his fate and the ring are intertwined. Others who also received a ring of power were excited about it. But it was a ruse. Their rings simply served to enslave them through his more powerful ring. "One ring to rule them all, one ring to find them, one ring to bring them all and in the darkness bind them." Satan's scheme is control, in order to enslave us like Sauron—just the opposite of what Jesus wants to do.

---

[189] φρονέω to have an opinion with regard to something., think, form/hold an opinion, judge. διάνοια, ας, ἡ (s. διανοέομαι; Aeschyl., Hdt+.; in LXX nearly always for לֵבָב, לֵב). the faculty of thinking, comprehending, and reasoning, understanding, intelligence, mind BDAG.

161

However, in light of all that we have seen thus far, we can paint a composite image of the initial rush the Marked-ones will experience when they receive their upgrade. They will possess superpowers unlike anything humans have ever experienced. They may feel the dark, overwhelming power rushing through their bodies. Each cell in their bodies will undergo a transformation; their DNA is rewritten with Satan's DNA. Their speed, strength, and abilities increase a thousandfold; they possess nearly the same powers as the Beast. Their minds flood with knowledge about humanity, the earth, and Satan's (Enlil's) ancient struggle against Israel's God. They may revel in the ecstasy of their power, ability, and knowledge and, along with it, a sense of pride and arrogance may rise to untold heights; each person feels he is the greatest that there ever was. They know they are gods. Everyone plans how he will rule the world, and do what is right in his own eyes; how he or she will ascend above the heights of the clouds and plant his or her throne above God himself. This ethereal moment is interrupted by an impulse to submit to Enlil.

JESUS PRAYS

Just the opposite of Satan's scheme, Jesus wants to free us rather than enslave us. In his famous prayer recorded in John 17, Jesus expressed his desire for unity for not only his then-current disciples but also for future disciples, "that they all may be one, as You, Father, are in Me, and I in You; that **they also may be one in Us** ..." (John 17:21). He wants us to have the same kind of unity that He and the Father have.

The idea is that when we go to be with the Lord, in His kingdom and under his rule, we as individuals are not annihilated or swallowed up. You do not cease being you; you are not lost into Nirvana. Rather, our historic and genetic traits stay the same, and we will each carry our "luggage" of talents, emotions and past experiences. We will keep our own personalities and preserve our free will as well. But there will no longer be division or philosophies contrary to God and our fellow man. We will enjoy complete harmony with one another, on the same frequency, just like what Jesus and the Father have been experiencing forever. There has never been a conflict of interest; they have always been united, in interest and in purpose.

That is what He wants for us, without taking away your individuality, without taking away your free will. "You are the body of Christ and members individually" (1 Cor 12:27).

"For as the body is one and has many members, but all the members of that one body, being many, are one body, so also is Christ" (1 Cor 12:12). Jesus wants us to come into this unit called the body. He does not want to diminish us but to augment and increase us in such a way that we have the same purpose and no conflict; fear that drives people to defensive actions will not be a factor anymore. He wants us to enjoy his glory and the unity He shares with the Father.

"And the glory which You gave Me I have given them, that they may be one just as We are one: I in them, and You in Me; that they may be made perfect in one, and that the world may know that You have sent Me, and have loved them as You have loved Me" (John 17: 22–23).

When the Holy Spirit comes in us, it is not to make us robots where we have no more choice, and we just do whatever the Father says. He wants to dwell with us, inhabit us, empower us, but not overpower us.

God has a bigger purpose; He is not trying to make us uniform or automatons. In God's kingdom, not everyone has to fit the same mold. He wants us all to have our own personalities, expressions, and character. When we come together in unity, He blends it together in such an incredibly masterful way that He creates this harmonic symphony composed of divergent sounds. They say that the human body is composed of about 50 trillion cells all working together; that is you. Teach singular cell does its part. And that is the same idea of how Jesus wants us to be.

Chapter 13: Death to Those Siding with the Invaders

or those who decide not to receive the "upgrade" and finally become gods in the Beast system, life will become increasingly difficult. We see this progression in Scripture where refusing the mark first results in not being able to buy or sell, and then leads to death, specifically by beheading. We see both of these scenarios in Revelation:

> "He was granted power to give breath to the image of the beast, that the image of the beast should both speak and cause as many as would not worship the image of the beast to be killed (Rev 13:15). He causes all, both small and great, rich and poor, free and slave, to receive a mark on their right hand or on their foreheads (Rev 13:16), and that no one may buy or sell except one who has the mark or the name of the beast, or the number of his name (Rev 13:17). Here is wisdom. Let him who has understanding calculate the number of the beast, for it is the number of a man: His number is 666" (Rev 13:18).

In fact, we learn the fate of those who refused the mark:

> "I saw the souls of those who had been **beheaded** for their witness to Jesus and for the word of God, who had **not** worshiped the beast or his image, and had not received his mark on their foreheads or on their hands" (Rev 20:4).

These seem contradictory at first since if a person is killed for not worshipping the image of the Beast, then being prohibited from buying or selling is a moot point. We can deduce, therefore, the Beast and/or False Prophet will first use a carrot to encourage compliance, and then later use the stick. We need to remember that the implementation of the mark of the Beast comes after the Beast kills the Two Witnesses who terrorized the world for 42 months. The Two Witnesses' message, and show of power, softened some to God's message and hardened others.

To justify their rejection of the Two Witnesses, a world that largely does not believe in the God of Abraham, and that claims evolution to be the story of man's origins, will likely interpret them as hostile aliens. Their resurrection and ascension to the sky will possibly be viewed as a temporary departure to get reinforcements. Hence, the need to upgrade to god-status is mandatory for the world to be able to fight.

The Beast will generously offer everyone the opportunity to take his DNA, which he promises will give everyone powers like his to fight against the coming enemy. If Satan can get the world to take the upgrade voluntarily, then all the better. And the reality is that many will. However, after some people resist and denounce it, his threat is implemented—that people will not be able to buy or sell unless they take it. How could the Beast / Satan effectively enforce such a threat? China's social credit system provides us with a prototype.

CHINA'S SOCIAL CREDIT SYSTEM

China's social credit system is like a FICO score. A person with a FICO score of 820 has great credit, meaning banks are more likely to give a loan for homes, cars, etc. since that person is more trustworthy. Your FICO score indicates that you manage your money well, your debt-to-income ratio is balanced; and loaning you $200,000 is not risky. It makes sense. Whereas a score of 600 or below typically means you do not handle money well and banks will probably not loan you money, or if they do it will be at a higher interest rate because you are a higher risk.

China has created sort of a FICO score for your whole life—a social credit system. They consider traditional input, such as your income tax payment, loan repayment, credit card bills, utility bills, payment of court judgments. They also factor in social input such as adherence to traffic rules, adherence to family planning limits, paying for public transportation, academic honesty, volunteer activity, filial piety, criminal record, etc. Then lastly, the score indicates your online input, like interactions with other internet users, the reliability of information posted or reposted online, and your shopping habits.

CHAPTER 13: DEATH TO THOSE SIDING WITH THE INVADERS

China's social credit system expands the idea of a standard credit check to all aspects of life. Each citizen is assigned 1000 points, monitored to judge their behavior, and rated accordingly. You can gain points by donating blood or money, engaging in charity work, praising the government on social media, and helping the poor. You can lose points by not visiting one's aging parents regularly, cheating in online games, insincere apologies for crimes committed or spreading rumors on the internet, etc.

Figure 25. Chinese Girls showing their social credit score; starts with 1000.

Of course, you should go visit your aging parents wherever they are. But would it be the same if your son or daughter came to visit you, and you knew that they were only trying to improve their credit score so they could get ahead in society? You might say, Hey, it is good to see you, son. Tell me: are you here because you love me or because you want to buy a house?

This system is already in place in China. In Figure 27 above, girls show their scores. Everyone starts with 1000 points. You can go up or down from that. You can gain a total of 1300 points, and you can go down as far as 600 points. These girls have 753, 724, 637, 668, and 690. This score does not merely determine if a person can get credit to buy something based on whether you are likely to pay the bank back or not. This score reflects what kind of person you are.

The idea makes sense on a certain level. After all, most of us desire a society where people are honest and true, do not jaywalk, and help people. The Chinese government takes the criteria and aggregates the data to determine how good you are. It comes with a cost. If your score goes too low, you could be banned from access to planes, high-speed trains, from access to the internet and other social services. It is kind of like the game of life.

However, what happens if the government gives an act a value disproportionate with the person's values? Certainly, some practices will lessen a person's score dramatically. Things like protesting the government, even for righteous causes, will bring down the score. Being part of the underground church instead of being part of the government-sanctioned Three-self Church will dramatically reduce a person's score.

China has close to 300 million cameras in which they use sophisticated facial recognition software to see when you have been naughty or nice, and they are keeping a list and checking it twice. If you jaywalk, you get points deducted. If you say something against the Chinese government, you get points deducted. This is now, and this is real in China.

None of these things in and of themselves are the Beast System. Yet when we start putting them together and look at the technology already available, we see the Beast System beginning to emerge. We see how it could be incredibly easy to implement globally, and to administer in a short amount of time.

It is not hard to imagine the addition of a few lines of code to check for the mark. Seeing that distinguishing mark would mean that this person is compliant. If no mark is seen, then your social credit score would be impacted, which could lead to you not being able to buy or sell.

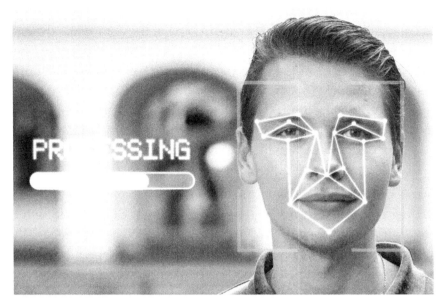

Figure 26 The essentials of facial recognition. Image by
https://pixabay.com/users/tumisu-148124

The Beast may give people a grace period of six months, for example, to upgrade and exhibit the mark. However, if a person persists in their refusal to be part of the solution, then they become a problem—indeed, a threat that must be dealt with or eliminated.

The world will take people's non-compliance very seriously because they will believe the earth will need to fight the coming hostiles (Rev 19:19). After Japan attacked Pearl Harbor, many patriotic Japanese Americans were seen as a threat and were rounded up, and sadly, were sent to internment camps. They were baselessly suspected of being Japanese spies. We can imagine the fear the world will have after living through forty-two months of genocidal governments terrorizing planet Earth while Two Witnesses call down plagues on the wicked and then resurrect! If people are not willing to be part of the solution, then they will be branded as Luddites, a danger to humanity and traitorous for siding with Earth's mortal enemy, the Master of the TWO!

Non-mark-takers will pose an existential threat to the survival of the Beast system type of the human race. Therefore, for the good of humanity, all traitors will be executed. Some of the Remnant, however, will have been strengthened in their faith because of the TWO. They might pray and lay hands on the executed and raise them back to life as hinted at in Daniel: "the people who know their God shall be strong, and **carry out great exploits**" (Dan 11:32). Thus, to ensure the executed stay dead, the Beast will issue a decree to behead non-mark takers; massive persecution will follow and hundreds of millions put to death:

"After these things I looked, and behold, **a great multitude** which no one could number, of all nations, tribes, peoples, and tongues, standing before the throne and before the Lamb, clothed with white robes, with palm branches in their hands (Rev 7:9), … "These are the ones who **come out of the great tribulation**, and washed their robes and made them white in the blood of the Lamb" (Rev 7:14).

Chapter 14: Gog, Son of Death / Perdition, the Ancient Leader Revealed

The Bible has a GREAT deal to say about the coming end-times leader who will unite the world in battle against Jesus. In *Corrupting the Image 2*, we studied about the coming of the Beast who "was, and is not, and will ascend out of the bottomless pit and **go to perdition**" (Rev 17:8), the one who is called "the son of perdition" (2 Thess 2:3–4). We determined that Satan and a man will fuse to become the god of death incarnate. We learned that Satan's many names, such as BAD, Nergal, Pabilsag, and many others, were all related to death. This hybridized individual will lead the world in a war against God Himself.

Ezekiel also prophesied about this individual known as Gog, who would come against Israel in the last days (Ezek 38:8) with his "great host" (Ezek 38:4), and "**his hordes and the many peoples who are with him**" whom God will destroy with "torrential rains and hailstones, fire and sulfur" (Ezek 38:22). God declares that Gog's presence will be overwhelming in Israel and, when he comes, God will be sanctified:

> "You will come up against My people Israel like a cloud, to cover the land. It will be in the **latter days** that I will bring you against My land, so that the nations may know Me, when I am sanctified in you, O Gog, before their eyes" (Ezek 38:16).

According to Ezekiel, God was declaring for years through the prophets that He would bring Gog against Israel.

> "Thus says the Lord GOD: 'Are you he of whom **I have spoken in former days by My servants the prophets of Israel**, who prophesied **for years** in those days that I would bring you against them?'" (Ezek 38:17).

But where in Scripture was God talking about Gog? By the name *Gog* we do not find any such occurrence. Gog[190] is used only in Ezekiel 38 and 39, and once in Revelation 20.[191]

---

[190] There was a Gog, son of Joel of the line of Reuben (1 Chr 5:4).
[191] See Appendix ## for Gog and Magog after the Millennium.

Modern lexicons, such as the *Dictionary of Deities and Demons in the Bible*, the NASB Lexicon, Strong's, and *Brown Driver Briggs Hebrew English Lexicon* all comment how the etymology of Gog is uncertain, which is to say, Gog from Ezekiel 38 and 39 is likely not of Hebrew origin. Consequently, scholars have looked for clues about Gog's identity in other languages, civilizations and events that might qualify linguistically; but ultimately they have failed, assuming they happened before Ezekiel.[192] Josephus suggested Gog as leaders of the Scythians,[193] a people (after Ezekiel) who lived on the fringe of the Roman Empire and invaded it from the northeast (ca. 3rd century BC).[194] Yet his suggestion also fails (like the others) because God said Gog would invade Israel, not the Roman Empire! Furthermore, God said Gog would come in the latter years and last days to a people brought back from the sword, whom we will see are the Jews who returned from the Holocaust.

SECOND TEMPLE LITERATURE ON GOG

Second Temple literature understood Gog to be the quintessential enemy of Israel, who would emerge in the last days, and then be destroyed by King Messiah. Interestingly, the Septuagint manuscripts seem to equate him with Og, king of [the] Bashan. *The Dictionary of Deities and Demons of the Bible* explains that Gog "is a **cipher** for the **evil darkness** of the north and personifies the powers hostile to the lord."[195]

---

[192] Gyges / Gugu in Ashurbanipal's records a seventh century king (670-652 B.C.) of Lydia, (ABD, vol. 2, p. 1056) (Also spelled Giges or Gogo, Encyclopedia Judaica, vol. 7, p. 691.). Gaga from the *Ras Shamra Texts* an Akkadian or Babylonian god (cf. Enuma Elish); Gagi, a ruler of the city of Sabi; Gasga, in Hittite texts (ca. 1300 or 1400 BC), a rebellious area on the border of Armenia and Cappadocia. (*Introduction To the OT* by R. K. Harrison, p. 842) (source: Utley: BDB 155, KB 182). Others have suggested it was the "name of a country, Gaga or Gagaia, allegedly mentioned in the El Amarna Letters (EA I:38)." DDDB

[193] (Josephus, Antiq. 1.6.1, ZPBE, vol. 2, p. 770),

[194] (*Introduction To the OT* by R. K. Harrison, p. 842) (source: Utley: BDB 155, KB 182)

[195] R. Ahroni. The Gog Prophecy and the Book of Ezekiel, HAR I (1977) 1-27 Cf. DDDB

The Targum of Palestine (Neofiti) in Numbers 11:26 says: "At the end, the end of the days, will Gog and Magog and his host come up against Jerusalem; but by the hand of the King Meshiha [Messiah] they will fall." The Babylonian Talmud Abuda Zara 3b (Idolatry) Chapter 1 echoes the Targum:

> "They will see the war of Gog and Magog, and will question them: 'With whom do you want to fight?' Whereto the answer will be: 'With the Lord and his Messiah' [as it reads [Psalm ii. 2]: 'Against the Lord and his anointed']"

The Jewish Encyclopedia notes that Rabbi R. Eliezer: "Mentions the **Gog** and Magog war together with the Messianic woes and the Last Judgment as the three modes of divine chastisement preceding the millennium. The **destruction of Gog** and Magog's army implies not ... the extermination of the Gentile world at the close of the Messianic reign, **but the annihilation of the heathen powers who oppose the kingdom of God and the establishing of the Messianic reign.**"[196]

In other words, the battle of Gog and Magog is the final conflict; it is the battle of the Day of the Lord as spoken of by Isaiah, Daniel, Habakkuk, and many others. These considerations harmonize perfectly with Revelation, which says that the whole world will make war against Jesus.

According to Syriac Apocalypse Baruch 11:1–2, Gog alone will survive the battle and will be brought "**bound before the Messiah on Mount Zion and judged and slain.**" According to II Esd. xiii. 9 *et seq.*, "fire will issue forth from the **mouth of the Messiah and consume the whole army.**" [197]

Such language readily identifies Gog with the Beast in both Daniel and Revelation; and the Son of Perdition from Paul's writings:

---

[196] https://jewishencyclopedia.com/articles/5849-eschatology, (in Meklita, Beshallaḥ, l.c.)
[197] https://jewishencyclopedia.com/articles/5849-eschatology

- the beast was **captured**, and with it the false prophet ... These two were **thrown** alive into the lake of **fire** that burns with sulfur (Rev 19:20).

- ... as I looked, the **beast** was **killed**, and its body **destroyed** and given over to be burned with fire (Dan 7:11).

- the lawless one will be revealed, whom the Lord will consume with the **breath** of His **mouth** and **destroy** with the brightness of His coming (2 Thess 2:8).

Paul was likely drawing upon Isaiah 11 where the Messiah: "with the breath of His lips He shall slay the wicked [LXX ungodly one]" (Isa 11:4).

The Babylonian Talmud, tractate Aboth, discusses how the Shekhina—the manifest presence of God—appears ten times throughout history. In the Garden of Eden, at the tower of Babel, at Sodom and Gomorrah, etc. Finally, "it will come down in the days of **Gog and Magog,** as it is written [Zech. xiv. 4]: **"And his feet will stand on that day upon the Mount of Olives."**[198]

The Babylonian Talmud, tractate Pesachim, chapter 10 pairs the battle of Gog and Magog with the time of Jacob's trouble: Dan. 12:1 and Jer. 30:7:

R. Johanan said that it refers to the time of the war of Gog and Magog (which **will occur just before** the coming of the Messiah and will be the **worst period** for the Israelites to pass through).[199]

Maimonides, the great medieval Jewish commentator, writes in *Guide for the Perplexed* about how the Day of the Lord, spoken of in Joel 3:3–5, may be interpreted as "an account of the defeat of Gog and Magog near Jerusalem in the days of the Messiah."[200]

In the sources we have just reviewed, Gog was clearly understood to be the definitive end-times enemy who will rise up against Israel in the final battle of the Day of the Lord, whom the Messiah would personally destroy with the breath of his mouth just before the establishment of the Messianic reign. Revelation calls this final battle, Armageddon. The names are slightly different, but the set and characters are all the same (which we will examine in more detail later).

---

[198] Tractate Aboth Babylonian Talmud
[199] Tractate Pesachim, chapter 10, Babylonian Talmud
[200] Maimonides – Guide for the Perplexed

While those ancient sources considered Gog to be equivalent to the Beast of Daniel and Revelation, Gog's name itself continues to shroud him in mystery. What is amazing is that Gog actually means death, enmity, and is yet another epithet for Satan.

GOG IS THE ENEMY (SUMERIAN EVIDENCE)

Just as we traced the great dragon, the Beast and the woman who rides it back to Shinar (some evidence being a review from *Corrupting the Image 2*), the solution to the Gog question is also resolved there as well. In 1914, A. Van Hoonacker suggested, "Gog" came from the Sumerian "gug" ('black spot', 'cornelian,' or 'shining') and is thus a metaphor for evil.[201] His suggestion is confirmed by the University of Pennsylvania Sumerian online lexicon, which lists variations of "gug," though Hoonacker may have stopped prematurely since he did not mention entries "gug5 "enmity, hostility" and the related gug6 "stick; weapon" and gug6 "tooth; blade; beak; dog bite" (Akk. Nišik).[202]

John A. Halloran, in his Sumerian Lexicon, points out that "gug5: hostility, war (might be reduplicated ug5,7,8, 'to kill; to die')."[203]

---

[201] Gog: A. VAN HOONACKER, ZA 28 [1914] 336. Cf. Dictionary of Deities and Demons in the Bible – by Karel van der Toorn, Bob Becking, Pieter Willem van der Horst. See also ABD, vol. 2, p. 1057, and W. F. Albright). F. Albright thought such a definition to be "highly implausible."

[202] 1) [BRIGHT] wr. gug "(to be) bright"... 3) [CARNELIAN] wr. na4gug "carnelian" Akk. Sāmtu; 4) [ENMITY] wr. gug5 **"enmity, hostility"** Akk. Nukurtu; 5) [GRASS] wr. u2gug4; gug4; gug; u2... "a grass; rush, sedge" Akk. šišnu; šuppatu; 6) [MOLE] wr. gug "mole, black spot; birthmark" Akk. halû; pendu; 7) [SEAL] wr. gug6 "to seal" Akk. Kanāku; 8) [STICK] wr. gug6 "stick; weapon" Akk. Kakku; 9) [TOOTH] wr. gug; gug6 "tooth; blade; beak; dog bite" Akk. nišik kalbi; šinnu.
http://psd.museum.upenn.edu/epsd/e1897.html

203 "ug(2): lion; anger, fury; storm. ug4,5,7,8: n., death; dead person. v., to kill; to die (singular and plural marû stem; plural hamtu, which is sometimes reduplicated; cf., úš). ug6, u6[IGI.É]: n., amazement; gaze, glance (['EYE' + 'HOUSE']). v., to look at; to stare at, gaze; to be impressed. adj., astonishing."

In linguistics, reduplication is the process in which a part of a word is repeated, sometimes with a slight change. Daniel A. Foxvog, in his *Introduction to Sumerian Grammar* explains the reduplication of a noun: "reduplication may signify either **intensification** of the adjectival idea or plurality of the modified noun. Thus, diĝir gal-gal might indicate 'the very great god' or more usually 'the great gods.'[204]

In *Corrupting the Image* Vol 2, we discovered the Sumerian logogram (pictogram, cuneiform symbol) BAD ⊨⊀ (IDIM) ▷══◁[205] (Akkadian mūtu and ÚŠ / UG) is written on the Mt. Hermon inscription and is the logogram of Enlil, Dagan, Ug (death), Nergal (god of death and the underworld). When the logogram BAD.BAD reduplicated i.e. "ug$_x$(|BAD.BAD|)"[206] it is written "GUG" and means "hostility, war," otherwise known as enmity.

This revelation is nothing short of mind-blowing. "Enmity" naturally draws our attention to Genesis 3:15, where Satan the dragon swindled Adam and Eve, and God declared war: "And I will put **enmity** between you and the woman and between your seed and her Seed" (Gen 3:15). This is an accurate description of Satan and his kingdom. He is the enemy; we often refer to him as the adversary.

---

https://www.sumerian.org/sumcvc.htm and
www.lexiline.com/lexiline/lexi37.htm

[204] Daniel A. Foxvog, "Introduction to Sumerian Grammar" Pg. 17. Posted to web: 4 January 2016. http://cdli.ucla.edu/?q=cuneiform-digital-library-preprints Hosted by the Cuneiform Digital Library Initiative (<http://cdli.ucla.edu>) Editor: Bertrand Lafont (CNRS, Nanterre) Number 2. pg. 23

[205] Instead of a large horizontal, as seen in the (digitized form, but one type of "bad"), the sign is seen in the Amarna letters as composed of two opposite facing (triangles), the wedges. https://en.wikipedia.org/wiki/Bad_(cuneiform)

[206] ug [DIE] ... wr. ug$_7$; ug$_5$; ug$_x$ (|BAD.BAD|) "plural and imperfect singular stem of uš [to die]" Akk. *mâtu*. http://psd.museum.upenn.edu/nepsd-frame.html [See also] mītu [ÚŠ:] (adj.) dead, deceased, departed; Cf. *mâtu, mītūtān* http://www.assyrianlanguages.org/akkadian/dosearch.php. See also https://prosobab.leidenuniv.nl/pdfs/logogram.pdf

Some of the other lexical entries for GUG reveal the notion of enmity and hostility. Satan, the enemy, has incited his followers to destroy us using weapons gug6 "stick; weapon" (Akk. Kakku) or by using "gug6 "tooth; blade," and the like. Peter tells us, "Your adversary the devil walks about like a roaring lion" (1 Pet 5:8).

Therefore, we have the attested linguistic evidence, which informs us that "gug" could become "gog," in addition to the many already noted parallels. Gog comes from Sumerian GUG meaning death, enmity, hostility. What an incredible description of the one who brings the world together to fight against the King of Kings! It is none other than Enmity / Death himself. It is BATios, Satan, the god of death, who we saw in *Corrupting the Image 2*: "According to the command of the great bull-god (Batios) Satan, those swearing an oath in this place go forth." Recall that the scribes likely called Satan, BATios because that one term described many conscious syncretisms such as Enlil, Dagan, Ninurta, and Baal.[207]

Hence, Satan, the god known by the logogram BAD (known locally as Enlil and his son Ninurta in Mesopotamia, and as Dagan and his son Ba'al in Syria) was sometimes represented by the reduplicated logogram ug.ug = BAD.BAD which when transliterated (spoken) was / is GUG. If the reduplication indicates intensification, then OG morphing to GOG tells us he is named the "Deadliest Death," the "Darkest Darkness," the most hateful hater-of-God and the #1 Enemy of man. Amazingly, there is yet another facet to this mystery!

---

[207] Private email communication with Professor Amar Annus of University of Tartu Natural History Museum and Botanical Garden, Mon, Sep 28, 2020. He states: "Dagan...and Enlil...sometimes share the logograms... dBAD and dKUR ...This cuneiform sign BAD has many logographic readings throughout history, including BAD for "dead" and BAD.BAD for ug in Sumerian." See also https://en.wikipedia.org/wiki/An_(cuneiform)

GOG IS ALSO NINURTA!

In *Corrupting the Image 2*, we considered extensive evidence showing that Ninurta was Nimrod, the rebel. We also discovered that Nimrod was the avatar of Satan and held his power, throne, and great authority, as the Beast will do. We have seen that Satan and the Beast are going to fuse into his avatar in the future; and what is so amazing is that the name "Gog" identifies as both Satan and Nimrod! Let's go back to Amos 5 where the prophet spoke of Nimrod and Satan:

> "You also carried along Sikkuth your king and Kiyyun, your images, the **star** of your gods which you made for yourselves" (Amos 5:26 NASB).[208]

Amar Annus notes that some scholars identify the astral divinity Sikkuth (Sakkud= skwt) with BAD (Ninurta):

> "… skwt originates from SAG.KUD and the deity Sakkuth was worshipped in Samaria during Amos' time (cf. 2 Kgs 17:30). What is curious in the biblical passage is the attribute "your king" (mlkkm) to skwt which fits Ninurta as the god of kingship. One might suggest that the Amos passage reflects peripheral Mesopotamian traditions diffused into Samaria. The second divine element, kywn, [Kiyyun] almost certainly corresponds to Akkadian *kajjamanu* (SAG.UŠ) "Saturn."[209]

---

[208] Amos 5:2 NASB note: "Or Sakkuth (Saturn) or shrine of your Moloch"
[209] Amar Annus, The God Ninurta in the Mythology and Royal Ideology of Ancient Mesopotamia, State Archives of Assyria Studies, Volume XIV Helsinki 2002.

CHIEF HEAD = ROSH SAG.UŠ

Saturn's Sumerian name is SAG.UŠ. SAG means "chief, head" saĝ, which in Old Babylonian, means "head; person; capital" and in Akkadian, qaqqadu; rēšu,[210] (similar to the Hebrew *"rosh."*) UŠ means "death, dead, dying," related to UG[211] and to GUG and to BATios. Therefore, SAG.UŠ means the "head of death!" Amos reports that Israel was worshiping their "king" Sikkut / Sakkuth. The association of chief (head) of death fits very well with what God said to Ezekiel: "Son of man, set your face toward Gog, of the land of Magog, the prince of Rosh, Meshech and Tubal, and prophesy against him" (Ezek 38:2).

The question arises as to whether '*Rosh*'[212] is a place name or a descriptive adjective modifying 'prince.' "Aquila, the Targum, and Jerome (Latin Vulgate) viewed rosh adjectively—'chief prince,'[213] which corresponds perfectly with the god Sikkuth / SAG.UŠ or head (*rosh*) of death. When we recall that Gog is the latest in a long line of epithets for Satan, then it makes sense that he is the chief prince. After all, though lesser demons are doing his bidding, he is king of them all. He is the chief prince of Tyre (Melqart, see *Corrupting the Image 2*) and the king of Babylon.

> "Take up this proverb against the **king of Babylon** … (Isa 14:4)
> "Hell from beneath is excited about you, to meet you at your coming; it stirs up the [Rephaim] (the dead), for you, **all the chief ones** of the earth; it has raised up from their thrones all the kings

---

[210] saĝ "head; person; capital" Akk. *qaqqadu*; *rēšu*
http://psd.museum.upenn.edu/nepsd-frame.html

[211] ug [DIE] … wr. ug₇; ug₅; ugₓ (|BAD.BAD|) "plural and imperfect singular stem of uš [to die]" Akk. *mâtu*. http://psd.museum.upenn.edu/nepsd-frame.html

[212] If Rosh is Russia, then Russia is necessarily an evil player. Russia has its problems but are they specifically the nation that God talked about? Is it possible Scofield mistakenly interpreted "the LXX's reading of the Hebrew *ros* as the proper name "Ros" ...as a code-name for 'Russia'"? *(Scofield Reference Bible;* GESENIUS. *Thesaurus* 1835. 1253).

[213] "Rethinking Ezekiel's Invasion by Gog" in Journal of the Evangelical Society, Mar. 1996, pg. 30.

of the nations (Isa 14:9). They all shall speak and say to you: 'Have you also become as weak as we? Have you become like us?'" (Isa 14:10) ... "How you are fallen from heaven, O Enlil [Heilel (הֵילֵל)], son of the morning! ..." (Isa 14:12).

This is showing that he is the chief above them all. Of course, we recall that Satan is called "the prince of the power of the air" (Eph 2:2) and "the ruler of this world" (John 12:31), just as Michael is "one of the chief princes" (Dan 10:13) of the good guys. So too, Satan is the head prince of the bad guys. Further corroboration comes from the name, Pabilsag.

Pabilsag comes from Old Babylonian and means a "relation." In Akkadian, it is "abu," which of course is related to the Hebrew אַבAb (father), or Aramaic, Abba. The infix "bilga," also Old Babylonian, means "male ancestor." Lastly, SAĜ means "head; person; capital," (Akkadian, qaqqadu; rēšu, like the Hebrew "rosh").[214]

Pabilsag, then, was the head / chief or "principal ancestor." Pabilsag, as indicated by his name, was clearly someone the Mesopotamians believed to be of great importance, who was the chief of all their ancestors. He was considered a son of the god Enlil and was syncretized with Ningirsu / Ninurta. Pabilsag's association with the netherworld could be due to his syncretism with the underworld deity, Nergal.[215] Thus, he is the principal ancestor and Ninurta / Nimrod, son of Enlil, who became a hybrid. When we compare Pabilsag's bio with Revelation 9, a startling realization comes into focus: The god that the House of Israel was worshiping will return in the last days.

---

[214] bilga... "fresh fruit; male ancestor"..."a kinship term" Akk. *Abu.* saĝ [HEAD] ...wr. saĝ "head; person; capital" Akk. *qaqqadu; rēšu*
http://psd.museum.upenn.edu/nepsd-frame.html
[215] http://oracc.museum.upenn.edu/amgg/listofdeities/pabilsag/index.html

NINURTA, SON OF ENLIL, IS THE ARROW

The name Sukuth was, probably from Assyro-Babylonian *Shukudu* … the brightest star in the night sky"[216] (recall that gug means "[to be] bright"). Amar Annus notes that "the arrow (*šukudu*) … Ninurta's star Sirius and … **might be a metaphor for Ninurta** himself…"[217] We learned how the theme of GUG "enmity" is also expressed as (gug6) "stick; weapon" (Akk. Kakku) and (gug6) "tooth; blade; beak; dog bite" (Akk. nišik kalbi; šinnu) which are tools of death, very much like how "Ninurta himself is an '**arrow.**'"

The first century Jewish apocalyptists used similar language suggesting Belial and his hordes will come out of the underworld with arrows flying. The apocalyptists were seeing what Satan (Mesopotamian Enlil) had been projecting all along; that he, or his proxy, was the great, invincible dragon that you did not want to mess with.[218]

In other words, Ninurta is known as the Arrow, which in an astronomical setting is the star, Sirius. The imagery of gods as stars reminds us of the language of Revelation in which angels are frequently symbolized as stars. In John's vision of Revelation, Jesus has seven stars in his right hand.

---

[216] http://usccb.org/bible/amos/5/

[217] Amar Annus, The God Ninurta in the Mythology and Royal Ideology of Ancient Mesopotamia, State Archives of Assyria Studies, Volume XIV Helsinki 2002. Pg. 104

[218] Yoder notes Ninurta / Nergal's epithet The majestic, great dragon who pours who venom upon them," and how Ninurta's mace consisted of seven snake-like heads. W. von Soden, "Die Unterweltsvision eines assyrischen Kronprinzen," *ZA* 43 [1936] 17:56; Angim III 38. For the Annunaki and Igigi gods, cf. W. von Soden, "Zur wiederherstellung der marduk-gebete bms 11 und 12," *Iraq* 31 (1969), 85:32; M. Civil, "Commentaries from Nippur," *JNES* 33 (1974), 336:13. Cited in: Pre-publication version: Tyler R. Yoder, "Ezekiel 29:3 and Its Ancient Near Eastern Context" Vetus Testamentum 63 (2013) 486-96. Nergal's title is [*ú-šum*]-*gal-lu ṣīru tābik imti elišunu*, cf (*CAD* U/W, Pg. 330)

Jesus reveals the mystery "... The seven stars are the angels of the seven churches... (Rev 1:20). Thus, there are seven stars or seven angels (messengers) to God's redeemed people. It is interesting that another word for "arrow" (*mulmullu*, Sumerian mul.mul) is related to the Pleiades, which again reminds us of Nergal's planet, Mars (Sal.bat.anu)[219]. Amar Annus explains that:

> The **Pleiades were thought to bring war and destruction** – "the warlike gods, who carry bow and arrow, whose rising means war." It is worth noting that the month of Ningirsu in Astrolabe B, Iyyar, is also referred to as "the month of the Pleiades, **the Seven Great Gods**" (KAV 218 A i 12f and 19).

The star was a symbol of Ninurta, the arrow, and even known as "gabbar" (like the Hebrew "gibbor" hero). Annus comments that, "Marduk's arrows (*mulmullu*) ...and *šukudu* **referred to the god's arrow which killed his enemy.**"[220]

From the previous evidence, we see that *Sukkut* refers to an arrow, as well as Ninurta. *Kiyyun* means "steady one." However, both names also refer to planets or a constellation and both are appellations that involve a hero, a bow, and an arrow. Nimrod was the one who became a gibbor ("hero"); he was a gibbor hunter, and of course, we positively identified him as Ninurta in *Corrupting the Image 2*. It may be significant that God says He will knock the arrow out of Gog's hand:

> "Then I will strike your bow from your left hand, and will make your arrows drop out of your right hand" (Ezek 39:3 ESV).

---

[219] Frans Wiggermann, Nergal, Reallexikon der Assyriologie (RlA) 9 1999 Pg. 215-226.

[220] Amar Annus, The God Ninurta in the Mythology and Royal Ideology of Ancient Mesopotamia, State Archives of Assyria Studies, Volume XIV Helsinki 2002. book 3 Pg. 135-138

CONCLUSION: GOG IS THE FUSION OF SATAN AND THE BEAST

Thus, Ninurta (biblical Nimrod "rebel") son of Enlil (BAD / BAT (=IDIM) was also known as the star Sirius, Nergal's Mars star which spreads plague, which was an arrow (šukudu, Sum. GAG); and Ninurta is a syncretism with Nergal, king of the dead. The Sumerian Gug "death, enmity, hostility" is a form of the logogram BAD. We have the linguistic evidence that the Sumerian "gug" could become "gog" and "gag" (arrow) could become "gog." Amazingly, both terms fit perfectly from the evidence we have examined. And what a picture! God said there would be enmity between Satan and the woman, between his seed and her seed (Gen 3:15), and Peter tells us, "your adversary the devil walks about like a roaring lion seeking whom he may devour." (1 Pet 5:8)[221]

In other words, GUG is the ancient enemy Satan (Enlil) and his son, Ninurta is GAG. We have determined Satan and a Nimrod / Ninurta antichrist-figure will merge into the Beast hybrid—the god of death and Sheol, the fallen star and king of the abyss. Who is also known as "destruction": *Abaddon, Apollyon,* who manifests in the last days as the Beast who ascends out of the abyss in the time of Jacob's trouble. Hence, together they become Gog (Enmity, Arrow) in the Bible. Thus Gug/Gag/Gog is yet another epithet for Satan / Enlil and or Ninurta / Nimrod, which answers the question: when did God speak by the prophets about Gog? Answer: all the time! Satan was the entity behind all those titles and the one of whom the prophets spoke, starting in Genesis 3, *"I will cause enmity between you and the woman."* Then every time there was a reference to Satan's many epithets such as: Heilel / Enlil / Ellil (King of Babylon) Isa 14:12, Melqart (King of Tyre) Ezek 28, Ninurta / Nergal / Pabilsag (2 Kings 17:30), Sikkut (Amos 5:26), Enlil (Satan)—the "father" of Ninurta, which the Bible deliberately transformed into "Nimrod" the Rebel.

---

[221] Hence we discover the following based on the nuances of GUG and UG: He who is at "enmity, hostility" (gug5) toward us was the "seal" (gug6) of perfection who was "exalted" (ug) and used "(to be) bright" (gug) lost God's "light" (ug2) and now appears with a "mole, black spot; birthmark" (gug) as a "furious" (ug2) "carnelian" (na4gug) (fiery red dragon) who slithers through the "grass" (gug4) and is seeking whom he may devour us like a like a "lion" (ugx) "offering" (gug2) with "tooth; blade (gug6) so that we die (ug7 ug5).

Enlil and Ninurta had many syncretisms such as Marduk / MARTU / Bel / Baal and many shared a common Sumerian logogram BAD/BAT/BE. Gog will simply be his final alias before being defeated by Jesus. In fact, in Revelation 13, John saw "a beast rising up" and "on his heads a blasphemous name" (Rev 13:1). Later in Revelation 17, John saw a "woman sitting on a scarlet beast which was **full of names of blasphemy**" (Rev 17:3). The **Beast has many names**, which defy and slander the good name and character of the God of Israel.

Chapter 15: A Fallen Star Opens the Gates of Hades

We started the book discussing how some UFO researchers believe the advanced beings inside the UFOs exist behind a "thin psychic dimensional membrane." And those who claim to have encountered the Draconians report the same thing. The Bible asserts that the portal to that other dimension will eventually be opened.

In the previous chapter, we learned about the link between the ancient god of death and the coming Beast. Our linguistic study has now brought us to the astounding fact that there is a surviving artifact that depicts the god of death; it is an ancient carving of Nergal, whose epithet was GAG (the arrow) AND who was the god of death, BAD / BAT / GUG. We examined this in *Corrupting the Image 2* in the context of Nimrod / Ninurta.

Yet, we know that the Beast is called the one who will ascend out of the abyss (Rev 17:8). Nimrod merged with Satan to be the Beast who once lived, but died and descended to the abyss to operate as the god of death, Nergal, et al.; and he is waiting to be freed. Nimrod was the first king to rule a kingdom for Satan; it was the first of five world kingdoms that have fallen. As we watch the final decline of the remnants of the Roman (6th) kingdom, we see the emerging Beast (7th) kingdom. This seventh king will be a modern-day man who embraces Satan as he is cast from the heavenly realm; and who also embraces Nimrod, as he bursts forth from the underworld of death with its hoards. The resulting merger is an eighth and final king. "The beast that was, and is not, is himself an eighth king and yet is one of the seven, and is going to destruction" (Rev 17:11NET). Make no doubt about it, Jesus will not return until this merger manifests. Paul made it clear:

> "Let no one deceive you by any means; for that Day will not come unless the falling away comes first, and the man of sin is revealed, the son of perdition" (2 Thess 2:3). Therefore:

Gog (GUG / GAG) must come before the Day of the Lord!

Figure 27 Nergal / Pabilsag from a 12th century entitlement
(Kudurru) Stone

We noted how Pabilsag / Nergal on the Kudurru stone is depicted having a bow and arrow (see Figure 29 above), in the same fashion as Sagittarius in the Greek tradition—also known as a "manticore." Nergal, of course, is god of war and is an underworld god who is also equated with Ninurta and the rebel Nimrod. *The Dictionary of Deities and Demons* notes some of the epithets Ninurta possesses:

> "Ninurta who has *qardu* 'fierce,' 'heroic' and *qarradu* 'warrior,' ''hero' among his standard epithets … Astronomers of the 8th-7th century added further connotations, identifying Ninurta (or Pabilsag) with Sagittarius or, alternatively, associating Ninurta with the planet Sirius (called Šukudu 'arrow'), the major star of Canis major (**Akk qatsu 'bow'**).[222]

---

[222] The Dictionary Of Deities And Demons In The Bible, Eds. K. Van Der Toorn, Bob Becking And Pieter W. Van Der Horst (Boston, 1999). Ninurta

Figure 28. Trace of Nergal / Pabilsag from a 12th century entitlement (Kudurru) Stone.

What emerges from our investigation is the image of the constellation Sagittarius, which is familiar to many of us as a horse-centaur that is armed with a bow and arrow. The centaur-like god, Sagittarius, turns out to be yet another version of Nimrod, whom the Bible revealed as the rebellious person who became a gibbor. The Mesopotamian version portrayed him as Lord of the Earth, the great mountain, the arrow, Sirius, the brightest star. Now we see his appearance as Pabilsag, and we learn he is also known as the chief ancestor and god of the netherworld, like Nergal. The ancient Mesopotamian versions reveal a composite being "with a number of features not seen in the Greek version, such as a set of wings, a scorpion's tail and the head of a dog."[223] We know exactly how Nergal looked due to the recently discovered iconography (see Table 7, next page). Remarkably, the image appears to be the same creature who comes out of the abyss in Revelation 9.

---

[223] (Richter 2004: 264).
http://www.skyscript.co.uk/babylonian_sagittarius.pdf

Composite Image of the Chimera in Revelation 9[224]	
9A (Rev 9:7–10) 1st Description	9B (Rev 9:17–19) 2nd Description
1. The shape of the locusts was like **horses** prepared for battle. 2. On their **heads** were **crowns** of something like gold, 3. and their faces were like the **faces of men** (Rev 9:7). They had hair like women's hair, 4. and their teeth were like **lions' teeth** (Rev 9:8). And they had **breastplates** like breastplates of iron, 5. and the sound of their wings (Rev 9:9) 6. They had **tails like scorpions**, and there were stings in their **tails**. Their power was to hurt men five months (Rev 9:10).	1. And thus I saw **the horses** in the vision: those who sat on them had **breastplates** of fiery red, hyacinth blue, and sulfur yellow; 2. and the **heads** of the **horses** were like the **heads of lions**; 3. and out of their mouths came fire, smoke, and brimstone (Rev 9:17). 4. the fire and the smoke and the brimstone which came out of their mouths (Rev 9:18). 5. For their power is in their mouth and in their **tails**; 6. for their **tails are like serpents**, **having heads**; and with them they do harm (Rev 9:19).

Table 7. Composite Image of the Chimera in Revelation 9.

---

[224] Note the composite features of this creature: 1) Like a horse running to battle, 2) Lion's head, 3) Man's face, 4) Something like crowns, 5) Woman's hair, 6) Lion's teeth, 7) Something like breastplates of iron, 8) Noisy wings, 9) Scorpion's tail with stingers, 10) Serpent-head tails, 11) Fiery red, hyacinth blue, and sulfur yellow iron-like breastplate, 12) Fire and brimstone from mouth.

The bow draws our attention to Revelation 6 and the rider of the white horse "who sat on it had a **bow**; and a crown was given to him, and he went out conquering and to conquer" (Rev 6:2). We also see in Ezekiel 39, God declared, "I will knock the **bow out of your left hand,** and cause the **arrows** to fall out of your right hand" (Ezek 39:3). This coming warrior is the hero of old: Nimrod, Ninurta, Pabilsag, Nergal (and other epithets) who were known as a warrior and as an archer; and his principal epithets were the arrow and the star, Sirius. "This arrow (Sirius) is frequently depicted on Kassite kudurrus"225 which we saw in *Corrupting the Image 2*.

The rider on the white horse [226] will have a bow, which is representative of his intentions of war made possible by the power that Satan gives to him. He will also be given a crown, and Satan will give the Beast his throne—both of which are symbols of a king. He will go out "conquering and to conquer." Satan will give him authority and an army will be given to him (Dan 8:12). We recall from *Corrupting the Image 2* how Enlil gave Ninurta his power, throne and authority. The rider on the white horse is the same figure. This king will have unique features and will be mighty. He will destroy many and will fight against the saints (the holy people). Comparing Daniel's descriptions in chapters seven and eight with the rider on the white horse gives us a strong match (see Table 8, below).

Revelation 6's White Rider	Daniel's Beast/Little Horn
• A bow for waging war, • Given a crown, kingship conferred • He goes out conquering	• He makes warfare • He is called a king • He is mighty and conquers many

Table 8. Comparison of Rev. 6's White Rider to Daniel's Beast/Little Horn.

---

[225] J. Black and A. Green, Gods, Demons and Symbols of Ancient Mesopotamia (1992), s.v. Arrow.

[226] Some have suggested that this is in fact Jesus himself, this interpretation seems very unlikely given that Jesus himself is the one who is opening the seals. Secondly, all the other seals result in a judgment on the earth. Thirdly, the nature of the other three riders is foreboding and catastrophic suggesting that the four riders are all on the same team.

John's description of the king of the abyss called, "Destruction" or *Abaddon* in Hebrew and *Apollyon* in Greek (Rev 9:11), is a perfect match to the underworld god, Nergal / Ninurta / son of Enlil, the son of perdition, GAG / GUG, the Beast who ascends from the abyss who brings war and destruction!

Mars Spreads Plague

With the number of syncretistic names for the Beast that we have seen so far, we probably should not be surprised to discover further astrological associations of BAD with the planet Mars, which is Nergal's planet.

According to Michiel de Vaan, in the *Etymological Dictionary of Latin and the other Italic Languages,* the oldest recorded form of Mars is *Mamart,* and is not Latin but of foreign origin.[227] We have learned already that there was Sumerian influence in the Italian peninsula in our discussion from *Corrupting the Image, 2* of BAD being found in a grotto in Mesapia (and the word Haruspex – HAR being Sumerian for liver). Thus, discovering that the name of the Roman god, Mars (Martis, genitive), is from Mesopotamian origins is not surprising.

Franz Wiggenner provides the etymology of "Nergal's planet … Mars (*salbatanu*)." He notes how "according to astrological omens Mars spreads death when he rises or flares up." He goes on to provide a tentative etymology that explains "this role of MUL tzal (sal) bat-a-nu as mushtabarru (ZAL) mutanu (BAD-a-nu) "(the planet) which spreads plague."[228] In other words, BAD, also spelled "BAT,"[229] which is synonymous with Nergal, the god of death.

[227] Michiel de Vaan, Etymological Dictionary of Latin and the other Italic Languages, Brill, 2008, p. 366.

[228] Frans Wiggermann, Nergal, Reallexikon der Assyriologie (RlA) 9 1999 Pg. 215-226.

[229] The cuneiform bad, bat, be, etc. sign is a common multi-use sign in the mid-14th-century BC Amarna letters, and the Epic of Gilgamesh.
https://en.wikipedia.org/wiki/Bad_(cuneiform)#:~:text=The%20cuneiform %20bad%2C%20bat%2C%20be,(capital%20letter%20(majuscule)).

CHAPTER 15: A FALLEN STAR OPENS THE GATES OF HADES

Wiggenner's etymology of "the planet which spreads plague" is incredibly revealing when compared with Bible prophecy.

"A great **star fell** from heaven, burning like a torch, and it fell on a third of the rivers and on the springs of water (Rev 8:10). The name of the star is Wormwood. A third of the waters became wormwood, and many men died from the water, because it was made bitter" (Rev 8:11).

The Revelation text seems to describe this: John saw a star that was burning while falling from heaven on the rivers and springs. It is significant to understand the ancients considered planets to be wandering stars and "according to astrological omens, Mars spreads death when he rises or flares up." John then says he saw: a star fallen from heaven to the earth. To him was given the key to the bottomless pit" (Rev 9:1). The star he sees "fallen" is the same star that was falling previously. Clearly the reference here it is not to your average night star twinkling in the sky, because this star is given the key to the abyss.

OPEN THE ABYSS—*BOR*

This time in chapter 9, John is revealing to us that the "fallen star from heaven" will be given the key to the bottomless pit; and will proceed to open the abyss. Clearly, Satan aka the Beast is ready to gather all his forces together in order to fight the King of Kings and Lord of Lords.

"I saw a star fallen from heaven to the earth. To him was given the key to the bottomless pit. And he opened the bottomless pit ..." (Rev 9:1–2).

The abyss or *Bor* (in Hebrew) is the lowest place in Sheol, the place that Peter reveals is the prison that the angels in the days of Noah, who crossed the line, were thrown into what is referred to as *Tartarus*, and understood to be the lowest rung of Hades:

"For if God did not spare the angels who sinned, but cast them down to hell [ταρταρόω, *tartaroó*] and delivered them into chains of darkness, to be reserved for judgment" (2 Pet 2:4).

This is also the very place where Satan is prophesied to be cast into for one thousand years. "Yet you shall be brought down to Sheol [ᾄδης, *hadēs* שְׁאוֹל], to the lowest depths of the Pit [בָּ *bor*]" (Isa 14:15). The rest of the fallen angels will likewise "be gathered together, as prisoners are gathered in the **pit [בָּוֹר *bor*]**, and will be shut up in the prison ..." (Isa 24:22).

Sheol and the *bor* are closely related and are perhaps the same place. The "key" to the bottomless pit may be the very covenant the world made with Satan. In other words, the key to opening the abyss was getting the world to agree to the covenant with death and Sheol. Instead of submitting to the One who conquered death (Rev. 21:14), people will seek immortality by making their own deal with death and Sheol. These scornful men have the audacity to brag to God that they made a covenant with Death, and that they have an agreement with Sheol, so God cannot touch them (Lit. "When the overflowing scourge passes through, it will not come to us") Isa 28:15. However, the Lord God says:

> "Your covenant with death will be annulled, and your agreement with Sheol will not stand; when the overcoming scourge passes through, then you will be trampled down by it" (Isa 28:18).

Despite their belief that they are immortal and beyond God's reach, God tells them that their contract with death won't protect them, they're not really immortal, and that they and Death itself will be cast into the Lake of Fire. Death and Sheol cannot offer immunity from the second death.

DARKNESS

> "And he opened the bottomless pit, and smoke arose out of the pit like the smoke of a great furnace. The **sun** and the **air** were **darkened** because of the smoke of the pit" (Rev 9:2).

Why will the sky become dark and why will the sun not give its light? The answer is simple: Because the smoke constantly billowing out of the abyss will be like the eruption of a subterranean volcano. When a volcano first erupts, the sun is still visible; but as time progresses more of the light of the sun is blotted out. In 2011,

CHAPTER 15: A FALLEN STAR OPENS THE GATES OF HADES

Eyjafjallajökull, an Icelandic volcano, erupted and the effects were felt around the world. Locally and in parts of Europe,[230] the sky was dark with black soot. The sun, when viewed through the smoke, looked like it was covered with sackcloth and the moon became blood red. Scripture alludes to this phenomenon by showing that the darkness starts by effecting "thirds" of the planet, and then it goes to "full blast."

"And a **third** of the sun was struck, a **third** of the moon, and a **third** of the stars, so that a third of them were darkened. A **third** of the day did not shine, and likewise the night" (Rev 8:12).

The sun is not giving the fullness of its light, because it has been blocked out by that strong ash; and it looks like it has been covered with sackcloth. The moon looks red due to the ash, which we are told specifically: **"The sun and the air were darkened because of the smoke of the pit (Rev 9:2).** That is the reason why the sun and the air will turn dark (**not due to a lunar eclipse**, as some theorize).

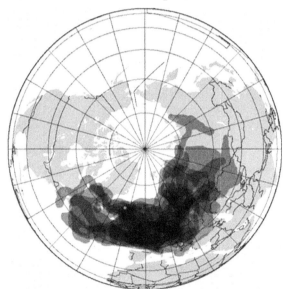

Figure 29. Extent of ash fallout from the eruption of Iceland's *Eyjafjallajökull* volcano.

---

[230] By Eyjafjallajökull_volcanic_ash_multilayer.xcf: *Blankmap-ao-090N-north_pole.xcf: Reisioderivative work: Cogiati (talk)derivative work: Cogiati (talk) - Eyjafjallajökull_volcanic_ash_multilayer.xcf, CC BY-SA 3.0, https://commons.wikimedia.org/w/index.php?curid=10122791

This is parallel to what we see in Joel: "For the day of the LORD is coming, for it is at hand (Joel 2:1): A **day** of **darkness** and gloominess, a day of clouds and **thick darkness**, like the morning clouds spread over the mountains (Joel 2:2). … the sun and moon grow dark, and the stars diminish their brightness" (Joel 2:10).

Many passages talk about the darkening of the sun, moon and sky.

- For the stars of heaven and their constellations will not give their light; the **sun** will be **darkened** in its going forth, and the **moon** will **not** cause its light to shine (Isa 13:9, 10).
- the **sun** became **black** as **sackcloth** of hair, and the moon became like blood (Rev 6:12).

When the abyss opens, there will be a great deal of smoke and ash; and it will progressively get darker until there is a "thick darkness" on the planet. Humanity is told to fear God; to give him glory for the hour of his judgment has come, but they do not repent. Eventually, the world will be full of darkness: "Then the fifth angel poured out his bowl on the throne of the beast, and his kingdom **became full of darkness**; and they gnawed their tongues because of the pain. They blasphemed the God of heaven because of their pains and their sores, and did not repent of their deeds" (Rev 16:10–11).

THE LOCATION OF THE ABYSS, GATES OF HADES

The location of the gates of Hades was squarely in the land of Bashan, at the foot of Mt. Hermon. It was the place where the angels had descended; and also where Og, King of the Bashan and the Amorite king—the kings of the Rephaim—were headquartered. It was at this place that "Canaanite mythology … locates … the abode of its deified dead kings, the mlk(m)/rpu(m) that dwell(s) in 'Štrt-hdr'y,"[231] that is, Og and Sihon, kings of the Rephaim that dwell in Ashtaroth and Edrei. In other words, **the underworld was known as a city**.

---

[231] Bashan: Dictionary of Deities and Demons in the Bible, eds. K. van der Toorn, Bob Becking and Pieter W. van der Horst (Boston, 1999). Pgs. 162-163.

W. F. Albright identifies "the City" as the netherworld, and equally of interest, the Ugaritic 'address' for Mlk, 'ttrt,' is likely to be identified with the city, Ashtaroth in Bashan, just north of Ammon. [232]

W. F. Albright's understanding of "the City" as the netherworld is based on the Old Babylonian *"irigal."* *Iri* is like the Hebrew *"ir"* (city) and *"gal"* is *"big."* It meant the underworld, and in Akkadian it was *erşetu; qabru* meaning "earth, land; underworld; grave." *Erşetu* (*ertzetu*) was also shorthand for *"daltu erşeti*: the door of the underworld."[233] Thus, the notion of the underworld having a gate, or a door is ancient and is found in the land of Shinar where Satan established his false religious system.

There may have been multiple gates to the underworld, just as there are multiple gates into a city. Nevertheless, the cave of Pan was considered to be one of those locations, and Jesus made that clear to his disciples. In his paper, The Gates of Hades and the Keys of the Kingdom, Joel Marcus confirms that Hades was "believed to house not only the human dead but also the demonic agents of death and destruction."[234] He further notes: "'gates of Hades' seems to stand for the entire underworld city of the dead."[235] Thus, Jesus' use of "Gates of Hades" is perfectly consistent with how the region of Bashan and Hermon itself have many underworld connections.

Jesus is not merely speaking about gates, but all of the underworld references represented by the logogram BAD / BAT, such as Enlil, Ninurta, Og, MLK (Milcom / Molech), Nergal, etc. Jesus declared to the great bull god *Batios*, king of the snake-dragons, stationed in Bashan, that he and his forces will not prevail against God's kingdom. Jesus' statement was a declaration of outright war against the rulers of the realm of the dead.

---

[232] Bashan: Dictionary of Deities and Demons in the Bible, eds. K. van der Toorn, Bob Becking and Pieter W. van der Horst (Boston, 1999). Pgs. 162-163. See: (KTU 1.1 08:2-3...)

[233] http://www.assyrianlanguages.org/akkadian/

[234] MARCUS, JOEL. "The Gates of Hades and the Keys of the Kingdom (Matt 16:18-19)." The Catholic Biblical Quarterly 50, no. 3 (1988): 443-55. Accessed September 30, 2020. http://www.jstor.org/stable/43717704.

[235] Ibid.

Marcus notes that:

The image of Matthew is of rulers of the underworld bursting forward from the gates of their heavily guarded, walled city to attack God's people on earth. When we speak of demonic powers flooding the earth, we are speaking the language of Jewish apocalypticists. Jewish apocalyptists believed that in the end-time, the powers of cosmic chaos—restrained since creation—would break forth from their restraint and bring unparalleled tribulation upon the world. Indeed, O. Betz has pointed out that there are remarkable parallels in the QL to the basic picture of Matt 16:18. In 1QH 3:17-18, e.g. the gates of Sheol open and the ungodly powers imprisoned in the underworld stream out to flood the earth.

As A. Cooper renders this passage:

"They open the gates of [Sheol for all] acts of wickedness; They close the doors of the pit behind the conceiver of mischief; The bars of eternity behind all spirits of wickedness. The gates of Sheol, after opening to release the demonic powers onto the earth, close behind them so that they could not return to the underworld even if they wished to; like wild animals shut up in a gladiatorial arena, they have no choice but to attack the human beings who share their confinement. Similarly, in 1QH 3:26-34 the 'time of the wrath of Belial' is described as one in which the gates of Sheol open and 'arrows of the pit' fly out."[236]

Jesus made the trek up toward Mt. Hermon and spoke to his disciples at Caesarea Philippi, making a direct reference to the "gates of Hell." This is highly suggestive that Satan had something planned for that time. Jesus went up to the Gates to meet the challenge. The events that Satan had planned might line up with the ideas of the apocalyptists of the day who believed the attack included the Gates of Hades opening and Satan's hordes flooding out. In the last days, the opening of the abyss may occur at none other than Caesarea Philippi at the base of Mt. Hermon.

---

[236] Ibid.

RELEASE OF THE DEMONIC ARMY

Why does Satan want to open the abyss? Because he will need to build up his forces before the Day of the Lord. Over the course of 3.5 years, the entire world is preparing "to make war against [Jesus] who sat on the horse and against His army" (Rev 19:19). Satan will need every principality and power available to wage war against his Creator. In *Corrupting the Image 2*, we learned that Satan, via his secret name BAD, was the one behind the angels descending on Mt. Hermon (also known as mount Bashan) in the days of Noah. At the base of that mountain was Caesarea Philippi, which was where Jesus took his disciples and proclaimed that the gates of Hades would not prevail against His kingdom. We determined that Satan had likely intended to open the portal at that time, and Jesus quashed his plans.

Opening the abyss will tap into "the spirits in prison, who formerly were disobedient ... in the days of Noah" (1 Pet 3:19–20). Scripture teaches us that they will be released for the final battle:

- the **angels** who did not keep their proper domain, but left their own abode ... **reserved** in **everlasting chains** under darkness for the **judgment** of the **great day**; (Jude 1:6).
- For if God did not spare the angels who sinned, but cast them down to hell [ταρταρόω *tartaru*] and delivered them into chains of darkness, to be reserved for **judgment**; (2 Pet 2:4).

The four specific angels who have been bound (lit. chained) at the Euphrates River will also be released.

"'Release the four angels who are **bound** at the great river Euphrates.' So the **four angels**, who had been prepared for the hour and day and month and year, were released to kill a third of mankind. Now the number of the army of the horses was two hundred million ..." (Rev 9:14–16).

This is the army spoken of by Daniel "because of transgression, an army was given over to the horn" (Dan 8:12). Herman Gunkel notes in *Zum religionsgeschichtlichen Verständnis des Neuen Testaments* that "The armies of the horsemen in v 16ff. are certainly 'composite creatures.'"[237]

---

[237] Zum religionsgeschichtlichen Verständnis des Neuen Testaments by Gunkel, Hermann, 1903 Göttingen, Vandenhoeck. pg., 52.

In other words, Gunkel believes that Revelation is speaking of hybridized monsters, as we have noted. The four angels that are released are initially "bound"—showing they are wicked principalities (kings) or generals who will serve in Satan's army. Related to that, "the great river Euphrates, and its water [will be] dried up, so that the way of the **kings from the east** might be prepared (Rev 16:12). These four angels who are bound at the Euphrates seem to be the kings of the east. Why the waters need to be dried up is not clear.

THE DAY OF THE LORD

What is the judgement of the great day? The battle of Armageddon, the Day of the Lord.

- The **great day** of the LORD is near; it is near and hastens quickly. The noise of the day of the LORD is bitter... (Zeph 1:14).
- For the **great day** of His wrath has come, and who is able to stand? (Rev 6:17).
- For they are spirits of demons, performing signs, which go out to the kings of the earth and of the whole world, to gather them to the battle of that **great day** of God Almighty (Rev 16:14).

The Day of Judgment, referred to in both, texts is not where angels stand before God's throne and receive their sentence. Rather, it refers to the judgment God will bring upon the world when He "will punish on high the host [army] of exalted ones ..." (Isa 24:21). They will be judged when:

The LORD will come with **fire** And with His chariots, like a whirlwind, to **render** His anger with fury, and His rebuke with flames of fire (Isa 66:15). For by fire and by His sword the LORD will **judge** all flesh; and the slain of the LORD shall be many (Isa 66:16).

Thus far, we have seen how these demonic forces will be released from their dark prison BEFORE the return of the Lord. It is quite likely Satan could not find a way to get them out of jail earlier. However, in *Corrupting the Image 2*, we considered how Satan likely tried to open the abyss in Jesus' time, but Jesus thwarted that plan.

Satan's next move will be using man's covenant with death and Sheol as the key that gives him power to open the gates of the underworld and release its denizens in preparation for the "great day."

TORMENTING THE NON-SEALED

"Then out of the smoke locusts came upon the earth. And to them was given power [authority εξουσια *exousia*], as the scorpions of the earth have power [authority εξουσια *exousia*] (Rev 9:3). They were commanded not to harm the grass of the earth, or any green thing, or any tree, but only those men who do not have **the seal of God on their foreheads** (Rev 9:4). And they were not given authority to kill them, but to torment them for **five months**. Their torment was like the torment of a scorpion when it strikes a man (Rev 9:5). **In those days men will seek death and will not find it; they will desire to die, and death will flee from them (Rev 9:6).** They had tails like scorpions, and there were stings in their tails. Their power was to hurt men **five months** (Rev 9:10). And they had as king over them the angel of the bottomless pit, whose name in Hebrew is *Abaddon*, but in Greek he has the name *Apollyon* (Rev 9:11)."

These Nergal-creatures are granted authority to torment all humanity, except for a very select group who have been "sealed … **on their foreheads** … the number of those who were sealed. One hundred and forty-four thousand of all the tribes of the children of Israel were sealed" (Rev 7:3–4). Thus, no one else will be immune to the locusts' attacks and torments.

The word "torment" is the Greek βασανίζω *basanizo*, which comes from βάσανος *basanos*. According to BDAG, it means "'touchstone, test', then of procedures or 'torment' used to extract a confession." It is also used for:

Of the tortures in the netherworld (cp. Wsd 3:1; 4 Macc 13:15) and as synon. of 'unquenchable fire' 2 Cl 17:7b; ὑπάρχειν ἐν β. be in torment Lk 16:23. Descriptive of place in the nether world τόπος τῆς β. place of torment.[238]

---

[238] BDAG βασανίζω

How significant that the Greek word *"basanizo"* for "torture" is associated with the netherworld. The word "Basan" in the Septuagint is the transliteration of Bashan (e.g. Num 21:32–33, etc.), which was the abode of the dead and an epithet for Satan, king of the netherworld. We might understand that the Nergal-creatures are coming to "Bashan-ize" the inhabitants of the earth, or to torment them to extract a confession.

This raises the question of what confession does Satan, the king of the underworld, seek from mankind by torturing them? Based on the authority afforded him through the covenant with Death and Sheol, Satan may use these creatures to incentivize humanity to completely upgrade to god status. We will not know their purpose for sure until the sequence plays out in real time and these creatures emerge from the abyss. Nevertheless, they would serve as a powerful incentive to take the mark, or else face their stings for five months.

The text tells us:

"In those days men will seek death and will not find it; they will desire to die, and death will flee from them" (Rev 9:5–6).

Why is it that men will seek death, but will be denied death? A healthy person does not want to die. They want to keep living; they want to have a family, and they want to achieve their dreams and goals. When people are suffering intense emotional or physical pain, sometimes all they can think about is escaping, and death is the escape and end of the suffering.

What will change in those days that people who want to die, cannot die? Simon & Garfunkel sang the song "50 Ways to Leave Your Lover": "You just slip out the back, Jack; Make a new plan, Stan; You don't need to be coy, Roy; Just get yourself free; Hop on the bus, Gus, etc."

Certainly, if someone wanted to die badly enough, it seems like there must be at least fifty ways to leave your life—Jump off a bridge, jump in front of a car, use a gun. Sadly, people often nowadays successfully commit suicide. Again, how could it be that people looking for death cannot find it? Something radical must have happened.

CHAPTER 15: A FALLEN STAR OPENS THE GATES OF HADES

The answer is simple: they have overcome their mortality and attained some type of immortality. Based on the research in this book, we conclude that they have taken the mark of the Beast, and it has transformed them into "gods," so they do not die. They have taken the mark of the Beast and have been transformed, and have achieved the transhumanist dream of immortality and divinity. However, once attained, they regret it. They will want to die; but then, it is too late.

MARK TAKERS BECOME ZOMBIES

They may want to die once they realize they are not in control of their lives anymore and are being manipulated and enslaved; or, they may realize that there is no undoing the fatal step they have taken. Whatever it may be, though they have become gods, with superhuman strength, intelligence and immortality, they will see that the mixture of Satan's seed with man's has a critical failure. The two components do not adhere properly, as Daniel 2 says:

"As you saw iron mixed with ceramic clay, they will mingle with the seed of men; but they will not **adhere** to one another, just as iron does not mix with clay" (Dan 2:43).

This critical failure alters their body so that "ugly and painful sores appeared on the people who had the mark of the Beast and who worshiped his image" (Rev 16:2 NET).

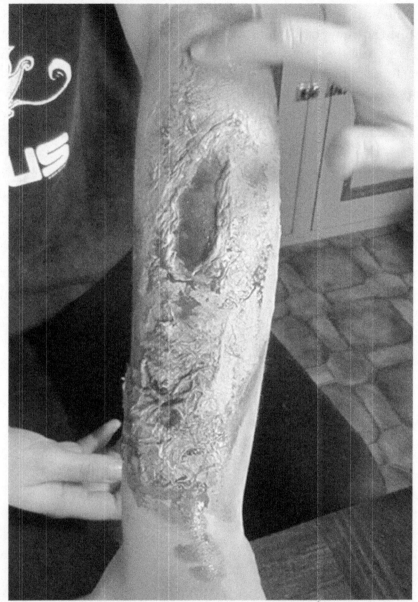

Figure 30. Necrotizing fasciitis.

They will suffer from foul and loathsome sores. According to the NET Bible notes, they suffer from "ulcerated sores."[239] The Greek word, ἕλκος (helkos), is a "wound, or sore, an abscess, ulcer, a foul and vile sore"[240] which reminds us of what happened during the 10 plagues of Egypt where there were "boils [שְׁחִין shechin] that break out in sores [אֲבַעְבֻּעֹת ababu'oth]." Gesenius defines ababu'oth as "pustules, boils, rising up in the skin, Ex. 9:9, 10; verbal from the root בעע...to boil up, to swell up."[241] The word shᵉchîyn is a boil or an inflamed spot[242] which is closely related to ababu'oth and is translated as "ἕλκος (helkos)" in the Septuagint.

These sores are ultimately a consequence of the marktakers' disregard for God's warnings and laws. God sent his messengers to warn people against taking the mark: "If anyone worships the beast and his image, and receives his mark ..." (Rev 14:9), "he himself shall also drink of the wine of the wrath of God ..." (Rev 14:10). But just as Pharaoh defiantly went against God and refused to heed warning after warning, and suffered the consequences, so too the world will disregard God's warning about the mark of the Beast. God finds no pleasure in the things that will happen to those who take the mark; these are simply the choices they will make.

---

[239] It says loathsome sore, but it is probably a reference to sores, many sores. "The Greek text is singular but is probably best understood as a collective singular." NET Notes. An example of the collective singular in English is the word "sugar." We say, "I need some sugar in my coffee." We do not say "sugars." That is a collective singular.

[240] BDAG ἕλκος (helkos

[241] Gesenius, H.W.F. *Hebrew and Chaldee Lexicon to the Old Testament Scriptures*, translated by Samuel Prideaux Tregelles, 7th ed., s.v. "Og," "Rachal." Ada: Baker Publishing Group, 1990. אֲבַעְבֻּעֹת ababu'oth.

[242] TWOT

According to *Robertson's Word Pictures of the New Testament*, *Helkos* is "a noisome and grievous sore; bad and malignant sore. *Helkos* is an old word for a suppurated wound that is an ulcer or something that opens on your body." Looking into modern medical descriptions helps us understand boils better:

> "Most boils are caused by staphylococcus aureus, a type of bacterium commonly found in the skin and inside the nose; a bump forms as pus collects under the skin. Boils sometimes develop at sites where the skin has been broken by a small injury, or an insect bite, which gives the bacteria easy entry. If your immune system is weakened for any reason, you are more susceptible to boils and carbuncles."[243]

Those people who take the mark (becoming hybrids), suffer from the wasting flesh condition because of the hybridized, demonic-human DNA they carry. When we consider that people will take Satan's DNA—and he is the god of death—then what they suffer from may be:

> "...necrotizing fasciitis, decaying skin or ... a flesh-eating bacteria, flesh-eating disease; a rapid progressing type of bacterial infection that destroys a skin fat and tissue that covers the muscle, in a short time span within 12 to 24 hours. Actually, the flesh is not eaten but the skin is dying as a result of the infection. The bacteria associated with the disease cuts off the blood supply; hence the tissue dies and goes through the process of decay, medically termed as necrosis."[244]

We may have a sense of what those people who take the Mark will look like based on reports of people who have taken the flesh-eating drug known as "krokodil."

---

[243] https://www.mayoclinic.org/diseases-conditions/boils-and-carbuncles/symptoms-causes/syc-20353770
[244] https://ehealthwall.com/flesh-eating-disease-pictures-symptoms-contagious-causes/

CHAPTER 15: A FALLEN STAR OPENS THE GATES OF HADES

Two sisters from Illinois have described how it feels to rot from the inside out, after using the flesh-eating drug krokodil, which emerged in Russia around 10 years ago. It is similar to heroin but is much cheaper as it is made from everyday household products, such as lighter fluid, gasoline, paint thinner and iodine.

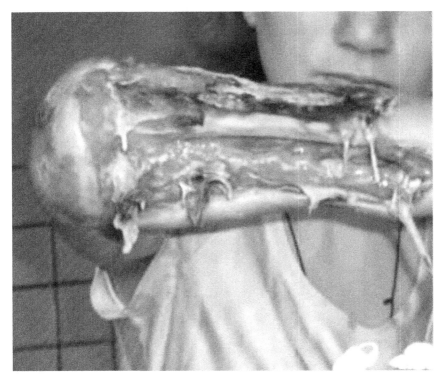

Figure 31. Necrotizing fasciitis after taking Krokodil
https://www.ibtimes.co.uk/krokodil-users-describe-rotting-inside-out-blister-514387

Speaking to ABC, Amber said she first noticed wounds on her skin: "It almost starts like a burn from a cigarette. It starts purple and then goes into a blister after five or six days." Krokodil has been dubbed a zombie or cannibal drug because it eats users' flesh from the inside out. The average user has a life expectancy of just three years.[245]

---

[245] https://www.ibtimes.co.uk/krokodil-users-describe-rotting-inside-out-blister-514387

Amber and her sister took the drug because they thought they would feel better. One person offered this reason for those who take it:

> "The people I have seen have not known what they were taking, but I believe some addicts will take it by choice despite the effects. There is an intense high and it's cheap, if people are desperate enough, they will use it."[246]

This is probably the same reason people will take the mark. They will believe the only way to stave off the hostile alien invasion (also known as the return of Jesus) is to upgrade to become a god by taking the mark—worshiping the Beast and the image of the Beast and becoming fully integrated into the hive mind.

However, in the end, taking the mark of the Beast appears to transform the person into a zombie. They will be a race of walking dead with a flesh-eating disease that decays their corpses. They desire death, but they cannot die.

Figure 32. Zombie Apocalypse Image by Ahmadreza Heidaripoor from Pixabay.

---

[246] https://www.ibtimes.co.uk/krokodil-users-describe-rotting-inside-out-blister-514387

CHAPTER 15: A FALLEN STAR OPENS THE GATES OF HADES

Not only will they be the walking dead; they will also have an insatiable appetite, like the demons and Nephilim before them. In *Corrupting the Image 2*, we studied how Satan and demons receive energy, much like in the movie, *The Matrix*, where people are actually the batteries powering the machines, except Satan's hordes crave the blood of their victims.

"They served their idols, which became a snare to them. They even sacrificed their sons and their daughters to demons, and shed innocent **blood**, the blood of their sons and daughters, whom they sacrificed to the idols of Canaan; and the land was polluted with **blood**" (Ps 106:36–38).

Thus, with every human sacrifice, every abortion, every war and every murder, Satan and his kin are recharging their batteries. The more innocent the blood, the more energy is derived. This bloodletting could explain why people are beheaded in the tribulation as well, but we cannot be sure. The book of 1 Enoch confirms how the Nephilim drank blood:

"the women conceiving brought forth giants, … it became **impossible to feed** them; when they turned themselves against men, in order to devour them; and began to injure birds, beasts, reptiles, and fishes, to eat their flesh one after another, and to drink their **blood**" (Enoch 7:10, 12, 14).

Even in medieval times, the notion of giants (Nephilim) eating blood persisted; as you recall, the giant bellowed: "Fe Fi Fo Fum, I smell the blood of an Englishmen." The rhyme appears in the 1596 pamphlet "Haue with You to Saffron-Walden" written by Thomas Nashe, who mentions that the rhyme was already old and its origins obscure.[247] "Fa fe fi fo fum" is actually a coherent phrase of ancient Gaelic meaning, "Behold food, good to eat, sufficient for my hunger!"[248]

---

[247] McCarthy, William Bernard; Oxford, Cheryl; Sobol, Joseph Daniel, eds. (1994). *Jack in Two Worlds: Contemporary North American Tales and Their Tellers* (illustrated ed.). UNC Press Books. p. xv. ISBN 9780807844434.

[248] Mackay, Charles (1877). *The Gaelic Etymology of the Languages of Western Europe: And More Especially of the English and Lowland Scotch, and Their Slang, Cant, and Colloquial Dialects*. Trübner. p. 160.

Historically, the places where demons gained a foothold and were worshipped, were also infamous for rites involving human blood. People becoming hybrids by taking the mark of the Beast become ravenous. They need energy to satiate themselves, and blood becomes the only food they find satisfying. Such a thirst for blood could be at least part of the reason why there is a judgment of the waters:

"Then the third angel poured out his bowl on the rivers and springs of water, and they became blood. And I heard the angel of the waters saying: 'You are righteous, O Lord, the One who is and who was and who is to be, because You have judged these things. For they have shed the **blood** of saints and prophets, and You have given them **blood** to drink. For it is their just due'" (Rev 16:4–6).

Taking the mark of the Beast is the future version of becoming a Nephilim. God judged it severely with the near-extinction-level Flood in the days of Noah and will do so again at his second coming.

Chapter 16: God's Plan Versus Gog's

We now come to the nail-biting, edge of your seat, hold your breath climax to Satan's long and terrible war he has waged against his Creator since the Garden of Eden. Satan has the "whole world in his hands" and under his authority, which gives him legal immunity to be able to fight against his all-powerful enemy.

Gog's first strategic move: He (Satan / the Beast) has established his army of two hundred million, ferocious Pabilsag-chimeras that can fly, breath fire, and sting (Rev 9). He did so when Satan, the fallen star, "opened the bottomless pit" (Rev 9:2), and a horde of hybridized creatures emerge. They will have "as king over them the angel of the bottomless pit, whose name in Hebrew is *Abaddon*, but in Greek he has the name *Apollyon*" (Rev 9:11). Satan (the Beast) is getting all of his forces together in order to fight the King of Kings and Lord of Lords.

Gog's next move: Perhaps more than a billion people have upgraded to "god" status and have taken the mark of the Beast, which Satan used to recreate mankind in his own image. They have been enveloped in the Hive mind, completely under Satan's control. Upon those not willing to take the mark, Satan has been waging war "and prevailing against them" (Dan 7:21). Billions have died and Satan's hordes will only stop "when the power of the holy people has been completely shattered" (Dan 12:7).

Things look very bleak, and the last ray of light is fading into darkness; hope seems lost. It would be like if Hitler were about to destroy the last standing Allied bunker; or as if Sauron were about to cast his shadow completely over Middle Earth. It is only a matter of days or weeks until life—as we know it—on earth is lost; and there is no one on earth left to stop the Beast.

The Beast's third move: His attention turns towards the Land of Israel, the modern State of Israel. Why would he need to invade Israel when he seemingly already has the entire world under his control? His dream of usurping and claiming the very Mountain of God, Mount Zion and Jerusalem, where God placed His name, seems to be coming true. The temptation of achieving victory runs high in Gog's camp—for him to assert his lifelong dream for which he had already been banished:

"For you have said in your heart: 'I will ascend into heaven, I will exalt my throne above the stars of God; I will also sit on the mount of the congregation on the farthest sides of the north' (Isa 14:13); 'I will ascend above the heights of the clouds, I will be like the Most High'" (Isa 14:14).

But God has His plan. Unbeknownst to Satan, God has set a trap for him. Satan thinks he will win, but it will be a deadly trap. Notice how God says He will bring the nations to Jerusalem:

- **I will make** Jerusalem a **cup of drunkenness** ... **I will make Jerusalem** a very heavy stone for all peoples; all who would heave it away will surely be cut in pieces, though **all nations** of the earth are gathered against it (Zech 12:2–3).
- For **I will gather** all the nations to battle against **Jerusalem** (Zech 14:2).
- **I will also gather** all nations, and bring them down to the Valley of Jehoshaphat; and I will enter into judgment with them there on account of My people, My heritage Israel ... (Joel 3:2).
- "I will turn you around, put **hooks** into your jaws, and **lead you out**, with all your army... (Ezek 38:4). It will be in the latter days that I will bring you **against My land**" (Ezek 38:16).

The language in the preceding verses is incredible! God will gather all the nations and "put a hook" into the Beast's / Gog's jaws to bring him to the modern state of Israel where he will fall. The Beast thinks he is invincible because he holds the contract of death and Sheol. He thinks he has God in an awkward position to such an extent that he has been blaspheming him and those who dwell in heaven. He has nearly complete victory, but will get sucked into a trap that God is laying for him. He wants to attack the modern state of Israel. And that is exactly where God wants him, by using the "hook" in his jaw to drive him into the trap. Gog does not understand God's ways, as Micah points out:

"Now also **many nations** have gathered against you, who say, 'Let her be defiled, and let our eye look upon Zion' (Mic 4:11). But **they do not know the thoughts of the LORD,** nor do they understand His counsel; for He will gather them like sheaves to the threshing floor" (Mic 4:12).

We will see how God threshes them like sheaves in a dramatic way in a later chapter. The Beast's plan nevertheless suffers a setback. While extending his power and subjugating Egypt, some shocking information will affect him. The news will be the "hook in his jaw," the very tool God will use.

"He shall stretch out his hand against the countries, and the land of **Egypt** shall not escape" (Dan 11:42). "He shall have power over the treasures of gold and silver, and over all the precious things of Egypt ..." (Dan 11:43). "News from the east and the north shall trouble him" (Dan 11:44).

Whatever the news is, it works. His fury escalates, and he becomes wrathful due to this news. "Therefore, he shall go out with great fury to destroy and annihilate many" (Dan 11:44). He sets out for Jerusalem, the holy mountain:

"And he shall plant the tents of his palace between the seas and the glorious holy mountain; yet he shall come to his end, and no one will help him" (Dan 11:45).

He will muster the swarm-hive-mind of the marked horde (Dan 8:12; 11:31) who resemble zombies coming from the world over (Ezek 38:15) to Jerusalem to destroy the last remnant of Jerusalemites (Zech 14:2).

ASSEMBLING SATAN'S ARMY

Despite the Beast's strategy, he does not know the mind of the Lord as Ezekiel records:

You will ascend, coming like a storm, covering the land like a cloud, you and all your troops and many peoples [*ammim rabbim* וְעַמִּים רַבִּים] with you (Ezek 38:9). Thus says the Lord GOD: "On that day it shall come to pass that thoughts will arise in your mind, and you will make an **evil plan** (Ezek 38:10): You will say, 'I will go up against a land of unwalled villages; I will go to a peaceful people, who dwell safely, all of them dwelling without walls, and having neither bars nor gates (Ezek 38:11) — to take plunder and to take booty, to stretch out your hand against the waste places that are again inhabited, and against a people gathered from the nations, who have acquired livestock and goods, who dwell in the midst of the land'" (Ezek 38:12).

211

Remember, God is putting a hook in his jaw to draw him to Israel. Surprisingly, his evil plan has to do with plunder and booty, possibly general terms for everything that is of value in Israel, including Israel's advanced achievements in science, works of art, warfare, temple artifacts and their scrolls, which are treasure. Other nations seem surprised by this when they ask:

"Have you come to take plunder? Have you gathered your army to take booty, to carry away silver and gold, to take away livestock and goods, to take great plunder?" (Ezek 38:13).

Their question may be one of incredulity—in other words: You have the entire world, and now you are coming to take plunder? Really? Perhaps they are surprised that such would be his excuse. In any case, we do not precisely know the intent behind the words. Nevertheless, we know for certain that God is drawing him and all the nations together against Jerusalem for a purpose:

"You will come up against My people Israel like a cloud, to cover the land. It will be in the latter days that I will bring you **against My land**, so that the nations may know Me, when I am hallowed in you, O Gog, before their eyes" (Ezek 38:16).

The modern state of Israel will suddenly find itself at the heart of the earth's ire. While this will not be the first time, it will look to be the last time. After all, who can make war with the Beast? There will be no earthly solution to this incredible predicament. But who is there? There is no one on earth that can do this, though there is One in heaven who can. But He will not come back until invited.

Gog Attacks Those Brought Back from the Sword

In the last days, Gog will come against a land restored from war whose people were brought back from the sword.

"In the latter years you will go against the land that is restored from war [שׁוֹבֶבֶת מֵחֶרֶב *those brought back from the sword*], the land whose people were gathered from many peoples upon the mountains of Israel, which had been a continual waste. Its people were brought out from the peoples" (Ezek 38:8a).

Figure 33. Hagana Ship arriving in Israel after WWII.

There can be no doubt that people of the modern state of Israel are those people who were gathered from many peoples, gathered from the sword, and came back to Israel, which was a continual waste (we will unpack that later).

Figure 34. Jews being rescued from a Nazi concentration camp.

213

Hitler's Final Solution was a "sword" of the most horrible kind; it was a deliberate, intentional, genocidal mass-murder of the Jewish people. In fact, just before committing suicide, Hitler dictated a document of how he wasn't responsible for the war, but the Jews were. In his closing line, he stated, "Above all I charge the leaders of the nation and those under them to scrupulous observance of the laws of race and to merciless opposition to the universal poisoner of all peoples, **International Jewry.**"[249]

Hitler wanted to kill every one of them; thankfully, he failed.

MODERN ISRAEL DWELLING SECURELY

A key feature that will be in place when Gog invades Israel is that the people who dwell [*labetach*] there feel that they are safe. Whether or not it is true, that is the sense.

And now [וְיֹשְׁבֵי לָבֶטַח כֻּלָּם] dwell securely, all of them [= for the security: *labetach* לָבֶטַח]. (Ezek 38:8b).

What does it mean to dwell securely? Is Israel dwelling securely today? There are still people who want to kill them; yet despite that, Israel enjoys a great deal of security. In fact, compared to the conditions the Jewish people have experienced over the past 1,800 years, they have never been more secure than they are today. Despite constant threats from the south and the north, ever since the State of Israel has been established, they have succeeded in developing a system of security that makes their lives practically undisturbed. This has been experienced by countless tourists visiting Israel throughout the years. Even with minor border wars and isolated incidents, the people and visitors to Israel have always pursued their activities unaffected and secure. This is a fact proven many times. Thus, God asks Gog, "On that day when My people Israel dwell safely [*labetach*, לָבֶטַח] will you not know it?" (Ezek 38:14).

---

[249] Rosenberg, Jennifer. (2021, July 31). Hitler's Political Statement Before His Suicide. Retrieved from https://www.thoughtco.com/hitlers-political-statement-1779643

The Security forces in Israel (also known as Israel security establishment) is in Hebrew [הבטחון מערכת] *Ma'arechetha'Bitachon* which comes from the same word *betach*. The security establishment includes a variety of organizations, including law enforcement, military, paramilitary, governmental, and intelligence agencies. Israel has a strong military; and a well-known secret is that they have nuclear weapons. They have an air force that is often considered to be second to none in the world. It is a tradition that every IDF recruit hikes up Masada to remember how the Romans slaughtered their people in AD 73, and then the recruits vow, "Never again."

According to the Gesenius Hebrew Lexicon *betach* (בֶּטַח) means:

"(1) confidence, and adv. confidently, with confident mind, Gen. 34:25., (2) security, Isa. 32:17. In other places always (לְבֶטַח) *labetach* and (בֶּטַח) *betach* adv.—(a) means without danger and/or fear, securely."[250]

Israeli Varda Spiegel, who was a Nurse-Director of the Bedouin Mobile Unit of the Negev, stated in the *Times of Israel* article, "When Israelis feel safe, and Americans don't":

"My friends and relatives in the U.S. were concerned for my safety, but I feel no sense of danger … It dawned on me that Israelis are trained from birth to **assume that they are safe** and to recite to themselves the reasons that they are in all likelihood safe whenever they face danger."[251]

There is a sense of security, even though it may not be completely real, or completely accurate, but there is a sense of having security. It is a feeling akin to that of a person who is safe in a lighthouse while dangerous waves are crashing around. We see this sense of security many times in the Scripture. "For You have been a shelter for me, a strong tower from the enemy" (Ps 61:3). Danger is out there, but in God, a person is safe.

---

[250] Gesenius, *Betach*

[251] https://blogs.timesofisrael.com/when-israelis-feel-safe-and-americans-dont/

- Therefore my heart is glad, and my glory rejoices; my flesh also will rest in hope [לָבֶטַח *labetach*] (Ps 16:9).
- And He led them on safely [לָבֶטַח *labetach*], so that they did not fear; but the sea overwhelmed their enemies (Ps 78:53).

The same phenomenon is described in Jeremiah 49; though Hazor is sitting safely, this security can be potentially threatened.

"For Nebuchadnezzar king of Babylon has taken counsel against you, and has conceived a plan against you (Jer 49:30). "Arise, go up to the wealthy nation that dwells securely [לָבֶטַח יוֹשֵׁב *yoshev labetach*]" (Jer 49:31).

This kind of safety means that life goes on undisturbed—business as usual—and those who dwell there are unsuspecting of changes, and are possibly overconfident in their own ability to defend themselves. Thus, God will destroy those who think they are safe. "And I will send fire on Magog and on those who live in security [לָבֶטַח *labetach*] in the coastlands (Ezek 39:6).

We see in Ezekiel 38:8 that they are sitting, they are dwelling securely [וְיָשְׁבוּ לָבֶטַח כֻּלָּם *yâshavu labetach kulám*].

There have been nations that were dwelling securely only to have it change quickly. Gideon, for example, went to the tents of "Nobah and Jogbehah and he attacked the army while the camp felt secure [וַיַּךְ אֶת־הַמַּחֲנֶה וְהַמַּחֲנֶה הָיָה בֶטַח]" (Judg 8:11). In the Hebrew, the word *felt* is missing; it actually says, "they were secure." We see this again regarding five men who went to Laish: "They saw the people who were there, how they dwelt safely [יוֹשֶׁבֶת־לָבֶטַח] ... quiet and secure" (Judg 18:7). In both cases, the people were safe, that is, at least until the Israelites attacked them.

Labetach does not mean that there is no threat of an enemy. It is the sense of being or feeling safe and secure. Israel will feel secure at the time of Gog's invasion, but it will not be an overall godly country. Unfortunately, not every Israeli knows God. Some do, with all their heart, passionately and fervently know and love God, but many do not.

PROFANING GOD'S NAME

We read in Ezekiel 39:7, "... I will give you [Gog] to birds; "I will make My holy name known in the midst of My people Israel, and I will not let them profane My holy name anymore... (Ezek 39:7). Israel is profaning God's name by many who live in contradiction to his Torah. Sadly, He is not known in their midst.

God will not allow His name to be profaned any longer, which means there are Israelis who are profaning his name. According to Wowtravel.me: "Tel Aviv" is the most gay-friendly city, not only in the Middle East, but in the entire world.[252]

Unfortunately, many people in Modern Israel, who ought to be living for God, are in many cases, far from him. To be clear, there are many Messianic Jewish believers who love Yeshua with all their heart, with all their strength, with all their soul. There are many Orthodox who fervently love the God of Abraham, Isaac, and Jacob. We must not paint too broadly here, but we also do not want to ignore the evidence that there are many in the land of Israel who are profaning God's name. Homosexuality is of course only one example. One of the reasons God says He is going to cause Gog to fall is because "... I will make My holy name known in the midst of My people Israel, and I will not let them profane My holy name anymore..." (Ezek 39:7).

The incredibly sophisticated prophecy of the children of Israel being brought back into their land has been fulfilled, despite Hitler trying to wipe them out. That is an astonishing fulfillment of prophecy that happened in 1948 when the nation was established. So they were brought back, but not everybody knows the name of the Lord.

---

[252] This vibrant city is an undisputed queer capital of the Middle East, It offers a 24/7 non-stop activities, all year-round great weather, great food, gay beaches and infinite of gay bars and night clubs. Every June Tel Aviv is celebrating the Gay Pride week, week of celebrations and happenings throughout the city with Pride Expo (Gay Culture Fair), LGBT Theater festival, LGBT Film Festival and the famous Pride Parade which is one of the most colorful gay parades in the world. http://wowtravel.me/11-most-gay-friendly-cities-in-the-world/

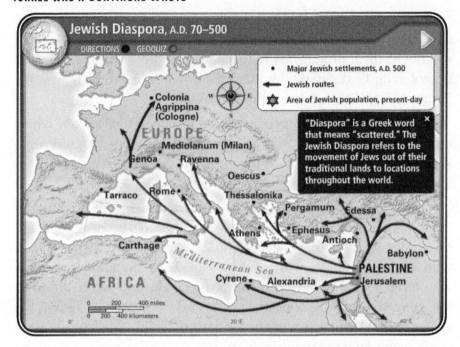

Figure 35. From Jews on the Move - https://bit.ly/3qSkuwW

"The land whose people were gathered from many peoples upon the mountains of Israel, which had been a continual waste" (Ezek 38:8a).

The Romans destroyed Jerusalem in 70 AD and again in 135 AD. After the second Jewish revolt in 135 AD, the Jews were warned not to return to Jerusalem, upon pain of death. They were then dispersed to the four corners of the earth—without a homeland for nearly 1,900 years in the Diaspora.

Figure 36. Jerusalem by David Roberts.

Interestingly, the American writer Mark Twain wrote in 1867 about the land of Israel, which at the time was called Palestine:

"Palestine sits in sackcloth and ashes ... the spell of a curse that has withered its fields and fettered its energies ... Palestine is desolate and unlovely ... It is a hopeless, dreary, heartbroken land."[253]

---

[253] Mark Twain. *The Innocents Abroad.*
http://www.literaturepage.com/read/twain-innocents-abroad-458.html

The Jerusalem Post writes:

"Six hundred years before Twain's visit, another famous visitor with a nom de plume was struck by Jerusalem's desolation. Rabbi Moses ben Nachman, known as Naḥmanides (1194-1270), fled Christian Spain for the Land of Israel. After a long and perilous journey, Naḥmanides arrived at the Port of Acre before traveling to Jerusalem in 1267, where he couldn't even find nine other Jews to pray with [He could not find a minion, you need 10 for a minion and he couldn't not find even nine other Jews]. He wrote to his son, "Many are Israel's forsaken places, and great is the desecration. The more sacred the place, the greater the devastation it has suffered. Jerusalem is the most desolate place of all."

Naḥmanides wrote concerning Israel's desolation, but he said it was a blessing in disguise. Commenting on a verse in Leviticus that describes the curses that will befall the land of Israel, Naḥmanides wrote that the devastation "constitutes a good tiding, proclaiming that during all our exiles, our land will not accept our enemies... Since the time that we left it, [the land] has not accepted any nation or people, and they all try to settle it... This is a great proof and assurance to us."[254]

Amazing! Even though the land had nothing, Naḥmanides said it was actually good news because nobody could settle there, and nobody would want the land. Not to say that it was completely devoid of people, but there was no major settlement in the area.

Rabbi Menachem Kohen of Brooklyn discovered that the land of Israel had: "suffered an unprecedented, severe and inexplicable (by anything other than supernatural explanations) drought that lasted from the first century until the 20th — a period of 1,800 years coinciding with the forced dispersion of the Jews."[255] And just as it says in Ezekiel 38: the land "... which had been a continual waste" (Ezek 38:8). This reminds us of Deuteronomy 29:

---

[254] https://www.jpost.com/Opinion/Unto-the-nations-505760
[255] https://www.wnd.com/2010/02/124106/

"So that the coming generation of your children who rise up after you, and the foreigner who comes from a far land, would say, when they see the plagues of that land and the sicknesses which the LORD has laid on it: 'The whole land is brimstone, salt, and burning; it is not sown, nor does it bear, nor does any grass grow there, like the overthrow of Sodom and Gomorrah, Admah, and Zeboiim, which the LORD overthrew in His anger and His wrath'" (Deut 29:22–23).

Journalist Joseph Farah, prompted by the research of Rabbi Kohen, later discovered that only after the Jews returned did the rain begin to come, he says, "For 1,800 years, it hardly ever rained in Israel. This was the barren land discovered by Mark Twain. So-called "Palestine" was a wasteland—nobody lived there. There was no indigenous Arab population to speak of. It only came *after* the Jews came back. Beginning in AD 70 and lasting until the early 1900s—about 660,000 days—no rain.

He examined the rainfall data for 150 years in Israel beginning in the early 1800s and leading up to the 1960s. He discovered "increasing rainfall almost every single year—with the heaviest rainfall coming in and around 1948 and 1967."[256] There was no rain until Judah came back. Jesus said the generation that sees these things will by no means pass away till all these things take place.

It is amazing when we put scriptures together and we look at the prophecies, how all this has come together. Jesus spoke of the desolation that was to come upon the leadership of Jerusalem because they rejected him as Messiah.

In the previous chapter, Jesus spoke of how He wanted to gather Jerusalem:

"O Jerusalem, Jerusalem, the one who kills the prophets and stones those who are sent to her! How often I wanted to gather your children together, as a hen gathers her chicks under her wings, but you were not willing!" (Matt 23:37). "See! Your house is left to you desolate" (Matt 23:38).

---

[256] https://www.wnd.com/2010/02/124106/

Shortly after stating their house would be desolate, as Jesus was coming up to Jerusalem, He cursed a fig tree:

"And seeing a fig tree by the road, He came to it and found nothing on it but leaves, and said to it, "Let no fruit grow on you ever again." Immediately the fig tree withered away" (Matt 21:19).

Jesus cursed that tree Monday morning. He then probably told the parable of the Fig Tree later Monday afternoon, or possibly on Tuesday.

Figure 37 Fig tree with unripe figs. Image by Vane Monte from Pixabay.

"A certain man had a fig tree planted in his vineyard, and he came seeking fruit on it and found none. Then he said to the keeper of his vineyard, 'Look, for three years I have come seeking fruit on this fig tree and find none. Cut it down; why does it use up the ground?' And his worker replied: 'Sir, let it alone this year also, until I dig around it and fertilize it. And if it bears fruit, well. But if not, after that you can cut it down'" (Lk 13:6–9).

Then, He told his disciples, in the Olivet Discourse: "Now learn this parable from the fig tree: (Matt 24:32–33). What are we supposed to learn from a fig tree? Jesus tells us: "When its branch has already become tender and puts forth leaves, you know that summer is near" (Matt 24:32–33).

The disciples who had studied the scriptures would have known that the scriptural references about the fig tree represent the house of Israel and the house of Judah.

- Speaking there of the House of Israel:
  - "… I saw your fathers as the firstfruits on the fig tree in its first season (Hos 9:10).
- Speaking of the House of Judah:
  - For a nation has come up against My land, … He has laid waste My vine, and ruined My fig tree; (Joel 1:6-7).
  - Thus says the LORD … "Like these good figs, so will I acknowledge those who are carried away captive from Judah, whom I have sent out of this place for their own good…the bad figs… will I give up Zedekiah the king of Judah, his princes, the residue of Jerusalem…" (Jer 24:3, 5, 8).

When Jesus said, learn a lesson from the fig tree, was He just giving an agricultural lesson? Jesus never wasted words. The parable of the fig tree was to teach us something important about the prophetic future of the whole House of Israel.

WHAT IS A GENERATION?

What is a generation? The biblical data suggests it equals the lifetime of a person, somewhere between 60 years and 100 years. Notice in Matthew 1: all the generations from Abraham to David are fourteen generations … (Matt 1:17). Also: "And Joseph died, all his brothers, and all that generation" (Exod 1:6). It equals the lifetime of a person.

A generation can have many overlapping generations. For example, my parent's generation lived, and many remain alive in my generation, and my kids can talk about my generation even though we are overlapping. We see this in Numbers 32:

"…none of the men … from twenty years old and above, shall see the land … He made them wander in the wilderness forty years, until all the generation that had done evil in the sight of the LORD was gone" (Num 32:11, 13).

It is simple math, 20 plus 40 is 60—that seems to be the minimum for a biblical generation. We read in Psalm 90:10, "The days of our lives are seventy years; and if by reason of strength they are eighty years ..." (Psa 90:10). This seems to be the golden mean—that is 70 or 80—it gives us a realistic picture of a generation.[257] We also have an upper limit God said to Abraham: "... your descendants will be strangers ... four hundred years (Gen 15:13). But in the fourth generation they shall return here" (Gen 15:16). 400 divided by 4; perhaps a generation is 100 years. It might even be 120 years since that is how long Moses lived. We cannot be dogmatic on this issue.

Jesus said, "... This[258] generation will by no means pass away till all these things take place" (Matt 24:34); And, "Learn this parable from the fig tree, when you see its branch become tender and put forth leaves, you know that summer is near, even at the doors." The generation He was talking about was not the generation that lived in His days, but the **generation that sees the things He spoke about**; that sees "the time of Jacob's trouble [tribulation .... [צָרָה]" (Jer 30:7), "... great tribulation, such as has not been [on the earth] since the beginning of the world until this time, no, nor ever shall be" (Matt 24:21). "That" generation will see how "unless those days were shortened, no flesh would be saved ..." (Matt 24:22a). "That" generation will see how "for the elect's sake those days will be shortened" (Matt 24:22b). "That" generation will be the one that calls upon Jesus.

Both the prophets and Jesus declared that Israel was a cursed fig tree. Israel's branches began budding in May 14, 1948. An ancient Christian confirmation of this is the *Apocalypse of Peter*, penned around the second Jewish revolt in 135 AD, when Hadrian told the Jews if they came back to Jerusalem they would die. The *Apocalypse of Peter* understood the fig tree to mean Israel, who would come back in the latter days.

---

257 https://https://www.cia.gov/library/publications/the-
worldfactbook/rankorder/2102rank.html
This and *that* in Greek are interchangeable.

"What are the **signs** of thy coming and of the **end of the world**, that we may perceive and mark the time of thy coming [...]? The answer is the **fig-tree**: so soon as the shoot thereof is come forth and the twigs grown, the end of the world shall come. ... the **fig-tree is the house of Israel** ... when the twigs thereof have sprouted forth in the **last days** ..."

Speaking of the birth of the fig tree and all the trees, we read in Isaiah 66:

"Who has heard such a thing? Who has seen such things? Shall the earth be made to give birth in one day? Or shall a nation be born at once? For as soon as Zion was in labor, she gave birth to her children" (Isa 66:8).

Figure 38. Palestine Post 1948: Israel is Born.

May 14, 1948, modern Israel (the fig tree) declared independence. This was ratified by the United Nations. Could it be that they were literally born in a day and the day in which a generation could be measured against? The evidence suggests —that Israel was born in a day.

"Look at the fig tree, **and all the trees**, When they are already budding, you see and know for yourselves that summer is now near. You also, when you see these things happening, know that the kingdom of God is near. Assuredly, I say to you, this generation will by no means pass away till all things take place" (Luke 21:29–32).

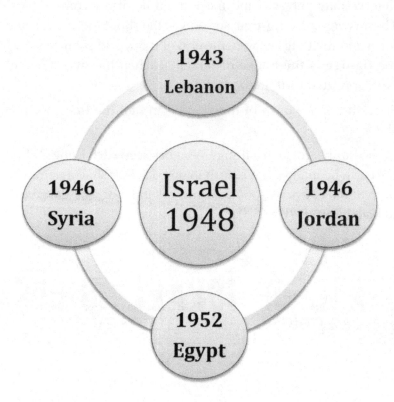

Figure 39. Analogy of "all these trees" budding together with Israel.

If the modern state of Israel is the fig tree, who are "all these trees"? If we are going to be consistent, and if we are going to say the fig tree represents Israel, then we should also deal with all these trees. And what is so astounding about this is that the nations that surround Israel were likewise established as nation states right around the time that Israel was established. Lebanon was established in 1943. Jordan was established in 1946. Egypt, established in 1952, and Syria, was established in 1946. It is amazing how all the other trees—the ones surrounding Israel—are budding as well.

If the evidence is suggesting that the fig tree is Israel, and that when you see it bud, you know that summer is near. This is a fulfillment of the prophecy in Ezekiel 38:

"In the latter years you will come into the land of those brought back from the sword [World War 2] and gathered from many people peoples [They were gathered from many, many nations] on the mountains of Israel, which had long been desolate; they were brought out of the nations, and now all of them dwell safely" (Ezek 38:8).

We saw that there was no rain for about 660,000 days. We have confirmation from Mark Twain and from Naḥmanides that the land was desolate. It began to rain right after the modern state of Israel was born. We know that in the modern state of Israel they are not all worshipping God. Many of them, sadly, are profaning his name. Nevertheless, we see these prophecies coming together, which tells us we are close. If we define a generation by taking the numbers from Psalm 90, (70 years are the days of our lives) that year has already passed. That means from 1948 to 2018, if that were the year, then we missed it. Could it be 2028? Maybe! Do not sell your house. Do not quit your job. If a generation is 100 years, that will take us to 2048, which is also incredibly significant if indeed that were the time of the Lord's return, which in turn would put the abomination of desolation 3.5 years earlier, which would be 2045. Is it just a coincidence that the transhumanists are telling us that they believe we will achieve, or maybe they will achieve, the singularity where man and machine meld into one by 2045? We will have to wait and see.

The Beast's 1260 days of horror

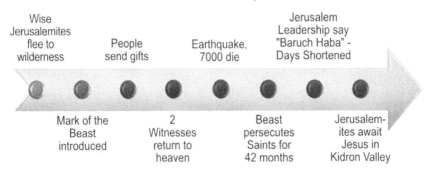

Table 9. The Beast's 1260 days of horror.

PART THREE:

HYBRIDS HAVE WON UNLESS ANCIENT LEADERS CALL THE SAVIOR

Chapter 17: The Chief Cornerstone is the Only Hope Against Genocide

There is ONE in heaven who will save his people and do his awesome work like at Mount Perazim and Gibeon, where He fought against the Nephilim. He will fight, but He will not come until the leadership of Jerusalem invites him back.

Jesus gave this ultimatum in Matthew 23: "For I tell you, you will not see me **from now until** [απ αρτι εως *ap arti eos*] you say, 'Blessed is the one who comes in the name of the Lord!'" (Matt 23:39 NET). Not long after that declaration, Jesus returned to his place, as prophesied:

> I will return again to My place till they acknowledge their offense. Then they will seek My face; In their affliction [tribulation צָרָה], they will earnestly seek Me" (Hos 5:15).

The leadership will recognize Jesus in the time of tribulation, "Alas! For that day is great, that none is like it; and it is the time of Jacob's trouble [tribulation צָרָה], but he shall be saved out of it" (Jer 30:7).

There will likely be a final meeting of the leaders of Jerusalem, the Sanhedrin, or possibly the Knesset (or whoever is left). They may be taking refuge in one of the many underground bunkers in Israel or in the tunnels under the old city. An overwhelming dread will hang over them as all the nations of the world, led by the Beast, are pressing down on Jerusalem to raze it to the ground and annihilate every last person. As they stare extinction in the face and acknowledge all their military strength is gone and they have no more ability to fight for their country or their lives, they will pray and wonder why *HaMashiach*, Messiah is delayed.

At that point, God will "pour out on the kingship of David and the population of Jerusalem a spirit of grace and supplication ..." (Zech 12:10NET2). God will give them what they need, which is to look deep into their nation's soul and consider why Messiah has not come.

BABYLONIAN TALMUD – HE WILL RAISE US UP

The Babylonian Talmud reveals a great deal as to why they think Messiah has not come. The rabbis considered the extent of human history to be analogous to a week, where each day represented one thousand years. Based on that understanding, we read in Sanhedrin 97a:

"Rabbi Kattina said: 'Six thousand years shall the world exist, and one [thousand], it shall be desolate,' as it is written, 'And YHVH alone shall be exalted in that day.' Abaye said: 'it will be desolate two [thousand],' as it is said, 'After two days will he revive us: in the third day, he will raise us up, and we shall live in his sight.'"

In a Rabbinic footnote to this passage, they interpreted the 'two days' in Hosea 6:2 to mean two thousand years. That means that after a period of two thousand years, and in the beginning of the next thousand years,[259] God would revive them so that they might live in his sight. The passage continues with the Tanna debe Eliyyahu who taught on the coming of Messiah within the six thousand plus one thousand year "week":

"The world is to exist six thousand years. In the first two thousand there was desolation; two thousand years the Torah flourished; and the next two thousand years is the Messianic era."

The first two thousand years of "desolation" include the Fall of Adam and Eve, the Nephilim incursion and the Flood, followed by the tower of Babel (Genesis 1–11). The next two thousand years in which Torah flourished, began with Abraham and then of course, Moses on down until the first century (Genesis 12–Malachi). According to the Hebrew calendar, which begins with the year of creation, Abraham was born 1,948 years after creation (*anno mundi*).

---

[259] "It has been taught in accordance with Rabbi Kattina: Just as the seventh year is one year of release in seven, so is the world: one thousand years out of seven shall be fallow, as it is written, 'And YHVH alone shall be exalted in that day,' ...and it is also said, "For a thousand years in your sight are but as yesterday when it is past.'" [Rabbinic Footnote: Ps XC, 4; thus 'day' in the preceding verses means a thousand years.]

The date of Abraham receiving the covenant in Genesis 15 was given as 2,018 years *anno mundi*. That means the last two thousand years of the Messianic era in which Messiah comes and the war of Gog & Magog takes place, began around the first century on the Gregorian calendar, around the time of Jesus. According to a rabbinic footnote in the text, Messiah will come within that period. In other words, 1st 2,000 Desolation + 2nd 2,000 Torah Flourished + 3rd 2,000 the Messianic Age.

The Talmud continues the discussion talking about the minimum time they calculated the world had to exist before Messiah would come.

"Elijah said to Rab Judah, the brother of R. Salia the pious: "The world shall exist not less than eighty-five jubilees … Before that, do not expect him; afterwards thou mayest await him.'"[260]

In other words, there would be a minimum of 85 Jubilees before Messiah would come. A Jubilee is calculated at either 49 or 50 years. If 49, then he would come after 4,165 years or if 50 years, then he would come 4,250 years after creation. In another text, a similar calculation is made based on "a scroll written in Hebrew in Assyrian characters" which had been discovered by a Jewish man "amongst the Roman archives."[261]

In it is stated that four thousand, two hundred and thirty-one years after the creation the **world will be orphaned**. [As to the years following,] some of them will be … in the war of Gog and Magog, and the remaining [period] will be the Messianic era.[262]

Based on these texts from the Babylonian Talmud, the Messiah should have come sometime around the first century on the Gregorian calendar. The text continues in Sanhedrin 97b, "but through our many iniquities all these years have been lost." Then the footnote states bluntly, "He should have come at the beginning of the last two thousand years; the delay is due to our sins."[263]

---

[260] http://www.come-and-hear.com/sanhedrin/sanhedrin_97.html
[261] http://www.come-and-hear.com/sanhedrin/sanhedrin_97.html
[262] http://www.come-and-hear.com/sanhedrin/sanhedrin_97.html
[263] The Babylonian Talmud: Mas. Sanhedrin 97a and b (Soncino Press)

According to their own texts, without the prompting of any Christian texts, the Jewish sages already have the answer, but simply cannot see it. It is like when people come to ask for advice and after they have shared their story, the answer comes to them. Eventually, based on their own texts, they will realize their Messiah was expected to come four thousand years after creation and then shortly thereafter it "would be orphaned." When they ask themselves why Messiah has not come, or "should have come at the beginning of the last two thousand years," the answer will be in the same text: "The delay is due to our sins." [264] Whereas their text told them the world would be orphaned; and they will discover Jesus' words, who said to his disciples "Let not your heart be troubled... I will not leave you orphans; I will come to you (John 14:1, 18).

THE COMMONERS WELCOMED JESUS

The masses of Jerusalem did accept Jesus as their king. On the first day of the week before Passover, which we often call Palm Sunday, Jesus instructed His disciples to go and fetch a young donkey, which He then rode into Jerusalem in the same fashion that Solomon did when he was coronated king.

"The king also said to them, 'Take with you the servants of your lord, and have Solomon my son ride on my own mule, and take him down to Gihon'" (1 Kgs 1:33).

When Jesus had his disciples borrow a donkey for his entry into Jerusalem, He was broadcasting that He was the rightful king in the line of David, and the promised Messiah.

"Rejoice greatly, O daughter of Zion! Shout, O daughter of Jerusalem! Behold, your King is coming to you; He is just and having salvation, Lowly and riding on a donkey, A colt, the foal of a donkey" (Zech 9:9).

---

[264] The Babylonian Talmud: Mas. Sanhedrin 97a and b (Soncino Press)

The people joyously welcomed Him in the name of YHWH as Messiah:

> "The next day a great multitude that had come to the feast, when they heard that Jesus was coming to Jerusalem, took branches of palm trees and went out to meet Him, and cried out: "[הוֹשִׁיעָה *Hoshianna*]! 'Blessed is He who comes in the name of the LORD!' The King of Israel!" (John 12:12–12).

Hoshianna is from the Hebrew root [ישע] yod-shin-'ayin and means, "please save." It is the same root as the name, Yeshua (Jesus) and *Yeshu-ah,* salvation. As Hebrew speakers, they almost certainly did not miss that they were calling out, "Please save" to him whose name is "salvation." They also said, "Baruch haba b'shem Adonai," acknowledging Yeshua as the king of Israel and Messiah, the long-waited One who would bring peace.

> "And when He had come into Jerusalem, all the city was moved, saying, 'Who is this?' the multitudes said, 'This is Jesus [Yeshua ישוע], the prophet from Nazareth of Galilee'" (Matt 21:10-11).

We see in Psalm 118:

> "I will praise You, for You have answered me, and have become my salvation [יְשׁוּעָה Yeshu'ah] … The **stone** which the **builders rejected** has become the **chief cornerstone** [פִּנָּה]. This was the LORD's doing; It is marvelous in our eyes … Save now, I pray, [הוֹשִׁיעָה *Hoshianna*] O LORD; blessed is he who comes in the name of the LORD! We have blessed you from the house of the LORD … You are my God, and I will praise You; You are my God, I will exalt You" (Ps 118:18–28).

The people probably had not connected all the theological dots about the hypostatic union—the triune nature of God. But what they did know was that He was the prophesied rightful king, the Messiah, and they put their hope in him. Sadly, the people in power refused to acknowledge him because He was a direct threat to their power; He was seen as a challenge to their leadership.

235

THE LEADERSHIP OF JERUSALEM REJECTED JESUS

Jesus' heartfelt cry, "O Jerusalem, Jerusalem," was directed toward the seat of power, those who made decisions. Just like when we speak of Washington D.C., we are not talking about the taxicab drivers, fast food workers etc., but about the President, Congress, and the Supreme Court.

The leadership of Jerusalem, like in a parable Jesus told, "hated him … saying, 'We will not have this man to reign over us'" (Luke 19:14). When they rejected Yeshua and did not welcome Him in the name of the Lord, which is from Psalm 118, then that song did not apply to them. The promise, "The LORD is on my side; I will not fear. What can man do to me?" (Ps 118:6) no longer applied to the leadership of Jerusalem and consequently, Jesus said to them. "See! Your house is left to you desolate" (Matt 23:38).

Why does it matter that the leadership rejected Jesus while the masses accepted Him? Isaiah laid it out plainly when he said, "The leaders of this people cause them to err, and those who are led by them are destroyed" (Isa 9:16).

We may not like where the captain is taking the ship, but if the captain sinks the ship, then we all die. The leaders are the ones who are steering our ship; the leaders of Jerusalem were the ones steering the national ship. What they decided was policy—for better or worse. The fate of the leaders was the national fate of the people:

- Thus says the LORD concerning the prophets who make my people stray (Mic 3:5).
- O My people! Those who lead you cause you to err, and destroy the way of your paths (Isa 3:12).
- If the blind leads the blind, both will fall into a ditch (Matt 15:14).

We also have several scriptures telling us "Judah is My lawgiver" (Ps 60:7),[265] and this position of lawgiver; or holding: "the scepter shall not depart from Judah, Nor a lawgiver from between his feet, until Shiloh comes; and to Him shall be the obedience of the people" (Gen 49:10).

---

[265] "Judah prevailed over his brothers, and from him came a ruler" (1 Chr 5:2).

In other words, Judah is the one who gives the law by which Israel is to live, until Shiloh comes. That is, Jesus is the one to whom it belongs. If the leadership of Judah refuses to recognize that the kingdom belongs to him, then their house would be left desolate, as Jesus said, until they welcome him in the name of the Lord. Jesus made it clear "For I tell you, you will not see me **from now until** [απ αρτι εως *ap arti eos*] you say, 'Blessed is the one who comes in the name of the Lord!'" (Matt 23:39 NET).

Those three little words "from now until" are Jesus' ultimatum: it is your move. Your house is desolate **from now** — this moment you have rejected me — **until** the time you welcome me in the name of the Lord.

"This is the day the LORD has made; we will rejoice and be glad in it (Ps 118:24). Save now, I pray, O LORD; O LORD, I pray, send now prosperity (Ps 118:25). Blessed is he who comes in the name of the LORD! We have blessed you from the house of the LORD." (Ps 118:26).

THE BUILDERS AND THE CORNERSTONE

Thus says the Lord GOD: "Behold, I lay in Zion a stone for a foundation, a tried stone, a precious **cornerstone**, a sure foundation; whoever believes will not act hastily" (Isa 28:16).

This is the same language as in Psalm 118:

"The **stone which the builders rejected has become the chief cornerstone**" (Ps 118:22). "This was the LORD's doing; it is marvelous in our eyes" (Ps 118:23).

The rejected stone is pivotal in understanding Israel's salvation. Jesus specifically directed this passage of Psalms against the leadership of Jerusalem and consequently the implications of Isaiah 28:16 as well:

"Have you not even read this Scripture: 'The **stone which the builders rejected Has become the chief cornerstone** (Mark 12:10). This was the LORD's doing, and it is marvelous in our eyes'?" (Mark 12:11). "And they sought to lay hands on Him, but feared the multitude, **for they knew He had spoken the parable against them**" (Mark 12:12).

237

Jesus was saying, "I am that stone." The leadership of Jerusalem, of the house of Judah, missed that Jesus was that stone. Nevertheless, it says, "This was the Lord's doing." We cannot overlook that! One of the saddest teachings over the last 2,000 years is when people suggest that the Jewish leadership put Jesus to death, and therefore deserve his wrath. We do not fully understand how it was God's doing, but it was. We must understand that when Jesus said, "O Jerusalem, Jerusalem ... How often I wanted to gather your children together ... but you were not willing!" (Matt 23:37), He was **not** talking about the average Joes. In fact, they received him.

NATIONAL RESTORATION WHEN THE "BUILDERS" WELCOME JESUS

After the ascension of Jesus, Peter said to his brethren, "I know that you did it [killed Jesus] in ignorance, as did also your rulers" (Acts 3:17). He calls on them to repent so that the times of refreshing may come.

> "... **Repent** therefore and **be converted**, that your sins may be blotted out, so that times of refreshing may come from the presence of the Lord, and that He may send Jesus Christ" (Acts 3:19–20).

The phrase "times of refreshing" implies relief from difficult, distressful, or burdensome circumstances. And according to the New English Translation Bible syntactical notes: it is generally regarded as a reference to the ushering in of the Messianic Age.

Peter followed this up by saying about Jesus, "Whom heaven must receive until the times of restoration of all things" (Acts 3:21). In other words, repent, be converted so Jesus may come, but until then, heaven will receive him until the right time.

The strong implication is if you, (Israel, Jerusalem) will repent, (even in Peter's day), then Jesus would come, which is exactly what Jesus was saying, "Until you repent and until you welcome me in the name of Yehovah, you're not going to see me again, but when you do repent, then you'll see me." If this—then that.

Peter was echoing Yeshua's prophecy, "you shall see Me no more ..." [And he says] You must obey him in everything he tells you," in Acts 3:22.

Peter "spoke to the rulers, the elders and the scribes as well as the high priest, Caiaphas, John, and Alexander ..." (Acts 4:6) who were attempting to quell the message:

> "Then Peter, filled with the Holy Spirit, said to them, 'Rulers of the people and elders of Israel' (Acts 4:8)... 'Jesus Christ of Nazareth, whom you crucified, whom God raised from the dead... (Acts 4:10) is the **stone which was rejected by you builders** which has become the **chief cornerstone** (Acts 4:11) nor is there salvation [Yeshuah] in any other, for there is no other name under heaven given among men by which we must be saved" (Acts 4:12).

He took that passage from Psalm 118, and of course, from Jesus' teachings.

> "The LORD is my strength and song, and He has become my **salvation [Yeshuah]**" (Ps 118:14). "I will praise You, for You have answered me, and have become my **salvation [Yeshuah]**" (Ps 118:21).

Peter is saying, "You leaders of Jerusalem are the builders, and you rejected Jesus, the chief cornerstone." Peter makes it clear that salvation [Hebrew: *Yeshua*] is only found in Yeshua-Jesus. Therefore, Peter was saying there would be no national restoration until the builders, that is, the leaders of Jerusalem, welcome Him in the name of the Lord.

Greed blinded the leadership from seeing what was right in front of them. It is such a sad testimony; how often we are blinded by greed for power, fame, or for something we do not have. The leaders knew Yeshua was doing miracles that were well attested. They said, we cannot deny it. We cannot deny that people are being healed, but we are still not going to believe.

For Jesus to come back, what must happen? The national leadership, the seat of authority now residing in Jerusalem, must repent. They are the ones that must make this call. Even though many believers around the world and throughout the ages (citizens of the commonwealth of Israel) have prayed "Lord come back." On this matter, it requires the leaders who sit in that seat of authority to issue a national decree in Jerusalem that will welcome Him back in the name of the Lord, just as Jesus said.

Chapter 18: Jerusalem Leaders will Look to Me

The spirit of grace and supplication will then cause the leadership to realize not all hope is lost; they will look to the only one who can save them.

"I will pour out on the kingship of David and the population of Jerusalem a spirit of grace and supplication so that they will look to [אל *el*] me, the one they have pierced" (Zech 12:10 [NET2]).

The preposition *el* [אל *el*] (Greek *pros*) means "to or toward" and not *al* which means "upon, over, above." Translations erroneously view this preposition as "*al*" which means upon, over, or above. Sadly, based on this unfortunate translation, commentators [266] have implied Jesus is returning to destroy the inhabitants of Jerusalem and when they look "upon" him they will cry with fear and terror, "Oh no!! Here comes Jesus, we are in trouble!" This false teaching, which also considers prophecies to be already fulfilled, such as the theory that Jesus already came back, is the essence of Preterism: Jesus came back on the dust clouds of the Roman army to destroy the Jews. That is not what the Bible teaches. **Jesus is not coming to destroy Israel, but to save her;**[267] and his people will call him with hope and expectation of final redemption, not with terror.

The Septuagint of Zech 12:10 reads *epiblepsontai pros me),* "they will look to me/toward me," which is the same preposition we find in "In the beginning was the Word, and the Word was with [*pros*] God," (John 1:1). Pros means "facing" or "toward"; it expresses a relationship. In this beautiful relationship recorded in John's gospel, the *Logos* (Jesus) and the Father are looking at each other.

The meaning of the preposition in Zechariah 12 is that they will look to Him as a little baby looks to his mother or father to give him sustenance and clothing and protection. This will occur when the leadership finally looks to Jesus to save them. Suddenly, many texts will flood into their minds, and they will have their "aha moment."

---

[266] Gill, John, et al. Gill's Commentary. Baker Book House, 1980. ZECH 12:10.
[267] For behold, the LORD comes out of His place To punish the inhabitants of the earth for their iniquity... (Isa 26:21). "Then the LORD will go forth and fight against those nations, As He fights in the day of battle." (Zech 14:3).

The passage from Numbers Rabbah could come to mind:

"When King Solomon speaks of his 'beloved,' he usually means Israel the nation. In one instance he compares his beloved to a roe, and therein he refers to a feature which marks alike Moses and the Messiah, the Two redeemers of Israel. Just as a roe comes within the range of man's vision only to disappear from sight and then appear again, so it is with these redeemers. Moses appeared to the Israelites, then disappeared, and eventually appeared once more, and the same peculiarity we have in connection with Messiah; He will appear, disappear, and appear again" (Numb. Rabba 11).

The meaning will become clear that Jesus the Messiah came then left and will return. Then the Midrash Ruth could come to mind:

"The fourteenth verse in the second chapter of Ruth is thus explained. 'Come thou hither' is the prediction of Messiah's kingdom. 'Dip the morsel in the vinegar,' foretells the agony through which Messiah will pass, as it is written in Isaiah (chpt. 53), 'He was wounded for our sins, He was bruised for our transgressions.' 'And she set herself beside the reapers' predicts the temporary departure of Messiah's kingdom. 'And he reached her a parched corn' means the restoration of His kingdom" (Midr. Ruth 5).

God will pour out his spirit of grace and supplication so that they can look to Yeshua for the first time in their collective history. The weight of the moment will be grave. Hours may pass until someone breaks the deafening silence with a verse:

"My servant grew up in the LORD's presence like a tender green shoot, sprouting from a root in dry and sterile ground. There was nothing beautiful or majestic about his appearance, nothing to attract us to him'" (Isa 53:2).

Another may add:

"He was despised and rejected—a man of sorrows, acquainted with bitterest grief. We turned our backs on him and looked the other way when he went by. He was despised, and we did not care" (Isa 53:3).

With hot tears running down her cheeks, another may interject:

"Yet it was our weaknesses he carried; it was our sorrows that weighed him down. And we thought his troubles were a punishment from God for his own sins!" (Isa 53:4).

There is silence for some time. Hearts are heavy, and then another with his face to the ground quietly says:

"But he was wounded and crushed for our sins. He was beaten that we might have peace. He was whipped, and we were healed!" (Isa 53:5).

Then they all confess together:

"All of us have strayed away like sheep. We have left God's paths to follow our own. Yet the LORD laid on him the guilt and sins of us all. He was oppressed and treated harshly, yet he never said a word. He was led as a lamb to the slaughter. And as a sheep is silent before the shearers, he did not open his mouth. From prison and trial they led him away to his death. But who among the people realized that he was dying for their sins—that he was suffering their punishment?" (Isa 53:6–8).

The painful reality of their rejection of *HaMashiach*, the only one who can save them, will truly sink in. They will contemplate how the one they had pinned their hopes on for thousands of years was the chief cornerstone that the builders, their leaders, had rejected; and who, though he had done no wrong, was whipped and sent to his death on a cross like a criminal and was put in a rich man's grave (Isa 53:8, 9).

THEY WILL MOURN

The gravity of having rejected the Messiah, the one they pierced, will be parallel to that of Joseph's brothers finally recognizing their brother as a fellow Hebrew and not a pagan Egyptian. When the leadership of Jerusalem sees Jesus as their brother and savior and not as a Christian (or pagan) invention, they will lament and weep bitterly, just as they would mourn at the death of an only child!

"Yes, they will mourn for Him as one mourns for his only son, and grieve for Him as one grieves for a firstborn. In that day there shall be a great mourning in Jerusalem … all the families that remain, every family by itself, and their wives by themselves" (Zech 12:10, 11–14).

Parents can imagine the sorrow they would feel at losing a child; their mourning would not last for five minutes but would carry on for days, weeks, even months. That will be the same heartfelt mourning they will feel when they realize they rejected the chief cornerstone. Each person will lament alone in profound sorrow, broken and in agony over the centuries of rejecting their Promised One—the very one who loved them more than any other and had come to His Own. Their hearts will be broken with contrition as they desperately call out to the One they had despised. Their hearts will be vexed realizing all the misery that might have been avoided if they had embraced him sooner.

They will mourn at how their leadership, two thousand years previously, did not see their true King "due to our sins." They will consider how the masses said, "Baruch Haba B'shem Adonai," but their leadership said, "Crucify him." They will weep, but for the first time ever, the leadership in Jerusalem will acknowledge their offense; and that will be the key to Messiah's return.

"I will return again to My place till they acknowledge their offense. Then they will seek My face; in their affliction [tribulation] they will earnestly seek Me" (Hos 5:15).

All these things will have led up to this grand-finale climactic moment where all is lost, but then a faint ray of hope begins to shine through. The Jewish people's history taught them that however deep the mourning and however grave the situation, they always kept a flicker of hope alive within their souls. Just as God had stated, through the tribulation of those days, they will earnestly seek him. It will be then that the "scornful men, who rule this people who are in Jerusalem" (Isa 28:14), who made a covenant with death and Sheol and said, "we have made lies our refuge, and under falsehood we have hidden ourselves" (Isa 28:15) will seek him. In their affliction—Jacob's trouble—they will fully understand Jesus to be the chief cornerstone.

I will praise You, for You have answered me, and have become my salvation (Yeshuah) (Ps 118:21). The stone which the builders rejected has become the chief cornerstone (Ps 118:22). This was the LORD's doing; it is marvelous in our eyes (Ps 118:23). This is the day the LORD has made; we will rejoice and be glad in it (Ps 118:24).

CHAPTER 18: JERUSALEM LEADERS WILL LOOK TO ME

In that day, the words of Isaiah the prophet will ring true:

Therefore thus says the Lord GOD: "Behold, I lay in Zion a stone for a foundation, A tried stone, a precious cornerstone,[268] a sure foundation; Whoever believes will not act hastily (Isa 28:16).

They will accept Yeshua as the sure foundation because the tribulation will have swept "away the refuge of lies" (Isa 28:17). It will be like a veil lifted from their eyes. They will see that:

It pleased the LORD to bruise Him; He has put Him to grief. When You make His soul an offering for sin, He shall see His seed, He shall prolong His days, and the pleasure of the LORD shall prosper in His hand (Isa 53:10).

God's spirit of grace and supplication will be at work telling them:

"So rend your heart, and not your garments; Return to the LORD your God, for He is gracious and merciful, slow to anger, and of great kindness; and He relents from doing harm" (Joel 2:13).

Thus, with all their heart they will call upon Jesus to save them. At the top of their lungs, they will shout and join the throngs of people who welcomed Jesus at his first coming by saying "Save now [Hoshianna], I pray, O LORD; O LORD, I pray, send now prosperity. Blessed is he who comes in the name of the LORD" "Baruch Haba B'shem Adonai," (Ps 118:25–26); come Yeshua, "We welcome you in the name of Yehovah." Just as they anticipated in the Babylonian Talmud, their confession will bring them to say:

"Come, and let us return to the LORD; For He has torn, but He will heal us; He has stricken, but He will bind us up. After two days He will revive us; On the third day He will raise us up, That we may live in His sight" (Hos 6:1–2).

Thomas Constable points out that "Corporate Israel has never prayed like this. The fulfillment must still be future, at the beginning of Christ's millennial reign."[269]

---

268 In Daniel 2 that there is a stone cut out of a mountain without hands, that will come, and will crush all the kingdoms of this world.

269 The Expository Notes of Dr. Thomas L. Constable, 2009. From theWord Bible Software.

REMARRIAGE

God divorced the ten northern tribes of Israel, but He intends to marry his bride upon his return. Judah was not divorced, but was declared an adulterous wife. How can the marriage supper of the Lamb take place under these circumstances? There must be a legal mechanism for the marriage to happen. The beautiful thing is that there is such a mechanism. Briefly stated, the "old covenant" was a marriage contract that God and Israel entered at Sinai.

- "I spread My wing over you and covered your nakedness. Yes, I swore an oath to you and entered into a covenant with you, and **you became Mine**," says the Lord GOD (Ezek 16:8).
- … the covenant that I made with their fathers in the day that I took them by the hand to lead them out of the land of Egypt, My covenant which they broke, though **I was a husband to them**, says the LORD (Jer 31:32).

However shocking it may sound, Scripture tells us clearly: God divorced the northern kingdom of Israel because of their adultery:

"Then I saw that for all the causes for which backsliding Israel had committed adultery, I had put her away and given her a **certificate of divorce**; yet her treacherous sister Judah did not fear, but went and played the harlot also" (Jer 3:8).

God did not divorce Judah "for the sake of My servant David, and for the sake of Jerusalem, the city which I have chosen out of all the tribes of Israel" (1 Kgs 11:32). Paul explains how the old marriage (old covenant) is annulled by the death of the husband.

"For the woman who has a husband is bound by the law to her husband as long as he lives. But if the husband dies, she is released from the **law of her husband**. So then if, while her husband lives, she marries another man, she will be called an adulteress; but if her husband dies, she is free from **that law** [of the husband], so that she is no adulteress, though she has married another man. Therefore, my brethren, you also have become dead to the law [of the husband] through the body of Christ, **that you may be married to another–to Him who was raised from the dead**, that we should bear fruit to God" (Rom 7:2–4).

246

CHAPTER 18: JERUSALEM LEADERS WILL LOOK TO ME

The northern tribes of Israel are forever mixed with the nations; but Judah is still under the old marriage covenant with its stains of adultery and infidelity. By welcoming Jesus in the name of the Lord, they recognize him as the husband who died and "the one they pierced" (Zech 12:10). Paul says, because of that "you also have become dead to the law [of the husband] through the body of Christ" (Rom 7:4). Isaiah speaks of this time when Jesus comes (Isa 4:2) and purges the blood of Jerusalem:

> "And it shall come to pass that he who is left in Zion and **remains in Jerusalem** will be called holy–everyone who is recorded among the living in Jerusalem. When the **Lord has washed away the filth** of the daughters of Zion, and **purged the blood of Jerusalem** from her midst, by the spirit of judgment and by the spirit of burning" (Isa 4:3–4).

Their acceptance of Jesus will bring many verses into focus:

> "And it will be said in that day: 'Behold, this is our God; we have waited for Him, and He will save us. This is the LORD; we have waited for Him; we will be glad and rejoice in His salvation [Yeshuah]'" (Isa 25:9).

Indeed, they will be comforted after the great tribulation of the time of Jacob's trouble through which they passed:

> "Comfort, yes, comfort My people!" Says your God (Isa 40:1). "Speak comfort to Jerusalem, and cry out to her, That her warfare is ended, That her iniquity is pardoned; For she has received from the LORD's hand Double for all her sins" (Isa 40:2).

Furthermore, the words of Joel will take on a greater significance:

> "And it shall come to pass that whoever calls on the name of the LORD shall be saved. For in Mount Zion and in Jerusalem there shall be deliverance, as the LORD has said, among the remnant whom the LORD calls" (Joel 2:32).

EPHRAIM RANSOMED

God also specifically states he will ransom Ephraim (the house of Israel) from Sheol and Death, the curse that has plagued man since the Fall in the Garden of Eden. The leadership of Jerusalem has repented and embraced Yeshua, the One who broke the curse of sin and death. This is the same duo with which the leaders of Jerusalem had made a deal:

"The iniquity of **Ephraim** is bound up; his sin is kept in store (Hos 13:12). Shall I ransom them from the power of **Sheol** [שְׁאוֹל]? Shall I redeem them from Death? O **Death** [מָוֶת *Mavet*], where are your plagues? O Sheol, where is your sting? Compassion is hidden from my eyes" (Hos 13:14).

Paul uses this passage to speak about the resurrection and the transformation that will take place at the gathering of the saints.

"So when this corruptible has put on incorruption, and this mortal has put on immortality, then shall be brought to pass the saying that is written: 'Death is swallowed up in victory" (1 Cor 15:54). "O **Death**, where is your sting? O **Hades**, where is your victory?" (1 Cor 15:55).

The confession of the Jerusalem leadership will bring forgiveness and reconciliation, and will turn the tables. Up until then, "The same horn was making war against the saints, and prevailing against them" (Dan 7:21) "**until** the Ancient of Days came, and a **judgment was made** *in favor* of the saints" (Dan 7:21-22). Just as Jesus said that they would not see him "**from now until** you say, 'Blessed is the one who comes in the name of the Lord!'" (Matt 23:39 NET). Nothing will change for the saints "until" then; and then the judgment is made for them because of what they confess.

FOR THE LOVE OF THE SAINTS

Jesus alluded to this shift as well when He said:

"For then there will be great tribulation, such as has not been since the beginning of the world until this time, no, nor ever shall be (Matt 24:21). And unless those days were shortened, no flesh would be saved; but for the elect's sake [δια δε τους εκλεκτους *dia de tous eklektos*] those days will be shortened" (Matt 24:22).

Why will they be shortened? It took me a long time to put the pieces together and to understand how it works. If we know that the tribulation will be 1,260 days long, how can the days be shortened?

When the word: sake, *Dia* is followed by an accusative (objective) case, according to BDAG Lexicon, it means, "the reason why something happens, results, exists: because of, for the sake of."[270] Based on the Greek grammar, the saints are not passive recipients of an act of pity from God. The shortening of the days of Tribulation is not done to them, but is caused by them, based on an action they performed.

Rather, the time of the affliction gets reduced "as a result of [something] the elect [did], those days will be shortened;" the elect cause the shortening of the days. What will they do? They will finally answer Jesus' challenge and welcome Him in the name of the LORD, and say "Baruch haba b'shem Adonai" (Matt 23:39).

Their welcoming Jesus in the name of the Lord will set in motion his return! Immediately prior to this, there seems to be a time of silence, "Be silent, all flesh, before the LORD; for He is aroused from His holy habitation" (Zech 2:13). It is as if He were drawing a deep breath followed by:

> The LORD also will roar from Zion, and utter His voice from Jerusalem; the heavens and earth will shake; but the LORD will be a shelter for His people, and the strength of the children of Israel (Joel 3:16).

The Day of the Lord will finally commence when, "the LORD comes out of His place to punish the inhabitants of the earth for their iniquity" (Isa 26:21). The world will shudder at his coming.

---

[270] Hated because of the name Mt 10:22; persecution arises because of teaching 13:21; because of unbelief vs. 58; because of a tradition 15:3; (BDAG)

Vignette 2: The Call to War behind the Veil

an a woman forget her nursing child, and not have compassion on the son of her womb? Surely they may forget, yet I will not forget them, Yeshua said, overwhelmed that the leadership of Jerusalem has finally called upon him. Leaning over, he blows the words gently through the veil to his people. "See, I have inscribed you on the palms of my hands. Your walls are continually before me. Your sons shall make haste; your destroyers and those who laid you waste shall go away from you. Don't you know? I am the eternal King, the Creator of the ends of the earth. I do not grow tired or weary; and my understanding cannot be fathomed."[271]

Yeshua was wearing many golden crowns; his face was like the sun. He was holding a sickle in his hand as the one who would administer justice and wage war with righteousness, his head and hair were white as wool or even snow, his eyes were like flames of fire, and his feet were like red-hot glowing metal. His perfect justice was like a breastplate on his chest and his ability to rescue and save his people was like a helmet on his head; his zeal to avenge his people was like a garment that covered him.[272]

"I am proclaiming the year of Adonai's favor, and the day of vengeance to comfort all who mourn in Jerusalem!" Yeshua thundered powerfully from upper Jerusalem to the earth so that the sky and the earth quaked.[273]

---

[271] Isa 49:15–17, Isa 40:28
[272] Rev 1:13–16, Isa 59:17; Mat 13:39; 24:42; Rev 14:16
[273] Joel 3:16

The Beast, Oracle, and Satan looked up to the sky after hearing the peals of thunder and considered what they might mean.

"I will have compassion on my people, the Hebrews," Yeshua proclaimed passionately as the sound of their cries and petitions mixed with the words *"Hoshianna! Baruch haba b'shem Adonai,"* rose up to his throne like incense. [274] Those were words that He had been waiting to hear from the leadership of the Hebrews. He had vowed to them: "You will not see my face again until you say, 'Blessed is he who comes in the name of Adonai,'"[275] and now after two-thousand years they were earnestly seeking him.[276] Finally, they saw with great clarity their need for the One who had come to his own, yet his own had not received him.[277]

"I will give them a beautiful headdress instead of ashes, the oil of gladness instead of mourning, the garment of praise instead of a faint spirit; that they may be called oaks of righteousness, the planting of Adonai, that he may be glorified. They shall build up the ancient ruins; they shall raise up the former devastations of many generations.[278] Look my people, you will be fully satisfied. I will never again make you an object of mockery among the nations."[279]

"I am displeased that there is no justice," Yeshua said as fiery lightning surged from his sides. "I am appalled that there is no one to intervene."[280]

"Great King, you are a refuge to your people, a stronghold to the Hebrews," someone shouted out, answering the audacious claims of the Beast to those around him.

---

274 Rev 5:8
275 Mat 23:39
276 Hos 5:15
277 John 1:10, 11
278 Isa 61:3, 4
279 Joel 2:18–19
280 Isa 59:15, 16; Mat 13:39; 24:42; Rev 14:16

"I am the one who has gathered them and the armies of the world into the valley of Jehoshaphat, for there I will judge them for harming my people, for scattering my inheritance among the nations, and for dividing up my land. They cast lots to decide which of my people would be their slaves and abused the little ones for their pleasures. I will bring them back again from all the places to which they were sold, and I will pay the nations back for all they have done.[281] I will strike the Beast from the house of the wicked, by laying his neck bare."[282]

"Satan, and his son, the Beast, and Oracle do not grasp my thoughts," Yeshua declared, "nor do they understand my counsel; for I am gathering them like sheaves to the threshing floor[283] because the time has come for the Hebrews to take possession of the kingdom.[284] I have made Jerusalem a trap and now I shall go and spring the trap!" Yeshua said in a mighty and thunderous voice, even as the Beast was boasting in his apparently unstoppable victory. "Look, I am making Jerusalem an unstable cup toward all of its surrounding armies as they lay siege against Judah and Jerusalem. I am making Jerusalem a heavy weight; so everyone who burdens themselves with it will be crushed, even though all of the nations of the earth have gathered themselves against it. I am about to strike every horse with panic and every rider with insanity. I will keep my eyes on the house of Judah, but I will blind every horse of the invading armies."[285]

"Swing your sickle, and gather the harvest," an Angel said in a loud voice coming out of the temple of Adonai, "for the hour has come to gather it, because the harvest of the earth is fully ripe."[286]

---

[281] Joel 3
[282] Hab 3:13
[283] Mic 4:12
[284] Dan 7:22
[285] Zech 12:2–4
[286] Rev 14:15

"Bring down your warriors, Yeshua!" the prophet Joel suddenly called out. "Rush forth with the sickle, for the harvest is ripe! Go, stomp the grapes, for the winepress is full! The vats overflow. Indeed, their wickedness is great! Crowds, great crowds are in the valley of threshing, the valley of Jehoshaphat, Armageddon!"[287]

"Michael," Yeshua said, "when you hear the trumpet blast, you will go out and gather my elect from the four winds, from one end of heaven to another.[288]

"The rest of you," Yeshua commanded the mighty Angels following him among the vast army, "Go and gather the weeds first and tie them in bundles for burning, but bring the wheat into my barn."[289]

Gabriel smiled, understanding exactly what Yeshua referred to. In fact, He had longed for this day when they would finally be authorized to go in every direction to first gather out of his kingdom all things that offend and those who practice lawlessness.[290] He peered through the veil to the earth noting the location of several of Satan's army of Watchers as well as the rulers of the earth[291] and all who had taken the mark and those who were attempting to destroy the Hebrews. Their vast numbers, He considered, were of no consequence, for they were like a drop in a bucket, and were reckoned as dust on the scales before Yeshua, the mighty! All the nations were as nothing before him, they were reckoned by him as nothing and chaos.[292]

---

[287] Joel 3:12–14
[288] Mat 24:29–31; Isa 11:12
[289] Mark 13:30
[290] Matt 13:41
[291] Isa 24:21
[292] Isa 40:15, 17

VIGNETTE 2: THE CALL TO WAR BEHIND THE VEIL

"The end of the age has come for the world to be harvested in judgment!" Yeshua proclaimed, and then stood up from his Father's throne and walked over to his majestic pure-white war-horse.[293] An astoundingly sharp, two-edged sword could be seen coming out of his mouth.[294] It was something like an intensified particle-wave beam of light.

"Go forth, great King, with your great army!" Enoch, the seventh from Adam, encouraged him. "Execute judgment on all; convict all who are wicked for all of the wickedness they have committed and of all the harsh things which the wicked have spoken against you."[295]

"Nations far and wide, get ready for war!" Gabriel taunted. "Call out your best warriors! Let all your fighting men advance for the attack!"[296] The cry for help of the Hebrews was the key to establishing Yeshua's kingdom, and He would not rest until[297] He had vanquished all their enemies[298] and established Jerusalem as a praise throughout the earth[299] and the Hebrews as the head of nations and no longer the tail.[300]

"The day of my vengeance has finally come," Yeshua bellowed, "The day to bring in the acceptable year of Adonai.[301] Now, my glory shall be revealed, and all the Adamites will see it at once."[302]

---

[293] 2Kgs 2:11; 6:17
[294] Rev 1:16
[295] Jude 1:14-15
[296] Joel 3
[297] Ruth 3:18
[298] Dan 7:22
[299] Isa 62:7
[300] Deut 28:13, 44
[301] Isa 34:8
[302] Isa 40:50

"Oh great King," Isaiah exclaimed, "rend the heavens and go down and may the mountains quake at your presence![303] Repay your enemies according to their actions: anger to your enemies, retribution to your foes; to the coastlands render their due!"[304] Isaiah was eager to see Yeshua defend the Hebrews; every one of her allies had forsaken her. He cried, "Go with strength, and may your arm rule for you."[305]

"It is done!" someone in a loud voice shouted from the throne in the temple.[306]

"The kingdoms of this world," others resonated in loud voices, "have become the kingdoms of Adonai and of Yeshua, and Adonai shall reign forever and ever! The nations were angry, and your wrath has come. Now is the time that the dead should be judged and that you should reward your servants the prophets, the saints, and those who fear your name, unimportant and important and for you to destroy those who have destroyed the earth." Suddenly the temple of Adonai began opening, exposing the ark of his covenant. Lightning and thundering booms emanated out of the place.[307]

All eyes were on Yeshua.

"I am coming quickly,"[308] He said with a voice like the sound of many waters. He was silent for a moment, and then ferociously roared out like a raging lion, shaking the throne itself. "I have heard you, my beloved, and I am coming!"[309]

The armies of Yeshua began taking their positions on their side of the veil ready for battle.[310]

---

[303] Isa 64:1
[304] Isa 59:18
[305] Isa 63:5
[306] Rev 16:17
[307] Rev 11:15-19
[308] Rev 22:20
[309] Joel 3:16
[310] Rev 19:14

Chapter 19: The Sky Opens at Jesus' Coming!

The leadership crying out "Baruch Haba B'shem Adonai" are the words that Jesus had waited two thousand years to hear. This is the time He "will have mercy on His afflicted" (Isa 49:13). Indeed God says, "The mountains shall depart and the hills be removed, but My kindness shall not depart from you" (Isa 54:10).

It will be the time that Isaiah pined for ages ago when he wrote, "Oh, that You would rend the heavens! That You would come down! That the mountains might shake at Your presence," (Isa 64:1). It will also be the time Jesus longed for, when He said, "I came to send fire on the earth, and how I wish it were already kindled!" (Luke 12:49).

The heavens will indeed open at that time, as John tells us:

"Now I saw heaven opened, and behold, a white horse. And He who sat on him was called Faithful and True, and in righteousness He judges and makes war" (Rev 19:11).

Earlier John said, "The sky receded as a scroll when it is rolled up..." (Rev 6:14). This is the epic moment when the veil between heaven and earth, or as investigative reporter George Knapp put it, the "thin psychic dimensional membrane," dissolves. Peter said that "The heavens will pass away with a great noise, and the elements will melt with fervent heat; both the earth and the works that are in it will be burned up" (2 Pet 3:10).

In *Corrupting the Image 2*, we studied how God's domain was one with ours before the Fall in the Garden of Eden. God and Man enjoyed fellowship in the same dimensional plane. When sin entered, a veil had to come between us for our protection.

The veil between our dimension and God's is analogous to the magnetosphere that surrounds the planet and protects us from solar and cosmic rays, so that we are not blasted by the sun. We cannot see it or touch it, but we know it is there. The veil is of a similar nature; it is a kind of shield—a force field or separating membrane—that shields us, and our corrupted degenerate earth, from God's righteous fire. Whose holiness is now incompatible with the fallen state of our domain.

The passage, "When the Lord Jesus is revealed (απoκαλυψει *apokalypsei*) from heaven with His mighty angels" (2 Thess 1:7), describes the moment He is "unveiled," and the barrier is removed, reuniting the two domains. Scripture declares, "He will destroy on this mountain the surface of the **covering** cast over all people, and the **veil** that is spread over all nations" (Isa 25:7).

There are four distinct places where the veil (heavens) opens:

- Ezekiel: "I saw the heavens were opened and I saw visions of God" (Ezek 1:1).
- ... Jesus came up ... and the heavens were opened to Him... (Matt 3:16).
- Stephen: "I see the heavens opened and the Son of Man standing at the right hand of God!" (Acts 7:55-56).
- John: "... I saw heaven opened ... Jesus was on a white horse..." (Rev 19:11).

What happened when Ezekiel was sitting with the captives by the River Chebar? Did all the planets move over, effectively opening a window, or was the sun knocked out of its place—or something like that? No. Ezekiel was able to see through this dimension into another dimension. At Jesus' baptism the heavens were opened, the planets and stars did not move over, but a portal was opened between these two places. The same is true for the other two passages.

"I saw heaven opened ... Jesus was on a white horse ..." (Rev 19:11).

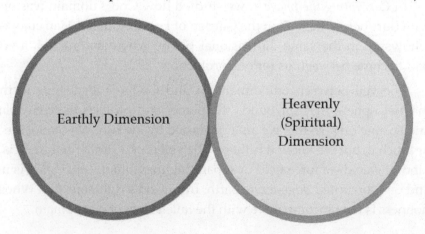

Figure 40. The two Dominions of Earthly and Heavenly Dimensions.

CHAPTER 19: THE SKY OPENS AT JESUS' COMING!

Heaven opening is the same as the "sky receding," and it is at this point that Scripture reveals. "The sky receded as a scroll when it is rolled up ..." (Rev 6:14).

In this age, we have the earthly dimension that Satan rules; he is the god of this world. God rules the heavenly—spiritual—realm. When Jesus comes back, the heavens will be opened, and He will make war against Satan, the Beast, and their forces. Isaiah 25 speaks of the veil between heaven and earth:

> "He will destroy on this mountain the surface of the covering cast over all people, and the **veil** that is spread over all nations" (Isa 25:7).

They are separated (see Figure 42). It was, "by Him to reconcile all things to Himself, by Him, whether things on earth or things in heaven, having made peace through the blood of His cross" (Col 1:20). Peter said in Acts 3 concerning Jesus, "Whom heaven must receive until the times of restoration of all things" (Acts 3:21). Jesus will remain in the spiritual (heavenly) dimension until the time of restoration.

John said,

> "His eyes were like a flame of fire, and on His head were many crowns. He had a name written that no one knew except Himself. He was clothed with a robe dipped in blood, and His name is called The Word of God. And the armies in heaven, clothed in fine linen, white and clean, followed Him on white horses. Now out of His mouth goes a sharp sword, that with it He should strike the nations. And He Himself will rule them with a rod of iron. He Himself treads the winepress of the fierceness and wrath of Almighty God" (Rev 19:12–15).

A sword is a tool that cuts and pierces. It may well be related to the quality of Jesus' voice which is described as "a loud voice, as of a trumpet" (Rev 1:10) and, "His voice as the sound of many waters," (Rev 1:15), and "Out of His mouth went a sharp two-edged sword" (Rev 1:16). If we combine these descriptions, we see his voice is piercing like a trumpet, weighty and voluminous like the sound of many waters and appears like a two-edged sword.

This same trumpeting quality is what was heard at Sinai, which is also a good preview of what we might hear as He comes into this realm.

"Then it came to pass on the third day, in the morning, that there were **thunderings** and **lightnings**, and a thick cloud on the mountain; and the **sound** of the **trumpet** was very loud, so that all the people who were in the camp trembled. And Moses brought the people out of the camp to meet with God, and they stood at the foot of the mountain. Now Mount Sinai was completely in **smoke**, because the **LORD descended** upon it in **fire**. Its smoke ascended like the smoke of a furnace, and the whole mountain quaked greatly" (Exod 19:16–18).

Just like at Mt. Sinai, there were thunderings and lightnings with smoke and fire causing the mountain to quake greatly, so too will the earth shake greatly and burn at the coming of Jesus. Due to the Jerusalem leadership calling upon Jesus, it will finally be the time for Jesus to repay his enemies according to their deeds (Isa 59:18), and to bring the restoration of all things in heaven and earth. An angel will come out of the heavenly temple and will cry, "Thrust in Your sickle and reap, for the time has come for You to reap, for the harvest of the earth is ripe" (Rev 14:15, Joel 3:13). The temple in heaven will open followed by lightning and thunder (Rev 11:15–19) Then, Jesus will "roar from Zion" and "the heavens and earth will shake" (Joel 3:16). Jesus' indignation (wrath) (Isa 26:20) begins when He "comes out of His place to punish the inhabitants of the earth for their iniquity" (Isa 26:21). Paul speaks of this in his letter to the Thessalonians: "the Lord Jesus is revealed from heaven with His mighty angels, in **flaming fire taking vengeance** on those who do not know God…" (2 Thess 1:7–8).

As noted above, the word "Revelation" is literally the "unveiling" which in Greek is αποκαλυψει *apokalypsei*. Paul was evidently drawing from the passages we have reviewed as well as Isaiah 66:

"The LORD will come with fire and with His chariots, like a whirlwind, to render His anger with **fury**, and His rebuke with flames of fire" (Isa 66:15).

Heaven is not the only realm to suffer dramatic and frightening changes once the barrier veil is removed. As we leaned from Peter, the Earth will also suffer an epic/ apocalyptic transformation:

CHAPTER 19: THE SKY OPENS AT JESUS' COMING!

"But the day of the Lord will come as a thief in the night, in which the heavens will pass away with a great noise, and the elements will melt with fervent heat; both the earth and the works that are in it will be burned up."

Why will the earth melt? Because He is coming back in flaming fire to take vengeance on those who do not know the Lord; and He is going to judge them. This is the day when Yeshua comes back, after the heavens will have receded like a scroll. And all people on planet Earth are going to say, "Uh oh!" They thought they could make war against Jesus and win. But once He is revealed, they will know they are in big trouble; the very elements are melting under their feet.

FURY WILL SHOW ON HIS FACE

In the heavenlies, dark, thick clouds will roll out, followed by flames of fire and raging bolts of lightning lighting (Ps 18), and then all the world will see His indignation.

The New English Translation brings out the grandeur of Jesus, the mighty warrior, in Habakkuk 3: "He took his battle position and shook the earth; with a **mere look** he frightened the nations" (Hab 3:6 NET). With "His eyes like a flame of fire, and on His head many crowns" (Rev 19:12): Jesus will take his position in the open heaven, filling the sky with his awe-inspiring presence and stand there for several moments surveying the earth, which has suffered incredible carnage during the time of Jacob's trouble; All the seas and rivers have turned to blood and everything in the seas has died: all the fish, the coral, the whales, dolphins, starfish, shellfish, even the plankton are dead. He will note the locations of Satan's armies of chimeras, zombies, and demons who are ostentatiously attempting to annihilate the Jerusalemites. Their vast numbers will be of no consequence, for they will be like a drop in a bucket, and will be reckoned as dust on the scales (Isa 40:15).

Ezekiel describes God's reaction:

"When Gog comes against the land of Israel," says the Lord GOD, "My **fury** will show in My **face** (Ezek 38:18). "For in My jealousy and in the fire of My wrath I have spoken," (Ezek 38:19).

The fury on his face (Eze 38:18) is exactly why the kings of the earth and the great men say to the rocks, "Fall on us and hide us from the **face** of Him who sits on the throne, for the great day of his **wrath** has come" (Rev 6:15–17). Isaiah says they will "go into the clefts of the rocks, and into the crags of the rugged rocks, from the **terror** of the LORD and the **glory of His majesty**, when He arises to shake the earth mightily" (Isa 2:21).

The return of Jesus will not be a surprise to those who love him. For those who are in the light, his return will not be like a thief; His return is like a thief to those in darkness, according to Paul:

"You yourselves know perfectly that the day of the Lord so comes as a thief in the night (1 Thess 5:2). For when they say, 'Peace and safety!' then sudden destruction comes upon them, as labor pains upon a pregnant woman. And they shall not escape (1 Thess 5:3). But **you, brethren, are not in darkness, so that this Day should overtake you as a thief** (1 Thess 5:4). You are all sons of light and sons of the day. We are not of the night nor of darkness (1 Thess 5:5)."

Yet his return will be a big shock to "those in darkness," who are in league with the Beast and Satan. Jesus says, "If you will not watch, I will come upon you as a thief, and you will not know what hour I will come upon you" (Rev 3:3). That is, to those who are watching, his coming is expected. To those who are not watching, his coming is an utter surprise, which He stated in Revelation after the demons go to collect the nations to war against him:

"For they are spirits of demons, performing signs, which go out to the kings of the earth and of the whole world, to gather them to the battle of that great day of God Almighty (Rev 16:14). 'Behold, **I am coming as a thief**. Blessed is he who watches, and keeps his garments, lest he walk naked and they see his shame' (Rev 16:15). And they gathered them together to the place called in Hebrew, Armageddon (Rev 16:16)."

The surprise at Jesus' return will not come to the believers but to the ungodly, who have likely convinced themselves that He, the almighty God of the Bible, does not exist as such; and they should be able to defeat him. When they see the skies receding like a scroll and the fury on Jesus' face, there will be much more than a surprise; there will be dread and fright:

> "All hands will be limp, every man's **heart will melt** (Isa 13:7), and they will be **afraid**. Pangs and sorrows will take hold of them; they will be in pain as a woman in childbirth; they will be **amazed** at one another; their faces will be like flames (Isa 13:8)."

Fear takes hold of them because the day of His wrath has come:

> "Behold, the **day of the LORD comes**, cruel, with both wrath and fierce anger, to lay the land desolate; and He will destroy its sinners from it. For the stars of heaven and their constellations will not give their light; the sun will be darkened in its going forth, and the moon will not cause its light to shine. 'I will punish the world for its evil, and the wicked for their iniquity; I will halt the arrogance of the proud, and will lay low the haughtiness of the terrible' (Isa 13:9–11)."

Satan may think he has a chance to beat Jesus, but most—even mildly sane mortals—will undoubtedly feel their hearts skip a beat as they fix their eyes on the champion towering over them and the armies of heaven coming behind him. Everyone on the planet will see his brighter-than-the-sun radiance, and the powerful beams of light coming out from his hands, and the sharp sword protruding out of his mouth.

There will be no doubt, when Jesus comes back, He will come as a lion, not as a lamb. "The LORD will go forth and fight against those nations, as He fights in the day of battle" (Zech 14:3). This will be the battle of the ages, when God comes to fight on behalf of his people!

COMING ON THE CLOUDS

After Jesus has ripped open the heavens and surveyed the earth, He will descend on the clouds to fulfill his epic mission: to make God's enemies a footstool, and to fight and subdue the Beast. We see the son of Man coming in several other places:

> "Then the sign of the Son of Man will appear in heaven, and then all the tribes of the earth will mourn, and they will see the Son of Man coming on the clouds of heaven with power and great glory" (Matt 24:30).

"Now I saw **heaven opened**, and behold, a white horse. And He who sat on him was called Faithful and True, and in righteousness He judges and makes war (Rev 19:11). And the armies in heaven, clothed in fine linen, white and clean, followed Him on white horses (Rev 19:14)."

Daniel says:

"I was watching in the night visions, and behold, one like the **Son of Man**, coming with the **clouds of heaven!** He came to the Ancient of Days, and they brought Him near before Him. Then to Him was given dominion and glory and a kingdom, that all peoples, nations, and languages should serve Him. His dominion is an everlasting dominion, which shall not pass away, and His kingdom the one which shall not be destroyed" (Dan 7:13–14).

Daniel first sees in the vision how the Ancient of Days / Son of Man will come to fight for the saints, who will then be given the kingdom, and then, in verses 26-27, he is given the interpretation of the vision.

"Until the Ancient of Days came, and a judgment was made in favor of the saints of the Most High, and the time came for the saints to possess the kingdom (Dan 7:22). But the court shall be seated, and they shall take away his dominion, to consume and destroy it forever (Dan 7:26). Then the kingdom and dominion, and the greatness of the kingdoms under the whole heaven, shall be given to the people, the saints of the Most High. His kingdom is an everlasting kingdom, and all dominions shall serve and obey Him (Dan 7:27)."

There can be no mistake; Jesus is coming to fight on behalf of his people! He will fight in favor of the leadership of Jerusalem and pour out his wrath on the Beast and his followers. Paul clearly states, Jesus will reserve his wrath for the enemies of God and not to those who serve Him.

"For God did **not appoint us to wrath**, but to obtain salvation through our Lord Jesus Christ" (1 Thess 5:9).

All who put their trust in Jesus, including the newly believing leadership of Jerusalem, will not face His wrath, but will enjoy his peace and protection.

Chapter 20: Satan's Air Cover

atan's army of two hundred million chimera-manticores were effective in dealing with people, but they will not stop Jesus. Nevertheless, as his airborne detachment, they will create a front line against Jesus. Recall how we discovered the god of death, Nergal, (yet another syncretism for Satan and or Nimrod) was described perfectly as the creature coming out of the abyss in Revelation 9. Satan very possibly had hoped to release that army on the world at Jesus' first coming, but he was thwarted by Jesus' decree: that the gates of Hades would not prevail; and by his actions on top of Hermon, and ultimately by his resurrection.

Figure 41. 8th century BCE Assyrian Cylinder Seal, Source: Walters Art Museum/Wikimedia Commons.

Nevertheless, once released, that army will quickly move into action. We know that they will use their serpent-head tails[311] to inflict pain on all who do not have the mark of God for five months. However, once that task is complete, we can infer that their job will be to defend Satan's strategic target of Jerusalem.

---

[311] We discussed how this word likely meant "phallus" in *Corrupting the Image 2*.

Satan had tried to stand in Jesus' way when Jesus was on a mission before. When Jesus crossed the Sea of Galilee with his disciples, Satan sent a furious storm to try to kill him and his disciples. The disciples panicked and woke their master, who seemed a bit disappointed that they interrupted his restful nap for such a small matter. 'Oh ye of little faith, why did you disrupt my nap?' While He was awakening from his sleep, He chastised them for having so little faith. Only after standing up did He rebuke the wind and waves! Satan had tried to put up a barrier to block Jesus from coming into his territory by stirring up the waves into a powerful storm. When they got to land, two demoniacs met them, at least one of whom had a legion of demons inside him, which is 4,000-6,000 demons! That was a whole army of unclean spirits that Satan had sent to prevent Jesus from accessing Bashan, the territory that formerly housed the "remnant of the giants" (Joshua 12:4) and was currently casting a "shadow of death" on the Galilee (Isa 9:2). Satan deployed a storm and legion of demons to shield the land of Bashan—his snake-dragon headquarters. Like Ronald Reagan envisioned his Strategic Defense Initiative, "Star Wars," Satan went on the defense and in essence, raised the deflector shield. In the end, Satan will again try to stop Jesus by raising a protective dome over the Jerusalemites that He is coming to rescue, the ones who had just said "Baruch Haba B'shem Adonai." Though Satan is on the defense, he may still have one final option. Because God said: "In that day the LORD will defend the inhabitants of Jerusalem" (Zech 12:8), Satan may believe if he can destroy all the inhabitants of Jerusalem, he can prove God a liar and then be able to negotiate a "cease-fire." Nevertheless, his back is now up against a wall; as this time, God is the one setting the trap.

Satan knows Jesus is coming in the air to rescue those in Jerusalem; He may send those wall-scaling, hive-minded chimeras to form an interlocking dome over Jerusalem.

> "They look like horses ... They scale walls like soldiers. Each one proceeds on his course; they do not alter their path. They do not jostle one another ... The earth quakes before them; the sky reverberates. The sun and the moon grow dark" (Joel 2: 4a, 7–8a; 10 NET).

266

They will provide air protection while his army of zombies attacks the remnant of Jerusalemites on the ground. We discover this from several passages. First of all, God says:

> "You will come up against My people Israel like a cloud, to cover the land. It will be in the latter days that I will bring you against My land, so that the nations may know Me, when I am hallowed in you, O Gog, before their eyes" (Ezek 38:16).

While we cannot deny that "like a cloud" could be interpreted just to mean something voluminous; alternatively, it may be understood to be a mimic of Jesus' departure and return on the clouds (Acts 1:9–11). It appears that 200 million, battle-ready, horse-like chimeras will thunder into Jerusalem like bees who swarm but don't bump into each other, to cover the land in a cloud-ceiling that blocks out the light from the sky. Satan has set his sights on defeating God, claiming Jerusalem (above and below) and sitting on God's throne. He may deploy his own version of an "iron dome," but God will fight in both realms. Isaiah tells us how God will fight at the time of the sky rolling up, and his sword will slaughter heavenly powers:

> "For the LORD is angry at all the nations and furious with all their armies. He will annihilate them and slaughter them (Isa 34:2). Their slain will be left unburied, their corpses will stink; the hills will soak up their blood (Isa 34:3). **All the stars in the sky will fade away, the sky will roll up like a scroll; all its stars will wither,** like a leaf withers and falls from a vine or a fig withers and falls from a tree (Isa 34:4). He says, 'Indeed, **my sword has slaughtered heavenly powers.** Look, it now descends on Edom, on the people I will annihilate in judgment' (Isa 34:5 NET)."

ANGELS ARE STARS

There are some important clues in this pericope: "All the stars in the sky will fade away" ("All the host of heaven shall be dissolved" NKJV). This refers to angelic beings, not the incandescent burning bodies that astronomy calls "stars." If it were talking about astronomical stars, then ALL the stars from Alpha Centari to Beetlejuice to the super giants and our own sun would need to fall to the earth. If that happened there would be no earth, the planet would be done.

267

Angels are often referred to as stars, especially in the book of Revelation. In chapter twelve, the "dragon" taking stars with its tail is the same as the dragon and his angels being cast to the earth.

- a great, fiery red dragon (Rev 12:3). His tail drew a third of the **stars** of heaven and threw them to the earth (Rev 12:4).
- the great dragon was cast out ... and his **angels** were cast out with him (Rev 12:9).
- The seven **stars** are the **angels** [*angeloi* ἄγγελοι] of the seven churches ... (Rev 1:20).
- it cast down some of the host [of heaven] and some of the stars to the ground, and trampled them (Dan 8:10).
- All the host of heaven [fallen angels] shall be dissolved ... All their host shall fall down ... as fruit falling from a fig tree (Isa 34:4; Rev 6:13).
- Then the third angel sounded: and a great star fell from heaven, burning like a torch, and it fell on a third of the rivers and on the springs of water (Rev 8:10).

In prophetic language, stars equal angelic beings.

"And I saw a star fallen from heaven to the earth. To him was given the key to the bottomless pit. And he opened the bottomless pit" (Rev 9:1-2).

That meaning is further underscored in the book of Job where the sons of God are also called stars. When the morning stars sang together, and all the sons of God (*benei ha'elohim*) shouted for joy? (Job 38:7). Nevertheless, the use of stars in the book of Revelation firmly establishes that "stars" is a reference to angels.[312] Thus, without doubt, the picture drawn is that of God doing battle against some of Satan's angels in the atmosphere, not on the planet's surface.

So, the "host" are bad angels that face judgment on the "day that the LORD will punish on high the host of exalted ones, and on the earth the kings of the earth" (Isa 24:21).

---

[312] As evidenced BDAG, classical Greek literature sometimes considered "stars" to be sentient beings. See: Stoicorum Veterum Fragmenta, coll. J(H)vArnim I–IV 1903–24. See also: Chrysippus, phil., ed. J(H) vArnim, Stoicorum veterum fragmenta II 1903 III b.c.

The "stars falling to the ground like figs" in Revelation are referred to as the "host of heaven falling" in Isaiah. We see that many other places in Scripture the term *tzevah hashamaim* is talking about the armies of heaven, which is the literal translation demonstrated in a scene in 1 Kings in which God is surrounded by the host of heaven [צְבָא הַשָּׁמַיִם *tzevah hashamaim*] (1 Kgs 22:19).

There are many examples that demonstrate that the phrase is typically referring to angels. In Jeremiah 19, the hosts of heaven are equated with "gods."

"Because of all the houses upon whose roofs they have burned incense unto **all the host of heaven** [הַשָּׁמַיִם [צְבָא], and have poured out drink offerings **unto other gods**" (Jer 19:13 KJV).

Those "gods," "host of heaven" or "fallen angels," are also referred to as the armies of exalted ones in the heavens, in Isaiah 24, which happens at "that time," which is a reference to the Day of the Lord.

"And it will come about at that time, the Lord will punish the **armies** [*tzevah* צְבָא] of the **exalted ones in the heavens**, and the rulers of the earth on earth" (Isa 24:21 ISV).

Paul, writing to the Ephesians, refers to the reality of the adverse cosmic powers (κοσμοκράτοράςας *cosmokratoras*). Those cosmic powers, which are all around us, are part of the spiritual forces that are in the heavenly realm, which is a reference to angels and not to balls of gas in outer space.

"For our struggle is not against human opponents, but against rulers, authorities, **cosmic powers** in the darkness around us, and evil spiritual forces in the **heavenly realm**" (Eph 6:12 ISV).

Now we are prepared to understand what Jesus meant when He said, "the **powers of heaven** will be shaken loose" (Matt 24:29 ISV). He was not referring to the sun, moon, and stars going away. Rather He was referring to the cataclysmic changes occurring among the heavenly powers and Satan's angelic servants.

Sword has Slaughtered Heavenly Powers

We remember that Satan and his angels were cast to the earth. They lost their ability to be on the other side of the veil. In *Corrupting the Image 2*, we considered how Satan and his angels yearn for a body; this led them to create the Nephilim to serve as bio-suits, but the experiment failed. In the end times, Satan has now fused with the Beast, and his angels have fused with the Manticores, and potentially also humans who have taken the mark.

Thus, Jesus is going to fight fleshly-spiritual beings; "Their slain will be left unburied, their corpses will stink; **the hills will soak up their blood**" (Isa 34:3). The location of this battle is clearly in the heavens, given the description, his **"sword has slaughtered heavenly powers."**

The heavenly powers that He slaughters are the lesser gods. God Almighty judges among the gods. The term "gods" does not mean entities that have real power to go against God, but angels, in the sense that He has arranged a hierarchy of positions. Some angels have been faithful; others have been unfaithful. And here He is speaking to the ones that have been unfaithful. This must be the fulfillment found in Psalm 82:

"I said, 'You are gods, and all of you are children of the Most High' (Ps 82:6). But you shall die like men, and fall like one of the princes" (Ps 82:7).

The fact that they will die like men is noteworthy. In other words, something has happened to them. We catch a glimpse of this in Isaiah 14 where God reveals what will happen to Babylon and the king of Babylon, who is Satan in this case. It says:

"The LORD's sword is dripping with blood, it is covered with fat; it drips with the blood of young rams and goats and is covered with the fat of rams' kidneys. For the LORD is holding a sacrifice in Bozrah, a bloody slaughter in the land of Edom" (Isa 34:6).

Dr. Bob Utley explains the imagery of the blood of young rams[313] and goats: "here Edom (like Moab earlier) is symbolic of all the arrogant nations who rebel against God." Lange and Schaff explain this section:

> "Isa 34:4 pictures the judgment that shall be executed on the heavens, but here the Prophet combines intention and performance. He contemplates the judgment of God as beginning in heaven, and continued on earth."[314]

Thus, the judgment begins with God's sword being bloody in the heavens, and then being bloody from activity on the earth.

> "Wild oxen will be slaughtered along with them, as well as strong bulls [אַבִּירִים]. Their land is drenched with blood, their soil is covered with fat (Isa 34:7). For the LORD has planned a day of revenge, a time when he will repay Edom for her hostility toward Zion (Isa 34:8 NET)."

In *Corrupting the Image 2*, we explored the phrase "bulls of Bashan," [אַבִּירֵי *abirei*] which TWOT defines as "mighty," "strong," or "brave," and carries a connotation of a bull-god. TWOT notes "'*ābîr* relates to the Akkadian *abāru* "be strong."… it may be an element in a divine name in Ugaritic "the Mighty One of Hadd." Psalm 78 says, "Men ate angels' [אַבִּירִים *abirim*] food … "(Ps 78:25), and the translators render it as angels, that is, mighty ones, instead of bulls. In other word, these bull are spiritual beings. They were present at the crucifixion, encompassing the crucified Jesus, with their hideous faces in a diabolic jubilation, thinking that Jesus and his work were defeated. They were so preoccupied with jeering and mocking Jesus, they were oblivious to the fact that Jesus was gaining supreme victory over death.

---

[313] UTLEY Isaiah 34:5. Consider also K&D Isaiah 35:5-7: "The lambs, he-goats, and rams, represent the Edomitish nation, which is compared to these smaller sacrificial animals. Edom and Bozrah are also placed side by side in Isa 63:1. The latter was one of the chief cities of the Edomites (Gen 36:33; Amo 1:12; Jer 49:13, Jer 49:22) - not the Bozrah in Auranitis (Haurân), however, which is well known in church history, but Bozrah in the mountains of Edom, upon the same site as the village of Buzaire (i.e., Minor Bozrah),"

[314] Lange Commentary Isaiah 34:7 J.P. Lange, Philip Schaff Isa 34:5-8.

Thus, Jesus is fighting angels who were "gods," but will die as men. In the end times, they will have become corporeal and flesh and will be attempting to stop Jesus from getting to Jerusalem; just as they once tried to stop him from crossing the Sea of Galilee. Jesus will go toe to toe with the mighty bulls of Bashan—clones of Batios, the great bull-god of Mt. Hermon!

"Look, it now descends on Edom, on the people I will annihilate in judgment" (Isa 34:5 NET).

Later the same prophet asks,

"Who is this who comes from Edom [מֵאֱדוֹם *me'Edom*], with dyed garments from Bozrah, this One who is glorious in His apparel, traveling in the greatness of His strength?– 'I who speak in righteousness, mighty to save' (Isa 63:1). Who is this who comes from Edom, Why is Your apparel red [אָדֹם *adom*], and Your garments like one who treads in the winepress? (Isa 63:2)."

This of course, is the very same place where God said he would bathe his sword in blood in heaven (and then turn it to the earth). There is a clear word play going on between Edom and red [אָדֹם *adom*] (Isa 63:2), which both share the same root [אדם] "'ādōm, 'ādēm. To be red."[315]

---

[315] Which in "Old Akkadian 'adāmu "dark red," as of a garment, Akkadian adamātu "dark red soil" and adamu "red blood," and Aramaic 'ādam, as of blood." Esau was given this name because he gave up his birthright when he said, "to Jacob, "Please feed me with that same red stew, for I am weary." Therefore his name was called Edom," (Gen 25:30).

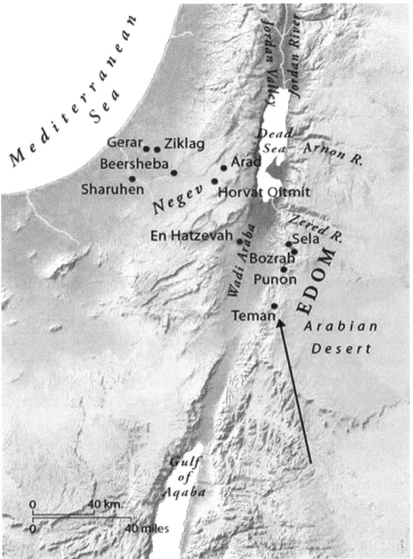

Figure 42. Map of Middle East showing Teman.

Isaiah is seeing that the one glorious in apparel and mighty to save (Yeshua) is coming from the same place where he said he would bathe his sword in blood in the heavens and on the earth. Jesus (Yeshua) answers:

"I have trodden the winepress alone, and from the peoples no one was with Me. For I have trodden them in My anger, and trampled them in My fury; their blood is sprinkled upon My garments, and I have stained all My robes" (Isa 63:3).

273

In other words, the same fury that would show on his face (Ezek 38:19), and the anger and fury toward the nations (Isa 34:2) will be expressed in part by a battle in the atmosphere. The prophet Habakkuk speaks of a battle in the same general area. We already noted from this passage how He will frighten the nations with a mere look (Hab 3:6 NET). The location of that event will be in Teman.

"God comes from Teman, the Holy One from Mount Paran. Selah. His splendor has covered the skies, the earth is full of his glory (Hab 3:3). His brightness will be as lightning; a two-pronged lightning bolt flashing from his hand. This is the outward display of his power (Hab 3:4). Plague will go before him; pestilence will march right behind him (Hab 3:5)."

The prophet notes that God (Jesus) is coming from a southernly direction to Israel. Both Teman and Bozrah are around Edom (modern day Jordan). Isaiah said He was glorious in his apparel, and Habakkuk notes his splendor covered the skies, revealing that Jesus is in the sky. The prophet also reveals his weapon; Jesus has bolts of lightning "flashing from his hand ... the outward display of his power." Clearly, Jesus is coming to do battle in the sky and He will shoot bolts of lightning against His enemies. Isaiah explains the motivation for this mighty warrior:

"For the day of vengeance is in My heart, and the year of My redeemed has come (Isa 63:4). I looked, but there was no one to help, and I wondered that there was no one to uphold; therefore My own arm brought salvation for Me; and My own fury, it sustained Me (Isa 63:5)."

Jesus does not come back and merely snap his fingers to end Satan's rule. As God, He presumably could do such a thing, but for a good reason He chooses not to. Rather than speculate why He does not, it is better to discuss what He does instead. He comes with lightning bolts in his hand and fights against the two hundred million Manticores that Satan has released from the abyss. Satan had prepared for this day, and like a good general, he brought out his secret weapon to use against his foe at an "above earth" level in the atmosphere. Nevertheless, Jesus will ultimately vanquish them; "Their slain will be left unburied, their corpses will stink; the **hills will soak up their blood**" (Isa 34:3). Ezekiel notes, concerning Satan's forces:

"You shall fall upon the **mountains** of Israel, you and all your troops and the peoples who are with you; I will give you to birds of prey of every sort and to the beasts of the field to be devoured" (Ezek 39:4).

Jesus eventually breaks through the manticore dome surrounding Jerusalem, which Satan hoped would stop Jesus from getting through to save His redeemed.

In Isaiah 63, the prophet asks,

"Why is Your apparel red ... (Isa 63:2) 'I have trodden the winepress alone [see also Revelation 14, Micah 4:12 and in Joel 3], and from the peoples no one was with Me. For I have trodden them in My anger, and trampled them in My fury; their blood is sprinkled upon My garments... (Isa 63:3) For the day of vengeance is in My heart, and the year of My redeemed has come (Isa 63:4). For I have trodden them in My anger, and trampled them in My fury; their blood is sprinkled upon My garments... (Isa 63:3) For the day of vengeance is in My heart, and the year of My redeemed has come' (Isa 63:4)."

JESUS' ARMY OF HOLY ONES

YHWH (LORD) of hosts is a common epithet of the God of Abraham, Isaac and Jacob. "Hosts" [צְבָאוֹת *Tsavoth*] means "armies." God came with his armies, that is, his holy angels when he came down to Sinai in a show of lightning, thunder, fire, and earthquake (Exod 19).

"The LORD came from Sinai, and dawned on them from Seir; He shone forth from Mount Paran, and He came with ten thousands of saints [holy ones]; from His right hand came a fiery law for them" (Deut 33:2).

King David describes the incredible number of chariots coming with God in the same Psalm where he talked about Bashan (Mt Hermon - the very place where Jesus later took three disciples and transfigured before them); and where the angels had descended in the days of Noah, as we studied in *Corrupting the Image 2*. "The chariots of God are twenty thousand, even thousands of thousands; the Lord is among them as in Sinai, in the Holy Place" (Ps 68:17).

"When Elisha and his servant woke to find themselves surrounded by the army of the Syrians, Elisha asked and "[YHWH] the LORD opened the eyes of the young man, and he saw. And behold, the mountain was full of horses and **chariots** of **fire** all around Elisha" (2 Kgs 6:17).

Notice how Isaiah envisions the Lord God when He comes down to judge the world:

"For behold, the LORD will come with **fire** and with His **chariots**, like a whirlwind, to render His anger with fury, and His rebuke with flames of fire. For by **fire** and by His **sword** the LORD will judge all flesh; and the slain of the LORD shall be many" (Isa 66:15–16).

This very description is said of Jesus who will be "revealed from heaven with His mighty angels, (2 Thess 1:7) in flaming **fire** taking vengeance on those who do not know God" (2 Thess 1:8).

Jesus himself said that he, "the Son of Man will come in the glory of His Father with His angels, and then He will reward each according to his works" (Matt 16:27, see also 25:31). John wrote of this retinue coming with Jesus, as well: "And the armies in heaven, clothed in fine linen, white and clean, followed Him on white horses" (Rev 19:14). It is impossible to say this retinue does not include humans. However, the emphasis is clearly on angels, in light of the other passages we have just reviewed; and, in light of Jude, who also states how the "Lord comes with ten thousands of His saints [holy ones], to execute judgment on all" (Jude 1:14–15). Jesus is coming to do battle against the millions in Satan's freshly created hybrid army.

Chapter 21: Rephaim Cast Down

Jesus' wrath is directed specifically against the Beast (Satan's Avatar). The leadership of Jerusalem and all who call upon the name of Jesus will be spared that wrath. "For God did not appoint us to wrath, but to obtain salvation through our Lord Jesus Christ" (1 Thess 5:9). Isaiah says that God's people will escape his wrath in rooms or chambers.

> "Come, my people, enter your chambers, and shut your doors behind you; hide yourself, as it were, for a little moment, until the indignation is past" (Isa 26:20).

In context, we see that this "hiding yourself" is happening concurrently with the time of the resurrection. It is very revealing to review the preceding verse in the NKJV, which reads:

> "Your dead shall live; together with my dead body they shall arise. Awake and sing, you who dwell in dust; for your dew is like the **dew of herbs**, and the earth shall cast out the dead" (Isa 26:19).

The use of the words "dew of herbs" and "dead," in the Hebrew text, present us with exciting details. The word translated as "dead" is actually "Rephaim," and is not rendered literally by many translations. Therefore, after a closer look, I decided to do my own translation, which is based on the Hebrew and corroborated by the Latin Vulgate:

> "Your dead will live, my corpse, they will rise; wake up [הָקִיצוּ *hakitzu*] and rejoice O dwellers of the dust because the dew of lights [טַל אֹורֹת *tal orot*] is your dew and the earth will cause the Rephaim [רְפָאִים] to fall [תַּפִּיל *tappil*]" (Isa 26:19 **My translation**).

The first thing we notice is the call to the dead (dwellers of the dust) to wake up [הָקִיצוּ *hakitzu*]. It is the same word used in Daniel, where those sleeping in the dust will wake. The only difference is Isaiah's version is a command to "wake!" and Daniel's is in the future tense, "will awake."

"And many of those who sleep **in the dust** of the earth **shall awake [יָקִיצוּ]**... (Dan 12:2) Those who are wise shall **shine** like the brightness of the firmament, and those who turn many to righteousness like the stars forever and ever" (Dan 12:3).

In Daniel's prophecy, we learn that those who wake will shine. In my translation of Isaiah 26, I translated *tal orot* [טַל אוֹרֹת] as "dew of lights." The idea is people are dwelling in the ground. When they awake, they will be covered with dew like someone who slept outside. However, this dew is not of herbs (grass), but of lights [אוֹרֹת]. When we compare this with Daniel's account ("shall shine"), we find they are parallel.

Lastly, Isaiah uses the feminine singular "hiphil" form of the verb *naphal* (to fall).[316] The hiphil is the causative aspect of the verb, which means: the earth will cause the Rephaim to fall. We examined the Rephaim in detail in *Corrupting the Image 2* and determined they are angel-human hybrids. The Latin Vulgate confirms our reading by translating it as *"et terram gigantum detrahes in ruinam* (Isa 26:19 VUL) "and the earth will drag down the giants in ruin."

God's Awesome and Unusual Work

In Isaiah 28, God revealed that He would do an amazing, unusual work where He says He will fight Rephaim (which are the transformed people who have taken the mark of the Beast, altering their core genetic makeup and rendering them hybrids). This transformation is almost certainly the reason we are told: "In those days men will seek death and will not find it; they will desire to die, and death will flee from them" (Rev 9:6).

With the call and supplication of Jerusalem's leadership to Jesus, God (Jesus) does an "unusual act."

"For the LORD will rise up as at Mount Perazim, He will be angry as in the Valley of Gibeon– that He may do His work, His **awesome** work, and bring to pass His act, His **unusual** act" (Isa 28:21).

---

[316] נָפַל 1392 nāpal TWOT: fall, lie, be cast down, fail... a violent or accidental circumstance is often indicated.

To understand the significance, we need to understand what happened at those two places. In the Valley of Gibeon, God listened to a man concerning the sun and moon.

"Then Joshua spoke to the LORD in the day when the LORD delivered up the Amorites before the children of Israel ... 'Sun, stand still over **Gibeon**; and Moon, in the Valley of Aijalon.' So the sun stood ... till the people had revenge upon their enemies..." (Josh 10:12–13).

Joshua and the children of Israel were facing the Amorites who were Rephaim, (genetic hybrids) that were an abomination in God's sight—beings emerging not from God's will but that of Satan's. We have seen this multiple times through the *Corrupting the Image* series. Here are summary verses:

- The **Amorites** ... are stronger than we are ... and all the people that we saw in it are of great height... we saw the **Nephilim** (the sons of **Anak**, who come from the Nephilim) ... (Numb 13:29–33, ESV).
- **Rephaim** ... a people great and many, and tall as the **Anakim** (Deut 2:20–21a, ESV).

God says it was He who "destroyed the Amorite ... whose height was like the height of the cedars" (Amos 2:9). God's "awesome work," and "unusual act" in the Valley of Gibeon was fighting against hybrids.

Next, at Mount Perazim, David fought the Philistines, some of whom were genetic hybrids, like Goliath and his brothers (who in Hebrew are called Rephaim and in Greek, *gigantes* / giants).

- At Gath, where there was a man of great stature ... and he also was descended from the **giants [רפה rapha]** (2 Sam 21:20 ESV).
- Lahmi the brother of Goliath the Gittite [Gath] ... he also was descended from the giants [Rephaim] ... These were descended from the giants in Gath (I Chron 20:5–6, 8 ESV).

David was fighting the Philistines who "went and deployed themselves in the Valley of Rephaim [רְפָאִים עֵמֶק *emek Rephaim*]" (2 Sam 5:18). The Septuagint reads "την κοιλαδα των τιτανων "the valley of the Titans."

We explored the Rephaim and Titans extensively in *Corrupting the Image 2* and concluded they were angel-human hybrids. Mount Perazim is the Valley of the Rephaim / Titans, a place where a battle occurred against hybrids and the principalities and powers which David intimates in this his victory cry:

"'The LORD has broken through my enemies before me, like a breakthrough of water.' Therefore he called the name of that place Baal Perazim" (2 Sam 5:20; 1 Chr 14:11).

Those who fled from before David (and ultimately YHWH), "left their images there... (2 Sam 5:21) to which: "David gave a commandment, and they were burned with fire" (1 Chr 14:12). God's "awesome work," and "unusual act" at Mount Perazim, which Isaiah spoke of (Isa 28:21) was that God was fighting against Rephaim / Titans and the principalities and powers; and He broke through like water. Then, the vestiges of the battle (the images) were burned with fire. God is saying He is going to do that amazing work again! He tells the mockers and scornful men in Jerusalem:

"Now therefore, do not be mockers, lest your bonds be made strong; for I have heard from the Lord GOD of hosts, a destruction determined even upon the whole earth" (Isa 28:22).

The destruction is coming upon the entire planet because the entire planet is coming against Israel. "The LORD will go forth and fight against those nations, as He fights in the day of battle" (Zech 14:3). When Jesus comes back, He will come as a lion, not a lamb. Ezekiel says,

"When Gog comes against the land of Israel," says the Lord GOD, "that My fury will show in My face (Ezek 38:18). "For in My jealousy and in the fire of My wrath I have spoken," (Ezek 38:19).

Jesus spoke of how He would bring fire on the earth one day: "I came to send fire on the earth, and how I wish it were already kindled!" (Luke 12:49).

This battle of the ages is what the Bible calls the Battle of Armageddon.

Chapter 22: Armageddon and the Valley of Jehoshaphat

The impending battle will be the cataclysmic, battle of the ages. Nothing will be bigger, and nothing will be more significant than this battle. World War I was astounding; World War II was mindboggling, but nothing will top the final battle known as Armageddon. Under the command of the Beast, all who have taken the mark and worshipped the Image from every nation will be united to fight against Jesus so Satan can keep earth as his domain.

All nations will assemble / gather there to battle and God himself will fight and judge in the Valley of Jehoshaphat [יְהוֹשָׁפָט *Yehoshafat*], which in Hebrew means: "Yehovah will judge."

"Prepare for war! Wake up the mighty men, let all the men of war draw near, let them come up. Beat your plowshares into swords …" (Joel 3:9) "Assemble and come, **all you nations…**" (Joel 3:11) "Let the nations be wakened, and come up to the **Valley of Jehoshaphat**; for there I will sit to **judge** all the surrounding nations" (Joel 3:12).

God tells us that many nations are going to come against Jerusalem, but they do not know the thoughts of the Lord (Mic 4:12). In Joel, God says, "Let the nations come to the Valley of Jehoshaphat" (where Yehovah judges) because that is where He is going to put in his sickle and harvest. He invites them to take part in this epic battle and advises them to make weapons by beating plowshares into swords so they can fight Him.

The world will come to Jerusalem to fight in the battle of all battles, as attested by many passages:

- I will make **Jerusalem** a cup of drunkenness to all the surrounding peoples, when they lay siege against Judah and **Jerusalem**. And it shall happen in that day that I will make **Jerusalem** a very heavy stone for all peoples; all who would heave it away will surely be cut in pieces, though **all nations** of the earth are gathered against it (Zech 12:2–3).
- It shall be in that day that I will seek to destroy **all the nations** that come against **Jerusalem** (Zech 12:9).

- For I will gather **all the nations** to battle against **Jerusalem** (Zech 14:2).
- And the winepress was trampled outside **the city** (Rev 14:20).
- You shall fall on the **mountains of Israel**, you and all your hordes … with you [Speaking of Gog] (Ezek 39:4).

These are all one and the same event. Next, Joel urges God to: "Put in the **sickle**, for the **harvest** is **ripe**. Come, go down; for the **winepress** is full, the vats overflow– for their wickedness is great" (Joel 3:13). This is the same language we find in Revelation where an angel calls out: "Thrust in Your **sickle** and reap, for the time has come for You to reap, for the **harvest** of the earth is **ripe**" (Rev 14:15). The result is that "the winepress [of God] was trampled "**outside the city**" (Rev 14:20). All nations of the world will come against Jerusalem, therefore, "outside the city" is not outside of Phoenix, Denver, or Tel Aviv. It is right outside of Jerusalem. This is where this winepress event is going to happen.

Figure 43. Ancient city of Jerusalem showing the Hinnom and Kidron Valleys.

The city in question is Jerusalem. Joel tells us about the hordes of people who will be in the valley at the end of the age, on the Day of the Lord, when the sun and moon will grow dark, as stated in the Revelation, Isaiah, and other passages.

> **"Multitudes**, multitudes in the valley of decision! For the day of the LORD is near in the valley of decision (Joel 3:14). The sun and moon will grow dark, and the stars will diminish their brightness (Joel 3:15). The LORD also will roar from Zion, and utter His voice from **Jerusalem**; the heavens and earth will shake (Joel 3:16)."

The winepress: Valley of Decision and Valley of Jehoshaphat (lit. Yehovah judges), are the same, which is just outside the city. The area is also known as the Kidron Valley, which is adjacent to Gehenna or Ge Ben-Hinnom Valley.

This location is historically significant. It's not by coincidence that the book of Joshua 18:6 calls this place "the Valley of Rephaim" and the Valley of Hinnom.

> "Then the border came down to the end of the mountain that lies before the Valley of the Son of **Hinnom** [גֵּ֣י בֶן־הִנֹּם֙ *gei-ben-Hinnom*], which is in the **Valley of Rephaim** on the north ..." (Josh 18:6) "... descended to the **Valley of Hinnom** [גֵּ֣י הִנֹּם֙ *gei-Hinnom*], to the side of the Jebusite city on the south, and descended to En Rogel" (Josh 18:16; see also Josh 15:8).

Rephaim are the same as the Anakim, which are Nephilim or hybrids. In other words, Gehenna was in the Valley of the Rephaim, the valley of Satan's hybrids (including King Og)! It was in the same area, on the Mount of Corruption, that Solomon demonstrated his lack of wisdom.

> "Then Solomon built a high place for Chemosh the abomination of Moab, on the **hill** that is east of Jerusalem, and for Molech the abomination of the people of Ammon" (1 Kgs 11:7).

Then, "he burned incense in the **Valley of the Son of Hinnom**, and burned his children in the fire, according to the abominations of the nations..." (2 Chr 28:3). Sadly, Israel's wisest king committed the very things God said not to do, lest their heart should depart from him.

Later Josiah, who was a good king—the one who found the Torah in the temple and tried to undo some of the heinous sins of the nation:

"He defiled Tophet, which is in the Valley of the Son of Hinnom [גֵּיא בֶן־הִנֹּם *gei-ben-Hinnom*], that no man might make his son or his daughter pass through the fire to Molech (2 Kgs 23:10). Then the king defiled the high places that were east of Jerusalem, which were on the south of the Mount of Corruption [next to the Mount of Olives], which Solomon king of Israel had built for Ashtoreth the abomination of the Sidonians, for Chemosh the abomination of the Moabites, and for Milcom the abomination of the people of Ammon" (2 Kgs 23:13).

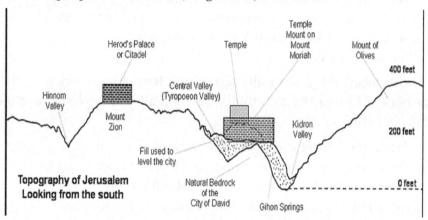

Figure 44. Topography and elevation of Jerusalem as viewed from the south. https://www.generationword.com/jerusalembook/8.html

The place was used for horrifically cruel sacrifices of the innocent to Ashtoreth and Baal.

"Because they have forsaken Me and made this an alien place, because they have burned incense in it to other gods whom neither they, their fathers, nor the kings of Judah have known, and have **filled this place with the blood of the innocents** (Jer 19:4) (they have also built the high places of Baal, to **burn their sons with fire for burnt offerings to Baal**, which I did not command or speak, nor did it come into My mind), (Jer 19:5) 'Therefore behold, the days are coming,' says the LORD, 'that this place shall no more be called **Tophet** or the **Valley of the Son of Hinnom**, but the Valley of Slaughter (Jer 19:6).'"

The word Tophet probably comes from the word *tupim*, drums. Tophet is superimposed with another word meaning *boshet*, which means, shame. It is thought they would beat the drums as they would burn the children to the false gods. Tophet and Gehenna are the same exact place (Jer 7:31). The Valley of the Son of Hinnom in Hebrew is *gei-ben-Hinnom*. *Gei* means Valley, *ben* is son and *Hinnom* is the family name. That same locale is Akeldama (field of blood), where, after Judas (who betrayed Jesus) realized what he had done, he went and hanged himself. It is in that same location. It all happens right here. Incredibly, in this little piece of real estate just down the hill from the Old City of Jerusalem, the great final conflict and judgement will take place.

Thus, the final defeat of the false gods will occur in the same location where they demanded human sacrifices; in the place where they trampled the innocent and demanded their blood, they themselves will be trampled and their blood will come up to the horses' bridles. No more than a few hundred meters east of the Mount of Corruption, where Solomon erected altars to the false gods, Jesus will touch down on the Mount of Olives, to bring divine retribution in the fullest sense. In a word, Armageddon will be fought in this place.

THE MEANING OF ARMAGEDDON

So where is Armageddon? And what does the word mean? A popular thought is that it will take place in the Megiddo Valley in the northern part of Israel, in the Jezreel Valley, near Galilee. This notion is based on the understanding that Armageddon comes from "Mountain of Megiddo." [הר מגידו *Har Megiddo*]: Yet if you go to Megiddo, you will not find a mountain. In fact, nowhere in the Bible is there talk of a "mountain of Megiddo." 2 Chronicles 35:22, speaks of the "Valley of Megiddo," and Zechariah 12:11 mentions the "plain of Megiddo." But there is no *har-megiddon* / mountain of Megiddo(n). Hence, this trail of explanation fails to match the geographic reality.

Even though there is a Tel Megiddo, from an ancient Akkadian word, which is an artificial mound created by the repeated destruction and rebuilding of a city. Tel Megiddo has been known for a long time. Nevertheless, it is not a *"har"* mountain, and thus there is no *Har Megiddo*. This means the etymology of Armageddon must be found elsewhere.

Another theory is that it comes from Har Moed [מועד] — that is, the mountain of appointed times or seasons. The rational is that the Hebrew letter: ע "ayin," present in the word, is often transliterated as the English letter "G." For example, Gomorrah is written with the Hebrew ayin, "'amorrah." Nevertheless, when we plug in those variables, we get Har-Moged or Armoged where the "a" changed to an "o" and the final "on" is missing. Simply stated, the suggestion of Har Moed, still falls short of the word Armageddon, and we ought to keep looking for another linguistic solution.

COMPARING SPELLINGS OF ARMAGEDDON

The spelling "Armageddon" is not attested in the Byzantine (majority texts), nor in the Alexandrus and Vaticanus (the oldest New Testament text families). The only vowel that would not fit both manuscript families is the spelling with one delta Αρμαγεδων "Armagedon." In Hebrew, Megiddo/n [מגדון] has a dagesh in the dalet, meaning it should be doubled. Hence the transliteration of this word requires two deltas. We do find two deltas in the Textus Receptus,[317] (the basis of the King James text), but in the overwhelming majority of texts and in the oldest texts, there is only one delta. Thus, we have a spelling problem with the consonants. Furthermore, of the twelve times this name appears in Scripture, eleven are spelled: Megiddo, and only once with the final *nun* (N) as: Megiddon. On top of that, we have a vowel problem. The Hebrew word [מגדון], Meg-i-don has vowels, which do not fit with Ar-ma-ge-don. Simply stated, Megiddon is not related to Armageddon.

---

[317] The Textus Receptus, which comes out of the Byzantine family, is a collection of a handful of manuscripts, somewhere between six to twelve manuscripts, which in turn came from the larger tradition called the Byzantine Majority text family, which were about five thousand manuscripts.

Instead of interpreting Armageddon as "mountain of Megiddo" (Har-Megiddon), which we saw does not exist physically or linguistically, another option that fits much better and falls into place with the themes in the Bible is interpreting Armageddon as three words Arema-gei-don,[318] which would translate as the "heaps of the valley of judgment."[319]

Alexandrus / Vaticanus (oldest)	Majority/Byzantine 5000+ copies	Textus Receptus only 6 mss	Original Hebrew
Αρμαγεδων	Αρμαγεδων	Αρμαγεδδών	מְגִדּוֹן
Harmagedon	Harmagedon	Harmageddon	Megiddon

Table 10. Comparing Spelling of Armageddon.

Figure 45 Heap of grain "arema"—Image by congerdesign from Pixabay.

---

[318] Arema fits phonetically that we have to imagine is the "e" that's in there.
[319] I first heard of this basic idea at:
http://biblefocus.net/consider/v01Armageddon/Word-Armageddon-is-Hebrew-for-a-Place.html

AREMA - HEAP

Arema is a heap of sheaves. For example, when Boaz "went to lie down at the end of the heap [הָעֲרֵמָה *ha'arema*] of grain" (Ruth 3:7). (We ought not to envision processed grain that comes out of a harvester-tractor). Boaz was lying on a heap of sheaves, like a straw bed.

The word is also used regarding the destruction of Babylon; Jeremiah wrote, "Cast her up as heaps [עֲרֵמִים *aremim*] of ruins" (Jer 50:26).

Aram means to be heaped up. It occurs once in the Bible in the verbal form; and we find it in other places as a noun or heap, and we also find in Micah 4:12.

"Now also many nations have gathered against you, who say, 'Let her be defiled, and let our eye look upon Zion.' But they do not know the thoughts of the Lord, nor do they understand His counsel; for He will gather them **like sheaves** [כֶּעָמִיר *k'amir*] to the threshing floor" (Micah 4:11-12).

In Hebrew, it is called a linguistic **metathesis** where two letters can switch, and this does happen. *Amir* and *arema* both have the same meaning, but the letters can change places because of the **metathesis**. There are many examples of this happening.[320] Thus, we have the same basic meanings in *Amir* and *arema*. God says He will gather like sheaves to the threshing floor, those who are coming against Jerusalem. This motif carries through in this Armageddon/ Second Coming event. Could *arema* transliterated into Greek become *arma-?* Based on the evidence of transliterated Hebrew words in the New Testament, the answer is yes. For example, the Hebrew: *Hoshianna* [הוֹשִׁיעָה] is transliterated and reduced to Hosanna [Ωσαννα]. We also have the curious word *Ephphatha* [ἐφφαθά], which I wrote about in *Discovering the Language of Jesus* (2005). The gospel of Mark tells us the word means, "be opened." It is a Niphal imperfect (future / command) of the Hebrew verb: *patach* [פתח].

---

[320] See: Isaac Kalimi, Metathesis in the Hebrew Bible: Wordplay as a Literary and Exegetical Device (Peabody, MA: Hendrickson, 2018).

Job 12:14, Job 32:19, Ezekiel 24:27, and Ezekiel 46:1 are the only verses with the form יפתח. Three of the four have the vocalization *yippate'ach* and the fourth has *yippatach*.[321] If Jesus were using the form *yippate'ach* for *Ephphatha* (versus *yippatach*) then we would see a reduction of the "e" vowel. This gives us a template for how *arema* may have been reduced to *arma* in the transliteration.

GEI - VALLEY

There are several words for valley in Hebrew: *Bakka is* בקעה *(Bi'kah)* indicates widely extended plains such as Babylon, Lebanon, and the area at the foot of Mt. Hermon. The Valley of Megiddo is the *Bik'at Megiddo*; a wide-open expanse that farmers love, due to the abundant flat area. *Emek* is a deeper valley of wide extent fit for agriculture and warfare. For example, the Valley of Jehoshaphat, *Emek Yehoshafat*, in Jerusalem. Lastly, *Gei* means a deep valley, canyon. *Gei Ben-Hinnom*, the Valley of the Son of Hinnom is just outside of Jerusalem where sacrifices were offered to Molech. In Zechariah 14: "And the Mount of Olives shall be split in two... Making a very large valley [גֵּיא gei]" (Zech 14:4).

DON - JUDGMENT

The last word is *don*, which comes from the Hebrew *din* or *ladon* and according to the *Theological workbook of the Old Testament*, "din" is nearly identical in meaning with *shaphat*"[322] which we have seen in the word Jehoshaphat. *Yeho-shaphat* is where God will judge and cast in his sickle: "I will also gather all nations, and bring them down to the Valley of Jehoshaphat; and I will enter into judgment with them there (Joel 3:2) Put in the sickle, for the harvest is ripe. Come, go down; for the winepress is full" (Joel 3:13). How do we get *dôn* from din? The same root is found in the word Dani-el, "God is my judge." The infinitive absolute always has the ô, e.g.: *mot* [מות môt] *sov* [סֹב sôv], *gol*, [גֹּול gôl] and *dom* [דֹּם dôm]. For example::

---

321 Hamp, Douglas. Discovering the Language of Jesus, Calvary Chapel Publishing, Santa Ana, CA, 2005.
322 TWOT shaphat

- Be silent [דֹם] in the LORD's presence... (Ps 37:7).
- You are to weep in silence [דֹם]..." (Ezek 24:17).

Hence, judgment is written as dôn [דוֹן].

SUMMARY

Putting it all together, we see that there is no mountain of Megiddo.[323] And no, the battle will not take place in the Jezreel (Megiddo) valley; rather, God will come like a man of war and will fight to save his people **in Jerusalem**. The battle takes place (initially) in the Valley of Jehoshaphat, next to the *Valley of Gei Ben-Hinnom* (Gehenna) where God is going to reap outside of the city (refer to Figure 45). Outside the city is where He is going to trample these grapes.

It should be noted here that this Valley of Judgment [גיא- דון *gei-don*] does not yet exist on the map. It will be created when Jesus' foot touches down on the Mt. of Olives and it cleaves in two, thereby creating the *"gei-don,"* and the "heap" will be the bodies of the Beast's army. We will consider this epic battle in the next chapter.

The pieces fit together with the Scriptural motifs of Jesus harvesting and treading grapes, and with the motif of the crossing of the Red Sea, (it appears God likes to recycle themes). Lastly, we will see how Satan will pull out all the stops to plan for this battle to take Jerusalem and defeat God; but in the end, he will be "hoisted with his own petard."[324] Just like in the Proverb "Whoever digs a pit will fall into it" (Prov 26:27), the Beast will fall in the trap that he sets for the Jerusalemites.

Our etymology of Armageddon as *arema-gei-don*, where *Arema* means harvested heap, *Gei* means valley and *Don* means judgment, yields: "the heap of the valley of the judgement," and fits far better than the nonexistent mountain of Megiddo, or the even weaker interpretation of the mountain of appointed times.

---

[323] Some people have suggested that this is the place of the crowds that is what the word means and maybe there is an underlying secondary use of that, though I rather doubt it. Dr. Michael Heiser has suggested Har-Moed "mountain of the appointed meeting time." However, that theory does not explain the differences in spelling.

[324] Hamlet, Act 3 Scene 4.

Chapter 23: Jesus Splits the Mt. of Olives

After saying, "Baruch Haba B'shem Adonai," the Jerusalemites will likely have to hide from the impending hordes of hybrids who want to kill them. We get the impression that nearly three days have passed since they called upon Jesus, based on Hosea:

"Come, and let us return to the LORD; for He has torn, but He will heal us; He has stricken, but He will bind us up (Hos 6:1). After two days He will revive us; on the third day He will raise us up, that we may live in His sight (Hos 6:2)."

Figure 46. Arrows represent the coming forces of the Beast to destroy the Jerusalem remnant. Photo by Bibleplaces.com.

However, the cataclysmic events will darken the sun and moon, and fill the air with smoke and gases from the elements that will melt. Mankind will panic, and it may not even be possible for them to determine the time that has passed since it all started; but it may be 3 literal days. Regardless, the Jerusalem remnant will try to make their way to the Mount of Olives because they know that is where Jesus will come. Jews have elected for centuries to be buried on the Mount of Olives, anticipating that will be where the resurrection occurs first—according to their expectations.

291

"Then the LORD will go forth and fight against those nations, as He fights in the day of battle (Zech 14:3). And in that day His feet will stand on the Mount of Olives, which faces Jerusalem on the east (Zech 14:4)."

The Jerusalemites may be trying to make it to the top of the Mount of Olives when they find themselves surrounded by what appears to be a pincer move from the Beast's forces who are coming from the north, and from the south to destroy them. Satan might once again think he has won, but he will again be outfoxed.

Even though the Remnant is surrounded by mountains on two sides and hybrid hordes on the other two, Jesus will give supernatural powers to the governors of Judah:

"In that day I will make the governors of Judah like a **firepan in the woodpile**, and like a **fiery torch in the sheaves**; they shall devour all the surrounding peoples on the right hand and on the left, but Jerusalem shall be inhabited again in her own place–Jerusalem." (Zech 12:6).

They are in the Valley of Jehoshaphat; the forces of antichrist are coming against them; and then the governors of Judah who are on the periphery receive power from the Lord to have fire shoot from their hands. This is more than feasible based on what the text says:

"In that day the LORD will defend the inhabitants of Jerusalem; the one who is feeble among them in that day shall be like David, and the house of David shall be like God, like the Angel of the LORD before them" (Zech 12:8).

In Habakkuk 3:4, we learn: "He had rays flashing from His hand" this means Jesus has rays of light flashing from his hand" (Hab 3:4)! This is far cooler than any superhero movie. Jesus will give them power; the strong among them will be like the angel of the Lord before them. They will have fire coming from their hands to defend themselves until Jesus gets there.

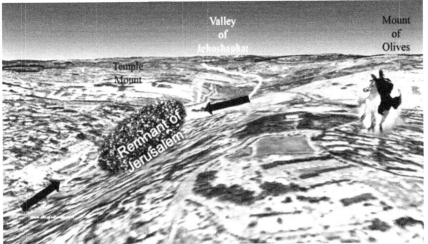

Figure 47. Jesus touching down on the Mount of Olives and with the Jerusalem remnant in the valley of Jehoshaphat.

The Jerusalemites in the Valley of Jehoshaphat, the Kidron valley are waiting for Jesus; they are fending off the people, the hybrid hordes of Gog that are coming and are devouring them on the right and on the left. The forces of antichrist are doing a pincer move, planning to conquer them from either side.

Finally, Jesus touches ground on the Mount of Olives, and when He dismounts his horse, then the mountain will split. Which might be the cause of the world's greatest ever earthquake (more on that later).

Suddenly, where there was no way to escape, God makes a way!

"The Mount of Olives shall be split in two, from east to west, making a very large valley; half of the mountain shall move toward the north and half of it toward the south (Zech 14:4). Then you shall flee through My mountain valley, for the mountain valley shall reach to Azal. Yes, you shall flee as you fled from the earthquake in the days of Uzziah king of Judah. Thus the LORD my God will come, and all the saints with You (Zech 14:5)."

We recall that Israel was in this predicament before. They were trapped between a rock and a hard place, with Pharaoh on one side and the Red Sea on the other side. This will be the second Exodus!

"For Pharaoh will say of the children of Israel, 'They are bewildered by the land; the wilderness has closed them in' (Exod 14:3). 'Then I will harden Pharaoh's heart, so that he will pursue them; and I will gain honor over Pharaoh and over all his army, that the Egyptians may know that I am the LORD.' And they did so (Exod 14:4)."

After the ten plagues, Pharaoh did not learn his lesson and thought he could trap the Israelites and enslave them again. However, it was God who was creating the trap for Pharaoh. In Exodus, we find the sea splitting down the middle, but in the last days, it will be a mountain splitting down the middle. Just as God said that He would "harden the hearts of the Egyptians so that they shall go in after them, and I will get glory over Pharaoh and all his host" (Exod 14:17), so too "the **LORD alone will be exalted in that day**" (Isa 2:17).

MOTHER OF ALL EARTHQUAKES

The earth will experience the greatest earthquake the world has ever seen and will ever see. Though Scripture does not specifically state it, we have good reason to believe that quake could be caused by Jesus' feet touching down on the Mt. of Olives. The Mount of Olives will open up wide enough for a multitude of people to flee through, similar to the parting of the Red Sea, and will cause tremendous shaking. We know that not many kilometers from Jerusalem, there is an area known as the Dead Sea Transform—"a transform plate boundary, along which two tectonic plates slide past one another."[325] Dr. Yariv Hamiel, head of the GSI's Geological Hazards and Geological Engineering Division in Israel cautions:

"In general, we're worried about the whole Dead Sea Transform (the Syrian-African great rift) from Eilat to Lebanon ... There could be a strong quake anywhere along it at any time."[326]

---

[325] https://www.usgs.gov/center-news/imaging-israel-s-dead-sea-fault-understand-how-continents-stretch-and-rift
[326] https://www.haaretz.com/israel-news/.premium.MAGAZINE-southern-israel-is-hundreds-of-years-overdue-for-an-earthquake-1.6933565

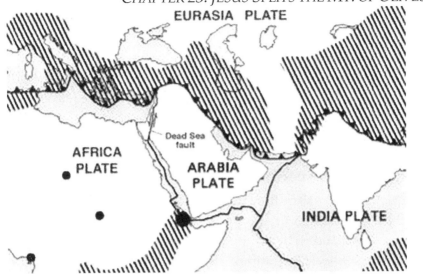

Figure 48. Dead Sea Transform Red lines are spreading boundaries, where new crust is generated as plates move away from one another; black lines are transform faults where plates slide past one another.

The Dead Sea Transform is itself at the center of four major plates: the African plate, the Anatolian plate, the Arabian plate, and the Eurasian plate. Jesus splitting the mountain could be the very domino that sets in motion the greatest of all earthquakes the world has ever seen. In fact, this is almost certainly the case based on the plethora of Scriptures that talk about massive earth shaking when God returns. Nevertheless, even if Jesus' foot stomping is not what causes the greatest of all earthquakes, the earth will experience a worldwide and unprecedented quake when He returns. It will be so monumental that it is mentioned repeatedly throughout Scripture.

"I will shake the heavens, and the **earth will move out of her place**, in the wrath of the LORD of hosts and in the day of His fierce anger" (Isa 13:13).

We find this same event repeated in Revelation where we learn that "**every mountain** and **island** was **moved** out of its place" (Rev 6:14). That is a big deal. This same event is repeated in chapter 16:

"There was a great earthquake, such a mighty and **great earthquake as had not occurred since men were on the earth**" (Rev 16:18). "Then **every island** fled away, and the **mountains were not found**" (Rev 16:20).

There will be the biggest earthquake in history. It will be so big that every mountain and island will move and flee away. The whole geographical structure of the surface of the earth as we know it will suffer dramatic changes. Nothing has or will ever compare to this event. In 2011, there was a 9.1 magnitude earthquake around Fukushima, Japan that caused unbelievable damage. They say that the earth shifted about an inch. Many of us watched in real time as tsunami waves overwhelmed houses, cars and people. That was just one island and just one inch. According to NASA,

"Calculations also show the Japan quake should have shifted the position of Earth's figure axis (the axis about which Earth's mass is balanced) by about 17 centimeters (6.5 inches), towards 133 degrees east longitude... This shift in Earth's figure axis will cause Earth to wobble a bit differently as it rotates."[327]

Now imagine if **every** island and **every** mountain moved out of its place! The prophet Isaiah described the event, "the **foundations** of the earth are **shaken**" (Isa 24:18); and,

"The earth is **violently broken**, The earth is split open, The earth is shaken exceedingly (Isa 24:19). The **earth shall reel to and fro like a drunkard**, and shall **totter** like a hut; Its transgression shall be heavy upon it, and it will fall, and not rise again (Isa 24:20)."

The devastation is so bad that Isaiah had to add, "it will fall and not rise again." The earth will never be the same. Jeremiah described it as the earth, "*tohu vavohu*," the same words used in Genesis 1:2 which describes a liquid:

"I beheld the earth, and indeed it was without form, and void [*tohu vavohu*]; and the heavens, they had no light (Jer 4:23). I beheld the mountains, and indeed they trembled, and all the hills moved back and forth (Jer 4:24)."

---

[327]

https://www.nasa.gov/topics/earth/features/japanquake/earth20110314.html

Figure 49. Some effects of soil liquefaction after the 1964 Niigata earthquake.

During sizeable earthquakes, the soil begins to act like quicksand, known as liquefaction, which is why buildings can just fall over; the soil under the foundation below them is eroded and becomes like liquid. [328]

In other words, the surface of the earth has lost its previous shape and consistency and lies marred, sunken and cracked. Jeremiah further explains the coming devastation:

"I beheld the mountains, and indeed they trembled, and all the hills moved back and forth (Jer 4:24). I beheld, and indeed there was no man, and all the birds of the heavens had fled (Jer 4:25). I beheld, and indeed the fruitful land was a wilderness, and all its cities were broken down At the presence of the LORD, By His fierce anger (Jer 4:26). For thus says the LORD: "The whole land shall be desolate; Yet I will not make a full end (Jer 4:27). For this shall the earth mourn, and the heavens above be black, Because I have spoken. I have purposed and will not relent, Nor will I turn back from it (Jer 4:28)."

Habakkuk states, "the perpetual mountains were shattered, the ancient hills collapsed" (Hab 3:6 NASB).

---

[328] http://www.sciencedaily.com/articles/e/earthquake_liquefaction.htm

How many times can the earth have every island and every mountain move from its place? It will only happen once because it will irreversibly destroy man's proud cities:

"And there were flashes of lightning, rumblings, peals of thunder, and a great earthquake such as there had never been ... (Rev 16:18) ... and the cities of the nations fell ... (Rev 16:19)."

The haughtiness of man has been brought to nothing: The factories of man's industry which produced tanks, planes, guns and bombs; the grand, magnificent skyscrapers, built ever higher, as well as the homes of both the humble and the proud; the stadiums full of idolatry; the great underground cities built for that very day; the glorious and stable pyramids, everything lies shattered in smoldering ruins, debris and rubble as if ripped apart by a tornado, crushed by Jesus' fierce anger.

However, this is not the end. We recall that the Beast and the Marked have prepared for this day by upgrading themselves into hybrid "gods" so that they could fight against Jesus. The earthquake certainly rocked their world, but they are not out of the fight yet. This reminds us of how after taking Israel out of Egypt, God was not done with Pharaoh. "And the Egyptians shall know that I am the LORD, when I have gotten glory over Pharaoh, his chariots, and his horsemen" (Exod 14:18). So too, in the battle of Armageddon, God says:

"You will come up against My people Israel like a cloud, to cover the land. It will be in the latter days that I will bring you against My land, so that the nations may know Me, when I am hallowed in you, O Gog, before their eyes" (Ezek 38:16). "Thus says the Lord GOD: 'Are you he of whom I have spoken in former days by My servants the prophets of Israel, who prophesied for years in those days that I would bring you against them?'" (Ezek 38:17). "So I will show my **greatness** and my **holiness** and make **myself known** in the eyes of many nations. Then they will know that I am the LORD" (Ezek 38:23).

In other words, God will be glorified when the boastful, blaspheming Gog is humbled and destroyed. It will also be on that day that an unprecedented earthquake will strike.

"For in My jealousy and in the fire of My wrath I have spoken: surely in that day there shall be a **great earthquake** in the land of Israel (Ezek 38:19), so that the fish of the sea, the birds of the heavens, the beasts of the field, all creeping things that creep on the earth, and **all men who are on the face of the earth** shall shake at My presence. The **mountains shall be thrown down**, the steep places shall fall, and every wall shall fall to the ground' (Ezek 38:20)."

Ezekiel describes this same event in which there will be an enormous earthquake that affects Israel and the whole world so that the mountains are thrown down and every wall falls. Every skyscraper will fall because every mountain and every island will move and it will be the greatest earthquake we will ever know.

"For the day of the LORD of hosts shall come upon everything proud and lofty..." (Isa 2:12). "Upon all the high mountains, and upon all the hills that are lifted up; (Isa 2:14) upon every high tower, and upon every fortified wall" (Isa 2:15) "... And the haughtiness of men shall be brought low; the LORD alone will be exalted in that day" (Isa 2:17).

Gog / the Beast has seen his fortune change, but his blasphemous arrogance will not allow him to throw in the towel. He will continue to fall into God's trap, just as Pharaoh did before him. In order to give time to prepare the way for Israel to go through the sea,

"The angel of God who was going before the host of Israel moved and went behind them, and the pillar of cloud moved from before them and **stood behind them** (Exod 14:19), coming **between** the **host of Egypt** and the **host of Israel**. And there was the cloud and the darkness. And it lit up the night without one coming near the other all night (Exod 14:20)."

God is going to make a way for the Jerusalem Remnant to get away. Rather than it being a wall of fire and cloud as between Israel and Egypt, this time it appears it will be a wall of gigantic hail, flooding rain, great hailstones, fire, and brimstone.

"And I will bring him to judgment with pestilence and bloodshed; I will rain down on him, on his troops, and on the many peoples who are with him, flooding rain, **great hailstones**, fire, and brimstone (Ezek 38:22). Thus I will magnify Myself and sanctify Myself, and I will be known in the eyes of many nations. Then they shall know that I am the LORD (Ezek 38:23)."

The same description is in the Revelation Armageddon passage:

"And there were noises and thunderings and lightnings; and there was a great earthquake, such a mighty and great earthquake as had not occurred since men were on the earth. (Rev 16:18) … And **great hail** from heaven fell upon men, each hailstone about the weight of a talent (Rev 16:21)."

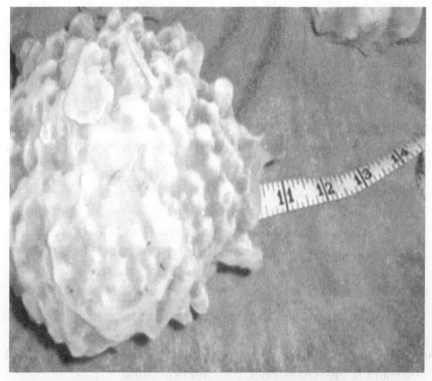

Figure 50. Softball (and larger)-sized hail fell during a severe thunderstorm that struck Vivian, S.D. on July 23. (Image: © NOAA).

A talent is roughly 75 pounds, or 34 kilos. The largest hailstone ever recorded was: "On June 22, 2003, chunks of ice the size of softballs rained down on Aurora, Nebraska. One, a jagged behemoth with a 7-inch (17.8-centimeter) diameter, entered the record books as the largest U.S. hailstone ever. Although large in size, it didn't unseat the champion by weight, which fell in Coffeyville, Kansas., in 1970, according to the National Center for Atmospheric Research (NCAR). That hailstone weighed more than a pound and a half (0.75 kg)."[329]

A pound and a half chunk of ice hitting someone at high speed could easily kill. Nevertheless, it will be dwarfed by the hailstones that will fall during the end of the Tribulation. A 75-pound hailstone falling is more like a cannonball.

Just as Pharaoh was blocked, while "the children of Israel went into the midst of the sea on the dry ground, and the waters were a wall to them on their right hand and on their left" (Exod 14:22). So also, falling hail will block the Beast / Gog and his hordes as the Jerusalem Remnant "shall flee through My mountain valley" (Zech 14:5), a canyon with steep walls on their right and left! However, as soon as possible, Pharaoh greedily led his army into the parted waters to capture his prey, and fell into God's trap.

"And the Egyptians pursued and went after them into the midst of the sea, all Pharaoh's horses, his chariots, and his horsemen" (Exod 14:23).

So too, the Beast and company will follow suit. The hail eventually stops, and we know that it has not killed Gog and the upgraded hybrid hordes because Revelation says that after the hail: "Men blasphemed God because of the plague of the hail, since that plague was exceedingly great" (Rev 16:21). Once the hail has stopped, then the Beast / Gog will hungrily pursue the Jerusalemites into the newly created Arema-Gei-Don, the Valley of Judgment of the Sheaves, and will fall like sheaves. They will do this because God is the one who put a hook in their jaws to lead them to Jerusalem to bring them into his valley of judgment, and they do not understand his thoughts:

---

[329] https://www.livescience.com/32694-how-big-was-the-biggest-hailstone-ever.html

"Now also many nations have gathered against you, who say, 'Let her be defiled, and let our eye look upon Zion.' But they **do not know the thoughts** of the Lord, nor do they understand His counsel; for He will gather them like **sheaves** to the threshing floor" (Micah 4:11–12).

In the Exodus, "the LORD looked down upon the army of the Egyptians through the pillar of fire and cloud, and He troubled the army of the Egyptians" (Exod 14:24). That is, God was present in the midst of the pillar of fire and cloud. He was personally overseeing Israel's rescue. The text says, "He took off their chariot wheels, so that they drove them with difficulty" (Exod 14:25). It quickly became apparent to the Egyptians that they were fighting a force far greater than themselves; and Pharaoh, the one they believed to be a god, was outmatched.

The Egyptians said, "Let us flee from the face of Israel, for the **LORD fights** for them against the Egyptians" (Exod 14:25).

This time, however, God will not be looking through a pillar of fire and cloud, but will be there, face to face with his adversary. Jesus will jump down about four hundred feet (yes, He can do that) and will interpose himself between his people who are fleeing behind him and the Beast and his hybrid hordes in front of him.

Figure 51. Jesus interposing in the newly formed valley "gei" of the judgment of the sheaves "Armageddon."

When they see Jesus, they will realize they are in trouble and will seek to go in reverse, but unfortunately for them, another wave of hybrids is pushing them toward Jesus, whose "face is like the sun" (Rev 1:16) and whose "brightness was like the light" (Hab 3:4). The brilliance of his visage "will strike every horse with confusion, and its rider with madness ... and will strike every horse of the peoples with blindness" (Zech 12:4). All the while, He will decimate the Beast and attackers with the "rays flashing from His hand," where "His power was hidden" (Hab 3:4). John also tells us, "out of His mouth goes a sharp sword, that with it He should strike the nations" (Rev 19:15).

When they want to get away from him and go back, they cannot; then what God said through the prophets Ezekiel and Zechariah will come to pass:

- "I will call for a sword against Gog throughout all My mountains," says the Lord GOD. "**Every man's sword will be against his brother**" (Ezek 38:21).
- "It shall come to pass in that day that a great panic from the LORD will be among them. Everyone will seize the hand of his neighbor, and **raise his hand against his neighbor's hand**" (Zech 14:13).

In the Exodus, the trap also became the Egyptians tomb:

Then the LORD said to Moses, "Stretch out your hand over the sea, that the waters may come back upon the Egyptians, on their chariots, and on their horsemen" (Exod 14:26). So too, Gog and his horde will meet their doom in the Arema-Gei-Don.

THEY MELT

Unable to retreat they will literally melt before the King of Kings and the Lord of Lords who has come to fight on behalf of his people, just as He promised.

"And this shall be the plague with which the LORD will strike all the people who fought against Jerusalem: their **flesh** shall **dissolve** while they stand on their feet, their **eyes** shall **dissolve** in their sockets, and their tongues shall dissolve in their mouths" (Zech 14:12).

Scripture is replete with passages stating how the mountains will melt at God's coming:

- The day of the Lord will come as a thief in the night, in which the heavens will pass away with a great noise, and the elements will **melt** with fervent heat; both the earth and the works that are in it will be burned up (2 Pet 3:10).
- The mountains **melt** like wax at the presence of the LORD, At the presence of the Lord of the whole earth (Ps 97:5).
- The mountains will **melt** under Him, and the valleys will split Like wax before the fire, Like waters poured down a steep place (Mic 1:4).
- The Lord GOD of hosts, He who touches the earth and it **melts**, and all who dwell there mourn. (Amos 9:5).
- I will send **fire** on Magog and on those who dwell securely in the coastlands,[330] and they shall know that I am the LORD (Ezek 39:6).

If the mountains and elements will melt, how much more will the Beast's / Gog's horde melt when confronted with the King? We should keep in mind that just as the entire earth did not melt when God came on Sinai, neither will the entire planet melt into goo when Jesus comes.

The melting seems to be localized on the surface of the planet. God put Moses in the cleft of the rock as He passed by, because the rocks offered some protection against His fiery presence. It is like passing your hand through a flame will not harm you, but leaving your hand on the flame, even for a few seconds, burns. It is God's fiery presence remaining in one place that does the damage. It will do so because creation is degenerate due to the Fall and has further

---

[330] The people of the coastlands were those we looked at in Genesis 10: ...Gomer, Magog, Madai [Persia], Javan [Greece], Tubal, Meshech, and Tiras. **[God is speaking to these ancestral people from whom we are descendants]** (Gen 10:2) ...From these the coastland peoples spread in their lands, each with his own language, by their clans, in their nations. (Gen 10:5). Fire on the cities of the sons of Japheth, which is related to Greece, in Greece went westward to Rome, and then they went westward to the UK, and then they went to the US, we are all related. We are descendants of these people. In Ezekiel 38 and 39 God through the prophet is speaking to those peoples, to us who came out of those places; it is the whole world.

degraded over time; but "creation itself also will be delivered from the bondage of corruption into the glorious liberty of the children of God" (Rom 8:21).

God set the trap, and Satan / the Beast and company fell into it. They had been exposed to God's fiery-lightning presence and were melted like wax. Paul corroborates this destruction caused by God's presence:

"These shall be punished with everlasting destruction **from** [*apo* απο – because of, by virtue of] the presence of the Lord and **from** [apo απο] the glory of His power" (2 Thess 1:9).

BDAG explains how *apo* can be used "to indicate cause, means, or outcome; gener., to show the reason for something. because of, as a result of, for (numerous ref.)"[331] Hence, they are not punished *away from his presence* but *because of, by virtue of Jesus' presence*. They are exposed to Jesus, who will consume them "with the breath of His mouth and destroy with the brightness of His coming" (2 Thess 2:8).

"Punished with everlasting destruction from the presence of the Lord and from the glory of His power"; we see this in the parallel passage of Isaiah 66:

"For behold, the LORD will come with fire and with His chariots, like a whirlwind, to render His anger with fury, and His rebuke with flames of fire. For by fire and by His sword the LORD will judge all flesh; and the slain of the LORD shall be many" (Isa 66:15–16).

Isaiah tells us the reason for God's wrath: "For the **indignation** of the LORD is against all nations, and His **fury** against all their armies" (Isa 34:2).

JESUS TREADS

The fury on Jesus' face will endure for some time; for even after Gog and his horde have been hit by the consuming fire of Jesus' presence and have begun melting before him, He will then execute judgment by treading them underfoot to the point that his garments are stained with their blood:

---

[331] BDAG

"He was clothed with a robe dipped in blood" (Rev 19:13), "He Himself treads the winepress of the fierceness and wrath of Almighty God" (Rev 19:15).

Jesus will cut down the wicked like sheaves with his sickle and then trample them in the "great winepress of the **wrath** of God" (Rev 14:19). He even states in Isaiah:

"I have trodden the winepress alone, and from the peoples no one was with Me. For I have trodden them in My anger, and trampled them in My fury; their blood is sprinkled upon My garments, and I have stained all My robes. I have trodden down the peoples in My anger, made them drunk in My fury, and brought down their strength to the earth" (Isa 63:2, 3, 6).

Jesus will trample like grapes the Beast[332] who "even **exalted** himself as high as the Prince of the host" (Daniel 8:10–11), who decided to "**exalt** himself in his heart ... (Dan 8:25), the one "who opposes and **exalts** himself above all that is called God or that is worshiped, (2 Thess 2:3–4), and the one who "was given a mouth **speaking** great things and **blasphemies** ... against God, to blaspheme His name (Rev 13:5-6). When Jesus returns to redeem His people, which God had long warned of through the prophets, that will be the Day of the Lord. Isaiah 2 tells us plainly, "the **LORD alone will be exalted in that day**" (Isa 2:17). The Day of the Lord is not the entirety of Daniel's seventieth week or even the three and a half year years of the great tribulation for the simple reason that the Beast / Gog /Antichrist is ostentatiously exalting himself and blaspheming God and those who dwell in heaven. Gog's humiliation will continue as wave after wave of attackers flow into Jesus' winepress of God's wrath. In Revelation, John writes:

"The winepress was trampled outside the city, and blood came out of the winepress, up to the horses' bridles, [for one thousand six hundred furlongs]" (Rev 14:20).

---

[332] Satan will likely decouple himself from his avatar at this point and try to save himself (though he ultimately is captured and sent into the abyss).

Figure 52. Blood up to the horse's bridle.

That is a lot of blood. If we are imagining that place up in the Megiddo Valley, up in the north, and if we are thinking about 4 and a half or 5 feet of blood, it seems nearly impossible. But if we imagine a narrow valley with steep canyon walls on the sides, while not a pretty picture, it at least makes more sense.

Thus Gog, the son of Perdition, Satan's avatar, the one who deceived the world into believing the delusion and boasted he and his army could defeat Jesus, has fallen and his reign of terror has ended just as God stated: "he shall be broken without human means" (Dan 8:25). He will fall in the Valley of YHWH Judges, Jehoshaphat, next door to Gehenna which God declared: "this place shall no more be called **Tophet** or the **Valley of the Son of Hinnom**, but the Valley of Slaughter" (Jer 19:6). Following his fall, God declared Gog's further humiliation:

"You shall fall upon the mountains of Israel, you and all your troops and the peoples who are with you; I will give you to birds of prey of every sort and to the beasts of the field to be devoured" (Ezek 39:4).

God further says in Ezekiel 39:

"… speak to the **birds** of every sort and to all beasts of the field, 'Assemble and come, **gather** from all around to the sacrificial **feast** that I am preparing for you, a great sacrificial feast on the mountains of Israel, and you shall eat flesh and drink blood (Ezek 39:17). You shall eat the **flesh** of the **mighty**, and drink the blood of the princes of the earth—of rams, of lambs, and of he-goats, of bulls, all of them fat beasts of Bashan (Ezek 39:18). And you shall eat fat till you are filled, and drink blood till you are drunk, at the sacrificial feast that I am preparing for you (Ezek 39:19). You shall be filled at My table with horses and riders, with mighty men and with all the men of war,' says the Lord GOD (Ezek 39:20)."

Jesus likewise spoke of the birds of prey that would follow: "So also will the coming of the Son of Man be. For wherever the carcass is, there the eagles will be gathered together" (Matt 24:27, 28).

The Greek word *aetos*, is a general word for carrion birds, such as the crow, eagle or vulture. It makes sense that carrion birds, birds that eat decaying flesh, will survive the longest after the waters have turned to "blood as of a dead man; and every living creature in the sea died" (Rev 16:3). Vegetation has burned up as well. Many land animals and many birds will have died, so the carrion birds will be quite busy. Because the carrion birds are the last ones around, they are invited to feast on all the dead in both Ezekiel and Revelation:

"An angel … cried with a loud voice, saying to all the **birds** that fly in the midst of heaven, 'Come and gather together for the **supper** of the great God (Rev 19:17), that you may eat the flesh of kings, the **flesh** of captains, the flesh of **mighty** men, the flesh of horses and of those who sit on them, and the flesh of all people, free and slave, both small and great' (Rev 19:18)."

The time of the battle of Armageddon will be at the *Fall Feasts*. The return of Jesus is most likely on *Yom Teruah* (*the Feast of Trumpets*), the day that no one knows the day or the hour because it falls on the first of the seventh month [*Rosh Chodesh*].

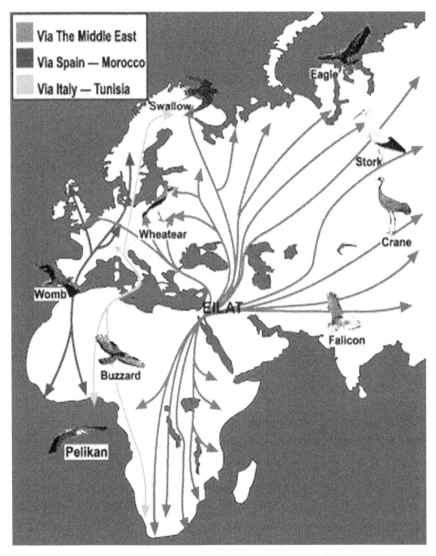

Figure 53. Migration of birds over Israel
https://spanishnature.blogspot.com/2011/12/tale-that-knows-no-boundaries-big-blog.html

In the Spring and Fall there is a massive migration of millions of birds, from Europe and Asia to Africa. Incredibly, the vast majority of birds fly over Israel. They do not fly over anywhere else primarily, but just almost completely over Israel. The angel will say to these birds, "Come on down, we've got this great feast, because the Lord has just trodden his enemies underfoot."

The Beast has now been thoroughly vanquished and humiliated. However, because he is a hybrid, he will sustain a lot of punishment until ultimately, the text says: "Then the beast was captured and with him the false prophet" (Rev 19:20).

After Jesus has vanquished all foes, He says:

"When the Son of Man comes in His glory, and all the holy angels with Him, then He will sit on the throne of His glory" (Matt 25:31).

Similar to the previous two texts, Daniel says fire comes from the Judge, court is in session, and the Beast is given to the fire:

"His throne was a fiery flame, his wheels a burning fire, a fiery stream, issued and came forth from before Him (Dan 7:9). Thousands, thousands ministered to Him, ten thousand times ten thousand stood before Him, the court was seated in the books were opened (Dan 7:10). I watched until the **beast** was **slain** and his body destroyed and given to the burning **flame** (Dan 7:11)."

John finishes with the same description of the end concerning the Beast and False Prophet:

"These two were cast alive into the lake of fire burning with brimstone (Rev 19:20). And the rest were killed with the sword which proceeded from the mouth of Him who sat on the horse. And all the birds were filled with their flesh (Rev 19:21)."

Following their judgment, a mighty angel will lead Satan bound in chains to the smoking and pitch-black abyss. "Then I saw an angel coming down from heaven, holding in his hand the key to the bottomless pit and a great chain (Rev 20:1). And he seized the dragon, that ancient serpent, who is the devil and Satan, and bound him for a thousand years (Rev 20:2), and threw him into the pit, and shut it and sealed it over him, so that he might not deceive the nations any longer, until the thousand years were ended. After that he must be released for a little while (Rev 20:3)."

Satan and the fallen will be put into the abyss, Sheol, the very prison they opened in order to fight Jesus. They will have their ultimate judgment deferred until one thousand years later, which we will explore in great detail in *Corrupting the Image 4.*

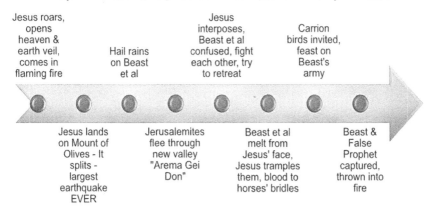

Day of the Lord, Jesus Comes in Fiery Wrath

Jesus roars, opens heaven & earth veil, comes in flaming fire

Hail rains on Beast et al

Jesus interposes, Beast et al confused, fight each other, try to retreat

Carrion birds invited, feast on Beast's army

Jesus lands on Mount of Olives - It splits - largest earthquake EVER

Jerusalemites flee through new valley "Arema Gei Don"

Beast et al melt from Jesus' face, Jesus tramples them, blood to horses' bridles

Beast & False Prophet captured, thrown into fire

Table 11. Day of the Lord, Jesus Comes in Fiery Wrath.

Epilogue: Good News of the Kingdom

The battle of Armageddon, the culmination of the great conflict between Jesus and his archenemy Satan, is now over. Nothing more will happen as far as the kingdom of the Beast-Gog is concerned. Satan successfully convinced the world to again give him their authority through the alien/UFO deception. While wielding authority over every tribe, tongue, and nation, he had immunity and could blaspheme God and those who dwell in heaven. It also granted him authority to make war against the saints and overcome them. It looked like Satan would be the victor; many were deceived into taking the mark of the Beast to become gods, only to suffer the fate of becoming the living dead, or zombies; and those who refused, died a martyr's death. However, God was always working through it all.

The time of Jacob's trouble caused the leadership in Jerusalem of the house of Judah, to finally call out, Baruch Haba b'shem Adonai. When they did that, they were inducted into the New Covenant causing the obligations associated with the Old (marriage) Covenant to be annulled. God then set up a trap for the Beast / Gog to want to attack Jerusalem without realizing they were playing right into his hands.

Jesus came back and did his awesome and unusual work when He destroyed the Rephaim hybrids. Jesus also destroyed with "the breath of his mouth and the brightness of his coming" (2 Thess 2:8), the Beast, Satan's god-man hybrid, who claimed to be a god and blasphemed the true God of heaven and earth. He trampled his enemies like one who is treading grapes in the winepress; then comes the time of judgment of the malefactors.

All these clashes have been for the purpose of God retaking the planet for a simple truth: God wants to dwell with us. Following the Feast of Trumpets, when Jesus will likely come back to save his people; and Yom Kippur, when Jesus will likely sit in judgment over his defeated foes; then comes Sukkot, the feast of tabernacles, when God dwells with us. The end goal for Jesus is to be our God and for us to be his people, which is the essence of the everlasting Gospel.

What is the Everlasting Gospel? We see this throughout Scripture.

- I have proclaimed the good news of righteousness in the great assembly … (Ps 40:9).
- Proclaim the good news of His salvation from day to day (Ps 96:2).
- How beautiful upon the mountains are the feet of him who brings good news, who proclaims peace, who brings glad tidings of good things, who proclaims salvation, who says to Zion, "Your God reigns!" (Isa 52:7).

The gospel was once preached to the people in the wilderness.

"For indeed the **gospel** was **preached to us as well as to them**; but the word which they heard did not profit them, not being mixed with faith in those who heard it." (Heb 4:2) "… they could not enter in because of unbelief" (Heb 3:19).

Were they hearing that Jesus would die for their sins? No. We recall that "Jesus went about all Galilee, teaching in their synagogues, preaching the gospel of the kingdom …" (Matt 4:23) Jesus also said: "The time is fulfilled, and the kingdom of God is at hand. Repent, and believe in the gospel" (Mark 1:15).

Jesus only spoke of his death and resurrection (essential parts of the good news, but not the entirety) at the very end of his ministry; yet, He was proclaiming the gospel, the good news before that.

The good news is you can be part of God's kingdom. You must repent. What does it mean to repent? When you meet Jesus personally, He impacts you. You will suddenly see that there is a right way that you should follow. You consciously decide to follow the "right way."

So repent means to have a change of mind; and then to make a turn in your actions—you are going one way, so you turn around and go the other direction. You think one thing about something that is incorrect, so turn it around and think the "right way." That will lead to different actions in your life. Don't expect perfection from the start. Failure happens, but lift up your eyes and persevere. With each bump, you will get stronger and more faithful to the Lord. Perseverance will lead to different actions in your life.

Jesus was asked:

"Teacher, what shall I do to inherit eternal life?" (Luke 10:25) He said to him, "What is written in the law? What is your reading of it?" (Luke 10:26) he answered and said, "'You shall love the LORD your God with all your heart, with all your soul, with all your strength, and with all your mind,' and 'your neighbor as yourself' " (Luke 10:27). [there he just condensed all the commandments] And He said to him, "You have answered rightly; do this and you will live" (Luke 10:28).

The good news is really this simple:

"'Only acknowledge your iniquity, that you have transgressed against the LORD your God ... and you have not obeyed My voice,' says the LORD" (Jer 3:13).

Without repentance you are excluded from God's good, beautiful, righteous, true, and joyous kingdom. But if you repent, you can be saved from death and live forever in the kingdom.

It is not enough to have an intellectual agreement that historically Jesus lived, died and was resurrected. Satan and his demons know Jesus rose. To just say yes, that He rose again, that is a good start, but it is not enough. There must be a change of heart. You have to say, I want to live for God's kingdom. I want to be part of what He is doing. I want to be part of his righteous kingdom.

Sadly, we, humans have gone away from God: Humanity, as well as Israel has gone astray.

We see in the Book of Hosea, God says, I will return again to My place Till they [Judah & Israel] acknowledge their offense (Hos 5:15).

Why did God say He will return again to his place? Because He kept calling out for Israel and Judah to come back to him and they said, "No, we don't want it." He finally said, "Okay, fine, one day you will seek me. I'm going to return again to My place until they acknowledge their offense and then they will seek My face and in their affliction, they will earnestly seek Me."

Just as Jesus gave the ultimatum to the leadership of Jerusalem "until you say, **'Blessed is He who comes in the name of the LORD!'"** (Matthew 23:39), you will not see my face," the same is true for us. Until each of us welcomes Jesus in the name of the Lord as our Savior, then we will not see his face. But once we do, then He will save us. Have you welcomed him? If not, do it today. The steps are simple: acknowledge your offense – that you have sinned against him. Then welcome him as your king and walk in his ways. Then you will be part of God's kingdom! And as soon as possible, be baptized in front of witnesses.

Appendices

APPENDIX 1: THE THEMATIC APPROACH TO INTERPRETING REVELATION

The book of Revelation is a very exciting book and comes with a blessing to those who read it. Nevertheless, it is far from being an easy book to understand. Part of the challenge is due to a tendency to interpret the book of Revelation chronologically rather than thematically. Though there is some chronology in the book, it is primarily laid out thematically.

If we read the judgments of the seals, trumpets, and bowls with a chronological-sequential method then those would represent nineteen completely separate judgments occurring at different times during the tribulation. That is, the seal judgments would all play out, then the trumpets would begin and then the bowls would follow after the last trumpet judgment (many scholars follow this scheme). It would look like this:

Chronological view of Revelation: First Seals, then Trumpets, then Bowls

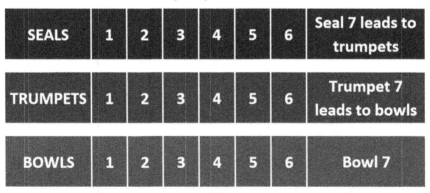

SEALS	1	2	3	4	5	6	Seal 7 leads to trumpets
TRUMPETS	1	2	3	4	5	6	Trumpet 7 leads to bowls
BOWLS	1	2	3	4	5	6	Bowl 7

Table 12. Chronological view of Revelation.

Nevertheless, within the seals, trumpets, and bowls, there are recurring, interrelated themes with various levels of detail, perspective, and intensity. This means John laid out the series of visions in the order that they were communicated to him and not as nineteen different and sequential judgments. It is like looking at a diamond with many facets and seeing inside the same thing.

Figure 54. Facets of a diamond.

Or it is like if John were given a tour of a television control room where before him were dozens of screens. All the scenes of a particular show are being shot at the same time. For the sake of illustration, let us imagine that the show has five distinct scenes. Each scene has separate cameras and cameraman to capture it. John merely sees the video feed. Each scene is complex and requires varying camera angles to appreciate the complexity.

Figure 55. TV control room.

Some cameras are placed above the set to get a wide angel – top-down approach. Other cameras zoom in on the face of the main characters. Finally other cameras pan to give the greater perspective. The seals, trumpets, and bowls are related events different vantage points (camera angles) so the readers get a more detailed understanding.

We could imagine this like a peanut butter and jelly sandwich. In the chronological approach, we first eat a piece of bread, then eat the peanut butter, then the jelly, and finally we eat the other slice of bread. In the thematic approach, however, we simply stack them on top of the other and eat them at the same time. In other words, the seals in Revelation 6 relate to the bowls in chapter 16. Just like a piece of layered cake, we slice through the cake and eat a cross-section all at once.

RECAPITULATION

Understanding the seals, trumpets, and bowls as a series of recapitulations or reiterations (stacked layers) means that John was initially given a grand, bird's eye view and then subsequent chapters go into supporting details of what has already been revealed. Using the stacking of layers idea like in an animated movie helps us picture how Revelation is organized.

Figure 56. Example of layering from the movie "Monsters."

Layering is illustrated nicely in modern animation techniques (like Monsters Inc.) which start with a basic story reel sketch that tells the story. Why don't they just stop there? Because it does not convey the entirety of the message. The subsequent layers add depth, color, detail, lighting, and animation to create a composite image. By the time we get to the final product right down here, it really feels like it is a feature film.

The seals are like the story reel giving us the basic story overview. While lacking depth, color, and detail, they take us from the beginning of the story to its finish. The trumpets and bowls add the texturing, color, and fine details to the same events so we have a rich composite image.

We see repeating themes (recapitulations) in many books of the Bible. For example, Genesis chapters one and two are often accused of being different accounts. Yet we see in chapter one an overview of the entire creation week, whereas chapter two focuses only on day six and the creation of man. Hence, we can conclude that chapter two is thematically related to chapter one. Sure, chapter one comes first in the book but the content of both chapters is thematically related and are the same story. Chapter two fits within the framework of chapter one. We see the same issue with Exodus 14 and 15 where the events happen in 14 and then Moses and Miriam recount the events in 15. They are the same events (themes) but told in different ways.

Hence, the seals, trumpets, bowls, and in fact all of Revelation chapters 6-19 are a series of visions of many layers to form a composite image. This means that there are repeating themes in the seals, trumpets, and bowls. Seals 1-7 are the overall plan of the great tribulation. The subsequent trumpets and bowls are looking at those events in either greater detail or from a different angle and with a progressive intensification of events (from 1/3 to everything). The seventh seal, trumpet and bowl all end at the same event: the return of Jesus. They are stacked one upon another or stair steps, if you will, where they keep getting more intense, and the timeframe keeps getting squished down, until finally they all culminate at the same moment with the return of Yeshua. We see the thematic arrangement throughout Revelation.

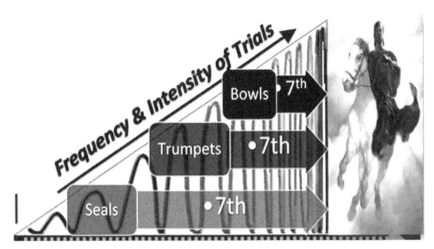

Figure 57. The seventh seal, trumpet, and bowl end with the return of Jesus.

EARTHQUAKES IN REVELATION SIX AND SIXTEEN ARE THE SAME

Let's consider how the earthquakes from chapters six and sixteen are one and the same event. There is an earthquake in the seventh and last bowl, which is described as:

"a great earthquake, such a mighty and **great earthquake as had not occurred** since men were on the earth" (Rev 16:18).

The language is very significant because it tells us that this would be the greatest of all time. John follows up with us by saying "every island fled away, and the mountains were not found" (Rev 16:20). This language is identical to the many descriptions of ultimate shaking that will take place on planet earth.

The mini apocalypse in Isaiah 24 describes how "the earth is **violently broken**, The earth is split open, The earth is **shaken exceedingly**" (Isa 24:19). This earth will be so utterly moved that it "shall reel to and fro like a drunkard, and shall totter like a hut; Its transgression shall be heavy upon it, and it will fall, and **not rise again**. (Isa 24:20). To fall and not rise again is parallel language to Revelation 16 – this is the worst ever earthquake never to be duplicated. We find many other passages of this as well:

- He stood and measured the earth; He looked and startled the nations. And the **everlasting mountains were scattered**, The perpetual **hills bowed**. His ways are everlasting. (Hab 3:6)
- The mountains melt like wax at the presence of the LORD, At the presence of the Lord of the whole earth. (Ps 97:5)

Isaiah 2 explains how:

the **day of the LORD** of hosts Shall come upon everything proud and lofty, Upon everything lifted up– And it shall be brought low– Upon **all the high mountains**, and upon all the hills that are lifted up; (Isa 2:12, 14)

That passage goes on to say in the Day of the Lord, when the mountains fall:

They shall go into the **holes** of the **rocks**, and into the **caves** of the earth, From the terror of the LORD And the glory of His majesty, When He arises to shake the earth mightily. (Isa 2:19)

In chapter thirteen, Isaiah says:

Therefore I will shake the heavens, and the **earth will move out of her place**, In the **wrath** of the LORD of hosts And in the **day** of His fierce anger. (Isa 13:13)

The description is identical to what we find in Revelation six in the sixth seal: "**every mountain** and **island** was moved out of its place" (Rev 6:14). Isaiah 2 merely says "they" whereas Revelation says:

"the **kings of the earth**, the **great men**, the rich men, the commanders, the mighty men, every slave and every free man, hid themselves in the **caves** and in the **rocks** of the mountains," (Rev 6:15).

Thus, we have an unprecedented earthquake in which earth's topography and geography change at a cataclysmic extent, so much so that mountains and islands move causing people to flee and hide in caves. Just like in Isaiah 2, they hide because it is the Day of the Lord.

and said to the mountains and rocks, "Fall on us and hide us from the face of Him who sits on the throne and from the wrath of the Lamb! (Rev 6:16) "For the **great day of His wrath has come**, and who is able to stand?" (Rev 6:17)

Are we to believe that the mighty men of the earth are throwing in the towel in Revelation 6 and fully admit that the day of Jesus' wrath has come? Yet in chapter 16 "the kings of the earth" and "the whole world" assemble for "the **battle of that great day of God Almighty**" (Rev 16:14)?

The thematic method sees parallel language and themes as being witnesses of the same event merely from different perspectives and with varying details. Revelation 6 and 16, Isaiah 2 and 24, Habakkuk 3, and others all speak of the kings of the earth gathered to the battle of the great Day of the Lord, the day of God and the mother of all earthquakes that will utterly shake the entire earth so that it will fall and not rise again and every mountain and island were moved out of their places. The day is so scary the kings, commanders, and all involved in the battle run into the caves for protection from the Day of the Lord.

Consider how the 2011 Fukushima 9.1 earthquake caused phenomenal damage to buildings and great loss of life. Now imagine the kind of destruction planet earth will experience when **every** island falling into the sea and **every** mountain crumbling! The word "every" precludes the event from happening twice; that means it happens once and there will be no repeat. Therefore, Revelation 6 is the same event as Revelation 16 and Isaiah 24, (etc.). Such an event will happen only once never to be repeated. The earth will fall and not rise again. The language in all the passages speaks of the Day of the Lord when this will happen.

HEAVENS OPEN

Another prevalent theme in Revelation (and other scriptures) is the opening of the heavens. We discussed the veil between heaven and earth in *Corrupting the Image 2* in great detail and we will not restate it here. Suffice it to say that the opening of the heavens is an end-of-the-world event that will only happen once when heaven itself and earth will pass. We should be aware that the opening of heavens is in direct connection with other phenomena:

- The Day of the Lord, since the Lord Jesus at this point is already engaged in the second coming
- the dramatic (structural) changes of heavens itself
- the elements of cataclysmic proportions accompanying these changes in heaven
- the oncoming great battle that Jesus is about to fight

By way of the heavens opened John directs our eyes to the temple of God in Rev 11 where the dramatic noises are accompanied by hail as well:

Then the **sky receded as a scroll** when it is rolled up, and every mountain and island was moved out of its place. (Rev 6:14)

This event is spoken of in Revelation 19 as well when Jesus is said to make war against the Beast and the world's armies.

Now I saw **heaven opened**, and behold, a white horse. And He who sat on him was called Faithful and True… And I saw the beast, the kings of the earth, and their armies, **gathered together to make war** against Him who sat on the horse and against His army. (Rev 19:11, 19)

This same battle (Armageddon) is described in Revelation 16 as well where the Beast, kings of the earth, and their armies are ready to fight against Jesus:

the beast…the kings of the earth and of the whole world…to **gather** them to the **battle of that great day of God** Almighty. (Rev 16:13, 14).

In the seventh and final bowl where the greatest earthquake also happens, we are told:

And there were **noises and thunderings and lightnings;** and there was **a great earthquake**, such a mighty and great earthquake as had not occurred since men were on the earth. (Rev 16:18) And **great hail** from heaven fell upon men… (Rev 16:21)

This is not the first time that we have encountered "noises and thunderings and lightnings" in Revelation. Those same **noises, thunderings, lightnings, and an earthquake** happen in the seventh seal. In that period, there is silence in heaven "for about half an hour and "the seven angels" are "given seven trumpets" (Rev 8:2). Next John saw:

"another angel, having a golden censer, came and stood at the altar. He was given much incense, that he should offer it with the prayers of all the saints upon the golden altar which was before the throne. (Rev 8:3) And the smoke of the incense, with the prayers of the saints, ascended before God from the angel's hand. (Rev 8:4) Then the angel took the censer, filled it with fire from the altar, and threw it to the earth. And there were **noises, thunderings, lightnings, and an earthquake**." (Rev 8:5)

We see this theme repeated in Revelation 11 which also includes hail falling:

Then the temple of God was opened in heaven, and the ark of His covenant was seen in His temple. And there were lightnings, noises, thunderings, an earthquake, and great hail. (Rev 11:19)

The opening of the heavenly temple happens in chapter fifteen as well: "the **temple** of the tabernacle of the testimony in **heaven was opened**" (Rev 15:5). After the opening of temple of God in heaven, the final judgments commence on the earth because, as we saw in chapter nineteen, that is when Jesus comes back to engage in the great battle of the Day of the Lord. The opening of the heavens is found in many other places in Scripture as well. Peter describes the Day of the Lord and the opening of the heavens:

But the **day of the Lord** will come as a thief in the night, in which the **heavens will pass away** with a great noise, and the elements will melt with fervent heat; both the earth and the works that are in it will be burned up. (2 Peter 3:10)

Isaiah 34:4 is identical to Revelation 6:13-14 where stars fall like figs and the sky recedes like a scroll:

the **heavens** shall be **rolled up like a scroll**; All their host shall fall down As the leaf falls from the vine, and as [fruit] falling from a fig tree. (Isaiah 34:4)

Isaiah speaks of this moment repeatedly again "the heavens will vanish away like smoke... (Isa 51:6) and then "Oh, that You would **rend the heavens**! That You would come down!" We have been granted a peek full of awe and drama from our earth into the events of heavens passing, as if we were looking up from earth and witnessing how the open heaven that had been hidden to us before by the veil, is passing away.

But we are also shown the frightening events happening at our level, our sky and earth level.

He gives the important detail "That the mountains might shake at Your presence" (Isa 64:1) which helps us provides us with the same details as we have seen in the other passages. Jesus then reiterates this moment concerning his return.

> "Immediately after the tribulation of those days the sun will be darkened, and the moon will not give its light; the **stars will fall from heaven**, and the powers of the heavens will be shaken. (Matt 24:29) "Then the sign of the Son of Man will appear in heaven, and then all the tribes of the earth will mourn, and they will see the Son of Man coming on the clouds of heaven with power and great glory. (Matt 24:30)

Jesus simply summarizes Joel about the sun, moon, and stars, and then Isaiah regarding the falling of the stars and then tells us how people will mourn (be distressed) when they see him, just like Isaiah said in chapter two.

Paul also spoke of this same event by mentioning the uncovering / unveiling / revealing of Jesus where apokalupsi, apo = "away from," kalupsis = veil to the Thessalonians: "when the **Lord Jesus is revealed** (apokalupsi) from heaven with His mighty angels, in **flaming fire** taking vengeance..." (2Thess 1:7-8). Paul's language of "revealing" is parallel to Isaiah: "the glory of the LORD shall be revealed, and all flesh shall see it together.." (Isa 40:5). Paul then combines that with the retributive nature of his coming, associated with fire and vengeance, just like Isaiah:

- For behold, the **LORD comes out of His place** To punish the inhabitants of the earth for their iniquity (Isa 26:21)
- "I have trodden the winepress alone...And trampled them in My fury; Their blood is sprinkled upon My garments... (Isa 63:3)
- For behold, the LORD will come with **fire** And with His chariots, like a whirlwind, To render His anger with fury, and His rebuke with **flames of fire**. (Isa 66:15)

Hence the opening of the heavens is an event that only happens once in the Day of the Lord which will cause the elements to melt, mountains to shake and the greatest of all earthquakes the world has ever known. The multitude of passages referring to the openings of heavens shows us that the thematic approach resolves the burden of trying to explain the different aspects of the judgments. Rather, the thematic interpretation says if one verse quacks and walks like a duck and another passage quacks and walks the same, then they are the same passage.

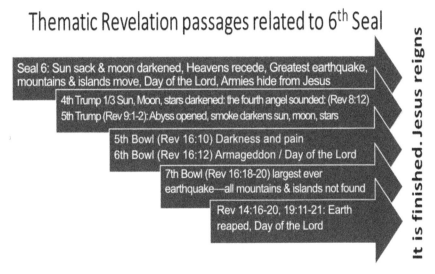

Thematic Revelation passages related to 6th Seal

Seal 6: Sun sack & moon darkened, Heavens recede, Greatest earthquake, mountains & islands move, Day of the Lord, Armies hide from Jesus

4th Trump 1/3 Sun, Moon, stars darkened: the fourth angel sounded: (Rev 8:12)
5th Trump (Rev 9:1-2): Abyss opened, smoke darkens sun, moon, stars

5th Bowl (Rev 16:10) Darkness and pain
6th Bowl (Rev 16:12) Armageddon / Day of the Lord

7th Bowl (Rev 16:18-20) largest ever earthquake—all mountains & islands not found

Rev 14:16-20, 19:11-21: Earth reaped, Day of the Lord

It is finished. Jesus reigns

Table 13. Thematic Revelation passages related to the 6th Seal.

THE SEVEN SEALS AS A TEMPLATE OF THE TRIBULATION

We have considered the earthquakes and opening of the heavens in detail to demonstrate that they are in synchrony with each other. The thematic approach inherently searches for multiple witnesses to establish sound doctrine. In Scripture matters are established by two or three witnesses. In other words, other passages support the contextual meaning of an event as the Holy Spirit revealed it in the text of the Scripture. Interpreting Revelation thematically reveals multiple witnesses which with varying and progressive perspectives. Using the seven seals as a template for the entire

1st Seal: rider on white horse with bow, crown, goes out conquering

- Rev 13:1-4: Beast w/ characteristics of former empires & 7 heads & 10 horns, receives dragon's power, throne, authority
- Rev 17:3 Beast with 7 heads & 10 horns carries the woman
- Other Scriptures of the Beast: Dan 7:7-8; 8:10-13, 23-25, Ezek 38:17; 39:8.

2nd Seal: rider on red horse takes away peace, men kill each other

- Rev 11:5-6: 2 witnesses strike earth w/ plagues
- Other Scriptures about no peace: Deut 17:6; Zech 4:14; Mal 4:4-6 (Moses & Elijah)

3rd Seal: scarcity of food (increasing intensity until Jesus' return)

- Rev 11:5-6: 2 witnesses strike earth w/ plagues
- Rev 8:7: 1st trump: 1/3 trees and grass burned up >> 4th bowl: sun scorches with heat
- Rev 8:8: 2nd trump: 1/3 of seas become blood, 1/3 die >> 2nd bowl: All seas blood and every creature dies. (Rev 16:3)
- 3rd trump: 1/3 of rivers blood and wormwood >> 3rd bowl: all rivers blood
- Other Scriptures: (Isa 24:6-7), (Joel 1:10-20) new wine fails, field wasted, barns broken, day of the Lord comes

4th Seal: Death and Sheol gain authority over all humans (around the middle of Daniel's 70th week) allowed to kill

- Rev 13:7 granted to make war with the saints and overcome them. **Authority** over every tribe, tongue, and nation.
- (Rev 9:11) Abaddon / death / Destruction / King of the Abyss / Sheol kills one third of mankind
- Other authority Scriptures: Isa 28:15; Dan 7:25; 8:25, 9:27

5th Seal: Martyred souls under altar given white garment

- Rev 7 – multitude from Trib in white
- Rev 12:13-17: "Flood" of people (per Jer 46:7-8 & Isa 8:7) persecute kill believers
- Rev 13: killed for not taking mark
- Rev 17:6 the woman, drunk with the blood of the saints and the martyrs of Jesus
- Rev 20 non-mark-takers beheaded, resurrected to reign with Jesus
  - o Other martyrs Scripture: Dan 12:1, 7, 10; Isa 24:4-6, 48:10
- Zech 13:8-9; Hos 5:14-15, Mal 3:3; Dan 11:35; Joel 2:12-14

6ᵗʰ Seal: sun, moon, stars darkened, sky recedes, mountains & islands move, battle-day of Lord, world armies hide from Jesus

- (6ᵗʰ seal) sun black as sackcloth, moon like blood. (Rev 6:12)
    - o He opened the sixth seal, and behold, there was a **great earthquake**; and the **sun** became black as sackcloth of hair, and the **moon** became like **blood. (Rev 6:12)**
    - o 4ᵗʰ Trump 1/3 Sun, Moon, stars darkened: Then the fourth angel sounded: And a third of the **sun** was struck, a third of the moon, and a third of the stars, so that a third of them were **darkened**. A third of the day did not shine, and likewise the night. (Rev 8:12)
    - o 5ᵗʰ trump Rev 9:1-2: abyss opened, sun, moon, stars darkened by smoke (increasing intensity)
        - ▪ And he opened the bottomless pit, and smoke arose out of the pit like the smoke of a great furnace. So the **sun** and the air were **darkened** because of the smoke of the pit. (Rev 9:2)
    - o >> 5ᵗʰ bowl Rev 16:10 Darkness and pain
        - ▪ Then the fifth angel poured out his bowl on the throne of the beast, and his kingdom became full of **darkness**. (Rev 16:10)
    - o Other darkening Scriptures:
        - ▪ "And I will show wonders in the heavens and in the earth: Blood and fire and pillars of smoke. (Joel 2:30) The **sun** shall be turned into **darkness**, and the **moon** into blood, Before the coming of the great and awesome day of the LORD. (Joel 2:31)
        - ▪ Behold, the day of the LORD comes, Cruel, with both wrath and fierce anger, To lay the land desolate; And He will destroy its sinners from it. (Isa 13:9) For the **stars** of heaven and their constellations Will not give their light; The **sun** will be darkened in its going forth, and the **moon** will not cause its light to shine. (Isa 13:10)
        - ▪ sun darkened; moon will not give its light (Matt 24:29)
    - o (6ᵗʰ seal) stars of heaven fell to the earth as a fig tree. (Rev 6:13)

- the LORD will punish on high the host of exalted ones. (Isa 24:21)
- All their host shall fall down…as fruit falling from a fig tree. (Isa 34:4)
- the stars will fall from heaven, and the powers of the heavens will be shaken. (Matt 24:29)

o (6th seal) the sky receded as a scroll when it is rolled up (Rev 6:14)

- Rev 11:19 the temple of God was opened in heaven
- Rev 19:11 heaven opened…He judges and makes war.
- Other Scriptures: Isa 34:4, 64:1; 2Pet 3:10

o (6th seal) Every mountain & island moved (Rev 6:14)

- 7th bowl Rev 16:18 largest ever earthquake - affects all mountains and islands (so they are not found Rev 16:20), hail,
- Isa 2:13-15; 13:13; 24:19-20; 40:4; Jer 4:24; Hab 3:6; (Ezek 38:19-20 all shake, all mountains thrown down)

o (6th seal) Battle w/ Jesus / kings, great men, commanders, hide in caves & in the mountains, "the great day of His wrath has come" (Rev 6:15, 17)

- 6th bowl Rev 16:12: Euphrates runs dry & nations gather to Armageddon for the battle / day of the Lord
- 6th trump: Rev 9: angels released from Euphrates, kill 1/3 mankind, Pabilsags on earth
- Rev 14:16-20 winepress, earth reaped, blood to horses' bridles
- Rev 19:11-21 Jesus treads winepress, Battle / Day of the Lord
  - Rev 19:17-18 Birds called to eat flesh of kings, commanders, etc., Ezek 39:4, 17-20
- Isa 2:10, 19; 26:21; 63:3; 66:15-16; Joel 2; 2Thess 1:7-8; Matt 24:30; Ezek 38:18 fury on my face

7ᵗʰ seal: (& trump & bowl): Lightning, thunders, noises, earthquake, It is finished, Babylon destroyed

- Lightning, thunders, noises, earthquake
    - the seventh seal...silence in heaven for about half an hour. (Rev 8:1) there were **noises, thunderings, lightnings**, and an **earthquake**. (Rev 8:5)
    - the temple of God was opened in heaven...there were lightnings, noises, thunderings, an earthquake, and great hail. (Rev 11:19)
    - And there were noises and thunderings and lightnings; and there was a great earthquake, (Rev 16:18)
    - Ezek 38:22 hail, brimstone
- Finished!
    - in the days of the **sounding** of the seventh angel...the **mystery of God would be finished**. (Rev 10:7)
    - the **seventh angel** sounded: And there were loud voices in heaven, saying, "The **kingdoms of this world have become the kingdoms of our Lord** and of His Christ, and He shall reign forever and ever!" (Rev 11:15) The nations were angry, and **Your wrath has come**, and the time of the dead, that they should be judged, and that You should reward Your servants the prophets and the saints...And should destroy those who destroy the earth." (Rev 11:18)
    - Then the seventh angel poured out his bowl into the air, and a loud voice came out of the <u>temple of heaven</u>, from the throne, saying, **"It is done!"** (Rev 16:17)
        - Ezek 39:29 God hides his face no longer
- Babylon judged
    - Rev 14:8 "Babylon is fallen, is fallen, that **great city**
    - **the great city** was divided...the cities of the nations fell. And great Babylon was remembered...(Rev 16:19)
    - Rev 18:2 Babylon is fallen
    - Rev 19:2 Jesus judged the harlot
    - Ezek 39:21 God sets glory among nations, Isa 48:1-8

CONCLUSION OF THEMATIC APPROACH

We have seen that the thematic method, with its many recapitulations, is used repeatedly in Scripture from Genesis to Revelation. Revelation takes us up to the end many times and then tells the story again from another perspective. Indeed, in the middle of the book, the angel told John: "You must prophesy again about many peoples, nations, tongues, and kings" (Rev 10:11). To interpret the book chronologically causes many problems such as every mountain and island moving out of their place twice which we are told is impossible. The thematic approach to the book focuses on parallel language and when we do that, we find an abundance of identical passages in the prophets and the words of Jesus - passages that superimpose showing they are referring to the same event.

APPENDIX 2: COMPARISON OF GOG AND BEAST / ANTICHRIST

In addition to the linguistic evidence, we also have a lot of Scriptural evidence that shows that Gog is the same person as the Beast. There are two different titles for the same individual. Gog in Ezekiel 38 and 39 is the same person that we read about as the little horn in the Book of Daniel and the beast in Revelation. He has a lot of different titles just as we discovered Satan had many titles in the ancient world such as Enlil, Marduk, Baal, etc.

To properly demonstrate they are the same, we also have to consider the Two passages that speak of the battle they fight. The timing of the battle of Gog and Magog is sometimes considered to be years before the battle of Armageddon and questioning that timing is difficult to entertain because it means radical changes in one's already crystalized beliefs eschatological systems which are built one on another. I am sympathetic if you consider them to be separate events; I once did as well. There have been many theologies I abandoned because I could not reconcile them with all of Scripture. If you are like me, however, knowing what really is going to happen is more exciting than holding on to a theology. Thus, I respectfully and sympathetically request you to consider the evidence with me to see if Gog's war in Ezekiel 38 and 39 is the same as Armageddon.

There are powerful reasons that Gog and Antichrist are the same person and Gog's war, and Armageddon are one and the same event. God established the principle of two or three witnesses (Deut 19:15). That means, for an event as epic and literally earth shaking as the Gog-war it must have another witness, it cannot be an outlier. Indeed, God gave multiple witnesses about the Gog war when he spoke "in former days by My servants the prophets of Israel, who prophesied for years" (Ezek 38:17).

The outline below presents a heading with the feature common to both Gog and his war and the Beast and Armageddon. The Ezekiel passage is first followed by other passages that speak of the Beast (Antichrist, man of sin, son of Perdition, little horn, etc.). We will see that many prophets before Ezekiel did indeed speak about Gog and his war. In another chapter we will consider the name Gog and how it is an excellent title of Israel's coming enemy.

1. Gog and the Beast at the end of days / end of years
   a. "After **many days** you will be visited. In the **latter years** you will come ...mountains of Israel... (Ezek 38:8) It will be in the **latter days** that I will bring you against My land...(Ezek 38:16)
      i. "what shall happen in **the latter time of the indignation;** for at the appointed time **the end shall be.** (Dan 8:19) "And in **the latter time** of their kingdom, When the transgressors have reached their fullness, A king shall arise, (Dan 8:23) "...it refers to **many days in the future.**" (Dan 8:26)
      ii. sealed till the time of the end. (Dan 12:9)
2. God will bring Gog / Beast to Israel
   a. "and I will turn you around and lead you on, bringing you up from the far north, and bring you **against the mountains of Israel.** (Ezek 39:2)
      i. "But **news from the east and the north** shall trouble him; therefore he shall go out with great fury to destroy and annihilate many. (Dan 11:44) "And he shall plant the tents of his palace between the **seas and the glorious holy mountain;** yet he shall come to his end, and no one will help him. (Dan 11:45)
      ii. they gathered them together to the place... called in **Hebrew, Armageddon.** (Rev 16:16)
3. God and the world nations (featured in Gen 10 table nations) attack Israel
   a. "Gog, of the land of **Magog,** the chief [rosh] prince of **Meshech** and **Tubal,** and prophesy against him **Persia, Cush,** and **Put**[333] are with them... **Gomer** and all his hordes; **Beth-Togarmah**...many peoples are with you. (Ezek 38:2, 5-6, ESV)

---

[333] NKJV incorrectly: Libya

b. "I will make Jerusalem a very heavy stone for all peoples; all who would heave it away will surely be cut in pieces, though **all nations of the earth are gathered** against it. (Zech 12:3) "It shall be in that day that I will seek to destroy **all the nations** that come against Jerusalem. (Zech 12:9)

c. I will gather **all the nations** to battle against Jerusalem. (Zech 14:2)

4. Evil plans (thoughts) and boastful

    a. **thoughts** will arise in your mind, and you will make an **evil plan**: (Ezek 38:10) "You will **say**, '**I will go up against** a land of unwalled villages; I will go to a peaceful people, who dwell safely….(Ezek 38:11)

        i. "And in the latter time …A king shall arise, Having **fierce features**, Who understands **sinister schemes**. (Dan 8:23) His power shall be mighty, but not by his own power; He shall destroy fearfully, and shall prosper and thrive; He shall destroy the mighty, and also the holy people. (Dan 8:24)

        ii. Then he opened his **mouth** in **blasphemy** against God…(Rev 13:6)

        iii. "Through his cunning He shall cause deceit to prosper under his rule; And he shall **exalt himself** in his **heart**. He shall destroy many in their prosperity. He shall even rise against the Prince of princes; (Dan 8:25)

5. Global shaking because of God's presence, walls fall

    a. "For in My jealousy and in the fire of My wrath I have spoken: 'Surely in that day there shall be a **great earthquake** in the land of Israel, (Ezek 38:19) 'so that the fish of the sea, the birds of the heavens, the beasts of the field, <u>all</u> creeping things that creep on the earth, and all men who are on the face of the earth shall **shake at My presence**. The **mountains shall be thrown down**, the steep places shall fall, and **every <u>wall</u> shall fall** to the ground.' (Ezek 38:20)

i. Upon all the high mountains, and upon all the hills that are lifted up; (Isa 2:14) Upon every high tower, and upon every fortified <u>wall</u>; (Isa 2:15)

ii. every mountain and island was **moved** out of its place. (Rev 6:14)

iii. there were noises, thunderings, lightnings, and an **earthquake**. (Rev 8:5)

iv. the temple of God was opened in heaven…there were <u>lightnings, noises, thunderings,</u> an **earthquake**. (Rev 11:19)

v. there were <u>noises</u> and <u>thunderings</u> and <u>lightnings;</u> and there was a **great earthquake**, such a mighty and **great earthquake** as **had not** occurred since men were on the earth. (Rev 16:18) (so they are not found Rev 16:20)

vi. Therefore I will **shake** the heavens, and the **earth** will **move** out of her place, In the wrath of the LORD of hosts And in the day of His fierce anger. (Isa 13:13)

vii. The **earth** is **violently** broken, The earth is **split** open, The earth is **shaken** exceedingly. (Isa 24:19) The **earth shall reel to and fro** like a drunkard, and shall totter like a hut; Its transgression shall be heavy upon it, and it will fall, and not rise again. (Isa 24:20)

viii. Every valley shall be exalted And **every mountain** and hill **brought low**; The crooked places shall be made straight And the rough places smooth; (Isa 40:4)

ix. He stood and measured the earth; He looked and startled the nations. And the everlasting **mountains were scattered**, The perpetual **hills bowed**. His ways are everlasting. (Hab 3:6)

6. God's Face is Seen, Fire and brimstone rain on Gog
   a. "when **Gog** comes against the land of Israel," says the Lord GOD, "that **My fury will show in My face**. (Ezek 38:18) "For in My **jealousy** and in the **fire** of My **wrath** (Ezek 38:19)
      i. the LORD will come with **fire** And with His chariots, like a whirlwind, To render His **anger** with **fury**, and His rebuke with **flames of fire**. (Isa 66:15) For by **fire** and by His sword The LORD will judge all flesh; And the slain of the LORD shall be many. (Isa 66:16)
      ii. when the Lord Jesus is **revealed** from heaven with His mighty angels, (2Thess 1:7) in **flaming fire** taking vengeance on those who do not know God (2Thess 1:8)
      iii. and said to the mountains and rocks, "Fall on us and hide us from the **face** of Him who sits on the throne and from the **wrath** of the Lamb! (Rev 6:16)
      iv. They shall go into the holes of the rocks, and into the caves of the earth, From the terror of the LORD And the **glory of His majesty**, When He arises to shake the earth mightily. (Isa 2:19)
      v. He stood and measured the earth; He **looked** and **startled** the nations. And the everlasting mountains were scattered, The perpetual hills bowed. His ways are everlasting. (Hab 3:6)
      vi. "Then the sign of the Son of Man will appear in heaven, and then all the tribes of the earth will mourn, and **they will see the Son of Man** coming on the clouds of heaven with power and great glory. (Matt 24:30)
      vii. The **day of the LORD** comes, Cruel, with both **wrath** and fierce **anger**, To lay the land desolate; And He will destroy its sinners from it. (Isa 13:9)

7. Their armies are confused and attack one another

    a. "I will call for a sword against Gog throughout all My mountains," says the Lord GOD. "**Every man's sword** will be **against** his **brother.** (Ezek 38:21)

        i. It shall come to pass in that day That a **great panic** from the LORD will be among them. **Everyone will seize the hand** of his neighbor, and raise his hand **against** his neighbor's hand; (Zech 14:13)

8. Great hailstones

    a. " <u>great</u> <u>hailstones</u>, fire, and brimstone. (Ezek 38:22)

        i. the temple of God was opened in heaven...there were lightnings, noises, thunderings, **an earthquake,** and <u>great hail</u>. (Rev 11:19)

    b. And <u>great hail</u> from heaven fell upon men, each <u>hailstone</u> about the weight of a talent. (Rev 16:21)

9. Pestilence, bloodshed, fire brimstone

    a. "And I will bring him to judgment with **pestilence** and **bloodshed**; I will rain down on him, on his troops, and on the many peoples who are with him, flooding rain, great hailstones, **fire**, and **brimstone**. (Ezek 38:22)

        i. Rev 19:11-21 Jesus treads winepress, Battle / Day of the Lord

        ii. Rev 14:16-20 winepress, earth reaped, **blood** to horses' bridles

        iii. "I have trodden the winepress alone...And trampled them in My fury; Their **blood** is sprinkled upon My garments... (Isa 63:3)

        iv. there was a great earthquake; and the sun became black as sackcloth of hair, and the moon became like **blood**. (Rev 6:12)

        v. "I will show wonders in the heavens and in the earth: **Blood** and **fire** and **pillars** of **smoke**. (Joel 2:30) The sun shall be turned into darkness, and the moon into **blood**, Before the coming of the great and awesome day of the LORD. (Joel 2:31)

10. Gog and the Beast are Destroyed at the end of the battle
   a. "I will give **Gog a burial place** there in Israel…Therefore they will call it the **Valley of Hamon Gog**. (Ezek 39:11)
      i. "the **beast** was **slain**, and its body destroyed and given to **the burning flame**. (Dan 7:11)
      ii. Then the **beast** was captured, and with him the false prophet …These two were cast alive into the **lake of fire** burning with brimstone. (Rev 19:20)
      iii. "And they shall go forth and look Upon the **corpses** of the men Who have **transgressed against Me**. For their worm does not die, and **their fire** is not quenched. They shall be an abhorrence to all flesh." (Isa 66:24)

11. Birds Feast on Kings and horses (Nergal) at God's supper
   a. 'Speak to every sort of **bird** and to every beast of the field: "Assemble yourselves and come; Gather **together** from all sides to My **sacrificial meal** Which I am sacrificing for you, A great sacrificial meal on the mountains of Israel, That you may eat flesh and drink blood. (Ezek 39:17) You shall **eat** the flesh of the **mighty**, Drink the blood of the **princes** of the earth… (Ezek 39:18) You shall be filled at My table With **horses** and **riders**, With mighty men And with all the men of war," says the Lord GOD. (Ezek 39:20)
      i. Then I saw an angel standing in the sun; and he cried with a loud voice, saying to all the **birds** that fly in the midst of heaven, "Come and **gather** together for the **supper of the great God**, (Rev 19:17) "that you may **eat** the **flesh** of **kings**, the flesh of captains, the flesh of **mighty** men, the flesh of **horses** and of those **who sit on them**, and the **flesh of all people**, free and slave, both small and great." (Rev 19:18)

12. After both battles weapons of war are destroyed
   a. "Israel will go out and set on fire and burn the **weapons**, both the shields and bucklers, the bows and arrows, the javelins and spears... (Ezek 39:9)
      i. They shall beat their swords into plowshares... (Isa 2:4)
13. God's name no longer be profaned...
   a. "Thus I will magnify Myself and sanctify Myself, and **I will be known** in the eyes of many nations. Then **they shall know that I am the LORD.**' (Ezek 38:23)
   b. "So I will make **My holy name known** in the midst of My people Israel, and I will not **let them profane** My holy name anymore. Then the **nations** shall **know** that **I am the LORD**, the Holy One in Israel. (Ezek 39:7)
      i. And the rest were killed with the sword which proceeded **from the mouth of Him who sat on the horse**. (Rev 19:21)
14. God pours out His Spirit and not hide face
   a. 'And I will **not hide My face** from them anymore; for I shall have **poured out My Spirit** on the house of Israel,' says the Lord GOD." (Ezek 39:29)
      i. With a little wrath **I hid My face** from you for a moment; But with everlasting kindness I will have mercy on you," Says the LORD, your Redeemer. (Isa 54:8)
      ii. "I will **pour on** the house of David and on the inhabitants of Jerusalem the **Spirit of grace** and supplication; then they **will look to Me** whom they pierced. Yes, they will mourn for Him as one mourns for his only son, and grieve for Him as one grieves for a firstborn. (Zech 12:10)
15. After both battles "It is done"
   a. "Surely it is coming, and **it shall be done**," says the Lord GOD. "This is the day of which I have spoken. (Ezek 39:8)

i. in the days of the **sounding** of the **seventh angel**...the **mystery of God would be** <u>finished</u>. (Rev 10:7)

ii. 7ᵗʰ **trumpet**: "The **kingdoms of this world have become the kingdoms of our Lord** and of His Christ, and He shall reign forever and ever!" (Rev 11:15) The nations were angry, and **Your wrath has come**, and the **time** of the **dead**, that they **should** be **judged**, and that You should reward Your servants the prophets and the saints...And should destroy those who destroy the earth." (Rev 11:18)

iii. 7ᵗʰ **Bowl** into the air, and a loud voice came out of the **temple of heaven**, from the throne, saying, **"It is done!"** (Rev 16:17)

16. After Battle - God shows his glory among the nations

a. "I will send fire on Magog and on those who live in security in the coastlands. Then they shall know that I am the LORD. (Ezek 39:6)

i. "I will set My glory among the **nations**; all the nations shall see My judgment (Ezek 39:21)

ii. **the great city** was divided...the cities of the **nations** fell. And great Babylon was remembered...(Rev 16:19)

TABLE OF NATIONS

All nations will come against Jerusalem. All the nations in Ezekiel 38 and 39 represent all the sons of Noah, which are the stock that all people came from. Not every nation is mentioned as that would take a while and they change their names over time. Nevertheless, by comparing the nations of Ezekiel 38-39, we can see how they represent the people from the Genesis 10 Table of Nations.

In Midrash Wayosha' (Jellinek, "B. H." i. 56) Gog is the leader of the seventy-two nations of the world, minus one (Israel), and makes war against the Most High; he is smitten down by God.[334]

---

[334] https://jewishencyclopedia.com/articles/5849-eschatology

Ezekiel 38 Reflecting the Table of Nations	Gen 10 Table of Nations	Common References in both & Modern equivalent[335]
"Son of man, set your face toward Gog, of the land of **Magog**, the chief [rosh] prince of **Meshech** and **Tubal**, and prophesy against him **Persia, Cush**, and **Put**[336] are with them… **Gomer** and all his hordes; **Beth-Togarmah**…many peoples are with you. (Ezek 38:2, 5-6, ESV)	The sons of Japheth *were* **Gomer, Magog,** Madai, Javan, **Tubal, Meshech,** and Tiras. (Gen 10:2) The sons of **Gomer**: Ashkenaz, Riphath, and **Togarmah**. (Gen 10:3) The sons of Javan: Elishah, **Tarshish**, Kittim, and Dodanim. (Gen 10:4)The sons of Ham: **Cush**, Egypt, **Put**, and Canaan. (Gen 10:6) The sons of **Cush**: Seba, Havilah, Sabtah, Raamah, and Sabteca. The sons of Raamah: **Sheba** and **Dedan**. (Gen 10:7) The sons of Shem were **Elam (Persia/Iran** cf AmTrac Dic), Asshur, Arphaxad, Lud, and Aram. (Gen 10:22)	Sons of Japheth Gomer = Turkey (Cimmerians) Magog = Turkey Tubal = Near Black Sea / Georgia Meshech =Turkey Beth-togarmah – Asia Minor Countries including the "istan" countries and Georgia, Armenia Sons of Ham Cush = Ethiopia Put = Somalia Son of Shem Elam = Iran

Table 14. Genesis 10 Table of Nations.

---

[336] NKJV incorrectly: Libya

The names in Genesis 10 were the descendants of Japhet, Ham, and Shem, the three sons of Noah. They all went to their respective places, and they had children, and they became people groups. Over time, continued to spread out all over the world. Rather than trying to pin a biblical place to a specific geographical location (e.g., Cush = Ethiopia), we get a much broader view if we realize that the text is talking about the nations of the world. The peoples in Ezekiel 38 are the same as those of the table of nations.

Figure 58. Division of peoples throughout the world based on Genesis 10.

Looking at the map, green are the sons of Ham, yellow are the sons of Shem, and pink are the sons of Japheth. These areas where the various people groups settled; and then they spread out from there. They went east to Asia, west to Europe, and eventually to America, and they went north and south. All these different groups have gone out from there. We do not have to look only exclusively around the nation of Israel. We do not have to only look in the Middle East even though it has a big part to play. The bottom line is we are looking at the entire world.

APPENDIX 3: GOG AND MAGOG IN THE MILLENNIUM?

Some have suggested *Gog* and *Magog* must be a reference to what is going to happen after the millennium since in Revelation 20:8 we read:

"Now when the thousand years have expired, Satan will be released from his prison Rev 20:7 and will go out to deceive the nations which are in the four corners of the earth, **Gog and Magog**, to gather them together to battle, whose number *is* as the sand of the sea. Rev 20:8"

After the thousand years have expired, when Satan has been put into the abyss, he is put into the *bôr* sometimes known as the bottomless pit, he will be there a thousand years and there will be this wonderful time on planet Earth. Satan will not be there, but then he will be released.

However, since we know the meaning of Gog as *enmity / death* the mention of Gog after the thousand years of bliss is readily understandable: the enemy or that which has enmity and is hostile toward God's kingdom, will reappear on earth after Satan's release will allow him again to regain his quality of opposer, enemy warrior like first time and challenge God one final time. Now it makes so much more sense. Now Rev 20 doesn't have to be placed before the tribulation. No, this can still happen after the thousand years reign of Christ. We are also told that there will be no more warfare in the age to come.

"He shall judge between the nations, and rebuke many people; they shall beat their swords into plowshares, and their spears into pruning hooks; nation shall not lift up sword against nation, neither shall they learn war anymore." Isa 2:4

The reference to bucklers and shields in Ezekiel 38 describes God's strategy of driving Gog's armies using the "hook" towards the great valley of Judgement. This event definitely happens before the great Armagedon battle. Hence we can exclude it from the Millennium time frame. After the thousand years, Satan the enemy will gather those with enmity against God after his release in Revelation 20. The only aggressive act that they perform is surrounding the beloved city. There is no mention of weapons; it does not say that they have any type of warfare other than that they surround the city and then fire comes down from God and destroys them. There is no reason that the *Gog* and *Magog* of Revelation 20 pose a conflict to what we see in Ezekiel 38-39; and that Ezekiel 38-39 is in fact the time of the tribulation.

APPENDIX 4: SUMERIAN LOAN WORDS IN HEBREW

Many Sumerian loan words made their way into Hebrew. What is a loan word? It is a word borrowed from one language & used in another: For example, "picnic," "coup d'état," and "jogging" are French loan words that English speakers liked and borrowed them.

An example is the word Palace. We see it borrowed from the "Akkadian ekallu" which means palace; we have Phoenician,היכל the Biblical Aramaic. We have היכלא Syriac, היכלא Mandaic היכלא Ugaritic hkl (palace or temple); from Arabic haykal which means a church and it's probably an Aramaic loan word; the Akkadian ekallu is probably a loan word from Sumerian e-gal which means great house.[337]

The words: heichal (היכל), Adrichal (אדריכל), and tarnegol (תרנגול) are loan words. "Adrichal" in Modern Hebrew means "architect," and first appears in the Talmudic literature. The etymology of this form, according to Even-Shoshan, is from the Akkadian erad-ekaly. This means "worker of the heichal" [which is the big house] – which we noted is originally Sumerian. Ilan points out that originally the adrichal was the builder, not the architect. Erad here is related to the Akkadian word aradu - "to serve" and ardu - "slave." This appears to be cognate with the Hebrew root " ירד to descend," and relates to the lower, subjugated status of the slave.

"Tarnegol" or "rooster" is also borrowed from Akkadian "tar lugallu," which is Sumerian "tar lugal" or "bird of the king," "Lugal" meant king in Sumerian, and it was made up of two parts - lu (man) and gal (great), like we had e-gal which was the big house.[338]

These are quick snapshots demonstrating how Sumerian loan words made their way into Hebrew and how "Gog" could come from Sumerian.

---

[337] http://www.balashon.com/2008/02/heichal-adrichal-and-tarnegol.html
[338] http://www.balashon.com/2008/02/heichal-adrichal-and-tarnegol.html

Despite the incredible number of parallels of GUG/UG, and the evidence of Sumerian loan words, Ezekiel wrote Gog not GUG. Do we have any linguistic attestation of Sumerian "u" becoming "o" in Hebrew, which is to ask can the Sumerian "Gug" turn into the Hebrew "Gog"? The answer is yes. An example, according to the lexicon Abraham Even-Shoshan, is that "the Hebrew word "Kor" comes from Sumerian "GUR, "a bundle of barley; standard unit of capacity."[339] The word was borrowed in Akkadian as "kurru," and then in Hebrew as kor [כֹּר] "Solomon's provision for one day was thirty kors [כֹּר] of fine flour..." (1Kgs 4:22)

What is surprising is that the Gog (hostility, death) was worshipped in Israel as a star. We have already examined variations of the name Gog, including UŠ.

---

339 Abraham Even-Shoshan (אַבְרָהָם אֱבֶן־שֹׁשָׁן) et al., הַמִּלּוֹן הֶחָדָשׁ (ha-milón he-khadásh, "The New Dictionary"), Kiryat-Sefer Ltd. (קִרְיַת־סֵפֶר בָּע"מ) (1984), volume 1 of 3 (א to כ), page 531. CF. https://en.wiktionary.org/wiki/Category:Hebrew_terms_derived_from_Sum erian

APPENDIX 5: LINGUISTIC STUDY GAG

The Akkadian words Šukudu, šiltāhu, and sikkatu, listed by Amar Annus (epithets of Ninurta and when seen in Sumerian) reveal a mystery and are certainly part of the cipher of Gog's name. The first word for arrow is Šukudu meaning "Sirius," in Sumerian is **GAG.SI.SÁ**. The suffix SI.SA means "righteous, straight, proper, make vertical,"[340] which is fitting since arrows are to go "straight" and "vertical."

The next Akkadian epithet is šiltāhu [GIŠ.**GAG**.U4.TAG.GA] means "an arrow; qaqqad šiltāhu: an arrowhead; 2) (epithet for divine name); 3) astronomy: [MUL.**GAG**.SI.SÁ]: Sirius."[341] GIŠ (wood) and MUL (star) are both determinatives, which was a device in Sumerian to let the reader know what kind of word they are looking at,[342] but not pronounced. Hence, the reader knew GIŠ had something to do with wood and MUL with stars. In MUL.**GAG**.SI.SÁ, MUL=star, GAG=arrow, SI.SÁ=straight /

---

340 There are many examples of si-sa in Gudea's inscriptions. First, si-sa means "righteous." It is equivalent to the meaning of nig-si-sa "social justice" in the law codes. lu lu-si-sa nig-erim-ak-gin7 "Like the man who does wrong to a righteous man," Gudea St. B, IX 24 zi-du-e su-si-sa-da erim-du-e gu gis ga-ga-da "to take care of the honest man righteously, and to beat the evil man," Gudea Cyl. B, VI 11-12 www.jstage.jst.go.jp/article/orient1960/21/0/21_0_31/_pdf#:~:text=Si%2Dsa %20means%20simply%20%22to,correctly%20yokes%20for%20the%20ox en.%22&text=There%20are%20other%20examples%20of,to%20the%20fu nctions%20of%20Lugalsisa. See also: si sa "to make straight; to make vertical" Akk. ešēru; šutēšuru http://psd.museum.upenn.edu/nepsd-frame.html

341 http://www.assyrianlanguages.org/akkadian/ Search term šiltāhu.

342 A determinative is one of a limited number of signs which, when placed before or after a sign or group of signs, indicates that the determined object belongs to a particular semantic category, e.g. wooden, reed, copper or bronze objects, or persons, deities, places, etc. Determinatives were still basically optional as late as the Ur III period (2114-2004). Daniel A. Foxvog, "Introduction to Sumerian Grammar" Pg. 17. Posted to web: 4 January 2016. http://cdli.ucla.edu/?q=cuneiform-digital-library-preprints Hosted by the Cuneiform Digital Library Initiative (<http://cdli.ucla.edu>) Editor: Bertrand Lafont (CNRS, Nanterre) Number 2.

vertical; hence the literal meaning is "straight-vertical arrow star" or "Sirius" with "GAG," being the key word. **Sikkatu.** wooden peg or a copper nail,[343] is GIŠ.GAG, in Sumerian.[344] GIŠ is a determinative for wood, which leaves just the word GAG.

Akkadian Epithet of Ninurta	Sumerian	meaning
ūṣu	ᴳᴵˢ.**GAG**.(TI) ti [ARROW] wr. ti "arrow"	arrow, arrowhead
sikkatu; ūṣu	ĝeš**gag**; gag; urudgag	"arrowhead; peg, nail"
šiltāḫu *qaqqad* *šiltāḫi*	ᴳᴵˢ.**GAG**.U₄.TAG.GA ᴹᵁᴸ.**GAG**.SI.SÁ	Arrow, arrowhead / Sirius
šukudu	**GAG**.SI.SÁ / astr. ᴹᵁᴸ.GAG.SI.SÁ	an arrow /Sirius
Mulmullu (Zappu)	mul.mul	arrow

Table 15. Epithets of Ninurta.

---

[343] 1) a wooden peg, a copper nail; 2) part of a chariot / a door / a lock; 3) the blade of a plough / a ploughshare / a plowshare; 4) a stake boundary-marker, *ša sikkatu*, a land surveyor (?); 5) mathematics: a cone, a pyramid; 6) Assyrian architecture, a foundation cone, a peg stone or terracotta in a wall: see karru (2); 7),: sikkat ṣēli / siqqa ṣēli: the breastbone / the sternum, [GAG.TI]
http://www.assyrianlanguages.org/akkadian/dosearch.php?searchkey=8776&language=id
[344] Is also listed as URUDU.GAG:
http://www.assyrianlanguages.org/akkadian/dosearch.php?searchkey=8776&language=id

Thus, "GAG" is present in three of Ninurta's arrow-epithets. When we consider the Sumerian word "GAG," irrespective of the determinatives and suffixes, we find the primary meaning is "arrowhead."[345]

In other words, Ninurta's epithet "arrow" (Akkadian šukudu, etc.) is GAG in Sumerian. Arrow in Akkadian and Sumerian was also a circumlocution for the star Sirius. Šukudu appears in Amos 5:26 as the "star of your gods" specifically speaking of Nimrod / Ninurta and the hidden Sumerian name is GAG.

We therefore conclude that Ninurta is Gag. GAG is to be pronounced like the "a" as in father.[346] Hence, The Sumerian word representing all those ideas is GAG which we discovered is also related to GUG enmity. Our discovery helps us understand why the LXX called Gog the king of a swarm of locusts: "a swarm of locusts coming from the east; and behold, one caterpillar, king Gog (γωγ ο βασιλευς)." (Amos 7:1 LXX Brenton) The correlations are astounding and are hard to take them all in.

---

[345] http://psd.museum.upenn.edu/nepsd-frame.html. Search term "gag."
[346] An example of Sumerian "a" becoming a Hebrew "o" is the Sumerian "allanum" (oak, acorn), borrowed by Akkadian ʾallānu, alyānu, "oak; acorn" which then came into Hebrew as "elon" [אֵלוֹן (elon)]. And "u" (oo) becoming an "a" is seen in Dumuzid into the Hebrew Tammuz as well as Sumerian "dub" "tablet" becoming "daf" in Hebrew. Abraham Even-Shoshan (אַבְרָהָם אֶבֶן־שֹׁשָׁן) et al., הַמִּלּוֹן הֶחָדָשׁ (ha-milón he-khadásh, "The New Dictionary"), Kiryat-Sefer Ltd. (בע״מ) (קִרְיַת־סֵפֶר) (1984), volume 1 of 3 (א to כ), page 531. CF. https://en.wiktionary.org/wiki/Category:Hebrew_terms_derived_from_Sum erian

APPENDIX 6: YARCHETEI TZAFON

Gog is said to come from the "the farthest sides of the North," a phrase used five times in Scripture. In Hebrew it is [יַרְכְּתֵי צָפוֹן *yarchetei tzafon*]. It is used to reference to God's abode.

> In the city of our God, In His holy mountain...Is Mount Zion on the **sides of the north** [יַרְכְּתֵי צָפוֹן *yarchetei tzafon*], The city of the great King (Psa 48:1-2).

That city is identified as heavenly: "Mount Zion and to the city of the living God, the heavenly Jerusalem" (Heb 12:22). We also recall how Satan said he wanted to:

> "'...ascend into heaven, [he said] I will exalt my throne above the stars [angels] of God; I will also sit on the mount(ain) of the congregation on the **farthest sides of the north**" [יַרְכְּתֵי צָפוֹן *yarchetei tzafon*] (Isa 14:13).

In Ezekiel 28, we are told that Satan was "on the holy mountain of God" (Ezek 28:14). These usages demonstrate how the phrase is not referring to a physical realm place but a spiritual / heavenly place. In other words, the spiritual dimension is a place. It is not just an abstraction; it is there in the geographical area compatible with God's presence, but is in a dimensionally different space that we cannot see, walk, drive, or fly to.

> When Ezekiel used the phrase three times in Ezekiel 38-39, it was already established as a spiritual place rather than purely physical.

- "Gomer and all its troops; the house of Togarmah *from* the far north [יַרְכְּתֵי צָפוֹן *yarchetei tzafon*], and all its troops–many people *are* with you. (Ezek 38:6)

- "Then you will come from your place out of the far north [יַרְכְּתֵי צָפוֹן *yarchetei tzafon*], you and many peoples with you, all of them riding on horses, a great company and a mighty army. (Ezek 38:15)

- "and I will turn you around and lead you on, bringing you up from the far north [יַרְכְּתֵי צָפוֹן *yarchetei tzafon*], and bring you against the mountains of Israel. (Ezek 39:2)

We may conclude that the army coming from the far north may not merely be a topographical reference but likely has a dual reality: partly physical and definitely spiritual. This makes perfect sense when we see Satan and his angels, who had previously been confined only to the spiritual realm, forced into this realm: "nor was a **place found for them in heaven** any longer, (Rev 12:8) the great dragon was cast out…to the earth" (Rev 12:9). We also see these beings go out to gather the nations to the great battle:

Figure 59. The approximate locations of people described in Ezekiel 38-39.

> For they are spirits of demons, performing signs, *which* go out to the kings of the earth and of the whole world, to gather them to the battle of that great day of God Almighty. (Rev 16:14)

So, we see the armies that will face each other: on one side Gog's hordes comprised of humans who have become hybrids. On the other side the heavenly hosts who will now operate openly in the earthly realm.

APPENDIX 7: SATAN IS THE GOD OF DEATH

For us to make sense of some of the end times prophecies about Satan (the great dragon), we need to recall that before the cross, Satan had the "power of death" (Heb 2:14) and ruled mankind "through fear of death [who] were all their lifetime subject to bondage" (Heb 2:15). Satan is the god of death, the god of the underworld (Sheol / Hades) and known as a mountain, three points that will connect many dots.

We recall from our studies in *Corrupting the Image 2* how Satan's secret logogram ⊨◁ BAD, hidden in the Hermon inscription (BATios), revealed him as the god of death. [347] The plural and imperfect singular stem of uš (to die) is ug7, [348] Sumerologist John Halloran points out how one of the words for lion in Sumerian was "ug(2): n., rage, anger, fury; storm(-demon); lion; wild animal; lamentation." He also notes it is related to "ug4,5,7,8: n., death; dead person. v., to kill; to die (singular and plural marû stem; plural ‹amu, which is sometimes reduplicated; cf., úš)." [349]

Professor Amar Annus notes that Dagan and Enlil "share the logogram BAD (=IDIM). The name of Dagan is written logographically dKUR ... a shortened form of Enlil's epithet KUR.GAL 'great mountain.'" [350] One of Enlil's major epithets was KUR-GAL (great mountain) which was also ascribed to god the Amorites (Amurru /

---

[347] BAD ⊨◁ represents the Sumerian word "úš = death, destruction" uš2 = die, kill; blood https://mugsarsumerian.com/default.htm#u12041. Proto-Semitic: *mūt, Arabic: māta مَاتَ Hebrew: māṯ מָת, Ugaritic: mt ⊤ ⊢ (mâtu in Akkadian), http://www.assyrianlanguages.org/akkadian/dosearch.php

[348] https://mugsarsumerian.com/default.htm#u12357_USH2_die_kill_blood

[349] https://www.sumerian.org/sumerfaq.htm His definition is confirmed by the University of Pennsylvania which states UG (BAD.BAD) means to die. http://psd.museum.upenn.edu/nepsd-frame.html

[350] Amar Annus, The God Ninurta in the Mythology and Royal Ideology of Ancient Mesopotamia, State Archives of Assyria Studies, Volume XIV Helsinki 2002. Pg. 178

MARTU) demonstrating that they were "one and the same god."[351] Furthermore Frans Wiggermann notes how Nergal, god of the underworld was another syncretism of Enlil and was explicitly called the "Enlil of the mountain (kur netherworld)." [352] Additionally, Nergal / Ninurta was "the **lion**, whom the Great Mountain (= Enlil) engendered,"[353] and also "Enlil the Great Mountain made obeisance to him."[354]

Hence Satan was the god of the dead (BAD), was god of the underworld (via Nergal) and was described as a mountain (KUR-GAL). These points are true for his aliases, the gods of death: Dagon, Molech, Addu, and Isthara.[355]

We also recall that Satan was known definitively as the great dragon in the ancient world by the names *Ushumgal, mušḫuššu and Basmu.*

"*Ušumgallu* also designates a host of Mesopotamian deities, including Marduk … His exalted position over humanity is expressed in the appellation, "great dragon of the heavens and earth." [356] The Ušumgallu was also known as the Anzu bird or 'lion-dragon' [357] whose foremost quality was "being a determined killer, killing probably with its venom, and frightening even the gods."[358]

---

[351] Clay, Albert T. "The Origin and Real Name of NIN-IB." Journal of the American Oriental Society 28 (1907): 135-44. Accessed September 11, 2020. doi:10.2307/592765.

[352] Frans Wiggermann, Nergal, Reallexikon der Assyriologie (RlA) 9 1999 Pg. 215-226.

[353] Amar Annus, The God Ninurta in the Mythology and Royal Ideology of Ancient Mesopotamia, State Archives of Assyria Studies, Volume XIV Helsinki 2002. Pg. 11

[354] Amar Annus, The God Ninurta in the Mythology and Royal Ideology of Ancient Mesopotamia, State Archives of Assyria Studies, Volume XIV Helsinki 2002. Pg. 122

[355] http://etcsl.orinst.ox.ac.uk/section1/tr162.htm

[356] Tyler R. Yoder, "Ezekiel 29:3 and Its Ancient Near Eastern Context" Vetus Testamentum 63 (2013) Pg. 486-96

[357] Ibid.

[358] "It is first attested by a 22nd-century BC cylinder inscription at Gudea." F. A. M. Wiggermann, *Mesopotamian Protective Spirits*, Pg. 167.

Figure 60. UŠUMGAL or Anzu bird Icon By editor Austen Henry Layard, drawing by L. Gruner - Monuments of Nineveh.

Another dragon was the Bašmu snake-dragon (Bashan in the Bible and sometimes as a catch all term for dragon). It was a determined killer, and was a suitable epithet for gods and kings! [359] Bashmu, in astronomy, was the constellation Hydra [360], the seven headed dragon[361] killed "by the god Ningirsu or Ninurta."[362] (See Figure 8). "Nergal's divine staff was as 'awe-inspiring as a serpent' and Ninurta's mace consisted of seven snake-like heads."[363] Furthermore, Nergal / Ninurta / Enlil) was described as: "[ú-šum]-gal-lu ṣīru tābik imti elišunu "The majestic, great dragon who pours his venom upon them." [364]

---

[359] Ibid.
[360]

http://www.assyrianlanguages.org/akkadian/dosearch.php?searchkey=4876&language=id

[361] According to Wiggermann: "Ereškigal...queen of the netherworld, rules the dead ... is associated with the constellation Hydra (MUL.dMUŠ) in late astrological texts ... the Babylonian constellation ... Its Babylonian name was probably Bašmu. Ereshkigal's messenger, Mutum "Death" ... He has the head of a mušḫuššu dragon." Transtigridian Snake Gods Wiggermann Pg. 35.

[362] God, Demons, and Symbols of Ancient Mesopotamia: Bašmu

[363] Ibid.6

[364] Tyler R. Yoder, "Ezekiel 29:3 and Its Ancient Near Eastern Context" Vetus Testamentum 63 (2013) Pg. 486-96

Figure 61. Ninurta killing one of the heads of the seven-headed serpent. Bible Review, Oct. 1992, 28 (=ANEP #671) (Early Dynastic). Courtesy of the Bible Lands Museum, Jerusalem.

Nergal god of the underworld and syncretism of Ninurta, Melqart, Marduk and Enlil, was called a seven-headed snake. The great dragon of Revelation has "seven heads and ten horns," (Rev 12:3) as does the Beast, who has "seven heads and ten horns" (Rev 13:1). Not only does the iconography reveal a great dragon,[365] but John saw "one of his heads as if it had been mortally wounded, and his deadly wound was healed. And all the world marveled and followed the Beast (Rev 13:3). Looking at Figure 22 above, we see that one of the heads is mortally wounded. God is revealing that the symbols in Revelation relate directly back to the false gods of Babylon.

---

[365] Yoder has shown how God, in Ezekiel, used the term "great dragon" to describe who Pharaoh thought he was. "Behold, I am against you, O Pharaoh king of Egypt, O great monster." The Greek Septuagint "great monster" as τον δρακοντα τον μεγαν "great dragon" (Ezek 29:3). Yoder explains "The prophet could easily have drawn from an existing cache of unambiguous expressions to portray Pharaoh, but instead chose a term suffused with mythological overtones." Tyler R. Yoder, "Ezekiel 29:3 and Its Ancient Near Eastern Context" Vetus Testamentum 63 (2013) 486-96.

Figure 62. Ninurta with wings.

There were many variations of the dragon, but they all lead back to a merging of Enlil and Ninurta (Satan and Nimrod). Jacobsen notes that with Ninurta "in time the animal forms were rejected in favor of imagining the god in human form only."[366] The lion with wings found in Old Babylonian, Akkadian (Assyrian), and Neo-Babylonian iconography is the same description we find in the Book of Daniel:

"The first was like a **lion**, and had **eagle's wings**. I watched till its wings were plucked off; and it was lifted up from the earth and made **to stand on two feet like a man**, and a man's heart was given to it" (Dan 7:4).

The next two creatures, the bear and leopard, are also predators like the lion.

"And suddenly another beast, a second, like a **bear**. It was raised up on one side, and had three ribs in its mouth between its teeth. And they said thus to it: 'Arise, devour much flesh!' (Dan 7:5) "After this I looked, and there was another, like a **leopard**, which had on its back four wings of a bird. The beast also had four heads, and dominion was given to it. (Dan 7:6)

---

[366] Jacobsen, Th. 1987 *The Harps that Once... Sumerian Poetry in Translation.* New Haven and London: Yale University Press. PG. 235.

The bear, "raised up on one side" appears unbalanced, a likely reference to the supremacy of the Persians in the Medo-Persian empire who came after the Neo-Babylonian empire. This same imbalance is present in the vision Daniel has in chapter eight: "was a ram which had two horns, and the Two horns were high; but **one was higher than the other**, and the higher one came up last" (Dan 8:3). The angel gives a plain interpretation about the ram with "two horns–*they are* the kings of Media and Persia" (Dan 8:20). The imbalanced bear in chapter seven is also Medo-Persia. The meaning of the three ribs is not clear but Persia did indeed devour much flesh in the amount of territory they conquered, which included Babylon.

In 331 BC, Darius III, the last Persian king, was defeated by Alexander the Great at the Battle of Gaugamela. The angel told Daniel "the male goat *is* the kingdom of Greece" (Dan 8:21). The leopard is known for its great speed and Alexander the great conquered Babylon and the entire Persian empire with incredible speed. The four wings and four heads are almost certainly referring to the four generals who succeeded Alexander the great. In chapter eight, the angel says plainly: "the male goat is the kingdom of Greece" (Dan 8:21a). He then follows up "The large horn that is between its eyes is the first king" (Dan 8:21b); the first king is Alexander the Great.

Lastly, he interprets: "As for the broken horn and the four that stood up in its place, four kingdoms shall arise out of that nation, but not with its power" (Dan 8:22). The vision of chapters seven and eight are one and the same though chapter eight focuses only on Medo-Persia and Greece (and its subsequent kingdoms). John also notes characteristics of "the beast... like a **leopard**, his feet were like the feet of a **bear**, and his mouth like the mouth of a **lion**" (Rev 13:2). In each succeeding kingdom, the management changed but Satan's (detestable) worship system remained in effect.

The Beast that will ascend out of the abyss, therefore, is the culmination and composite of the three kingdoms which ruled Babylon and supported the woman. The Beast will possess all their power, strength, speed, influence, authority, glory, and pride. The Beast will have a fierce countenance (Dan 8:23) and his power will not be his own (Dan 8:24).

The source of the beast's power will come from Satan himself. "The dragon gave him his power, his throne, and great authority. (Rev 13:2) It will be a repeat of what he previously did with Nimrod (Ninurta), "whom Enlil has exalted above himself" [367]

These dragons and amalgamated creatures represent Enlil and his various syncretisms such as Nergal, Ninurta, Marduk, etc. Their common identifier is that they are fierce killers which is why their impersonator himself is called "death" and are often known as the god of the underworld. Hence Satan is the king (god) of death, the god of the underworld (Sheol / Hades). Put another way, Death (מָוֶת Mavet) and Sheol or Death and Hades are epithets of Satan. It is important for us to have the right understanding of what comes next: the covenant with death and Sheol / Hades grants Satan authority over mankind.

---

[367] Amar Annus, The God Ninurta in the Mythology and Royal Ideology of Ancient Mesopotamia, State Archives of Assyria Studies, Volume XIV Helsinki 2002. Pg. 122

Bibliography

"Ancient Mesopotamian Gods and Goddesses," ORACC Museum, based on data prepared by the UK HEA-funded AMGG project, May 2011, oracc.museum.upenn.edu/ amgg/index.html.

Abraham Even-Shoshan (אַבְרָהָם אֶבֶן־שׁוֹשָׁן) et al., הַמִּלוֹן הֶחָדָשׁ (ha-milón he-khadásh, "The New Dictionary"), Kiryat-Sefer Ltd. (קִרְיַת־סֵפֶר בְּע״מ) (1984), volume 1 of 3 (א to כ), page 531. CF. en.wiktionary.org/wiki/Category:Hebrew_terms_derived_from_S umerian

According to MUFON reporting as seen on Netflix: Hangar 1: The UFO Files

Ahroni, R. *The Gog Prophecy and the Book of Ezekiel*, HAR I (1977) 1-27 Cf. DDDB

Akkadian Dictionary, s.v. "Cherub," "Ug." Accessed through Association Assyrophile de France, www.assyrianlanguages.org/akkadian/.

Albert T. Clay, "Ellil, the God of Nippur" AJSL 23 (1907) 277.

All quotations from Dr. John Mack retrieved July 14, 2010 from: www.pbs.org/wgbh/nova/aliens/johnmack.html

Annus, Amar. *The God Ninurta in the Mythology and Royal Ideology of Ancient Mesopotamia*. State Archives of Assyria Studies, Volume 14. Helsinki: Neo-Assyrian Text Corpus Project, 2002.

Austin Feff - Own work, CC BY-SA 4.0, commons.wikimedia.org/w/index.php?curid=79121417

basarab-nicolescu.fr/Docs_articles/CHK_3.pdf Cybernetics and Human Knowing. Vol. 23 (2016), no. 4, pp. 77-81 The Dark Side of Technological Singularity: New Barbarism Basarab Nicolescu1

biblefocus.net/consider/v01Armageddon/Word-Armageddon-is-Hebrew-for-a-Place.html

Biblical Studies Foundation. New English Translation Bible. Richardson: Biblical Studies Press, L.L.C., 1996. Accessed at netbible.org/.

Black, Jeremy and Anthony Green. *Gods, Demons and Symbols of Ancient Mesopotamia An Illustrated Dictionary*, Illustrator: Tessa Rickards. London: British Museum Press, 1992.

Black, Jeremy, and Green, Anthony. *Gods, Demons, and Symbols of Ancient Mesopotamia: An Illustrated Dictionary*. Austin: University of Texas Press, 1992.

blogs.timesofisrael.com/when-israelis-feel-safe-and-americans-dont/

Brisch, Nicole. *Ancient Mesopotamian Gods and Goddesses*. "Pablisag." 2013. Accessed through ORACC, oracc.museum.upenn.edu/amgg/listofdeities/pabilsag/index.html.

Bromiley, G. W. *The International Standard Bible Encyclopedia*. Grand Rapids: W. B. Eerdsmans, 1979. Accessed through TheWord Bible Software.

Brown, Francis, S. R. Driver and Charles A. Briggs. *A Hebrew and English Lexicon of the Old Testament*. Oxford: The Clarendon Press, 1907.

Campbell, Mike. "Sumerian Mythology Names," s.v. "Gilgamesh." Behind the Name. www.behindthename.com/names/usage/sumerian-mythology.

Cassius Dio, *Roman History*, published in Vol. VIII of the Loeb Classical Library edition, 1925. Pg. 419.

Charles, R. H., ed. *The Book of Enoch*, 63. Oxford: The Clarendon Press, 1893.

Christopher B. Hays, Enlil, Isaiah, and the Origins of the 'ĕlilim: A Reassessment, ZAW 2020; 132(2): 224–235, doi.org/10.1515/zaw-2020-2002

Clay, Albert T. "The Origin and Real Name of NIN-IB." Journal of the American Oriental Society 28 (1907): 135-44. doi.org/10.2307/592765.

Constable, Thomas L. Expository Notes, 2009. From theWord Bible Software.

Converging Technologies for Improving Human Performance (pre-publication on-line version), June 2002, U.S. National Science Foundation, U.S. Department of Commerce, pp. 164, 165

creation.com/transhumanism-mankinds-next-step-forward

Crick F. (1981). *Life itself.* Simon & Schuster, p. 148. See also ofbacteriaandmen.blogspot.com/2012/08/francis-crick-and-directed-panspermia.html

Damien Echols, *Angels and Archangels: The Western Path to Enlightenment* (Boulder, CO: Sounds True, 2020), pp. 261–263. Cf Second Coming of Saturn pg. 290.

Definitions.net. "Chernobyl." www.definitions.net/definition/Chernobyl.

disruptionhub.com/edit-rise-human-hive-mind/ Jun 2017

Dittenberger, W., ed. Orientis Graeci Inscriptiones Selectae. Leipsiae: S Hirzel, 1903.

Doniger, Wendy. *Merriam-Webster's Encyclopedia of World Religions*, 120, 140. Springfield: Merriam-Webster, Inc., 1990.

Edzard, D.O. "Mesopotamien. Die Mythologie der Sumerer und Akkader." Götter und Mythen im Vorderen Orient Wörterbuch der Mythologie, H.W. Haussig, and E. Schmalzriedt, eds. 17-140. Stuttgart: Klett-Cotta Verlag, 1965.

ehealthwall.com/flesh-eating-disease-pictures-symptoms-contagious-causes

Even-Shosan, Avraham (אַבְרָהָם אֶבֶן־שֹׁשָׁן). The New Dictionary (ha-milón he-khadásh הַמִּלּוֹן הֶחָדָשׁ), 1 ed., s.v. "Hebrew Terms Derived from Sumerian." Jerusalem: Kiryat-Sefer Ltd. (קִרְיַת־סֵפֶר בְּע"מ), 1984. en.wiktionary.org/wiki/Category: Hebrew_terms_derived_from_Sumerian.

Expelled: No Intelligence Allowed, Directed by Nathan Frankowski, written by Kevin Miller and Ben Stein, starring Ben Stein. 2008.

Eyjafjallajökull_volcanic_ash_multilayer.xcf: *Blankmap-ao-090N-north_pole.xcf: Reisioderivative work: Cogiati (talk)derivative work: Cogiati (talk) - Eyjafjallajökull_volcanic_ash_multilayer.xcf, CC BY-SA 3.0, commons.wikimedia.org/w/index.php?curid=10122791

fathersforlife.org/culture/Hive_Mind.htm

Foxvog, Daniel A. "Introduction to Sumerian Grammar," Jan. 4, 2016. In Cuneiform Digital Library Preprints, 2.0. Bertrand Lafont, ed. cdli.ucla.edu/?q=cuneiform-digital-library-preprints.

George, Andrew (2007) "The Tower of Babel: Archaeology, history and cuneiform texts" Archiv für Orientforschung, 51 (2005/2006). Pg. 75–95. pdf document.

Gesenius, H.W.F. *Hebrew and Chaldee Lexicon to the Old Testament Scriptures, translated by Samuel Prideaux Tregelles, 7th ed.*, s.v. "Og," "Rachal." Ada: Baker Publishing Group, 1990.

Gill, John, et al. *Gill's Commentary*. Baker Book House, 1980. ZECH 12:10.

Gudea Cyl. B, VI 11-12
www.jstage.jst.go.jp/article/orient1960/21/0/21_0_31/_pdf#:~:text=Si%2Dsa%20means%20simply%20%22to,correctly%20yokes%20for%20the%20oxen.%22&text=There%20are%20other%20examples%20of,to%20the%20functions%20of%20Lugalsisa.

Halloram, John A. Sumerian Language Page, s.v. "gug5." www.sumerian.org/sumcvc. htm.

Hamp, Douglas. *Discovering the Language of Jesus*, Calvary Chapel Publishing, Santa Ana, CA, 2005.

Hangar 1: The UFO Files, "Star People" Episode, aired May 8, 2015. www.imdb.com/title/tt4535058/?ref_=nm_flmg_slf_2

Hangar 1: The UFO Files, "UFO Superpowers" Episode aired Jun 26, 2015. www.imdb.com/title/tt4535112/?ref_=tt_ch

Harris, Laird R., Gleason L. Archer, Jr. and Bruce K. Waltke. *Theological Wordbook of the Old Testament*. Chicago: Moody Publishers, 1980. (TWOT)

Heiser, Michael. (Mysteries of Mt. Hermon) Interview with Douglas Hamp. The Awakening Report, podcast video. August 25, 2020. youtu.be/yjiZHLnhIRQ.

Hermann, Gunkel. Zum religionsgeschichtlichen Verständnis des Neuen Testaments by 1903 Göttingen, Vandenhoeck. pg., 52.

Introduction To the OT by R. K. Harrison (quoted in Utley)

io9.gizmodo.com/could-humans-evolve-into-a-giant-hive-mind-5891143 issuu.com/mytheory/docs/becoming_transhuman

Jacobsen, Thorkild. *The Harps that Once… Sumerian Poetry in Translation*. New Haven and London: Yale University Press, 1987.

jewishencyclopedia.com/articles/5849-eschatology, (in Meklita, Beshallah, l.c.)

journals.plos.org/plosone/article?id=10.1371/journal.pone.0105225

K&D Isaiah 35:5-7.

Kalimi, Isaac *Metathesis in the Hebrew Bible: Wordplay as a Literary and Exegetical Device* (Peabody, MA: Hendrickson, 2018).

Kaulins, Andis. Lexiline: *History of Civilization*. www.lexiline.com/lexiline/lexi37.htm.

knowingneurons.com/2018/01/31/emergence-hive-mind/

Krieger, Douglas. *The Two Witnesses Vol 1*. Tribnet Publishing. Sacramento, CA, 2014. pgs. 9-40.

Lange, Philip Schaff. *Lange Commentary* Isaiah 34:7 J.P. Isa 34:5-8.

Lewis, David A., and Robert Shreckhise. *UFO: End-Time Delusion*. New Leaf Press, 1992.

Liddell, H. G. and R. Scott. *A Greek-English Lexicon, s.v. "Beta: B."* Oxford: Clarendon Press, 1996. Accessed through Greek Alphabet, www.greekalphabeta.com/learn-about-beta-b-2.html, definitions culled from LSJ.

Liddell, H. G., Robert Scott and Henry Stuart Jones, eds. *Lexicon of Classical Greek, 9th ed.*, Oxford: Oxford University Press, 1925.

Lindsey, Hal. *The Late Great Planet Earth*. Grand Rapids: Zondervan Academic, 1970.

link.springer.com/article/10.1140/epjc/s10052-021-08851-0

Mackay, Charles (1877). *The Gaelic Etymology of the Languages of Western Europe: And More Especially of the English and Lowland Scotch, and Their Slang, Cant, and Colloquial Dialects*. Trübner. p. 160.

Maimonides, Moses. *Guide for the Perplexed*. 2021.

Manly P. Hall, *The Lost Keys of Freemasonry*, Macoy Publishing and Masonic Supply Co. Richmond, Va., 1976. P. 65

MARCUS, JOEL. "The Gates of Hades and the Keys of the Kingdom (Matt 16:18-19)." The Catholic Biblical Quarterly 50, no. 3 (1988): 443-55. Accessed September 30, 2020. www.jstor.org/stable/43717704.

Mark Twain. *The Innocents Abroad.* www.literaturepage.com/read/twain-innocents-abroad-458.html

McCarthy, William Bernard; Oxford, Cheryl; Sobol, Joseph Daniel, eds. (1994). *Jack in Two Worlds: Contemporary North American Tales and Their Tellers* (illustrated ed.). UNC Press Books. p. xv. ISBN 9780807844434.

medium.com/@BJ_Murphy/a-transhumanists-journey-becoming-gods-angels-and-ghosts-826c81bb5b33

Michiel de Vaan, Etymological Dictionary of Latin and the other Italic Languages, Brill, 2008, p. 366.

mindmatters.ai/2021/10/could-advanced-aliens-have-fine-tuned-earth-for-life/

mindmatters.ai/2021/10/harvard-astronomer-advanced-aliens-engineered-the-big-bang/

mindmatters.ai/2021/10/if-extraterrestrials-didnt-fine-tune-earth-maybe-there-is-a-god/

Molteni, Megan (October 18, 2019). "A Netflix Series Explores the Brave New World of Crispr - From malaria-ridden villages in Burkina Faso to fertility clinics in Ukraine, Unnatural Selection takes viewers deep into the gene-editing revolution." Wired. Retrieved October 18, 2019. www.wired.com/story/a-netflix-series-explores-the-brave-new-world-of-crispr/

mugsarsumerian.com/default.htm#u12041. www.assyrianlanguages.org/akkadian/dosearch.php

mugsarsumerian.com/default.htm#u12357_USH2_die_kill_blood

Murphy, Heather. "Man who had transplant finds out months later his DNA has changed to that of donor 5,000 miles away." New York Times. Accessed through The Independent, pub. Dec. 9, 2019. www.independent.co.uk/news/world/americas/dna-bone-marrow-transplant-man-chimera-chris-long-forensic-science-police-a9238636.html.

news.bbc.co.uk/2/hi/science/nature/1513342.stm

Parpola, Asko. "Studia Orientalia." Finnish Oriental Society, 84 (1998). ISBN 9789519380384

Parrot, André. *The Tower of Babel, Studies in Biblical Archaeology 2*, 64. New York: The Philosophical Library Inc., 1955.

Pearsall, Paul. The Heart's code: tapping the wisdom and power of our heart energy. New York; Broadway Books, 1999.

Personal email communication and Interview Awakening Report with Tyler H. who asked for his last name to remain undisclosed.

Philo, "De Execrationibus," 8; Targ. Yer. to Isa. xxxv. 10, jewishencyclopedia.com/articles/5849-eschatology#anchor8

prosobab.leidenuniv.nl/pdfs/logogram.pdf

psd.museum.upenn.edu/epsd/e1897.html

"Rethinking Ezekiel's Invasion by Gog" in Journal of the Evangelical Society, Mar. 1996, pg. 30.

Richter 2004: 264. www.skyscript.co.uk/babylonian_sagittarius.pdf

Robertson, Archibald Thomas. Robertson's Word Pictures. Ada: Baker Publishing Group, 1923.

Rosenberg, Jennifer. (2021, July 31). Hitler's Political Statement Before His Suicide. Retrieved from www.thoughtco.com/hitlers-political-statement-1779643

royalsocietypublishing.org/doi/abs/10.1098/rstb.2009.0095

Sayce, Archibald Henry (1911). "Babylon." In Chisholm, Hugh (ed.). Encyclopædia Britannica. 3 (11th ed.). Cambridge University Press. pp. 98–99.

scienceaccessibly.wordpress.com/2016/09/27/crispr-how-genome-editing-will-change-the-world-forever/

Scofield Reference Bible; GESENIUS. Thesaurus 1835. 1253.

See also en.wikipedia.org/wiki/An_(cuneiform)

Stoicorum Veterum Fragmenta, coll. J(H) vArnim I–IV 1903–24. See also: Chrysippus, phil., ed. J(H) vArnim, Stoicorum veterum fragmenta II 1903 III b.c.

Tate, Karl. "How Quantum Entanglement Works." LiveScience, April 8, 2013. www. livescience.com/28550-how-quantum-entanglement-works-infographic.html.

The Associated Press, "Arguments Conclude in 'West Memphis Three' Appeals." Arkansas Democrat-Gazette, Oct. 2, 2009. www.arkansasonline.com/news/2009/oct/02/appeals-continue-slayings-arkboys-93/, retrieved 5/4/21. Cf The Second Coming of Saturn. Derek P. Gilbert, 2021. Pg. 290.

The Babylonian Talmud: Mas. Sanhedrin 97a and b (Soncino Press)

The Extraterrestrial Species Almanac: The Ultimate Guide to Greys, Reptilians, Hybrids, and Nordics (MUFON) Publisher: MUFON, Publication Date: January 1st, 2021, By Craig Campobasso.

The Pennsylvania Sumerian Dictionary, s.v. "gug." Last updated June 26, 2006. psd. museum.upenn.edu/epsd/e1897.html.

The priests of Baal (synonymous with Melqart, King of Tyre, AKA Satan) with whom Elijah contends (1 Kgs 18:20–40) would thus be the priests of Melqart. Erdman's Bible Dictionary: MELQART.

The Second Coming of Saturn. Derek P. Gilbert, 2021. Pg. 290.

thehill.com/opinion/international/579303-nasa-chief-bill-nelson-latest-official-to-suggest-ufos-have?rl=1

thesiliconreview.com/2017/03/neuralink-is-developing-neural-lace-technology-to-augment-the-cognitive-abilities-of-the-human-brain

TMZ INVESTIGATES: UFOs: THE PENTAGON PROOF

Tobler et al. (1995)The Global Demography Project (Natl. Center for Geographic Information and Analysis, Univ. California, Santa Barbara), Tech. Rep. 95–6.

Tractate Aboth Babylonian Talmud

Tractate Pesachim, chapter 10, Babylonian Talmud

Trustees of the British Museum. World History Encyclopedia, s.v. "Cylinder Seal with Ninurta." Feb. 1, 2017. British Museum, London. Photograph. www.ancient.eu/image/6317/ cylinder-seal-with-ninurta/.

usccb.org/bible/amos/5/

Utley, Bob. *You Can Understand the Bible*. Marshall: Bible Lessons International, March 2013. Retrieved from TheWord Bible Software.

Vallée, Jacques. Dimensions: A Casebook of Alien Contact. New York: Ballantine Books, 1988.

Vallée, Jacques. *The Invisible College*, 233. Boston: Dutton, 1975.

Van der Toorn, Karel, Bob Becking and Pieter W. van der Horst, eds. *Dictionary of Deities and Demons in the Bible*. Grand Rapids: Wm. B. Eerdmans Publishing Co., 1999.

venturebeat.com/2021/02/13/thought-detection-ai-has-infiltrated-our-last-bastion-of-privacy/

Walter Bauer. *A Greek-English Lexicon of the New Testament and Other Early Christian Literature*, Frederick W. Danker, ed. Chicago: University of Chicago Press, 2000. Accessed through TheWord Bible Software, v.9.

Werner, Gitt. *In the Beginning Was Information*. Translated by Jaap Kies. Bielefeld: Christliche Literatur-Verbreitung, 2000.

White, Gavin. *"The Winter Solstice Period."* Nov. 2009. Accessed through Skyscript, www .skyscript.co.uk/babylonian_sagittarius.pdf.

Wiggermann, F. A. M. *Mesopotamian Protective Spirits, The Ritual Texts* - Styx & PP Publications Groningen 1992.

Wiggermann, F. A. M. Nergal, *Reallexikon der Assyriologie*, 215-26. Berlin: De Gruyter, 1999.

Wiggermann, F. A. M., *Sumerian Gods and their Representations*. "Transtigridian Snake Gods," 33-35. Groningen: Styx Publications, 1997.

wiki2.org/en/John_A._Samford

Wikipedia. "Bad (cuneiform)." en.wikipedia.org/wiki/Bad_(cuneiform)#:~:text= The%20cuneiform%20bad%2C%20bat%2C%20be,(capital%20lette r%20(majuscule)).

William, Whiston, ed. and transl. Flavius Josephus, *Antiquities of the Jews*. Auburn and Buffalo: John E. Beardsley, 1895.

wowtravel.me/11-most-gay-friendly-cities-in-the-world/

www.americanveterinarian.com/journals/amvet/2018/november2018/pet-cloning-where-we-are-today

www.assyrianlanguages.org/akkadian/

www.balashon.com/2008/02/heichal-adrichal-and-tarnegol.html

www.bloomberg.com/news/articles/2021-02-01/elon-musk-wired-up-a-monkey-s-brain-to-play-videogames

www.cbsnews.com/news/crispr-jennifer-doudna-walter-isaacson-the-code-breaker/

www.cbsnews.com/news/ex-air-force-personnel-ufos-deactivated-nukes/

www.cbsnews.com/news/ufo-military-intelligence-60-minutes-2021-05-16/

www.cia.gov/library/publications/the-worldfactbook/rankorder/2102rank.html

www.come-and-hear.com/sanhedrin/sanhedrin_97.html

www.desiringgod.org/articles/the-tornado-the-lutherans-and-homosexuality

www.dnascript.com/products/

www.edge.org/conversation/kevin_kelly-the-technium-and-the-7th-kingdom-of-life

www.endtime.com/blog/book-revelation-chronological-order/

www.fool.com/investing/2018/06/18/is-gene-editing-dangerous-4-things-you-should-know.aspx

www.fox.com/watch/2c2489402d90e9cf47fe5ec0eff0250f/

www.haaretz.com/israel-news/.premium.MAGAZINE-southern-israel-is-hundreds-of-years-overdue-for-an-earthquake-1.6933565

www.history.com/news/ufos-washington-white-house-air-force-coverup

www.history.com/news/wooly-mammoth-resurrection-cloning-genesis

www.ibtimes.co.uk/krokodil-users-describe-rotting-inside-out-blister-514387

www.ibtimes.co.uk/ray-kurzweil-human-brains-could-be-connected-cloud-by-2030-1504403

www.iflscience.com/brain/direct-brain-brain-communication-used-humans/

www.imdb.com/title/tt15163678/?ref_=ttep_ep3

www.ipsos.com/en-us/americans-believe-in-ufos-aliens.

www.jpost.com/Opinion/Unto-the-nations-505760

www.livescience.com/28550-how-quantum-entanglement-works-infographic.html

www.livescience.com/32694-how-big-was-the-biggest-hailstone-ever.html

www.mayoclinic.org/diseases-conditions/boils-and-carbuncles/symptoms-causes/syc-20353770

www.merriam-webster.com/dictionary/quantum%20entanglement

www.nasa.gov/topics/earth/features/japanquake/earth20110314.html

www.nationalgeographic.com/news/2017/01/human-pig-hybrid-embryo-chimera-organs-health-science/

www.netflix.com/watch/81066340?trackId=14170287 Episode 3, Code Named Aurora, minutes 26-27.

www.newadvent.org/fathers/0103530.htm

www.pewresearch.org/fact-tank/2021/06/30/most-americans-believe-in-intelligent-life-beyond-earth-few-see-ufos-as-a-major-national-security-threat See also www.studyfinds.org/ufo-alien-invasion-inevitable/

www.psychologytoday.com/blog/owning-pink/201308/the-nocebo-effect-negative-thoughts-can-harm-your-health

www.sciencealert.com/wealthy-humans-could-live-forever-as-cyborgs-within-200-years-expert-predicts

www.sciencedaily.com/articles/e/earthquake_liquefaction.htm

www.space.com/ufos-are-real-leslie-kean-interview

www.studyfinds.org/ufo-alien-invasion-inevitable/

www.sumerian.org

www.theguardian.com/technology/2014/oct/27/elon-musk-artificial-intelligence-ai-biggest-existential-threat

www.the-sun.com/lifestyle/tech/2713352/first-human-monkey-embryo-created/

www.the-sun.com/news/3008383/ufos-coming-from-space-sea-aliens/

www.the-sun.com/news/3125848/ufos-shut-down-nukes-us-base/

www.un.org/sustainabledevelopment/wp-content/uploads/2017/05/Ocean-fact-sheet-package.pdf

www.usgs.gov/center-news/imaging-israel-s-dead-sea-fault-understand-how-continents-stretch-and-rift

www.vice.com/en/article/5db4ma/starlight-could-really-be-a-vast-alien-quantum-internet-physicist-proposes

www.vice.com/en/article/z3vkny/scientists-have-proposed-a-new-particle-that-is-a-portal-to-a-5th-dimension

www.wired.com/2011/12/the-true-hive-mind-how-honeybee-colonies-think

www.wnd.com/2010/02/124106/

www.youtube.com/watch?v=5gQGWJraptU

www.youtube.com/watch?v=rD5uNAMbDaQ&feature=colike

Yoder, Tyler R. "Ezekiel 29:3 and Its Ancient Near Eastern Context." Vetus Testamentum. Vol. 63, Issue 3 (Jan. 1, 2013).

Yonge, Charles Duke, ed. *The Works Of Philo Judaeus, Complete And Unabridged*. Peabody: Hendrickson Publishers, 1993.

Made in the USA
Las Vegas, NV
22 February 2022

44407168R00236